Rick Steves'

SNAPSHOT

Sevilla, Granada & Southern Spain

CONTENTS

INTRODUCTION

This Snapshot guide, excerpted from my guidebook *Rick Steves' Spain*, introduces you to southern Spain's two top cities—Sevilla and Granada—and the surrounding Spanish heartland. When Americans think of Spain, they often picture this region, with its massive cathedrals, Moorish palaces, vibrant folk life, whitewashed villages, bright sunshine, and captivating rat-a-tat-tat of flamenco.

Sevilla is the soulful cultural heart of southern Spain, with an atmospheric old quarter and riveting flamenco shows. Granada, formerly the Moorish capital, is home to the magnificent Alhambra palace. Córdoba features Spain's top surviving Moorish mosque, the Mezquita. Make time to delve into Andalucía's sleepy, whitewashed hill towns: Arcos de la Frontera, Ronda, and Grazalema. Spain's south coast, the Costa del Sol, is a palm-tree jungle of beach resorts and concrete, but has some appealing destinations—Nerja, Tarifa, and Gibraltar—beyond the traffic jams. And since it's so easy, consider an eye-opening side-trip to another continent by hopping the ferry to Tangier, the newly revitalized gateway to Morocco (and to Africa).

To help you have the best trip possible, I've included the following topics in this book:

• **Planning Your Time,** with advice on how to make the most of your limited time

• **Orientation,** including tourist information (abbreviated as TI), tips on public transportation, local tour options, and helpful hints

• **Sights** with ratings:

▲▲▲—Don't miss

▲▲—Try hard to see

▲—Worthwhile if you can make it

No rating—Worth knowing about

- **Sleeping** and **Eating,** with good-value recommendations in every price range
- **Connections,** with tips on trains, buses, and driving

Practicalities, near the end of this book, has information on money, phoning, hotel reservations, transportation, and more, plus Spanish survival phrases.

To travel smartly, read this little book in its entirety before you go. It's my hope that this guide will make your trip more meaningful and rewarding. Traveling like a temporary local, you'll get the absolute most out of every mile, minute, and dollar.

Buen viaje!

Rick Steves

SEVILLA

Flamboyant Sevilla (seh-VEE-yah) thrums with flamenco music, sizzles in the summer heat, and pulses with the passion of Don Juan and Carmen. It's a place where bull-fighting is still politically correct and little girls still dream of growing up to become flamenco dancers. While Granada has the great Alhambra and Córdoba has the remarkable Mezquita, Sevilla has a soul. (Soul—or *duende*—is fundamental to flamenco.) It's a wonderful-to-be-alive-in kind of place.

The gateway to the New World in the 16th century, Sevilla boomed when Spain did. The explorers Amerigo Vespucci and Ferdinand Magellan sailed from its great river harbor, discovering new trade routes and abundant sources of gold, silver, cocoa, and tobacco. In the 17th century, Sevilla was Spain's largest and wealthiest city. Local artists Diego Velázquez, Bartolomé Murillo, and Francisco de Zurbarán made it a cultural center. Sevilla's Golden Age—and its New World riches—ended when the harbor silted up and the Spanish empire crumbled.

In the 19th century, Sevilla was a big stop on the Romantic "Grand Tour" of Europe. To build on this tourism and promote trade among Spanish-speaking nations, Sevilla planned a grand exposition in 1929. Bad year. The expo crashed along with the stock market. In 1992, Sevilla got a second chance at a world's fair. This expo was a success, leaving the city with impressive infrastructure: a new airport, a train station, sleek bridges, and the super AVE bullet train (making Sevilla a 2.5-hour side-trip from Madrid). In 2007, the main boulevards—once thundering with noisy traffic and mercilessly cutting the city in two—were pedestrianized, dramatically enhancing Sevilla's already substantial charm.

SEVILLA

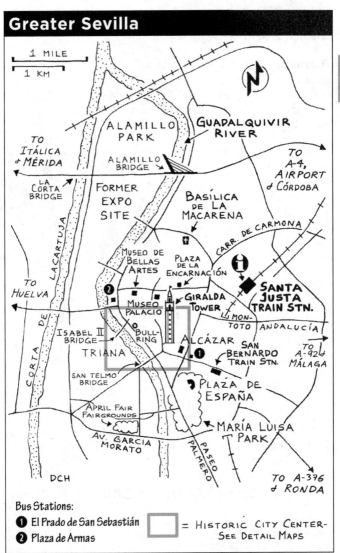

Greater Sevilla

1 MILE
1 KM

N

ALAMILLO PARK

GUADALQUIVIR RIVER

TO ITÁLICA & MÉRIDA

ALAMILLO BRIDGE

TO A-4, AIRPORT & CÓRDOBA

LA CORTA BRIDGE

FORMER EXPO SITE

BASÍLICA DE LA MACARENA

LA CARTUJA

CARR. DE CARMONA

TO HUELVA

MUSEO DE BELLAS ARTES

PLAZA DE LA ENCARNACIÓN

SANTA JUSTA TRAIN STN.

CORTA DE

❷

MUSEO PALACIO

GIRALDA TOWER

LI MONTOTO

ANDALUCÍA

ISABEL II BRIDGE

BULL-RING

ALCÁZAR

SAN BERNARDO TRAIN STN.

TO A-92 MÁLAGA

TRIANA

❶

SAN TELMO BRIDGE

PLAZA DE ESPAÑA

APRIL FAIR FAIRGROUNDS

MARÍA LUISA PARK

AV. GARCIA MORATO

PASEO PALMERO

DCH

TO A-376 & RONDA

Bus Stations:
❶ El Prado de San Sebastián
❷ Plaza de Armas

☐ = HISTORIC CITY CENTER—SEE DETAIL MAPS

Today, Spain's fourth-largest city (pop. 704,000) is Andalucía's leading destination, buzzing with festivals, color, guitars, castanets, and street life, and enveloped in the fragrances of orange trees, jacaranda, and myrtle. James Michener wrote, "Sevilla doesn't *have* ambience, it *is* ambience." Sevilla also has its share of impressive sights. Its cathedral is Spain's largest. The Alcázar is a fantastic royal palace and garden ornamented with Mudejar (Islamic) flair. But the real magic is the city itself, with its tangled former Jewish Quarter, riveting flamenco shows, thriving bars, and teeming evening paseo.

Planning Your Time

On a three-week trip, spend two nights and two days here. On even the shortest Spanish trip, I'd zip here on the slick AVE train for a day trip from Madrid. With more time, if ever there was a Spanish city to linger in, it's Sevilla.

The major sights are few and simple for a city of this size. The cathedral and the Alcázar are worth about three hours, and a wander through the Santa Cruz district takes about an hour. You could spend a day touring Sevilla's other sights. Stroll along the bank of the Guadalquivir River and cross Isabel II Bridge to explore the Triana neighborhood and to savor views of the cathedral and Torre del Oro. An evening in Sevilla is essential for the paseo and a flamenco show. Stay out late at least once to appreciate Sevilla on a warm night—one of its major charms.

Bullfights take place on most Sundays in May and June, on Easter and Corpus Christi, daily through the April Fair, and in late September. The Museo de Bellas Artes is closed on Monday. Tour groups clog the Alcázar and cathedral in the morning; go late in the day to avoid the crowds, or at least buy your Alcázar ticket online to avoid the lines.

Córdoba is a convenient and worthwhile side-trip from Sevilla, or a handy stopover if you're taking the AVE to or from Madrid or Granada.

Orientation to Sevilla

For the tourist, this big city is small. The bull's-eye on your map should be the cathedral and its Giralda Bell Tower, which can be seen from all over town. Nearby are Sevilla's other major sights, the Alcázar (palace and gardens) and the lively Santa Cruz district. The central north-south pedestrian boulevard, Avenida de la Constitución, stretches north a few blocks to Plaza Nueva, gateway to the shopping district. A few blocks west of the cathedral are the bull-ring and the Guadalquivir River, while Plaza de España is a few blocks south. Triana, the colorful working-class area on the west bank of the Guadalquivir River, has a thriving market but lacks tourist sights. With most sights walkable, and taxis so friendly, easy, and affordable, you probably won't even bother with the bus.

Tourist Information

Sevilla has tourist offices at the **airport** (Mon-Fri 9:00-19:30, Sat-Sun 9:30-15:00, tel. 954-782-035), at **Santa Justa train station** (overlooking tracks 6-7, same hours as airport TI, tel. 954-782-003), and near the cathedral on **Plaza del Triunfo** (Mon-Fri 9:00-19:30, Sat-Sun 9:30-19:30, tel. 954-210-005).

At any TI, ask for the city map, the English-language magazine *The Tourist,* and a current listing of sights with opening times. The free monthly events guide—*El Giraldillo,* written in Spanish basic enough to be understood by travelers—covers cultural events throughout Andalucía, with a focus on Sevilla. At the TI, ask for information you might need for elsewhere in the region (for example, if heading south, pick up the free *Route of the White Towns* brochure and a Jerez map). Helpful websites are www.turismosevilla.org and www.andalucia.org.

Sightseeing Pass: The **Sevilla Card** covers admission to most of Sevilla's sights (including the cathedral, Alcázar, Flamenco Dance Museum, Basílica de la Macarena, Bullfight Museum, and more), and gives discounts at some hotels and restaurants (sold at the ICONOS shop on Avenida de la Constitución, near the Alcázar, Mon-Sat 10:00-20:00, Sun 11:00-19:00; or at the "INFHOR" stand—the train station's hotel room-finding booth, overlooking track 11). It's doubtful whether any but the busiest sightseer would save much money using the card (€33/24 hours—includes choice of 2 museums and river cruise; €53/48 hours—includes all sights and choice of river cruise or bus tour; €71/72 hours or €77/120 hours—includes all sights plus cruise and bus tour; www.sevillacard.es). If you're over 65, keep in mind that even without the Sevilla Card, you'll get into the Alcázar and the cathedral almost free.

Arrival in Sevilla

By Train: Most trains arrive at sublime Santa Justa Station, with banks, ATMs, bike rental, and a TI. Baggage storage *(cosigna)* is below track 1, next to the bike-rental office (€3-5/day depending on size of bag, security checkpoint open 6:00-24:00). The TI overlooks tracks 6-7. If you don't have a hotel room reserved, INFHOR, the room-finding booth above track 11, can help; you can also get maps and other tourist information here—a good idea if the TI line is long (Mon-Sat 9:30-14:30 & 15:30-20:00, Sun 9:30-16:30). The plush little AVE Sala Club, designed for business travelers, welcomes those with a first-class AVE ticket and reservation (across the main hall from track 1). The town center is marked by the ornate Giralda Bell Tower, peeking above the apartment flats (visible from the front of the station—with your back to the tracks, it's at 1 o'clock). To get into the center, it's a flat and boring 25-minute walk or about a €6 taxi ride. By city bus, it's a short ride on #C1 to the El Prado de San Sebastián bus station (find bus stop 100 yards in front of the train station, €1.40, pay driver), then a 10-minute walk or short tram ride (see next section).

By Bus: Sevilla's two major bus stations—El Prado de San Sebastián and Plaza de Armas—both have information offices, basic eateries, and baggage storage.

The **El Prado de San Sebastián bus station,** often called just "El Prado," covers most of Andalucía (daily 7:00-22:00, information tel. 954-417-111, generally no English spoken; baggage storage/*consigna* at the far end of station—€1.50-3.50/day depending on size, daily 9:00-21:00). From the bus station to downtown (and Barrio Santa Cruz hotels), it's about a 10-minute walk: Exit the station to the right, and cross the busy street at the big roundabout. Turn right and keep the fenced-in gardens on your left. At the end of the fence, duck left through the Murillo Gardens and into the heart of Barrio Santa Cruz (use the color map in the front of this book to navigate). Sevilla's tram connects the El Prado station with the city center (and many of my recommended hotels): Turn left as you exit the bus station and walk to Avenida de Carlos V (€1.40, buy ticket at machine before boarding; ride it two stops to Archivo de Indias to reach the cathedral area, or three stops to Plaza Nueva).

The **Plaza de Armas bus station** (near the river, opposite the Expo '92 site) serves long-distance destinations such as Madrid, Barcelona, Lagos, and Lisbon. Ticket counters line one wall, an information kiosk is in the center, and at the end of the hall are luggage lockers (€3.50/day). Taxis to downtown cost around €5. Or, to take the bus, exit onto the main road (Calle Arjona) to find bus #C4 into the center (stop is to the left, in front of the taxi stand; €1.40, pay driver, get off at Puerta de Jerez).

By Car: To drive into Sevilla, follow *centro ciudad* (city center) signs and stay along the river. For short-term parking on the street, the riverside Paseo de Cristóbal Colón has two-hour meters and hardworking thieves. Ignore the bogus traffic wardens who direct you to an illegal spot, take a tip, and disappear later when your car gets towed. For long-term parking, hotels charge as much as a normal garage. For simplicity, I'd just park at a central garage (€15-22/day) and catch a taxi to my hotel. Try the big one under the bus station at Plaza de Armas, the Cristóbal Colón garage by the bullring and river, the Plaza Nueva garage on Albareda, or the one at Avenida Roma/Puerta de Jerez (cash only). For hotels in the Santa Cruz area, the handiest parking is the Cano y Cueto garage near the corner of Calle Santa María la Blanca and Avenida de Menéndez Pelayo (about €18/day, open 24/7, at edge of big park, unsigned and underground).

By Plane: Sevilla's San Pablo Airport (airport code: SVQ) sits about six miles east of downtown (tel. 954-449-000, www .aena-aeropuertos.es). The Especial Aeropuerto (EA) bus connects the airport with both train stations, both bus stations, and several stops in the town center (2/hour, 30-45 minutes, €4, buy ticket from driver). The two most convenient stops downtown are south of the Alcázar gardens on Avenida de Carlos V, near El Prado de San Sebastián bus station (close to my recommended Santa Cruz hotels); and on the Paseo de Cristóbal Colón, near the Torre del Oro. Look for the small *EA* sign at bus stops. If you're going from downtown Sevilla *to* the airport, verify bus stops with your hotel or the TI, as locations can change. To taxi into town, go to one of the airport's taxis stands to ensure a fixed rate (€22 by day, €24 at night and on weekends, extra for luggage, confirm price with the driver before your journey).

Getting Around Sevilla

Most visitors have a full and fun experience in Sevilla without ever riding public transportation. The city center is compact, and most of the major sights are within easy walking distance (the Basílica de la Macarena is a notable exception). On a hot day, air-conditioned buses can be a blessing.

By Taxi: Sevilla is a great taxi town. You can hail one anywhere, or find a cluster of them parked by major intersections and sights (weekdays: €1.30 drop rate, €1/kilometer, €3.60 minimum; Sat-Sun, holidays, and after hours, 21:00-7:00: €2 drop rate, €1.40/kilometer, €4.50 minimum; calling for a cab adds about €3). A quick daytime ride in town will generally fall within the €3.60 minimum. Although I'm quick to take advantage of taxis, because of one-way streets and traffic congestion it's often just as fast to hoof it between central points.

By Bus, Tram, and Metro: Thanks to ongoing construction projects in the city center, bus routes often change. It's best to check with your hotel or the TI for the latest updates.

SEVILLA

A single trip on any form of city transit costs €1.40. For half-price trips, you can buy a Tarjeta Multiviajes card that's rechargeable and shareable (€7 for 10 trips, €1.50 deposit; buy at kiosks or at the TUSSAM transit office near the bus stop on Avenida de Carlos V, next to El Prado de San Sebastián bus station; scan it on the card reader as you board; for transit details, see www.tussam.es).

The various #C **buses,** which are handiest for tourists, make circular routes through town (note that all of them eventually wind up at Basílica de La Macarena). For all buses, buy your ticket from the driver. The #C3 stops at Murillo Gardens, Triana, then La Macarena. The #C4 goes the opposite direction, but without entering Triana. And the spunky little #C5 is a minibus that winds through the old center of town, including Plaza del Salvador, Plaza de San Francisco, the bullring, Plaza Nueva, the Museo de Bellas Artes, La Campana, and La Macarena, providing a relaxing joyride that also connects some farther-flung sights.

A new **tram** *(tramvia)* makes just a few stops in the heart of the city, but can save you a bit of walking. Buy your ticket at the machine on the platform before you board (runs about every 7 minutes until 1:45 in the morning). It makes five stops (from south to north): San Bernardo (at the San Bernardo train station), Prado San Sebastián (next to El Prado de San Sebastián bus station), Puerta Jerez (south end of Avenida de la Constitución), Archivo de Indias (next to the cathedral), and Plaza Nueva.

Sevilla also has a brand-new underground **metro,** but most tourists won't need to use it. It's designed to connect the suburbs with the center and only has one line. There are stops downtown at the San Bernardo train station, El Prado de San Sebastián bus station, and Puerto Jerez.

Helpful Hints

Festivals: Sevilla's peak season is April and May, and it has two one-week festival periods when the city is packed: Holy Week and April Fair.

While **Holy Week** (Semana Santa) is big all over Spain, it's biggest in Sevilla. It's held the week between Palm Sunday and Easter Sunday (April 13-20 in 2014). Locals start preparing for the big event up to a year in advance. What would normally be a five-minute walk can take an hour if a procession crosses your path. But even these hassles become totally worthwhile as you listen to the *saetas* (spontaneous devotional songs) and let the spirit of the festival take over.

Then, after taking enough time off to catch its communal breath, Sevilla holds its **April Fair** (April 29-May 4 in 2014). This is a celebration of all things Andalusian, with plenty of eating, drinking, singing, and merrymaking (though most of the revelry takes place in private parties at a large fairground).

Book rooms well in advance for these festival times. Prices can go sky-high, many hotels have four-night minimums, and food quality at touristy restaurants can plummet.

Rosemary Scam: In the city center, and especially near the cathedral, you may encounter women thrusting sprigs of rosemary into the hands of passersby, grunting, *"Toma! Es un regalo!"* ("Take it! It's a gift!"). The twig is free...and then they grab your hand and read your fortune for a tip. Coins are "bad luck," so the minimum payment they'll accept is €5. While they can be very aggressive, you don't need to take their demands seriously—don't make eye contact, don't accept a sprig, and say firmly but politely, *"No, gracias."*

Internet Access: Almost every hotel in town has Wi-Fi, and many also have computers for guests to use. The city itself is fairly Wi-Fi friendly. Find free Wi-Fi on the tram, at the Museo de Bellas Artes, and in Plaza de la Encarnación, among other public spaces.

Post Office: The post office is at Avenida de la Constitución 32, across from the cathedral (Mon-Fri 8:30-20:30, Sat 9:30-13:00, closed Sun).

Laundry: Lavandería Roma offers quick and economical drop-off service (€6/load wash and dry, Mon-Fri 10:00-14:00 & 17:30-20:30, Sat 10:00-14:00, closed Sun, a few blocks west of the cathedral at Calle Arfe 22, tel. 954-210-535). Near the recommended Santa Cruz hotels, **La Segunda Vera Tintorería** has two machines for self-service (€10/load wash-and-dry, €10/load drop-off service, Mon-Fri 9:30-14:00 & 17:30-20:300, Sat 10:00-13:30, closed Sun, about a block from the eastern edge of Santa Cruz at Avenida de Menéndez Pelayo 11, tel. 954-536-376).

Bike Rental: Sevilla is an extremely biker-friendly city, with designated bike lanes and a public bike-sharing program (€11 one-week subscription, first 30 minutes of each ride free, €1-2 for each subsequent hour, www.sevici.es). Ask the TI about this and other bicycle rental options. **BiciBike** rents bikes at the Santa Justa train station, and will even deliver them to your hotel at no charge (€8/3 hours, €10/6 hours, €15/24 hours, tel. 955-514-110, www.bicibike.es).

Train Tickets: For schedules and tickets, visit a RENFE Travel Center, either at the **train station** (daily 8:00-22:00, take a

Holy Week (Semana Santa) in Andalucía

Holy Week—the week between Palm Sunday and Easter—is a major holiday throughout the Christian world, but nowhere is it celebrated with as much fervor as in Andalucía, especially Sevilla. Holy Week is all about the events of the Passion of Jesus Christ: his entry into Jerusalem, his betrayal by Judas and arrest, his crucifixion, and his resurrection. In Sevilla, on each day throughout the week, 60 neighborhood groups (brotherhoods, called *hermandades* or *cofradías*) parade from their neighborhood churches to the cathedral with floats depicting some aspect of the Passion story.

As the week approaches, the anticipation grows: Visitors pour into town, grandstands are erected along the parade routes, and TV stations anxiously monitor the weather report. The floats are so delicate that rain can force the processions to be called off—a crushing disappointment.

By mid-afternoon of any day during Holy Week, thousands line the streets. The parade begins. First comes a line of "penitents" carrying a big cross, candles, and incense. The *penitentes* perform their penance publically but anonymously, their identities obscured by pointy, hooded robes. (The penitents' traditional hooded garb has been worn for centuries—long before such hoods became associated with racism in the American South.) Some processions are silent, but others are accompanied by beating drums, brass bands, or wailing singers.

A hush falls over the crowd as the floats *(los pasos)* approach. First comes a Passion float, showing Christ in some stage of the drama—being whipped, appearing before Pilate,

number and wait, tel. 902-320-320 for reservations and info) or near **Plaza Nueva** in the city center (Mon-Fri 9:30-14:00 & 17:30-20:00, Sat 10:00-13:30, closed Sun, Calle Zaragoza 29, tel. 954-211-455). You can also check schedules at www.renfe .com. Many travel agencies sell train tickets; look for a train sticker in agency windows.

Tours in Sevilla

Guided City Walks by Concepción

Concepción Delgado, an enthusiastic teacher who's a joy to listen to, takes small groups on English-only walks. Using me as her guinea pig, Concepción has designed a fine two-hour **Sevilla Cultural Show & Tell** walk. In this introduction to her home-

or carrying the cross to his execution. More penitents follow—with dozens or even hundreds of participants, a procession can stretch out over a half-mile. All this sets the stage for the finale—typically a float of the Virgin Mary, who represents the hope of resurrection.

The elaborate floats feature carved wooden religious sculptures, some embellished with gold leaf and silverwork. They can be adorned with fresh flowers, rows of candles, and even jewelry on loan from the congregation. Each float is carried by 30 to 50 men, who labor unseen (you might catch a glimpse of their shuffling feet). The bearers wear turban-like headbands to protect their heads and necks from the crushing weight (the floats can weigh as much as two tons). Two "shifts" of float carriers rotate every 20 minutes. As a sign of their faith, some men carry the float until they collapse.

As the procession nears the cathedral, it passes through the square called La Campana, south along Calle Sierpes, and through Plaza de San Francisco. (Some parades follow a parallel route a block or two east.) Grandstands and folding chairs are filled by VIPs and Sevilla's prominent families. Thousands of candles drip wax along the well-trod parade routes, forming a waxy buildup that causes car tires to squeal for days to come.

Being in Sevilla for Holy Week is both a blessing and a curse. It's a remarkable spectacle, but it's extremely crowded. Parade routes can block your sightseeing for hours. Check printed schedules if you want to avoid them. If you do find a procession blocking your way, look for a crossing point marked by a red-painted fence, or ask a guard. Even if all you care about on Easter is a chocolate-bearing bunny, the intense devotion of the Andalusian people during their Holy Week traditions is an inspiration to behold.

town, she shares important insights the average visitor misses. Her tour rounds out the rest of your Sevilla experience, brilliantly complements your independent vis-its to major sights, and clues you in on what's new and what's going on around town during your visit. I think it's worthwhile even if you're only in town for one day (€15/person, minimum 4 people, Feb-July and Sept-Dec Mon-Sat at 10:30; Jan and Aug on Mon, Wed, and Fri only; meet at statue in Plaza Nueva).

For those wanting to really understand the city's two most

SEVILLA

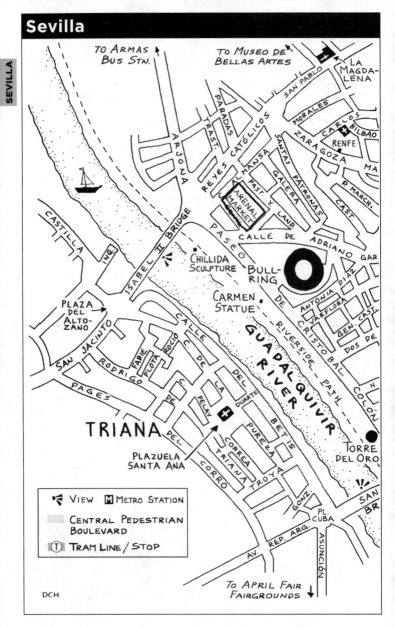

Sevilla

TO ARMAS BUS STN.

TO MUSEO DE BELLAS ARTES

LA MAGDALENA

SAN PABLO

MORALES

CARLOS

BILBAO

RENFE

ZARAGOZA

PARADAS

TRAST.

ARJONA

REYES CATÓLICOS

ALMANSA

SANTAS PATRONAS

GALERA

PAST. Y LAND.

P. MARCH.

CAST.

MA

ARENAL MARKET

CASTILLA

INQ.

ISABEL II BRIDGE

PASEO

CALLE DE ADRIANO

GAR

CHILLIDA SCULPTURE

BULL-RING

ANTONIA DIAZ

VARFLORA

GEN. CAST.

DOS DE

CARMEN STATUE

GUADALQUIVIR RIVER

RIVERSIDE PATH

DE CRISTOBAL

N. COLON

PLAZA DEL ALTOZANO

SAN JACINTO

CALLE DE RODRIGO

FABIE

FLOTA

ROCIO

C. DE

LA

PAGES

DE

PELAY

DUARTE

DEL

BETIS

TRIANA

PUREZA

TORRE DEL ORO

PLAZUELA SANTA ANA

CORRO

TRIANA

CORREA

TROYA

GONZ.

SAN BR

REP. ARG.

PL. CUBA

ASUNCIÓN

AV.

To APRIL FAIR FAIRGROUNDS

Legend

- VIEW
- M METRO STATION
- CENTRAL PEDESTRIAN BOULEVARD
- T TRAM LINE / STOP

DCH

To Museo Palacio & Plaza de la Encarnación

IGLESIA DEL SALVADOR

To Casa de Pilatos

200 YARDS
200 METERS

CANAL

TETUAN

SIERPES

PL. SAN FRAN.

CITY HALL

PLAZA NUEVA

DRID

S. ISIDRO

ALVAREN QUINTERO

FRANCOS

FERN. COLON

PAJARITOS

ARGOTE DEL MOLINA

FLAMENCO MUSEUM

N

GATAZO

JIMIOS

CIA DE VINUESA

ARFE

ALEMANES

SEGOVIAS

GIRALDA

MATEOS

GAGO

XIMÉNEZ

BARRIO SANTA CRUZ
(SEE DETAIL MAPS)

CATHEDRAL

HOSPITAL DE LOS VENERABLES

MAYO

ALM.
Post

ARCHIVO DE INDIAS

PLAZA D. TRIUMFO

HOSPITAL DE LA CARIDAD

IBARRA

TEMPRADO

BAL.

SANTANDER

M. MARARA

PLAZA CONT.

M. PIN.

AGUA

ALCÁZAR

EA AIRPORT BUS

B

A LOBO

PUERTA DE JEREZ

M T

ALCÁZAR GARDENS

TELMO SANJURO

PASEO

IDGE

ROMA

PALOS

AV.

SAN FERNANDO

HOTEL ALF XIII

MENÉNDEZ

EL PRADO BUS STN.

EA AIRPORT BUS

CARLOS V

T B

TO SAN BERNARDO TRAIN STN.

DELICIAS

UNIV.

MARIA LUISA PARK

PLAZA DE ESPAÑA →

M

PRADO SAN SEB.

PORTUGAL

important sights—which are tough to fully appreciate on their own—Concepción also offers in-depth tours of the **cathedral** and the **Alcázar**, each lasting about 1.25 hours (€7 each plus entrance fees, €2 discount if you also take the Show & Tell tour; meet at 13:00 at statue in Plaza del Triunfo; minimum 4 people; cathedral tours—Mon, Wed, and Fri; Alcázar tours—Tue, Thu, and Sat; no Alcázar tours Jan and Aug).

Although you can just show up for Concepción's tours, it's smart to confirm the departure times and reserve a spot (tel. 902-158-226, mobile 616-501-100, www.sevillawalkingtours.com, info @sevillawalkingtours.com). Concepción does no tours on Sundays or holidays. Because she's a busy mom of two young kids, Concepción sometimes sends her colleague Alfonso (who's also excellent) to lead these tours.

All Sevilla Guided Tours

This group of three licensed guides (Susana, Estela, and Elena) offers good English-language private tours and day trips (€120/3 hours, €160/half-day, tel. 954-638-883, mobile 606-217-194, www .allsevillaguides.com, info@allsevillaguides.com).

Really Discover Seville

Englishman David and Sevillan Luis have teamed up to show off their city with several creatively conceived, good-value walks and bike rides—all run with small groups and a personal touch. Their **Seville Bike Tour** takes up to 10 riders on a 2.5-hour journey around the city, stopping at—but not entering—all the major sights (€25, 3-10 people per group, includes bike, daily at 10:30, meet near the cathedral by the tall white monument in Plaza del Triunfo). Each morning they also lead a two-hour **Seville Walking Tour** (€20, 3-10 per group, daily at 10:30), then give you the option to tack on a one-hour boat tour (€19 more, 10-seat electric boat with guide). Call or email to confirm before showing up, as tours may be canceled for lack of interest (tel. 955-113-912, www.reallydiscover.com, davidcox@reallydiscover.com).

BiciBike

This outfit offers several guided bike tours of Sevilla (€20/2 hours, €30/3 hours, includes bike and helmet, daily at 10:00, leaves from their office on ground floor of Santa Justa train station, best to reserve ahead, tel. 955-514-110, www.bicibike.es). They also rent bikes from the same office.

Hop-On, Hop-Off Bus Tours

Two competing city bus tours leave from the curb near the riverside Torre del Oro. You'll see the parked buses and salespeople handing out fliers. Each tour does about an hour-long swing through the city with recorded narration. The tours, which allow hopping on and off at four stops, are heavy on Expo '29 and Expo '92 neighborhoods—both zones of little interest in 2014. While the narration does its best, Sevilla is most interesting in places buses can't go (€17, daily 10:00-21:00, green route has shorter option).

Horse and Buggy Tours
A carriage ride is a classic, popular way to survey the city and a relaxing way to enjoy María Luisa Park (€45 for a 45-minute clip-clop, much more during Holy Week and the April Fair, find a likable English-speaking driver for better narration). Look for rigs at Plaza América, Plaza del Triunfo, the Torre del Oro, Alfonso XIII Hotel, and Avenida Isabel la Católica.

Boat Cruises
Boring one-hour panoramic tours leave every 30 minutes from the dock behind the Torre de Oro. The low-energy recorded narration is hard to follow, but there's little to see anyway (overpriced at €15, tel. 954-561-692).

More Tours
Visitours, a typical big-bus tour company, does €95 all-day trips to Córdoba, as well as several other locations in Andalucía (Tue, Thu, and Sat; tel. 955-999-760, mobile 686-413-413, www.visitours.es, visitours@visitours.es). For other guides, contact one of the **Guide Associations of Sevilla:** AUITS (mobile 699-494-204, www .auits.com, guias@auits.com) or APIT (tel. 954-210-044, www .apitsevilla.com, visitas@apitsevilla.com).

Self-Guided Walk

Barrio Santa Cruz
Of Sevilla's once-thriving Jewish Quarter, only the tangled street plan and a wistful Old World ambience survive. This classy maze

of lanes (too narrow for cars), small plazas, tile-covered patios, and whitewashed houses with wrought-iron latticework draped in flowers is a great refuge from the summer heat and bustle of Sevilla. The streets are narrow—some with buildings so close they're called "kissing lanes." A happy result of the narrowness is shade: Locals claim the Barrio Santa Cruz is three degrees cooler than the rest of the city.

Orange trees abound—because they never lose their leaves, they provide constant shade. But forget about eating the oranges. They're bitter and used only to make vitamins, perfume, cat food, and that marmalade you can't avoid in British B&Bs. But when they blossom (for three weeks in spring, usually in March), the aroma is heavenly.

The barrio is made for wandering. Getting lost is easy, and

SEVILLA

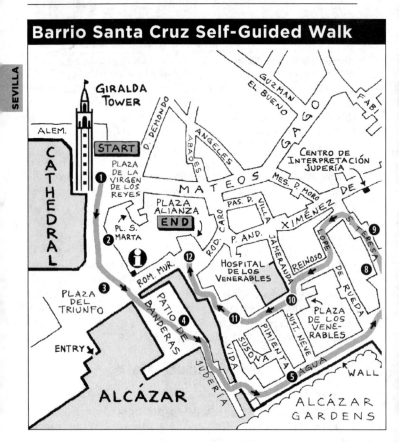

Barrio Santa Cruz Self-Guided Walk

I recommend doing just that. But to get started, here's a plaza-to-plaza walk that loops you through the *corazón* (heart) of the neighborhood and back out again.

Tour groups often trample the barrio's charm in the morning. I find that early evening (around 18:00) is the ideal time to explore the quarter.

❶ **Plaza de la Virgen de los Reyes:** Start in the square in front of the cathedral, at the base of the Giralda Bell Tower. This square is dedicated to the Virgin of the Kings—see her tile on the white wall facing the cathedral. She is one of several different versions of Mary you'll see in Sevilla, each appealing to a different type of worshipper. This particular one is big here because the Spanish king reportedly carried her image with him when he retook

1. Plaza de la Virgen de los Reyes
2. Nun Goodies
3. Plaza del Triunfo
4. Patio de Banderas
5. Calle Agua
6. Plaza de la Santa Cruz
7. Plaza de Refinadores
8. Casa de Murillo
9. Monasterio de San José del Carmen
10. Plaza de los Venerables, Hospital de los Venerables & Centro Velázquez
11. Plaza de Doña Elvira
12. Plaza de la Alianza

50 YARDS

50 METERS

⬅ WALKING TOUR

the town from the Moors in 1248. The fountain dates from 1929. The reddish Baroque building across the square is the Archbishop's Palace.

Notice the columns and chains that ring the cathedral, as if put there to establish a border between the secular and Catholic worlds. Indeed, that's exactly the purpose they served for centuries, when Sevillans running from the law merely had to cross these chains—like crossing the county line. (People in trouble didn't escape justice; they just had a bit of a choice as to who would administer it.) Many of these columns are far older than the cathedral, having originally been made for Roman and Visigothic buildings, and later recycled by medieval Catholics.

From this peaceful square, look up the street leading away from the cathedral and notice the characteristic (government-protected) 19th-century architecture. The ironwork, typical of Andalucía, is the pride of Sevilla. Equally ubiquitous is the traditional whitewash-and-goldenrod color scheme.

Another symbol you'll see throughout Sevilla is the city insignia: "NO*8*DO," the letters "NODO" with a figure-eight-like shape at their center. *Nodo* meant "knot" in the old dialect, and this symbol evokes the strong ties between the citizens of Sevilla and King Alfonso X (during a succession dispute in the 13th century, the Sevillans remained loyal to their king).

• *Keeping the cathedral on your right, walk toward the next square.*

❷ **Nun Goodies:** The white building on your left was an Augustinian convent. At #3, step inside to meet (but not see) a cloistered nun behind a *torno* (the lazy Susan the nuns spin to sell their goods while staying hidden). The sisters raise money by producing local goodies—like tasty communion wafer *tabletas* (€1—eating them is like having sin-free cookies) and lovely rosaries (€4). Consider buying something here just as a donation. The sisters, who speak only Spanish, have a sense of humor (daily 9:00-13:00 & 16:45-18:15).

• *Then step into...*

❸ **Plaza del Triunfo:** The "Plaza of Triumph" is named for the 1755 earthquake that destroyed Lisbon, but only rattled Sevilla, leaving most of this city intact. A statue thanking the Virgin for protecting the city is at the far end of the square, under a stone canopy. That Virgin faces another one (closer to you), atop a tall pillar honoring Sevillan artists, including the painter Murillo.

• *Before leaving the square, consider stopping at the TI for a map or advice. Then pass through the arched opening in the Alcázar's crenellated wall. You'll emerge into a courtyard called the...*

❹ **Patio de Banderas:** The Banderas Courtyard (as in "flags," not Antonio) was once a military parade ground for the royal guard. The barracks surrounding the square once housed the king's bodyguards. Farther back, a Moorish palace stood on this spot; archaeologists are busy excavating what remains of it. Today, the far end of this square is a favorite spot for snapping a postcard view of the Giralda Bell Tower.

• *Exit the courtyard at the far corner, through the Judería arch. Go down the long, narrow passage. Emerging into the light, you'll be walking*

Sevilla's Jews

In the summer of 1391, smoldering anti-Jewish sentiment flared up in Sevilla. On June 6, Christian mobs ransacked the city's Jewish Quarter (Judería). Around 4,000 Jews were killed, and 5,000 Jewish families were driven from their homes. Synagogues were stripped and transformed into churches. The former Judería eventually became the neighborhood of the Holy Cross-Barrio Santa Cruz. Sevilla's uprising spread through Spain (and Europe), the first of many nasty pogroms during the next century.

Before the pogrom, Jews had lived in Sevilla for centuries as the city's respected merchants, doctors, and bankers. They flourished under the Muslim Moors. After Sevilla was "liberated" by King Ferdinand III (1248), Jews were given protection by Spain's kings and allowed a measure of self-government, though they were confined to the Jewish neighborhood.

But by the 14th century, Jews were increasingly accused of everything from poisoning wells to ritually sacrificing Christian babies. Mobs killed suspected Jews, and some of Sevilla's most respected Jewish citizens had their fortunes confiscated.

After 1391, Jews faced a choice: Be persecuted (even killed), relocate, or convert to Christianity. The newly Christianized—called *conversos* (converted) or *marranos* (swine)—were always under suspicion of practicing their old faith in private, and thereby undermining true Christianity. Longtime Christians were threatened by this new social class of converted Jews, who now had equal status, fanning the mistrust.

To root out the perceived problem of underground Judaism, the "Catholic Monarchs," Ferdinand and Isabel, established the Inquisition in Spain (1478). Under the direction of Grand Inquisitor Tomás de Torquemada, these religious courts arrested and interrogated *conversos* suspected of practicing Judaism. Using long solitary confinement and torture, they extracted confessions.

On February 6, 1481, Sevilla hosted Spain's first auto-da-fé ("act of faith"), a public confession and punishment for heresy. Six accused *conversos* were paraded barefoot into the cathedral, made to publicly confess their sins, then burned at the stake. Over the next three decades, thousands of *conversos* were tried and killed in Spain.

In 1492, the same year the last Moors were driven from Spain, Ferdinand and Isabel decreed that all remaining Jews convert or be expelled (to Portugal and ultimately to Holland). Spain emerged as a nation unified under the banner of Christianity.

alongside the Alcázar wall. Take the first left, then right, through a small square and follow the narrow alleyway called...

❺ **Calle Agua:** As you walk along the street, look to the left, peeking through iron gates for occasional glimpses of the flower-smothered patios of exclusive private residences. The patio at #2

is a delight—ringed with columns, filled with flowers, and colored with glazed tiles. The tiles are not merely decorative; they keep buildings cooler in the summer heat. Emerging at the end of the street, turn around and look back at the open-ings of two old pipes built into the wall. These 12th-century Moorish pipes once carried water to the Alcázar (and today give the street its name). You're standing at an entrance into the pleasant Murillo Gardens (to the right), formerly the fruit-and-vegetable gardens for the Alcázar.

• *Don't enter the gardens now, but instead cross the square diagonally to the left, and continue 20 yards down a lane to the...*

❻ **Plaza de la Santa Cruz:** Arguably the heart of the barrio, this pleasant square, graced by orange trees and draping vines, was once the site of a synagogue (there used to be four in the barrio; now there are none), which Christians destroyed. They replaced the synagogue with a church, which the French (under Napoleon) later demolished. It's a bit of history that locals remember when they see the blue, white, and red French flag marking the French consulate, now overlooking this peaceful square. A fine 16th-century iron cross marks the center of the square and the site of the church the French destroyed. The Sevillan painter Murillo, who was buried in that church, lies somewhere below you.

At #9, you can peek into a lovely courtyard that's proudly been left open so visitors can enjoy it. The square is also home to the recommended Los Gallos flamenco bar, which puts on nightly performances.

• *At the far end of the square, a one-block detour along Calle Mezquita leads to nearby...*

❼ **Plaza de Refinadores:** Sevilla's most famous (if fictional) 17th-century citizen is honored here with a statue (see photo). Don Juan Tenorio—the original Don Juan—was a notorious sex addict and atheist who proudly thumbed his nose at the stifling Church-driven morals of his day.

• *Backtrack to Plaza de la Santa Cruz and turn right*

(north) on Calle Santa Teresa. At #8 (on the left) is...

8 Casa de Murillo: One of Sevilla's famous painters, Bartolomé Esteban Murillo (1618-1682), lived here, soaking in the ambience of street life and reproducing it in his paintings of cute beggar children.

• *Directly across from Casa de Murillo is the...*

9 Monasterio de San José del Carmen: This is where St. Teresa stayed when she visited from her hometown of Ávila. The convent (closed to the public) keeps artifacts of the mystic nun, such as her spiritual manuscripts.

Continue north on Calle Santa Teresa, then take the first left on Calle Lope de Rueda, then left again, then right on **Calle Reinoso**. This street—so narrow that the buildings almost touch—is one of the barrio's "kissing lanes." A popular explanation suggests the buildings were built so close together to provide maximum shade. But the history is more complex than that: this labyrinthine street plan goes back to Moorish times, when this area was a tangled market. Later, this was the Jewish ghetto, where all the city's Jews were forced to live in a very small area.

• *Just to the left, the street spills onto...*

10 Plaza de los Venerables: This square is another candidate for "heart of the barrio." The streets branching off it ooze local

ambience. When the Jews were expelled from Spain in 1492, this area became deserted and run-down. But in 1929, for its world's fair, Sevilla turned the plaza into a showcase of Andalusian style, adding the railings, tile work, orange trees, and other too-cute, Epcot-like adornments. A different generation of tourists enjoys the place today, likely unaware that what they're seeing in Santa Cruz is far from "authentic" (or, at least, not as old as they imagine).

The large, harmonious Baroque-style Hospital de los Venerables (1675), once a retirement home for old priests (the "venerables"), is now a cultural foundation worth visiting for its ornate church and excellent collection of paintings.

• *Continue west on Calle de Gloria, past an interesting tile map of the Jewish Quarter (on the right). You'll soon come upon...*

Sevilla at a Glance

▲▲▲**Flamenco** Flamboyant, riveting music-and-dance performances, offered at clubs throughout town. **Hours:** Shows start as early as 19:00. See page 59.

▲▲**Cathedral and Giralda Bell Tower** The world's largest Gothic church, with Columbus' tomb, treasury, and climbable tower. **Hours:** July-Aug Mon-Sat 9:30-17:00, Sun 14:30-18:00; Sept-June Mon-Sat 11:00-17:00, Sun 14:30-18:00. See page 24.

▲▲**Alcázar** Palace built by the Moors in the 10th century, revamped in the 14th century, and still serving as royal digs. **Hours:** April-Sept daily 9:30-19:00, Oct-March daily 9:30-17:00. See page 32.

▲▲**Hospital de la Caridad** Former charity hospital (funded by the likely inspiration for Don Juan) with gorgeously decorated chapel. **Hours:** Mon-Sat 9:00-13:00 & 15:30-19:00, Sun 9:00-12:30. See page 43.

▲▲**Basílica de la Macarena** Church and museum with the much-venerated Weeping Virgin statue and two significant floats from Sevilla's Holy Week celebrations. **Hours:** Daily 9:30-14:00 & 17:00-20:30. See page 51.

▲▲**Triana** Energetic, colorful neighborhood on the west bank of the river. **Hours:** Always strollable. See page 53.

▲▲**Bullfight Museum** Guided tour of the bullring and its museum. **Hours:** Daily May-Oct 9:30-20:00, Nov-April 9:00-19:00, on fight days until 14:00. See page 56.

▲▲**Evening Paseo** Locals strolling in the cool of the evening, mainly along Avenida de la Constitución, Barrio Santa Cruz, the

---

⓫ Plaza de Doña Elvira: This small square—with orange trees, tile benches, and a stone fountain—sums up our barrio walk. Shops sell work by local artisans, such as ceramics, embroidery, and fans.
• *Cross the plaza and head north along Calle Rodrigo Caro into the...*
⓬ Plaza de la Alianza: Ever consider a career change? Gain inspiration at the site that once housed the painting studio of John Fulton (1932-1998; find the small plaque on the other side of the square), an American

Calle Sierpes and Tetuán shopping pedestrian zone, and the Guadalquivir River. **Hours:** Spring through fall; best paseo scene 18:00-20:00, until very late at night in summer. See page 58.

▲**Archivo de Indias** Fantastic Renaissance building (Lonja Palace) housing Spain's national archives. **Hours:** Mon-Sat 9:30-17:00, Sun 10:00-14:00. See page 41.

▲**Church of the Savior** Sevilla's second-biggest church, bristling with Baroque altarpieces. **Hours:** July-Aug Mon-Sat 9:30-17:00, Sun 14:30-18:00; Sept-June Mon-Sat 11:00-17:00, Sun 14:30-18:00. See page 45.

▲**Museo Palacio de la Condesa de Lebrija** A fascinating 18th-century aristocratic mansion. **Hours:** July-Aug Mon-Fri 9:00-15:00, Sat 10:00-14:00, closed Sun; Sept-June Mon-Fri 10:30-19:30, Sat 10:00-14:00 & 16:00-18:00, Sun 10:00-14:00. See page 47.

▲**Flamenco Dance Museum** High-tech museum explaining the history and art of Sevilla's favorite dance. **Hours:** Daily 10:00-19:00. See page 47.

▲**Museo de Bellas Artes** Andalucía's top paintings, including works by Spanish masters Murillo and Zurbarán. **Hours:** Tue-Sat 10:00-20:30, Sun 10:00-17:00, closed Mon. See page 48.

▲**Bullfights** Some of Spain's best bullfighting, held at Sevilla's arena. **Hours:** Fights generally at 18:30 on most Sundays in May and June, on Easter and Corpus Christi, and daily through the April Fair and in late September. Rookies fight small bulls on Thursdays in July. See page 55.

who pursued two dreams. Though born in Philadelphia, Fulton got hooked on bullfighting. He trained in the tacky bullrings of Mexico, then in 1956 he moved to Sevilla, the world capital of the sport. His career as matador was not top-notch, and the Spaniards were slow to warm to the Yankee, but his courage and persistence earned their grudging respect. After he put down the cape, he picked up a brush, making colorful paintings in his Sevilla studio.

• *From Plaza de la Alianza, you can return to the cathedral by turning left (west) on Calle Joaquin Romero Murube (along the wall). Or, if you're ready for a bite, head northeast on Calle Rodrigo Caro, which intersects with Calle Mateos Gago, a street lined with tapas bars.*

Sights in Sevilla

▲▲Cathedral and Giralda Bell Tower

Sevilla's cathedral is the third-largest church in Europe (after St. Peter's at the Vatican and St. Paul's in London) and the largest

Gothic church anywhere. When they ripped down a mosque of brick on this site in 1401, the Reconquista Christians announced their intention to build a cathedral so huge that "anyone who sees it will take us for madmen." They built for about a hundred years. Even today, the descendants of those madmen proudly display an enlarged photocopy of their *Guinness Book of Records* letter certifying, "Santa María de la Sede in Sevilla is the cathedral with the largest area: 126.18 meters x 82.60 meters x 30.48 meters high."

Cost and Hours: €8, €3 for students and those over age 65 (must show ID), kids under age 18 free; keep your ticket, which includes free entry to the Church of the Savior—you'll save €3; July-Aug Mon-Sat 9:30-17:00, Sun 14:30-18:00; Sept-June Mon-Sat 11:00-17:00, Sun 14:30-18:00; closes 30 minutes earlier on Mondays year-round; last entry to cathedral one hour before closing, last entry to bell tower 30 minutes before closing; WC and drinking fountain just inside entrance and in courtyard near exit, tel. 954-214-971. Most of the website www.catedraldesevilla.es is in Spanish, but following the "vista virtual" links will take you to a virtual tour with an English option.

Crowd-Beating Tip: Though there's usually not much of a line to buy tickets, you can avoid the queue altogether by buying your €8 combo-ticket at the Church of the Savior, a few blocks north. See that church first, then come to the cathedral and waltz past the line to the turnstile.

Tours: My self-guided tour covers the basics. The €3 audioguide explains each side chapel for anyone interested in all the old paintings and dry details. For €7, you can enjoy Concepción Delgado's tour instead (see "Tours in Sevilla," earlier).

⊙ Self-Guided Tour: Enter the cathedral at the south end (closest to the Alcázar, with a full-size replica of the Giralda's

Bartolomé Murillo
(1617-1682)

The son of a barber of Seville, Bartolomé Murillo got his start selling paintings meant for export to the frontier churches of the Americas. In his 20s, he became famous after he painted a series of saints for Sevilla's Franciscan monastery. By about 1650, Murillo's sugary, simple, and accessible religious style was spreading through Spain and beyond.

Murillo painted street kids with cute smiles and grimy faces, and radiant young Marías with Ivory-soap complexions and rapturous poses (Immaculate Conceptions). His paintings view the world through a soft-focus lens, wrapping everything in warm colors and soft light, with a touch (too much, for some) of sentimentality.

Murillo became a rich, popular family man, and the toast of Sevilla's high society. In 1664, his wife died, leaving him heartbroken, but his last 20 years were his most prolific. At age 65, Murillo died after falling off a scaffold while painting. His tomb is lost somewhere under the bricks of Plaza de la Santa Cruz.

weathervane statue in the patio).

• *First, you pass through the...*

❶ **Art Pavilion:** Just past the turnstile, you step into a room of paintings that once hung in the church, including works by Sevilla's two 17th-century masters—Bartolomé Murillo (*St. Ferdinand,* depicting the king who freed Sevilla from the Moors) and Francisco de Zurbarán *(St. John the Baptist in the Desert).* Find a painting showing two of Sevilla's patron saints—Santa Justa and Santa Rufina, killed in ancient Roman times for their Christian faith. Potters by trade, these two are easy to identify by their pots and palm branches (symbolic of their martyrdom), and the bell tower symbolizing the town they protect. As you tour the cathedral, keep track of how many depictions of this dynamic and saintly duo you spot. They're everywhere.

• *Walking past a rack of church maps and a WC, enter the actual church. In the center of the church, sit down in front of the...*

❷ **High Altar:** Look through the wrought-iron Renaissance grille at what's called the largest altarpiece *(retablo mayor)* ever made—65 feet tall, with 44 scenes from the life of Jesus and Mary carved from walnut and chestnut, blanketed by a staggering amount of gold leaf. The work took three generations to complete

Sevilla's Cathedral

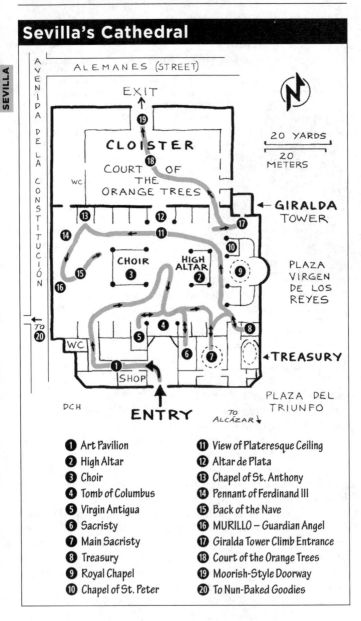

❶ Art Pavilion	⓫ View of Plateresque Ceiling
❷ High Altar	⓬ Altar de Plata
❸ Choir	⓭ Chapel of St. Anthony
❹ Tomb of Columbus	⓮ Pennant of Ferdinand III
❺ Virgin Antigua	⓯ Back of the Nave
❻ Sacristy	⓰ MURILLO – Guardian Angel
❼ Main Sacristy	⓱ Giralda Tower Climb Entrance
❽ Treasury	⓲ Court of the Orange Trees
❾ Royal Chapel	⓳ Moorish-Style Doorway
❿ Chapel of St. Peter	⓴ To Nun-Baked Goodies

(1481-1564). The story is told left to right, bottom to top. Find Baby Jesus in the manger, in the middle of the bottom row, then follow his story through the miracles, the Passion, and the Pentecost. Crane your neck to look way up to the tippy-top, where a Crucifixion adorns the dizzying summit.

• *Turn around and check out the...*

❸ Choir: Facing the high altar, the choir features an organ of more than 7,000 pipes (played Mon-Fri at the 10:00 Mass, Sun at the 10:00 & 13:00 Mass, not in July-Aug, free for worshippers). A choir area like this one—enclosed within the cathedral for more intimate services—is common in Spain and England, but rare in churches elsewhere. The big, spinnable book holder in the middle of the room held giant hymnals—large enough for all to chant from in a pre-Xerox age when there weren't enough books for everyone.

• *Now turn 90 degrees to the left and march to find the...*

❹ Tomb of Columbus: In front of the cathedral's entrance for pilgrims are four kings who carry the tomb of Christopher Columbus. His pallbearers represent the regions of Castile, Aragon, León, and Navarre (identify them by their team shirts). Notice how the cross held by Señor León has a pike end, which is piercing an orb. Look closer: It's a pomegranate, the symbol of Granada—the last Moorish-ruled city to succumb to the Reconquista (in 1492).

Columbus didn't just travel a lot while alive—he even kept it up posthumously. He was buried first in northwestern Spain (in Valladolid, where he died), then moved to a monastery here in Sevilla, then to what's now the Dominican Republic (as he'd requested), then to Cuba. Finally—when Cuba gained independence from Spain, around 1900—his remains sailed home again to Sevilla. After all that, it's fair to wonder whether the remains in the box before you are actually his. Sevillans like to think so. (Columbus died in 1506. Five hundred years later, to help celebrate the anniversary of his death, DNA samples did indeed give Sevillans some evidence to substantiate their claim.)

Immaculate Conception

Throughout Sevilla—and all of Spain—you'll see paintings titled *The Immaculate Conception,* all looking quite similar (see example on page 25). Young, lovely, and beaming radiantly, these virgins look pure and untainted...you might even say "immaculate." According to Catholic doctrine, Mary, the future mother of Jesus, entered the world free from the original sin that other mortals share. When she died, her purity allowed her to be taken up directly to heaven (in the Assumption).

The doctrine of Immaculate Conception can be confusing, even to Catholics. It does not mean that the Virgin Mary herself was born of a virgin. Rather, Mary's mother and father conceived her in the natural way. But at the moment Mary's soul animated her flesh, God granted her a special exemption from original sin. The doctrine of Immaculate Conception had been popular since medieval times, though it was not codified until 1854. It was Sevilla's own Bartolomé Murillo (1617-1682) who painted the model of this goddess-like Mary, copied by so many lesser artists. In Counter-Reformation times (when Murillo lived), paintings of a fresh-faced, ecstatic Mary made abstract doctrines like the Immaculate Conception and the Assumption tangible and accessible to Catholics across Europe.

Most images of the Immaculate Conception show Mary wearing a radiant crown and with a crescent moon at her feet; she often steps on the heads of cherubs. Paintings by Murillo frequently portray Mary in a blue robe with long, wavy hair—young and innocent.

On the left is a 1584 mural of St. Christopher, patron saint of travelers. The clock above has been ticking since 1788.

• *Facing Columbus, turn right and duck into the first chapel (on your left) to find the...*

❺ **Virgin Antigua:** Within this chapel is a gilded fresco of the Virgin delicately holding a rose and the Christ Child, who's holding a bird. It's the oldest art here, even older than the cathedral itself: It was painted onto a horseshoe-shaped prayer niche of the mosque that formerly stood on this site. After Sevilla was reconquered in 1248, the mosque served as a church for about 120 years—until it was torn down to make room for this huge cathedral. The Catholic builders, who were captivated by the fresco's beauty and well aware of the Virgin Antigua's status as protector of sailors (important in this port city), decided to save the fresco.

• *Exiting the Virgin Antigua Chapel, begin your counterclockwise tour of the cathedral. As you explore, note that its many chapels are described in English, and many of the windows have their dates worked into the design.*

Just on the other side of Columbus, walk through the next small chapel and into the...

❻ **Sacristy:** This space is where the priests get ready each morning before Mass. The Goya painting above the altar features another portrayal of Justa and Rufina with their trademark bell tower, pots, and palm leaves.

• *Two chapels down is the entrance to the...*

❼ **Main Sacristy:** Marvel at the ornate, 16th-century dome of the main room, a grand souvenir from Sevilla's Golden Age.

The intricate masonry, called Plateresque, resembles lacy silverwork (*plata* means "silver"). God is way up in the cupola. The three layers of figures below him show the heavenly host; relatives in purgatory—hands folded—looking to heaven in hope of help; and the wretched in hell, including a topless sinner engulfed in flames and teased cruelly by pitchfork-wielding monsters.

Dominating the room is a nearly 1,000-pound, silver-plated monstrance (vessel for displaying the communion wafer). This is the one locals use to parade the holy host through town during Corpus Christi festivities.

• *At the far end of the main sacristy, at the left-hand corner, is a door leading to our next stop.*

❽ **Treasury:** The *tesoro* fills several rooms in the corner of the church. Wander deeper into the treasury to find a unique oval dome. It's in the 16th-century chapter room *(sala capitular),* where monthly meetings take place with the bishop (he gets the throne, while the others share the bench). The paintings here are

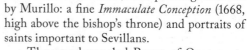

by Murillo: a fine *Immaculate Conception* (1668, high above the bishop's throne) and portraits of saints important to Sevillans.

The wood-paneled Room of Ornaments shows off gold and silver reliquaries, which hold hundreds of holy body parts, as well as Spain's most valuable crown. This jeweled crown (the Corona de la Virgen de los Reyes, by Manuel de la Torres) sparkles with thousands of tiny but precious stones, and the world's largest pearl—used as the torso of an angel. This amazing treasure was paid for by locals who donated their wealth to royally crown their Madonna.

• *Leave the treasury and cross through the church to see...*

More Church Sights: First you'll pass the closed-to-tourists ❾ **Royal Chapel,** the burial place of several of kings of Castile (open for worship only—access from outside), then the also-closed ❿ **Chapel of St. Peter,** which is filled with paintings showing scenes from the life of St. Peter. In the far corner—past the glass case displaying the *Guinness Book* certificate declaring that this is indeed the world's largest church by area—is the entry to the Giralda Bell Tower; we'll finish our visit there. But for now, continue your counterclockwise circuit. Near the high altar, in the middle, crane your neck skyward to admire the ⓫ **Plateresque tracery** on the ceiling, and take in the enormous ⓬ **Altar de Plata** rising up in a side chapel. The gleaming silver altarpiece adorned with statues looks like a big monstrance.

The ⓭ **Chapel of St. Anthony** (Capilla de San Antonio), the last chapel on the right, is used for baptisms. The Renaissance baptismal font has delightful carved angels dancing along its base. In Murillo's painting, *Vision of St. Anthony* (1656), the saint kneels in wonder as a Baby Jesus comes down surrounded by a choir of angels. Anthony, one of Iberia's most popular saints, is the patron saint of lost things—so people come here to pray for Anthony's help in finding

jobs, car keys, and life partners. Above the *Vision* is *The Baptism of Christ,* also by Murillo. You don't need to be an art historian to know that the stained glass dates from 1685. And by now you must know who the women are....

Nearby, a glass case displays the ⓮ **pennant of Ferdinand III,** which was raised over the minaret of the mosque on November 23, 1248, as Christian forces finally expelled the Moors from Sevilla. For centuries, it was paraded through the city on special days.

Continuing on, stand at the ⓯ **back of the nave** (behind the choir) and appreciate the ornate immensity of the church. Can you see the angels trumpeting on their Cuban mahogany? Any birds? The massive candlestick holder to the right of the choir dates from 1560. And before you is the gravestone of Ferdinand Columbus, Christopher's second son. Having given the cathedral his collection of 6,000 precious books, he was rewarded with this prime burial spot.

Turn around. To the left, behind an iron grille, is a niche with ⓰ **Murillo's** *Guardian Angel* pointing to the light and showing an astonished child the way.

• *Backtrack the length of the church toward the Giralda Bell Tower, and notice the back of the choir's Baroque pipe organ. The exit sign leads to*

the Court of the Orange Trees and the exit. But first, some exercise.

⑰ Giralda Tower Climb: Your church admission includes entry to the bell tower. Notice the beautiful Moorish simplicity as you climb to its top, 330 feet up, for a grand city view. The spiraling ramp was designed to accommodate a donkey-riding muezzin, who clip-clopped up five times a day to give the Muslim call to prayer.

• *Back on the ground, head outside to the...*

⑱ Court of the Orange Trees: Today's cloister was once the mosque's Court of the Orange Trees (Patio de los Naranjos).

Twelfth-century Muslims stopped at the fountain in the middle to wash their hands, face, and feet before praying. The ankle-breaking lanes between the bricks were once irrigation streams—a reminder that the Moors introduced irrigation to Iberia. The mosque was made of bricks; the church is built of stone. The only large-scale remnants of the mosque today are the Court of the Orange Trees, the Giralda Bell Tower, and the site itself.

• *You'll exit the cathedral through the Court of the Orange Trees (WCs are at the far end of the courtyard, downstairs). As you leave, look back from the outside and notice the arch over the...*

⑲ Moorish-Style Doorway: As with much of the Moorish-looking art in town, this doorway is actually Christian—the two coats of arms are a giveaway. The relief above the door shows the Bible story of Jesus ridding the temple of the merchants...a reminder to contemporary merchants that there will be no retail activity in the church. The plaque on the right honors Miguel de Cervantes, the great 16th-century writer. It's one of many plaques scattered throughout town showing places mentioned in his books. (In this case, the topic was pickpockets.) The huge green doors predate the church. They are bits of the pre-1248 mosque—wood covered with bronze. Study the fine workmanship.

Giralda Tower Exterior: Step across the street from the exit gate and look at the bell tower. Formerly a Moorish minaret from which Muslims were called to prayer, it became the cathedral's bell tower after the Reconquista. A 4,500-pound bronze statue symbolizing the Triumph of Faith (specifically, the Christian faith over the Muslim one) caps the tower and serves as a weather vane (in Spanish, *girar* means "to rotate"; a *giraldillo* is something that rotates). In 1356, the original top of the tower fell. You're looking at a 16th-century Christian-built top with a ribbon of letters proclaiming, "The strongest tower is the name of God" (you can see *Fortísima*—"strongest"—from this vantage point).

Now circle around for a close look at the corner of the tower at ground level. Needing more strength than their bricks could provide for the lowest section of the tower, the Moors used Roman-cut stones. You can actually read the Latin that was chiseled onto one of the stones 2,000 years ago. The tower offers a brief recap of the city's history: It sits on a Roman foundation, has a long Moorish section, which is capped by the current Christian age.

Today, by law, no building in the center may be higher than the statue atop the tower. (But the new Cajasol Tower, just across the river, is by far the tallest erection in the greater city—and that offends locals in this conservative town. The fact that it's the headquarters of one of Spain's major banks, which many Spaniards blame for the economic crisis, hasn't helped its popularity.)

• *Your cathedral tour is finished. If you've worked up an appetite, get out your map and make your way a few blocks for some...*

❷⓿ **Nun-Baked Goodies:** Stop by the El Torno Pastelería de Conventos, a co-op where various orders of cloistered nuns send their handicrafts (such as baptismal dresses for babies) and baked goods to be sold. You won't actually see *el torno* (a lazy Susan), since this shop is staffed by non-nuns, but this humble little hole-in-the-wall shop is worth a peek, and definitely serves the best cookies, bar nun. It's located through the passageway at 24 Avenida de la Constitución, immediately in front of the cathedral's main front door: Go through the doorway marked *Plaza del Cabildo* into the quiet courtyard (Mon-Fri 10:00-13:30 & 17:00-19:30, Sat-Sun 10:30-14:00, closed Aug, Plaza del Cabildo 2, tel. 954-219-190).

▲▲Alcázar

Originally a 10th-century palace built for the governors of the local Moorish state, this building still functions as a royal palace—the oldest in Europe that's still in use. The core of the palace features an extensive 14th-century rebuild, done by Muslim workmen for the Christian king, Pedro I (1334-1369). Pedro was nicknamed either "the Cruel" or "the Just," depending on which end of his sword you were on. Pedro's palace embraces both cultural traditions.

Today, visitors can enjoy several sections

SEVILLA

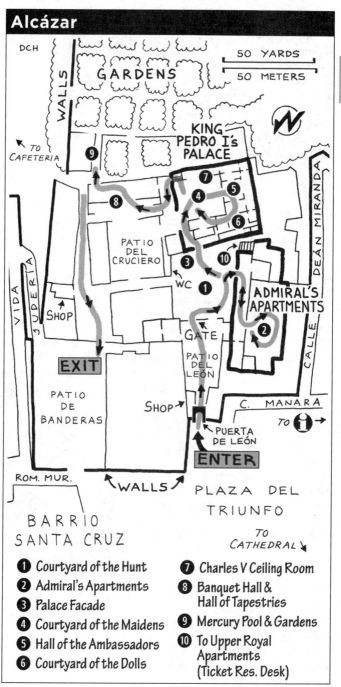

Alcázar

DCH

WALLS

GARDENS

50 YARDS
50 METERS

N

← TO
CAFETERIA

KING
PEDRO I's
PALACE

DEÁN MIRANDA

9

8

7

4

5

6

PATIO
DEL
CRUCIERO

3

10

WC

1

JUDERÍA

VIDA

SHOP

ADMIRAL'S
APARTMENTS

2

CALLE

GATE

EXIT

PATIO
DEL
LEÓN

PATIO
DE
BANDERAS

SHOP

C. MANARA

TO ℹ →

PUERTA
DE LEÓN

ENTER

ROM. MUR.

WALLS

PLAZA DEL
TRIUNFO

BARRIO
SANTA CRUZ

TO
CATHEDRAL ↘

1 Courtyard of the Hunt

2 Admiral's Apartments

3 Palace Facade

4 Courtyard of the Maidens

5 Hall of the Ambassadors

6 Courtyard of the Dolls

7 Charles V Ceiling Room

8 Banquet Hall &
Hall of Tapestries

9 Mercury Pool & Gardens

10 To Upper Royal
Apartments
(Ticket Res. Desk)

of the Alcázar. Spectacularly decorated halls and courtyards have distinctive Islamic-style flourishes. Exhibits call up the era of Columbus and Spain's New World dominance. The lush, sprawling gardens invite exploration.

Cost and Hours: €9 (free Mon after 15:00), €2 for students and seniors over 65—must show ID, free for children under 16, open April-Sept daily 9:30-19:00, Oct-March daily 9:30-17:00, tel. 954-502-324, www.alcazarsevilla.org.

Crowd-Beating Tips: To skip the ticket-buying line, reserve a time slot ahead online (https://oberonsaas.com/realalcazarsevilla). Mornings are the busiest with tour groups (especially on Tuesdays). It's less crowded late in the day—but note that the Royal Apartments can only be visited before 13:30.

Tours: The fast-moving, €4 audioguide gives you an hour of information as you wander. My self-guided tour hits the highlights, or you could consider Concepción Delgado's Alcázar tour.

The **Upper Royal Apartments** can only be visited with a separate tour (€4.35, includes separate audioguide, must check bags in provided lockers). For some, it's worth the extra time and cost just to escape the mobs in the rest of the palace. If you're interested, once inside the Alcázar go directly to the desk and reserve a spot. Groups of 15 leave every half-hour from 10:00 to 13:30, listening to the 30-minute audio tour while escorted by a security guard.

◉ Self-Guided Tour: This royal palace is decorated with a mix of Islamic and Christian elements—a style called Mudejar. It offers a thought-provoking glimpse of a graceful Al-Andalus world that might have survived its Castilian conquerors...but didn't. The floor plan is intentionally confusing, to make experiencing the place more exciting and surprising. While Granada's Alhambra was built by Moors for Moorish rulers,

what you see here is essentially a Christian ruler's palace, built in the Moorish style by Moorish artisans.

• *Buy your ticket and enter through the turnstiles. Pass through the garden-like Patio of the Lions (Patio del León), with the rough stone wall of the older Moorish fortress on your left (c. 913), and through the arch into a courtyard called the . . .*

❶ Courtyard of the Hunt (Patio de la Montería): Get oriented. The palace's main entrance is directly ahead, through the elaborately decorated facade. WCs are in the far-left corner. In the far-right corner is the staircase and ticket booth for the Upper Royal Apartments—if you're interested, reserve an entry time now.

SEVILLA

Christopher Columbus
(1451-1506)

This Italian wool-weaver ran off to sea, was shipwrecked in Portugal, married a captain's daughter, learned Portuguese and Spanish, and convinced Spain's monarchs to finance his bold scheme to trade with the East by sailing west. On August 3, 1492, Columbus set sail from Palos (near Huelva, 60 miles west of Sevilla) with 3 ships and 90 men, hoping to land in Asia, which Columbus estimated was 3,000 miles away. Ten weeks—and yes, 3,000 miles—later, with a superstitious crew ready to mutiny after they'd seen evil omens (including a falling meteor and a jittery compass), Columbus landed on an island in the Bahamas, convinced he'd reached Asia. He and his crew traded with the "Indians" and returned home to Palos harbor, where they were received as heroes.

Columbus made three more voyages to the New World and became rich with gold. But he gained a bad reputation among the colonists, was arrested, and returned to Spain in chains. Though pardoned, Columbus fell out of favor with the court. On May 20, 1506, he died in Valladolid. His son said he was felled by "gout and by grief at seeing himself fallen from his high estate," but historians speculate that diabetes or syphilis may have contributed. Columbus died thinking he'd visited Asia, unaware he'd opened up Europe to a New World.

The palace complex was built over many centuries, with rooms and decorations from the various rulers who've lived here. Moorish

caliphs first built the original 10th-century palace and gardens. Then, after Sevilla was Christianized in 1248, King Pedro I built the most famous part of the complex. During Spain's Golden Age, it was home to Ferdinand and Isabel and, later, their grandson Charles V (a.k.a. Carlos I); they all left their mark. Successive monarchs added still more luxury. And today's king and queen still use the palace's upper floor as one of their royal residences.

• *Before entering the heart of the palace, start in the wing to the right of the courtyard. Step inside.*

❷ **Admiral's Apartments (Cuarto del Almirante):** When Queen Isabel debriefed Columbus here after his New World discoveries, she realized what he'd found could be big business. She created this wing in 1503 to administer Spain's New World ventures. In these halls, Columbus recounted his travels, Ferdinand

Magellan planned his around-the-world cruise, and mapmaker Amerigo Vespucci tried to come up with a catchy moniker for that newly discovered continent.

In the pink-and-red Audience Chamber (once a chapel), the **altarpiece painting** is of St. Mary of the Navigators (*Santa María de los Navegantes*, by Alejo Fernández, 1530s). The Virgin—the patron saint of sailors and a favorite of Columbus—keeps watch over the puny ships beneath her. Her cape seems to protect everyone under it—even the Native Americans in the dark background (the first time "Indians" were painted in Europe).

Standing beside the Virgin (on the right, dressed in gold, joining his hands together in prayer) is none other than Christopher Columbus. He stands on a cloud, because he's now in heaven (this was painted a few decades after his death). Notice that Columbus is blond. Columbus' son said of his dad: "In his youth his hair was blond, but when he reached 30, it all turned white." Many historians believe this to be the earliest known portrait of Columbus. If so, it's also likely to be the most accurate. The man on the left side of the painting, with the gold cape, is King Ferdinand.

Left of the painting is a **model** of Columbus' *Santa María*, his flagship and the only of his three ships not to survive the 1492 voyage. Columbus complained that the *Santa María*—a big cargo ship, different from the sleek *Niña* and *Pinta* caravels— was too slow. On Christmas Day it ran aground off present-day Haiti and tore a hole in its hull. The ship was dismantled to build the first permanent structure in America, a fort for 39 colonists. (After Columbus left, the natives burned the fort and killed the colonists.) Opposite the altarpiece (in the center of the back wall) is the family **coat of arms** of Columbus' descendants, who now live in Spain and Puerto Rico. Using Columbus' Spanish name, it reads: "To Castile and to León, Colón gave a new world."

Return to the still-used reception room, filled with big canvases. The **biggest painting** (and most melodramatic) shows a key turning point in Sevilla's history: King Ferdinand III humbly kneels before the bishop, giving thanks to God for helping him liberate the city from the Muslims (in 1248). Ferdinand promptly turned the Alcázar of the caliphs into the royal palace of Christian kings.

Pop into the room beyond the grand piano for a look at some ornate **fans** (mostly foreign and well-described in English). A long painting (designed to be gradually rolled across a screen and viewed like a primitive movie) shows 17th-century Sevilla during Holy Week. Follow the procession, which is much like today's, with traditional floats carried by teams of men and followed by a retinue of penitents.

• *Return to the Courtyard of the Hunt. Face the impressive entrance in the...*

❸ **Palace Facade:** This is the entrance to **King Pedro I's Palace** (Palacio del Rey Pedro I), the Alcázar's 14th-century nucleus. The facade's elaborate blend of Islamic tracery and Gothic Christian elements introduces us to the Mudejar style seen throughout Pedro's part of the palace.

• *Enter the palace. Pass through the vestibule (impressive, yes, but we'll see better), and continue left through the maze of rooms and passageways until you emerge into the big courtyard with a long pool in the center. This is the...*

❹ **Courtyard of the Maidens (Patio de las Doncellas):** You've reached the center of King Pedro's palace. It's an open-air

courtyard, surrounded by rooms. In the center is a long, rectangular reflecting pool. Like the Moors who preceded him, Pedro built his palace around water.

King Pedro cruelly abandoned his wife and moved into the Alcázar with his mistress, then hired Muslim workers from Granada to re-create the romance of that city's Alhambra in Sevilla's stark Alcázar. The designers created a microclimate engineered for coolness: water, sunken gardens, pottery, thick walls, and darkness. This palace is considered Spain's best example of the Mudejar style. Stucco panels with elaborate designs, colorful ceramic tiles, coffered wooden ceilings, and lobed arches atop slender columns create a refined, pleasing environment. The elegant proportions and symmetry of this courtyard are a photographer's delight.

• *Explore the rooms branching off the courtyard. Through the door at the end of the long reflecting pool is the palace's most important room, called the...*

❺ Hall of the Ambassadors (Salón de Embajadores): Here, in his throne room, Pedro received guests and caroused

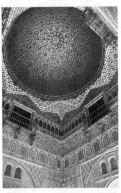

in luxury. The room is a cube topped with a half-dome, like many important Islamic buildings. In Islam, the cube represents the earth, and the dome is the starry heavens. In Pedro's world, the symbolism proclaimed that he controlled heaven and earth. Islamic horseshoe arches stand atop recycled columns with golden capitals.

The stucco on the walls is molded with interlacing plants, geometrical shapes, and Arabic writing. Here, in a Christian palace, the walls are inscribed with unapologetically Muslim sayings: "None but Allah conquers" and "Happiness and prosperity are benefits of Allah, who nourishes all creatures." The artisans added propaganda phrases, such as "Dedicated to the magnificent Sultan Pedro—thanks to God!"

The Mudejar style also includes Christian motifs. Find the row of kings, high up at the base of the dome, chronicling all of Spain's rulers from the 600s to the 1600s. Throughout the palace (as in the center of the dome above you), you'll see coats of arms—including the castle of Castile and the lion of León. There are also natural objects (such as shells and birds), which you wouldn't normally find in Islamic decor, as it traditionally avoids realistic images of nature.

Wander through adjoining rooms. Notice how it gets cooler as you go deeper into the palace. Straight ahead from the Hall of the Ambassadors, in the **Philip II Ceiling Room** (Salón del Techo de Felipe II), look above the arches to find peacocks, falcons, and

other birds amid interlacing vines. Imagine day-to-day life in the palace—with VIP guests tripping on the tiny steps.

• *Make your way to the second courtyard, nearby (in the Hall of the Ambassadors, face the Courtyard of the Maidens, then walk to the left). This smaller courtyard is the...*

❻ Courtyard of the Dolls (Patio de las Muñecas): This delicate courtyard was reserved for the king's private family life. Originally, the center of the courtyard had a pool, cooling the residents and reflecting decorative patterns that were once brightly painted on the walls. The columns—recycled from ancient Roman and Visigothic buildings—are of alternating white, black, and pink marble. (Pedro's original courtyard was a single story; the upper floors and skylight were added centuries later.) The courtyard's name comes from the tiny doll faces found at the base of one of the arches. Circle the room and try to find them. (Hint: While just a couple of inches tall, they're eight feet high.)

• *The long adjoining room with the gilded ceiling, the* **Prince's Room** (Cuarto del Príncipe), *was Queen Isabel's bedroom, where she gave birth to a son, Prince Juan.*

Return to the Courtyard of the Maidens. Look up and notice the second story. Isabel's grandson, Charles V, added it in the 16th century. See the difference in styles: Mudejar below (lobed arches and elaborate tracery), and Renaissance above (round arches and less decoration).

As you stand in the courtyard with your back to the Hall of the Ambassadors, the door in the middle of the right side leads to the...

❼ **Charles V Ceiling Room (Salón del Techo del Carlos V):** Emperor Charles V, who ruled Spain at its peak of New World wealth, expanded the palace. The reason? His marriage to his beloved Isabel—which took place in this room—that joined vast realms of Spain and Portugal. Devoutly Christian, Charles celebrated his wedding night with a midnight Mass, and later ordered the Mudejar ceiling in this room to be replaced with the less Islamic (but no less impressive) Renaissance one you see today.

• *We've seen the core of King Pedro's palace, with the additions by his successors. Return to the Courtyard of the Maidens, then turn right. In the corner, find the staircase built in a strikingly different style: a century older than its surroundings, it was originally Gothic, then renovated in Renaissance times. Follow the stairs up to rooms decorated with bright ceramic tiles and Gothic vaulting. Pass through the chapel and into two big, long, parallel rooms, the...*

❽ **Banquet Hall (Salón Gótico)** and **Hall of Tapestries (Salón Tapices):** The first room you enter is the big, airy banquet

hall where Charles and Isabel held their wedding reception. Tiles of yellow, blue, green, and orange line the room, some decorated with whimsical human figures with vase-like bodies. The windows open onto views of the gardens.

Next door, the walls are hung with 18th-century Spanish copies of 16th-century Belgian tapestries showing the conquests, trade, and industriousness of Charles' prosperous reign. (The highlights are described in Spanish along the top, and in Latin along the bottom.) The map tapestry of the Mediterranean world has south pointing up. Find Genova, Italy, on the bottom; Africa on top; Lisbon *(Liboa)* on the far right; and the large city of Barcelona in between. The artist included himself holding the legend—with a scale in both leagues and miles.

Facing the map, head to the far left end of room, where the wall is filled by a dramatic portrayal of the Spanish navy. Spain ruled the waves—and thereby an empire upon which the sun never set. Its reign lasted from 1492 until the Battle of Trafalgar in 1805; after that, Britannia's navy took the helm, and it was her crown that controlled the next global empire.

• *At the far end of the Banquet Hall, head outside to the...*

❾ **Mercury Pool and Gardens:** The Mercury Pool, a reservoir fed by a 16th-century aqueduct, irrigated the palace's entire garden. As only elites had running water, the fountain was an extravagant show of power. Check out the bronze statue of Mercury, with his cute little winged feet. The wall defining the east side of the garden was  part of the original Moorish castle wall. In the early 1600s, when fortifications were no longer needed here, that end was redesigned to be a grotto-style gallery.

From the Mercury Pool, steps lead into the formal gardens. Just past the bottom of the steps, a tunnel on the right leads under the palace to the coolest spot in the city.

Finally, explore the gardens. The intimate geometric zone nearest the palace is the Moorish garden. The far-flung garden beyond that was the backyard of the Christian ruler.

Here in the gardens, as in the rest of the palace, the Christian and Islamic traditions merge. Both cultures used water and nature as essential parts of their architecture. The garden's pavilions and fountains only enhance this. Wander among palm trees, myrtle hedges, and fragrant roses. While tourists pay to be here, this is actually a public garden, and free to locals. It's been that way since 1931, when the king was exiled and Spanish citizens took ownership of royal holdings. In 1975, the Spanish people allowed the king back on the throne—but on their terms...which included keeping this garden.

• *On the other side of the east wall is an air-conditioned **cafeteria** with a nice terrace overlooking the gardens.*

If you've booked a spot to visit the Upper Royal Apartments, return to the Courtyard of the Hunt, and head upstairs.

❿ Upper Royal Apartments (Cuarto Real Alto): This is the royal palace of today's monarchs. Fifteen public reception rooms are open to visitors: the official dining room, Audience Hall, and so on. The rooms are amply decorated with Versailles-like furniture, chandeliers, carpets, and portraits of 19th-century nobility. The highlight is the Audience Room, a Mudejar-style room overlooking the Patio de la Montería.

• *Your Alcázar tour is over. From the Moors to Pedro the Cruel to Ferdinand and Isabel, and from Charles V to King Juan Carlos and Queen Sofía, we've seen the home of a millennium of Spanish kings and queens. When you're ready to go, head out through the **Patio de Banderas**, once the entrance for guests arriving by horse carriage. Enjoy a classic Giralda Bell Tower view as you leave.*

Near the Cathedral
▲Archivo de Indias in the Lonja Palace

The Lonja Palace, across the street from the Alcázar, houses the historic archives for all of Spain. Its four miles of shelving contain the precious documents of a once-mighty empire. While little of interest is actually on show, a visit is free, easy, and gives a look at one of the finest Renaissance palaces in Spain. Designed by royal architect Juan de Herrera, the principal designer of El Escorial, the building evokes the greatness of the Spanish empire at its peak (c. 1600).

Cost and Hours: Free, Mon-Sat 9:30-17:00, Sun 10:00-14:00, Avenida de la Constitución 3, tel. 954-500-528.

Visiting the Palace: Originally this was a market for traders—an early stock market. But by the end of the 1600s, Sevilla had become a backwater (after suffering plagues and the silting up of its harbor, which allowed Cádiz to overtake Sevilla as Spain's main port of embarkation), and in 1717, the building was abandoned. In 1785, it was put to new use as the storehouse for all the documents the country was quickly amassing from its discovery and conquest of the New World.

Start you visit on the ground floor, where an interesting 15-minute intro video plays in a continuous loop. Then climb the extravagant stairs to the top floor and make a big circle to check out the temporary exhibits.

Avenida de la Constitución

Old Sevilla is bisected by this grand boulevard. Its name celebrates the country's 1978 adoption of a democratic constitution, as the Spanish people moved quickly to re-establish their government after the 1975 death of longtime dictator Francisco Franco.

The busy avenue was converted into a pedestrian boulevard in 2007. Overnight, the city's paseo route took on a new dimension.

Suddenly cafés and shops here had fresh appeal. (Two Starbucks moved in, strategically bookending the boulevard, but they're having a tough time winning over locals who prefer small €1 coffees to mammoth €4 ones.) The new tram line (infamously short, at only about a mile long) is controversial, as it violates what might have been a more purely pedestrian zone.

In Barrio Santa Cruz

Hospital de los Venerables

Buried in the Barrio Santa Cruz, this former charity-run old-folks' home and hospital comes with a Baroque church and an exquisite painting gallery that includes the Centro Velázquez, which displays works by one of Spain's premier artists. Everything is well-explained by the included audioguide.

Cost and Hours: €5.50, free on Sunday evenings, open daily 10:00-14:00 & 16:00-20:00, Plaza de los Venerables 8, tel. 954-562-696, www.focus.abengoa.es.

Visiting the Hospital: In the **courtyard,** with its sunken fountain, you get a sense of how this facility housed retired priests and Sevilla's needy.

The **church,** which takes you back to the year 1700, is bursting with Baroque decor, one of Spain's best pipe organs, and frescoes by Juan de Valdés Leal. The decor exalts the priesthood and Spain's role as standard-bearer of the pope.

The top-notch **painting gallery** is dedicated to one of the world's greatest painters, Diego Velázquez (1599-1660), who was born here in Sevilla, where he also worked as a young man. Velázquez's *Vista de Sevilla* helps you imagine the excitement of this thriving city in 1660 when, with 140,000 people, it was the fourth-largest in Europe. You'll recognize landmarks like the Giralda Tower, the cathedral, and the Torre del Oro. The pontoon bridge leads to Triana—where citizens of all ranks strolled the promenade together, as they still do today.

The Sevilla that shaped Velázquez was the gateway to the New World. There was lots of stimulation: Adventurers, fortune hunters, and artists passed through here, and many stayed for years. Of the few Velázquez paintings remaining in his hometown, three are in this gallery.

Centro de Interpretación Judería de Sevilla

This small, overpriced interpretive museum, standing in the heart of Barrio Santa Cruz, chronicles the history of Sevilla's Jews, who once called this neighborhood home. Bilingual placards and a few displays give visitors a glimpse of Sevilla's Sephardic heritage. However, most find the Casa de Sefarad in Córdoba more interesting.

Cost and Hours: €6.50, Mon-Sat 10:30-15:30 & 17:00-

20:00, Sun 11:00-19:00, guided tours in English may be available on request, Calle Ximénez de Enciso 22, tel. 954-047-089, www .juderiadesevilla.es.

Between the River and the Cathedral
▲▲Hospital de la Caridad

This charity hospital, which functioned as a place of final refuge for Sevilla's poor and homeless, was founded in the 17th century by the nobleman Don Miguel Mañara. Your visit includes an evocative courtyard, his office, a church filled with powerful art, and a good audioguide that explains it all. This is still a working hospice, so when you pay your entrance fee, you're advancing the work Mañara started back in the 17th century.

Cost and Hours: €5, includes good audioguide, Mon-Sat 9:00-13:00 & 15:30-19:00, Sun 9:00-12:30, last entry 30 minutes before closing, Calle Temprado 3, tel. 954-223-232, www.santa -caridad.es.

Background: The Hospice and Hospital of the Holy Charity in Sevilla was founded by the Venerable Servant of God, Don Miguel Mañara (1626-1679). Mañara was a big-time playboy and enthusiastic sinner who, late in life, had a massive change of heart. He spent his last years dedicating his life to strict worship and taking care of the poor. In 1674, Mañara acquired some empty warehouses in Sevilla's old shipyard and built this 150-ward "place of heroic virtues."

Mañara could well have been the inspiration for Don Juan, the quasi-legendary character from a play set in 17th-century Sevilla, popularized later by Lord Byron's poetry and Mozart's opera *Don Giovanni* ("Don Juan" in Italian). While no one knows for sure, I think it makes sense...and it adds some fun to the visit.

One thing's for sure: Mañara is on the road to sainthood. His supporters request that you report any miraculous answers to prayers asking him to intercede—you need to perform miracles to become a saint.

Visiting the Hospital: The **courtyard** gives a sense of the origin of the building and its ongoing work as a hospice for the poor. The statues come from Genova, Italy, as Mañara's family were rich Genova merchants who moved to Sevilla to get in on the wealth from New World discoveries. The Dutch tiles (from Delft), depicting scenes from the Old and New Testament, are a reminder that the Netherlands was under Spanish rule in centuries past.

The **Sala de Cabildos,** a small room at the end of the courtyard, is Mañara's former office. Here you'll see his original desk, a painting of him at work (busy preaching against materialism and hedonism), a treasure box with an elaborate lock mechanism, his sword (he killed several people in his wilder days), a whip that was part of his austere style of worship, and his death mask.

The **chapel,** which Mañara had built, is the highlight. Once inside, notice the graphic painting over the door you entered that provided a vivid Mañara-style sendoff to worshippers.

Juan de Valdés Leal's *The End of the Glories of the World* shows Mañara and a bishop decaying together in a crypt, with worms and roaches munching away. Above, the hand of Christ—pierced by the nail—holds the scales of justice: sins (on the left) and good deeds (on the right).

Immediately opposite is Leal's *In the Blink of an Eye* (*In ictu oculi*). In it, the Grim Reaper extinguishes the candle of life. Filling the canvas are the ruins of worldly goods, knowledge, power, and position. It's all gone in the blink of an eye—true in the 1670s...and true today.

Sit in a pew and take it in: This is Sevillan Baroque. Seven original or replica Murillo paintings celebrate good deeds and charity: feeding the hungry, tending the sick, and so on. The altar is carved wood with gold leaf. A dozen hardworking cupids support the Burial of Christ. The duty of the order of monks here was to give a Christian burial to the executed and drowned. See the tombstone worked into the altar scene (on the right). Above are the three main Christian virtues (left to right): faith, charity, hope.

Before leaving the church, do Don Miguel Mañara a favor. Step on his **tombstone.** Located just outside the central door in the back, it's served as a welcome mat since 1679. He requested to be buried outside the church where everyone would step on him as they entered. It's marked "the worst man in the world."

Leaving the church, return to the courtyard, go straight across, and around to the left. Wander around, noticing the brick Gothic arches of the huge halls of the 13th-century shipyards, whose original floors are 15 feet below. Overlooking the courtyard, immediately behind the church's altar, were the rooms where Mañara spent his last years. Here he could be close to his charity work and his intensely penitent place of worship.

Across the street from the entry is a park. Pop in and see Don Juan—wracked with guilt—carrying a poor, sick person into his hospital.

Torre del Oro (Gold Tower) and Naval Museum

Sevilla's historic riverside Gold Tower was the starting and end-ing point for all shipping to the New World. It's named for the golden tiles that once covered it—not for all the New World booty that landed here. Ever since the Moors built it in the 13th cen-tury, it's been part of the city's fortifications, and long anchored a heavy chain that draped from here across the river to protect the harbor. Today it houses a dreary little naval museum. Looking past the dried fish and knot charts to find the mural showing the world-spanning journeys of Vasco da Gama, the model of Columbus' *Santa María* (the first ship to land in the New World), and an interesting mural of Sevilla in 1740. Enjoy the view from the balconies upstairs. The Guadalquivir River is now just a trickle of its former self, after canals built in the 1920s siphoned off most of its water to feed ports downstream.

Cost and Hours: €3, €2 audioguide, Mon-Fri 9:30-18:45, Sat-Sun 10:30-18:45, tel. 954-222-419.

North of the Cathedral
Plaza Nueva
This pleasant "New Square" is marked by a statue of King Ferdinand III, who liberated Sevilla from the Moors in the 13th century and was later sainted. For centuries afterward, a huge Franciscan monastery stood on this site; it was a spiritual home to many of the missionaries who colonized the California coast. (It was destroyed in 1840, following the disbanding of the monastic system under a government keen to take back power from the Church.) Today it's the end of the line for Sevilla's short tram system (which zips down Avenida de la Constitución to the San Bernardo train station).

Running along the top of the square is the relatively modern **City Hall.** For a more interesting look at this building, circle around to the other end (on the smaller square, called Plaza de San Francisco) where you can see how the structure has expanded right along with the city it governs: architectural styles evolve, from left to right, along the facade. The newest, right part of the facade is more or less undecorated—a blank canvas for future artists to leave their mark. This square has been used for executions, bullfights, and (today) big city events.

▲Church of the Savior (Iglesia del Salvador)
Sevilla's second-biggest church, built on the site of a ninth-century mosque, gleams with freshly scrubbed Baroque pride. While the larger cathedral is a jumble of styles, this church is uniformly Andalusian Baroque—the architecture, decor, and statues are all from the same time period. The church is home to some of the most beloved statues that parade through town during religious festivals.

Cost and Hours: €3, or free with €8 cathedral ticket (also sold here, with shorter lines), audioguide-€2.50, same hours as cathedral, Plaza del Salvador, tel. 954-211-679.

Visiting the Church: The church's 14 richly decorated altarpieces, many from the 18th century, are its highlight (and come with excellent English descriptions). Start at the **high altar,** with the whirling pair of angels holding lamps with red ropes. Then look high above to see frescoes that, once long forgotten, were revealed by a recent cleaning.

In the right transept stands another venerable Mary; this one is **Our Lady of the Waters,** who predates this church by about 400 years. Though permanently parked now, for centuries she was paraded through Sevilla in times of drought.

In the left transept is the chapel with one of the city's most beloved statues (visible through the bars): the gripping **Christ of the Passion,** who is carrying the cross to his death (from 1619, by Juan Martínez Montañés). The statue is so revered by pilgrims and worshippers that the chapel has its own separate entrance (access through the courtyard, free, daily 10:00-14:00 & 17:00-21:00). For centuries the faithful have come here to pray, marvel at the sadness that fills the chapel, then kiss Jesus' heel (to join them, head up the stairs behind the altar). Jesus is flanked by a red-eyed John the Evangelist and a grieving María Dolorosa, with convincing tears and a literal dagger in her heart. Under the chapel's main altar, notice the skulls of two Jesuit missionaries who were martyred in Japan. In the adjacent shop, a wall tile shows the statue in a circa-1620 procession.

In the **courtyard,** you can feel the presence of the mosque that once stood on this spot. Its minaret is now the bell tower, and the mosque's arches are now halfway underground. What's left of the structure functions today as part of the church's crypt.

Nearby: Finish your visit by enjoying **Plaza del Salvador,** a favorite local meeting point. Strolling this square, you become part of the theater of life in Sevilla.

Casa de Pilatos

This 16th-century palace offers a scaled-down version of the royal Alcázar (with a similar mix of Gothic, Moorish, and Renaissance styles) and a delightful garden. The nobleman who built it was inspired by a visit to the Holy Land, where saw the supposed mansion of Pontius Pilate. If you've seen the Alcázar, this might not be worth the time or money. Your visit comes in two parts: the stark ground floor and garden (with audioguide); and a plodding, 25-minute guided tour of the lived-in noble residence upstairs (English/Spanish spiel, about 2/hour, check schedule at entry).

Cost and Hours: €8, includes audioguide and tour, daily 10:00-19:00, 9:00-18:00 off-season, Plaza de Pilatos 1.

SEVILLA

▲Museo Palacio de la Condesa de Lebrija

This aristocratic mansion takes you back into the 18th century like no other place in town. The Countess of Lebrija was a passionate collector of antiquities. Her home's ground floor is paved with Roman mosaics (which you can actually walk on) and lined with musty old cases of Phoenician, Greek, Roman, and Moorish artifacts—mostly pottery. To see a plush world from a time when the nobility had a private priest and their own chapel, take a quickie tour of the upstairs, which shows the palace as the countess left it when she died in 1938.

Cost and Hours: €5 for unescorted visit of ground floor, €8 includes English/Spanish tour of "lived-in" upstairs offered every 45 minutes; July-Aug Mon-Fri 9:00-15:00, Sat 10:00-14:00, closed Sun; Sept-June Mon-Fri 10:30-19:30, Sat 10:00-14:00 & 16:00-18:00, Sun 10:00-14:00; free and obligatory bag check, Calle Cuna 8, tel. 954-227-802, www.palaciodelebrija.com.

Plaza de la Encarnación

Several years ago, in an attempt to revitalize this formerly nondescript square, the city unveiled what locals call "the mush-

rooms": a gigantic, undulating canopy of five waffle-patterned, toadstool-esque, hundred-foot-tall structures. Together, this structure (officially named *Metropol Parasol*) provides shade, a gazebo for performances, and a traditional market hall. While the market is busy each morning, locals don't know what to make of the avant-garde structure, and the square is pretty lifeless in the afternoon and evening. A ramp under the canopy leads down to ancient-Roman-era street level, where a museum displays Roman ruins found during the building process. From the museum level, a €1.30 elevator takes you up top, where you can do a loop walk along the terrace to enjoy its commanding city views. It feels like walking on a roller-coaster track. Although the structure is a bit newsy, I found it not worth the time or trouble. Other views in town are free, more central, and just as good (such as from the rooftop bar of the EME Catedral Hotel, across the street from the cathedral).

▲Flamenco Dance Museum (Museo del Baile Flamenco)

Though small and pricey, this museum is worthwhile for anyone looking to understand more about the dance that embodies the spirit of southern Spain.

The main exhibition, on floor 1, takes about 45 minutes to see. It features well-produced videos, flamenco costumes, and other artifacts collected by the grande dame of flamenco, Christina

Hoyos, including a collection of posters celebrating notable flamenco artists of yore (be sure to stand directly under the "sound showers"). The top floor and basement house temporary exhibits, mostly of photography and other artwork. On the ground floor and in the basement, you can watch flamenco lessons in progress— or even take one yourself (one hour, first person-€60, €20/person after that, shoes not provided).

Cost and Hours: €10, €24 combo-ticket includes evening concert, 10 percent discount with this book, daily 10:00-19:00, pick up English booklet at front desk, about 3 blocks east of Plaza Nueva at Calle Manuel Rojas Marcos 3, tel. 954-340-311, www .flamencomuseum.com.

Performances: Live flamenco performances take place here nightly, just after the museum closes.

▲Museo de Bellas Artes

Sevilla's passion for religious art is preserved and displayed in its Museum of Fine Arts. While most Americans go for El Greco, Goya, and Velázquez (not a forte of this collection), this museum gives a fine look at other, less-appreciated Spanish masters: Zurbarán and Murillo. Rather than exhausting, the museum is pleasantly enjoyable.

Cost and Hours: €1.50, Tue-Sat 10:00-20:30, Sun 10:00-17:00, closed Mon, tel. 955-542-942, www.museosdeandalucia.es.

Getting There: The museum is at Plaza Museo 9, a 15-minute walk from the cathedral, or a short ride on bus #C5 from Plaza Nueva. If coming from the Basílica de la Macarena, take bus #C4 to the Torneo stop and walk inland four blocks. Pick up the English-language floor plan, which explains the theme of each room.

Background: Sevilla was once Spain's wealthy commercial capital (like New York City) at a time when Madrid was a newly built center of government (like Washington, DC). Spain's economic Golden Age (the 1500s) blossomed into the Golden Age of Spanish painting (the 1600s), especially in Sevilla. Several of Spain's top painters—Zurbarán, Murillo, and Velázquez—lived here in the 1600s. Like their contemporaries, they labored to make the spiritual world tangible, and forged the gritty realism that marks Spanish painting. You'll see balding saints and monks with wrinkled faces and sunburned hands. The style suited Spain's spiritual climate, as the Catholic Church used this art in its Counter-Reformation battle against the Protestant rebellion.

In the early 1800s, Spain's government, in a push to take

some power from the Church, began disbanding convents and monasteries. Secular fanatics had a heyday looting churches, but fortunately, much of Andalucía's religious art was rescued and hung safely here in this convent-turned-museum.

🡒 **Self-Guided Tour:** The permanent collection features 20 rooms in neat chronological order. It's easy to breeze through once with my tour, then backtrack to what appeals to you.

• *Enter and follow signs to the permanent collection, which begins in Sala I (Room 1).*

Rooms 1-4: Medieval altarpieces of gold-backed saints, Virgin-and-babes, and Crucifixion scenes attest to the religiosity that nurtured Spain's early art. Spain's penchant for unflinching realism culminates in Room 2 with Pedro Torrigiano's 1525 statue of an emaciated San Jerónimo, and in Room 3 with the painted clay head of St. John the Baptist—complete with severed neck muscles, throat, and windpipe. This kind of warts-and-all naturalism would influence the great Sevillan painter Velázquez (some of whose works are often displayed in Room 4).

• *Continue through the pleasant outdoor courtyard to the former church that is now Room 5.*

Room 5: This room shows off the works of another hometown boy, **Bartolomé Murillo** (mur-EE-oh, 1617-1682). His signature subject is the Immaculate Conception, the doctrine that holds that Mary was exempt from original sin. Several *Inmaculadas* may be on display. Typically, Mary is depicted as young, dressed in white and blue, standing atop the moon (crescent or full). She clutches her breast and gazes up rapturously, surrounded by tumbling winged babies. Murillo's tiny *Madonna and Child* (*Virgen de la Servilleta*, 1665; at the end of  the room in the center, where the church's altar would have been) shows the warmth and appeal of his work.

Murillo's sweetness is quite different from the harsh realism of his fellow artists, but his work was understandably popular. For many Spaniards, Mary is their main connection to heaven. They pray directly to her, asking her to intercede on their behalf with God. Murillo's Marys are always receptive and ready to help.

Besides his *Inmaculadas,* Murillo painted popular saints. They often carry sprigs of plants, and cock their heads upward, caught up in a heavenly vision of sweet Baby Jesus. Murillo is also known for his "genre" paintings—scenes of common folk and rascally street urchins—but the museum has few of these.

Also in Room 5 is *The Apotheosis of St. Thomas Aquinas (Apteosis de Santo Tomás de Aquino)* by Francisco de Zurbarán—considered to be Zurbarán's most important work. It was done at the height of his career, when stark realism was all the rage. In a believable, down-to-earth way, Zurbarán presents the pivotal moment when the great saint-theologian experiences his spiritual awakening. We'll see more of Zurbarán upstairs in Room 10.

• *Now head back outside and up the stairs to the first floor.*

Rooms 6-9: In Rooms 6 and 7, you'll see more Murillos and Murillo imitators. Room 8 is dedicated to yet another native Sevillan (and friend of Murillo), Juan de Valdés Leal (1622-1690). He adds Baroque motion and drama to religious subjects. His surreal colors and feverish, unfinished style create a mood of urgency.

Room 10: Francisco de Zurbarán (thoor-bar-AHN, 1598-1664) painted saints and monks, and the miraculous things they experienced, with an unblinking, crystal-clear, brightly lit, highly detailed realism. Monks and nuns could meditate upon Zurbarán's meticulous paintings for hours, finding God in the details.

In Zurbarán's *St. Hugo Visiting the Refectory (San Hugo en el Refectorio)*, white-robed Carthusian monks gather together for  their simple meal in a communal dining hall. Above them hangs a painting of Mary, Baby Jesus, and John the Baptist. Zurbarán created paintings for monks' dining halls like this. His audience: celibate men and women who lived in isolation, as in this former convent, devoting their time to quiet meditation, prayer, and Bible study. Zurbarán shines a harsh spotlight on many of his subjects, creating strong shadows. Zurbarán's people often stand starkly isolated against a single-color background—a dark room or the gray-white of a cloudy sky. He was the ideal painter for the austere religion of 17th-century Spain.

Find *The Virgin of the Caves (La Virgen de las Cuevas)* and study the piety and faith in the monks' weathered faces. Zurbarán's Mary is protective, with her hands placed on the heads of two monks. Note the loving detail on the cape embroidery, the brooch, and the flowers at her feet. But also note the angel babies holding the cape, with their painfully double-jointed arms. Zurbarán was no Leonardo.

The Rest of the Museum: Spain's subsequent art, from the 18th century on, generally followed the trends of the rest of Europe. Room 12 has creamy Romanticism and hazy Impressionism. You'll see typical Sevillan motifs such as matadors, cigar-factory girls, and river landscapes. Enjoy these painted slices of Sevilla, then exit to experience similar scenes today.

Far North of the Cathedral
▲▲Basílica de la Macarena

Sevilla's Holy Week celebrations are Spain's grandest. During the week leading up to Easter, the city is packed with pilgrims wit-

nessing 60 processions carrying about 100 religious floats. If you miss the actual event, you can get a sense of it by visiting the Basílica de la Macarena and its accompanying museum to see the two most impressive floats and the darling of Semana Santa, the statue of the Virgen de la Macarena. Although far from the city center, it's located on Sevilla's ring road and easy to reach. (While La Macarena is the big kahuna, for a more central look at beloved procession statues, consider stopping by the Church of the Savior, described earlier; or Tirana's Church of Santa Ana, described later.)

Cost and Hours: Church-free, treasury museum-€5, audioguide-€1, daily 9:30-14:00 & 17:00-20:30.

Getting There: Wave down a taxi and say "Basilica Macarena" (about €6 from the city center). All the #C buses go there, including bus #C3 and #C4 from Puerta de Jerez (near the Torre de Oro) or Avenida de Menéndez Pelayo (the ring road east of the cathedral), tel. 954-901-800, www.hermandaddelamacarena.es.

◑ Self-Guided Tour: Despite the long history of the Macarena statue, the Neo-Baroque church was only built in 1949 to give the oft-moved sculpture a permanent home.

• *Grab a pew and study the...*

Weeping Virgin: La Macarena is known as the "Weeping

Virgin" for the five crystal teardrops trickling down her cheeks. She's like a Baroque doll with human hair and articulated arms, and is even dressed in underclothes. Sculpted in the late 17th century (probably by Pedro Roldán), she's become Sevilla's most popular image of Mary.

Her beautiful expression—halfway between smiling and crying—is ambiguous, letting worshippers project their own emotions onto her. Her weeping can be contagious—look around you. She's also known as La Esperanza, the Virgin of Hope, and she promises better times after the sorrow.

Installed in a side chapel (on the left) is the **Christ of the Judgment** (from 1654), showing Jesus on the day he was condemned. This statue and La Macarena stand atop the two most important floats of the Holy Week parades.

• *To see the floats and learn more, visit the treasury museum (exit the church; museum entrance is on the left side of the church).*

Tesoro (Treasury Museum): This small three-floor museum tells the history of the Virgin statue and the Holy Week parades. Though rooted in medieval times, the current traditions developed around 1600, with the formation of various fraternities *(hermandades)*. During Holy Week, they demonstrate their dedication to God by parading themed floats throughout Sevilla to retell the story of the Crucifixion and Resurrection of Christ. The museum displays ceremonial banners, scepters, and costumed mannequins; videos show the parades in action (some displays in English).

The three-ton float that carries the Christ of the Judgment is slathered in gold leaf and shows a commotion of figures acting out the sentencing of Jesus. (The statue of Christ—the one you saw in the church—is placed before this crowd for the Holy Week procession.) Pontius Pilate is about to wash his hands. Pilate's wife cries as a man reads the death sentence. During the Holy Week procession, pious Sevillan women wail in the streets while relays of 48 men carry this float on the backs of their necks—only their feet showing under the drapes—as they shuffle through the streets from midnight until 14:00 in the afternoon every Good Friday. The men rehearse for months to get their choreographed footwork in sync.

La Macarena follows the Christ of the Judgment in the procession. Mary's smaller 1.5-ton float seems all silver and candles—"strong enough to support the roof, but tender enough to quiver in the soft night breeze." Mary has a wardrobe of three huge mantles, worn in successive years; these are about 100 years old, as is her six-pound gold crown/halo. This float has a mesmerizing effect on the local crowds. They line up for hours, then clap, weep, and throw roses as it slowly sways along the streets, working its way through town. A Sevillan friend once explained, "She knows all the problems of Sevilla and its people; we've been confiding in her for centuries. To us, she is hope."

The museum collection also contains some matador paraphernalia. La Macarena is the patron saint of bullfighters, and they give thanks for her protection. Copies of her image are popular in bullring chapels. In 1912 the bullfighter José Ortega, hoping for protection, gave La Macarena the five emerald brooches she wears. It worked for eight years...until he was gored to death in the ring. For a month, La Macarena was dressed in widow's black—the only time that has happened.

Macarena Neighborhood: Outside the church, notice the best surviving bit of Sevilla's old walls. Originally Roman, what remains today was built by the Moors in the 12th century to (unsuccessfully) keep the Christians out. And yes, it's from this city that a local dance band (Los del Río) changed the world by giving us the popular 1990s song "The Macarena." He-e-y-y, Macarena!

South of the Cathedral

University

Today's university was yesterday's *fábrica de tabacos* (tobacco factory), which employed 10,000 young female *cigareras*—including the saucy femme fatale of Bizet's opera *Carmen*. In the 18th century, it was the second-largest building in Spain, after El Escorial. Wander through its halls as you walk to Plaza de España. The university's bustling café is a good place for cheap tapas, beer, wine, and conversation (Mon-Fri 8:00-21:00, Sat 9:00-13:00, closed Sun).

Plaza de España

This square, the surrounding buildings, and the nearby María Luisa Park are the remains of the 1929 international fair, where for

a year the Spanish-speaking countries of the world enjoyed a mutual-admiration fiesta. When they finish the restoration work here (it's taking years), this delightful area—the epitome of world's fair-style architecture—will once again be great for people-watching (especially during the 19:00-20:00 peak paseo hour). The park's highlight is the former Spanish Pavilion. Its tiles—a trademark of Sevilla—show historic scenes and maps from every province of Spain (arranged in alphabetical order, from Álava to Zaragoza). Climb to one of the balconies for a fine view. Beware: This is a classic haunt of thieves and con artists; many pose as lost tourists, and may come at you with a map unfolded to hide their speedy, greedy fingers. Believe no one here.

▲▲Triana, West of the River

In Sevilla—as is true in so many other European cities that grew up in the age of river traffic—what was long considered the "wrong side of the river" is now the most colorful part of town. Sevilla's Triana is a proud neighborhood, famed for its flamenco soul (characterized by the statue that greets arrivals from across the river) and its independent spirit. Locals describe crossing the bridge toward the city center as "going to Sevilla."

Visiting Tirana: From downtown Sevilla, head southwest on the busy Calle Reyes Católicos (which passes just north of the bullring), crossing the Puente de Isabel II. Just off the bridge, on the right as you cross into Triana, is the neighborhood's covered **market.** Built in 2005 in the Moorish Revival style, it sits upon the ruins of an Inquisition-era castle (the scant remains of which you can see). The market bustles in the mornings and afternoons with traditional fruit and vegetable stalls as well as colorful tapas bars and cafés.

Calle San Jacinto, straight ahead just beyond the bridge, was recently liberated from car traffic. It's the hip center of the people scene—a festival of life each evening. Venturing down side lanes, you find classic 19th-century facades with fine ironwork and colorful tiles. Long home to several tile factories, the district's crusty and flamenco-flamboyant character was shaped by its working-class industrial heritage and a sizeable Roma (Gypsy) population. You can still see a few flowery back courtyards that were once the *corrales* (communal patios) of Roma clans who shared one kitchen, bathroom, and fountain.

The first cross-street intersecting Calle San Jacinto, Calle Pureza, cuts (left) through the historic center of Triana, passing the **Church of Santa Ana,** nicknamed "the Cathedral of Triana." It's the home of the beloved Virgin statue called Nuestra Señora de la Esperanza de Triana (Our Lady of Hope of Triana). She's a big deal here—in Sevilla, upon meeting someone, it's customary to ask not only which football team they support, but which Virgin Mary they favor. The top two in town are the Virgen de la Macarena and La Esperanza de Triana. On the Thursday of Holy Week, it's a battle royale of the Madonnas, as Sevilla's two favorite Virgins are both in processions on the streets at the same time.

As you wander, pop into bars and notice how the decor mixes bullfighting lore with Virgin worship. Keep your eyes peeled for *abacerías,* traditional neighborhood grocers who also function as neighborhood bars (such as La Antigua Abacería, at Calle Pureza 12).

Near Sevilla

Itálica

One of Spain's most impressive Roman ruins is found outside the sleepy town of Santiponce, about six miles northwest of Sevilla. Founded in 206 B.C. for wounded soldiers recuperating from the Second Punic War, Itálica became a thriving town of great agricultural and military importance. It was the birthplace of famous Roman emperors Trajan and Hadrian. Today its best-preserved ruin is its amphitheater—one of the largest in the Roman Empire—with a capacity for 30,000 spectators. Other highlights include beautiful floor mosaics, such as the one in Casa de los Pájaros (House of the Birds), with representations of more than 30 species of birds. In summer, plan your visit to avoid the midday heat—arrive either early or late in the day, and definitely bring water.

Cost and Hours: €1.50; April-May Tue-Sat 9:00-20:00, Sun 10:00-17:00; June-mid-Sept Tue-Sat 9:00-15:30, Sun 10:00-17:00, mid-Sept-March Tue-Sat 9:00-18:30, Sun 10:00-17:00; closed Mon year-round; last entry 30 minutes before closing, tel. 955-123-847, www.museosdeandalucia.es.

Getting There: You can get to Itálica on bus #M-172A (30-minute trip, frequent departures from Sevilla's Plaza de Armas station). If you're driving, head west out of Sevilla in the direction of Huelva; after you cross the second branch of the river, turn north on SE-30/A-66, and after a few miles, get off at Santiponce. Drive past pottery warehouses and through the town to the ruins at the far (west) end.

Experiences in Sevilla

Bullfighting
▲Bullfights
Some of Spain's most intense bullfighting is done in Sevilla's

14,000-seat bullring, Plaza de Toros. Fights are held (generally at 18:30) on most Sundays in May and June; on Easter and Corpus Christi; daily during the April Fair; and at the end of September (during the Feria de San Miguel). These serious fights, with adult matadors, are called *corrida de toros* and often sell out in advance. On many Thursday evenings in July, the *novillada* fights take place, with teenage novices doing the killing and smaller bulls doing the dying. *Corrida de toros* seats range from €25 for high seats looking into the sun to €150 for the first three rows in the shade under the royal box; *novillada* seats are half that—and easy to buy at the arena a few minutes before show time (ignore scalpers outside; get information at a TI, your hotel, by phone, or online; tel. 954-210-315, www.plazadetorosdelamaestranza.com).

▲▲Bullring (Plaza de Toros) and Bullfight Museum (Museo Taurino)

Follow a bilingual (Spanish and English) 40-minute guided tour through the bullring's strangely quiet and empty arena, its museum, and the chapel where the matador prays before the fight. (Thanks to readily available blood transfusions, there have been no deaths in nearly three decades.) The two most revered figures of Sevilla, the Virgen de la Macarena and the Jesús del Gran Poder (Christ of All Power), are represented in the chapel. In the museum, you'll see great classic scenes and the heads of a few bulls—awarded the bovine equivalent of an Oscar for a particularly good fight. The city was so appalled when the famous matador Manolete was killed in 1947 that even the mother of the bull that gored him was destroyed. Matadors—dressed to kill—are heartthrobs in their "suits of light." Many girls have their bedrooms wallpapered with posters of cute bullfighters.

Cost and Hours: €7, entrance with escorted tour only—no free time inside, 3/hour, daily May-Oct 9:30-20:00, Nov-April 9:00-19:00, until 14:00 on fight days, when chapel and horse room are closed. The last tour departs 15 minutes before closing. While they take groups of up to 50, it's still wise to call or drop by to reserve a spot in the busy season (tel. 954-224-577, www.realmaestranza.com).

The April Fair

For a seven-day period that falls a week or two after Easter, much of Sevilla is packed into its vast fairgrounds for a grand party (April 29-May 4 in 2014). The fair, seeming to bring all that's Andalusian together, feels friendly, spontaneous, and very real. The local passion for horses, flamenco, and sherry is clear—riders are ramrod straight, colorfully clad girls ride sidesaddle, and everyone's drinking sherry spritzers. Women sport outlandish dresses that would look clownish elsewhere, but  are somehow brilliant here en masse. Horses clog the streets in an endless parade until about 20:00, when they clear out and the streets fill with exuberant locals. The party goes on literally 24 hours a day for the entire week.

Countless private party tents, called *casetas*, line the lanes. Each tent is the private party zone of a family, club, or association. You need to know someone in the group—or make friends quickly—to get in. Because of the exclusivity, it has a real family-affair feeling. In each *caseta*, everyone knows everyone. It seems like a thousand wedding parties being celebrated at the same time.

Any tourist can have a fun and memorable evening by simply crashing the party. The city's entire fleet of taxis (who'll try to charge double) and buses seems dedicated to shuttling people from downtown to the fairgrounds. Given the traffic jams and inflated prices, you may be better off hiking: From the Torre del Oro, cross the San Telmo Bridge to Plaza de Cuba and hike down Calle Asunción. You'll see the towering gate to the fairgrounds in the distance. Just follow the crowds (there's no admission charge). Arrive before 20:00 to see the horses, but stay later, as the ambience improves after the *caballos* giddy-up on out. Some of the larger tents are sponsored by the city and open to the public, but the best action is in the streets, where party-goers from the livelier *casetas* spill out. Although private tents have bouncers, everyone is so happy that it's not tough to strike up an impromptu friendship, become a "special guest," and be invited in. The drink flows freely, and the food is fun and cheap.

Shopping in Sevilla

For the best local shopping experience, follow my shopping stroll (described next). The popular pedestrian streets Sierpes and Tetuán/Velázquez—along with the surrounding lanes near Plaza Nueva—are packed with people and shops.

Clothing and shoe stores stay open all day. Other shops generally take a siesta, closing between 13:30 and 16:00 or 17:00 on weekdays, as well as on Saturday afternoons and all day Sunday. Big stores such as El Corte Inglés stay open (and air-conditioned) right through the siesta.

El Corte Inglés also has a supermarket downstairs and a good but expensive restaurant (Mon-Sat 10:00-22:00, closed Sun). Popular souvenir items include ladies' fans, shawls, *mantillas,* other items related to flamenco (castanets, guitars, costumes), ceramics, and bullfighting posters.

Collectors' markets hop on Sunday: stamps and coins at Plaza del Cabildo (near the cathedral) and art on Plaza del Museo (by the Museo de Bellas Artes).

Mercado del Arenal, the covered fish-and-produce market, is perfect for hungry photographers (Mon-Sat 9:00-14:30, closed Sun, least lively on Mon, on Calle Pastor y Landero at Calle Arenal, just beyond bullring).

▲▲Shopping Paseo Tour

Although many tourists never get beyond the cathedral and the Santa Cruz neighborhood, it's important to wander west into the lively pedestrian shopping center of town. The best shopping streets—Calle Tetuán, Calle Sierpes, and Calle Cuna—also happen to be part of the oldest section of Sevilla. A walk here is a chance to join one of Spain's liveliest paseos—that bustling celebration of life that takes place before dinner each evening, when everyone is out strolling, showing off their fancy shoes and checking out everyone else's. This walk, if done between 18:00 and 20:00, gives you a chance to experience the paseo scene while getting a look at the town's most popular shops. You'll pass windows displaying the best in both traditional and trendy fashion. The walk ends at a plush mansion of a local countess (open to the public).

Start on the pedestrianized **Plaza Nueva,** a 19th-century square facing the ornate city hall, which features a statue of Ferdinand III, a local favorite because he freed Sevilla from the Moors in 1248. From here wander the length of **Calle Tetuán** (notice the latest in outrageous shoes). Calle Tetuán becomes **Calle Velázquez,** and ends at La Campana (a big intersection and popular meeting point, with the super department store, El Corte Inglés, just beyond, on Plaza del Duque de la Victoria).

Turn right. At the corner of **Calle Sierpes** awaits a venerable pastry shop, Confitería La Campana, with a fine 1885 interior...and Sevilla's most tempting sweets. From here, head down Calle Sierpes, which is great for shopping and strolling. Calle Sierpes is the main street of the Holy Week processions—imagine it packed with celebrants and its balconies bulging with spectators. At the corner of Sierpes and Jovellanos/Sagasta, you're near several fine shops featuring Andalusian accessories. Drop in to see how serious local women are about their fans, shawls, *mantillas* (ornate head scarves), and *peinetas* (combs designed to secure and prop up the *mantilla*). The most valuable *mantillas* are silk, and the top-quality combs are made of tortoise shell (though most women opt for much more affordable polyester and plastic). Andalusian women have various fans to match different dresses—they're considered an accessory. The *mantilla* comes in black (worn only on Good Friday and by the mother of the groom at weddings) and white (worn at bullfights during the April Fair).

From here turn left down **Calle Sagasta.** Notice that the street has two names—the modern version and a medieval one: Antigua Calle de Gallegos ("Ancient Street of the Galicians"). With the Christian victory in 1248, the Muslims were given one month to evacuate. To consolidate Christian control during that time, settlers from Galicia, the northwest corner of Iberia, were planted here; this street was the center of their neighborhood.

Finally, you'll arrive at charming Plaza del Salvador. It's teeming with life at the foot of the Church of the Savior (well worth a visit). Backtrack left along **Calle Cuna,** famous for its exuberant flamenco dresses and classic wedding dresses. Local women save up to have flamenco dresses custom-made for the April Fair: They're considered an important status symbol. If all this shopping wasn't enough to make you feel like a countess, follow Calle Cuna to the Museo Palacio de la Condesa de Lebrija. Nearby is the mod, mushroom-shaped structure that towers over Plaza de la Encarnación.

Nightlife in Sevilla

▲▲▲Flamenco

This music-and-dance art form has its roots in the Roma (Gypsy) and Moorish cultures. Even at a packaged "flamenco evening," sparks fly. The men do most of the flamboyant machine-gun foot-work. The women often concentrate on the graceful turns and smooth, shuffling step of the *soléa* version of the dance. Watch the musicians. Flamenco guitarists, with their lightning-fast finger-roll strums, are among the best in the world. The intricate rhythms are set by casta-nets or the hand-clapping (called  *palmas*) of those who aren't dancing at the moment. In the raspy-voiced wails of the singers, you'll hear echoes of the Muslim call to prayer.

Like jazz, flamenco thrives on improvisation. Also like jazz, good flamenco is more than just technical proficiency. A singer or dancer with "soul" is said to have *duende.* Flamenco is a happening, with bystanders clapping along and egging on the dancers with whoops and shouts. Get into it.

Hotels push tourist-oriented, nightclub-style flamenco shows, but they charge a commission. Fortunately, it's easy to book a place on your own. And if you don't care to see an actual show, you can still clap your castanets at the Flamenco Dance Museum.

Sevilla's flamenco offerings tend to fall into one of three categories: serious concerts (usually about €18 and about an hour long), where the singing and dancing take center stage; touristy dinner-and-drinks shows with table service (generally around €35—not including food—and two hours long); and—the least touristy option—casual bars with late-night performances, where for the cost of a drink you can catch impromptu (or semi-impromptu) musicians at play. Here's the rundown for each type of performance:

Serious Flamenco Concerts

While it's hard to choose among these three nightly, one-hour flamenco concerts, I'd say enjoying one is a must during your Sevilla visit. To the novice viewer, each company offers equal quality. They cost about the same, and each venue is small, intimate, and air-conditioned. For most, they are preferable to the "shows" listed later (which are half the cost, half the length, and have half as many seats). They also take place relatively early in the evening, especially compared with the flamenco you can see for free in various bars around town (that scene doesn't ignite until very late at night).

My recommended concerts are careful to give you a good overview of the art form, covering all the flamenco bases. At each venue you can reserve by phone and pay upon arrival, or drop by early to pick up a ticket. While La Casa del Flamenco is the nicest and most central venue, the other two have exhibits that can add to the experience.

La Casa de la Memoria is a strangely wide venue (just two rows deep), where everyone gets a close-up view and room to stretch out (€16, nightly at 19:30 and 21:00, no drinks, no children under six, 80 seats, Calle Cuna 6, tel. 954-560-670, www.casadelamemoria.es, flamencomemoria@gmail.com, run by Rosanna). They also have an exhibit on one easy, well-described floor, with lots of photos and a few artifacts (€3, or free with concert ticket—but only open 10:00-18:00).

The **Flamenco Dance Museum,** while the most congested venue (with 115 tightly packed seats), has a bar and allows drinks, and you can visit the museum immediately before the show. It has festival seating—the doors open at 18:00, when you can grab the seat of your choice, then spend an hour touring the museum and enjoying a drink before the show (€20, nightly at 19:00, €24 combo-ticket includes the museum and a show).

La Casa del Flamenco is in a delightful arcaded courtyard right in the Barrio Santa Cruz (€18, €2 discount when booking direct with this book, nightly at 21:00 in April-Sept, at 19:30 in Oct-March, no drinks, no kids under 6, 60 spacious seats, reception at adjacent Hotel Alcántara serves as the box office, Calle

Ximénez de Enciso 33, tel. 954-500-595).

Razzle-Dazzle Flamenco Shows

These packaged shows can be a bit sterile—and an audience of tourists doesn't help—but I find both Los Gallos and El Arenal entertaining and riveting. While El Arenal may have a slight edge on talent, and certainly feels slicker, Los Gallos has a cozier setting, with cushy rather than hard chairs—and it's cheaper.

Los Gallos presents nightly two-hour shows at 20:15 and 22:30 (€35 ticket includes a drink, €3/person discount with this book in 2014—but limited to two people, arrive 30 minutes early for best seats, noisy bar but no food served, Plaza de la Santa Cruz 11, tel. 954-216-981, www.tablaolosgallos.com, owners José and Blanca promise goose bumps).

Tablao El Arenal has arguably more professional performers and a classier setting for its show—but dinner customers get the preferred seating, and waiters are working throughout the performance (€38 ticket includes a drink, €60 includes tapas, €72 includes dinner, 1.5-hour shows at 20:00 and 22:00, near bullring at Calle Rodó 7, tel. 954-216-492, www.tablaoelarenal.com).

El Patio Sevillano is more of a variety show, with flamenco as well as other forms of song and dance. While hotels may recommend this, they're just working for kickbacks. I like the other two much better.

Impromptu Flamenco in Bars

Spirited flamenco singing still erupts spontaneously in bars throughout the old town after midnight—but you need to know where to look. Ask a local for the latest.

La Carbonería Bar, the sangria equivalent of a beer garden, is a few blocks north of the Barrio Santa Cruz. It's a sprawling place with a variety of rooms leading to a big, open tented area filled with young locals, casual guitar strummers, and nearly nightly flamenco music from about 22:30 to 24:00. Located just a few blocks from most of my recommended hotels, this is worth finding if you're not quite ready to end the day (no cover, €2.50 sangria, daily 20:00-3:00 in the morning; near Plaza Santa María—find Hotel Fernando III, the side alley Céspedes dead-ends at Levies, head left to Levies 18, unsigned door; tel. 954-214-460).

While the days of Gypsies and flamenco throbbing throughout Triana are mostly long gone, a few bars still host live dancing; **Lo Nuestro** and **Rejoneo** are favorites (at Calle Betis 31A and 31B).

▲▲Evening Paseo

Sevilla is meant for strolling. The paseo thrives every non-winter evening in these areas: along either side of the river between the San Telmo and Isabel II bridges (Paseo de Cristóbal Colón and Triana district), up Avenida de la Constitución, around Plaza Nueva, at Plaza de España, and throughout the Barrio Santa Cruz. On hot summer nights, even families with toddlers are out and about past midnight. Spend some time rafting through this river of humanity.

Nighttime Views

Savor the view of floodlit Sevilla by night from the Tirana side of the river—perhaps over dinner.

For the best late-night drink with a cathedral view, visit the trendy top floor of EME Catedral Hotel (at Calle Alemanes 27). Ride the elevator to the top, climb the labyrinthine staircases to the bar, and sit down at a tiny table with a big view.

Sleeping in Sevilla

All of my listings are centrally located, mostly within a five-minute walk of the cathedral. The first are near the charming but touristy Santa Cruz neighborhood. The last group is just as central but closer to the river, across the boulevard in a more workaday, less touristy zone.

Room rates as much as double during the two Sevilla fiestas (Holy Week and the weeklong April Fair, held a week or two after Easter). In general, the busiest and most expensive months are April, May, September, and October. Hotels put rooms on the discounted push list in July and August—when people with good sense avoid this furnace—and from November through February. A price range indicates low- to high-season prices (but I have not listed festival prices).

If you do visit in July or August, you'll find the best deals in central, business-class places. They offer summer discounts and provide a (necessary) cool, air-conditioned refuge. But be warned that Spain's air-conditioning often isn't the icebox you're used to, especially in Sevilla.

Santa Cruz Neighborhood

These places are off Calle Santa María la Blanca and Plaza Santa María. The most convenient parking lot is the underground Cano y Cueto garage. A self-service launderette is a couple of blocks away up Avenida de Menéndez Pelayo.

$$$ Hotel Casa 1800, well-priced for its elegance, is worth

Sleep Code

(€1 = about $1.30, country code: 34)
S = Single, **D** = Double/Twin, **T** = Triple, **Q** = Quad, **b** = bathroom, **s** = shower only. Unless otherwise noted, credit cards are accepted, hoteliers speak enough English, and breakfast costs extra. Some hotels include the 10 percent IVA tax in the room price; others tack it onto your bill.

To help you easily sort through these listings, I've divided the accommodations into three categories based on the price for a double room with bath during high season:

$$$ Higher Priced—Most rooms €110 or more.
  $$ Moderately Priced—Most rooms between €60-110.
    $ Lower Priced—Most rooms €60 or less.

Prices can change without notice; verify the hotel's current rates online or by email. For the best prices, always book direct.

the extra euros. Located dead-center in the Barrio Santa Cruz (facing a boisterous tapas bar that quiets down after midnight), its 24 rooms circle an elegant chandeliered patio lounge that hosts a daily free afternoon tea for guests. With a rooftop terrace offering an impressive cathedral view and elegantly appointed rooms with high, beamed ceilings, it's a winner (standard Db-€147, superior Db with private patio-€164, deluxe Db with terrace and outdoor Jacuzzi-€194, "grand deluxe" Db with all of the above and more-€320, breakfast-€9.50, air-con, elevator, guest computer, free Wi-Fi, Calle Rodrigo Caro 6, tel. 954-561-800, www .hotelcasa1800.com, info@hotelcasa1800.com).

$$$ Hotel Las Casas de la Judería has 178 quiet, elegant rooms and suites, many of them tastefully decorated with hardwood floors and a Spanish flair. The service can be stiff and stuffy, but the rooms, which surround a series of peaceful courtyards, are a romantic splurge. Some are rather dated, though, so request one of the newer ones (Sb-€110-160, Db-€120-244 depending on season, mention this book for 10 percent discount, check their website for even better rates, expensive but great buffet breakfast-€19, air-con, elevator, free Wi-Fi in lobby, pool in summer, valet parking-€20/day, Plaza Santa María 5, tel. 954-415-150, www.casasypalacios .com, juderia@casasypalacios.com).

$$$ El Rey Moro encircles its spacious, colorful patio (which tourists routinely duck into for a peek) with 19 rooms. Colorful

Santa Cruz Hotels, Restaurants & Flamenco

and dripping with quirky Andalusian character, and thoughtful about including extras (such as free loaner bikes and private rooftop Jacuzzi time), it's a class act (Sb-€79-99, Db-€100-129, breakfast-€9—or free if you reserve on their website, check their site for other specials, air-con, elevator, guest computer, free Wi-Fi, Calle Lope de Rueda 14, tel. 954-563-468, www.elreymoro .com, hotel@elreymoro.com).

$$$ Hotel Amadeus is a little gem that music lovers will appreciate (it even has a couple of soundproof rooms with pianos— something I've never seen anywhere else in Europe). The rooms, lovingly decorated with a musical motif, are situated around small courtyards. Elevators take you to two roof terraces (one with an under-the-stars Jacuzzi). Though small, this 24-room place is classy and comfortable, with welcoming public spaces and a very charming staff. The €8.50 breakfast comes on a trolley—enjoy it in your room, in the lounge, or on a terrace (Sb-€90, Db-€105,

① Hotel Casa 1800
② Hotel Las Casas de la Judería
③ El Rey Moro
④ Hotel Amadeus, La Música de Sevilla & Pensión Córdoba
⑤ Hotel Palacio Alcázar
⑥ YH Giralda
⑦ Hotel Alcántara & La Casa del Flamenco
⑧ Hotel Murillo
⑨ Plaza Santa Cruz Hostal
⑩ To Samay Hostel & Launderette
⑪ Bodega Santa Cruz
⑫ Las Teresas Bar
⑬ Cervecería Giralda
⑭ Restaurante San Marco
⑮ Casa Roman Taberna
⑯ Taberna Poncio
⑰ Tapas Trio
⑱ Restaurante Modesto
⑲ Freiduría Puerta de la Carne
⑳ Bar Restaurante El 3 de Oro
㉑ Café Bar Carmela
㉒ Villar Ice Cream
㉓ Los Gallos (Flamenco)
㉔ To La Carbonería Bar

big Db-€120, suites-€165-195, cheaper July-Aug, air-con, eleva-tor, guest computer, free Wi-Fi—plus iPads in every room, laun-dry-€15, parking-€20/day, Calle Farnesio 6, tel. 954-501-443, www.hotelamadeussevilla.com, reservas@hotelamadeussevilla .com, wonderfully run by María Luisa and her staff—Zaida and Cristina). Their next-door annex is every bit as charming, and a similarly good value: **$$$ La Música de Sevilla** offers six beau-tifully appointed rooms—three facing the interior patio, and three streetside rooms with small balconies (patio Db-€110, exte-rior Db-€130, air-con, reserve through and check in at Hotel Amadeus).

$$$ Hotel Palacio Alcázar is the former home and studio of John Fulton, an American who moved here to become a bullfighter and painter. This charming boutique hotel has 12 crisp, modern rooms, and each soundproofed door is painted with a different scene of Sevilla. Triple-paned windows keep out the noise from

SEVILLA

Sevilla Hotels

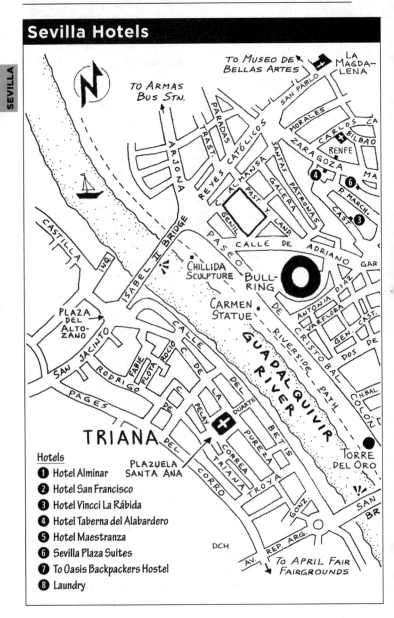

Hotels
1. Hotel Alminar
2. Hotel San Francisco
3. Hotel Vincci La Rábida
4. Hotel Taberna del Alabardero
5. Hotel Maestranza
6. Sevilla Plaza Suites
7. To Oasis Backpackers Hostel
8. Laundry

SEVILLA

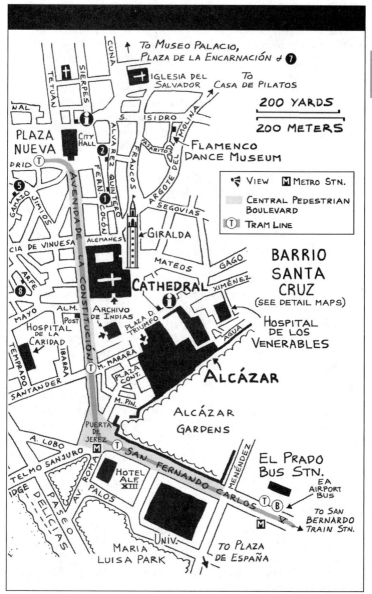

To Museo Palacio, Plaza de la Encarnación & ❼

IGLESIA DEL SALVADOR

To Casa de Pilatos

CUNA

TETUAN

SIERPES

ALVAREZ QUINTERO

S. ISIDRO

PIZARRITOS

FRANCOS

ARGOTE DEL MOLINA

200 YARDS

200 METERS

NAL

PLAZA NUEVA

CITY HALL

❷

FERN COLON

❶

Flamenco Dance Museum

DRID

☂ T

❺

GARAZO

JIMIOS

CIA DE VINUESA

AVENIDA DE LA CONSTITUCIÓN

ALEMANES

SEGOVIAS

GIRALDA

MATEOS

GAGO

🔭 VIEW   Ⓜ METRO STN.

CENTRAL PEDESTRIAN BOULEVARD

Ⓣ TRAM LINE

ARFE

❽

MAYO

CATHEDRAL

BARRIO SANTA CRUZ

(SEE DETAIL MAPS)

XIMÉNEZ

ALM.

Post

ARCHIVO DE INDIAS

PLAZA D. TRIUMFO

HOSPITAL DE LOS VENERABLES

HOSPITAL DE LA CARIDAD

TEMPRADO

IBARRA

M. MARARA

PLAZA CONT.

AGUA

ALCÁZAR

SANTANDER

M. PIN.

ALCÁZAR GARDENS

A. LOBO

TELMO

SANJURO

PUERTA DE JEREZ

Ⓜ Ⓣ

SAN FERNANDO CARLOS

MENÉNDEZ

EL PRADO BUS STN.

EA AIRPORT BUS

IDGE

DELICIAS

PASEO

AV

ROMA

PALOS

HOTEL ALF. ✠XIII✠

Ⓣ Ⓑ

Ⓜ

TO SAN BERNARDO TRAIN STN.

MARIA LUISA PARK

UNIV.

TO PLAZA DE ESPAÑA

the plaza (Sb-€85-120, Db-€95-130, Tb-€130-145, prices depend on room size and season, breakfast-€9, air-con, elevator, free Wi-Fi, rooftop terrace with bar and cathedral views, Plaza de la Alianza 11, tel. 954-502-190, www.hotelpalacioalcazar.com, hotel @palacioalcazar.com).

$$ YH Giralda, once an 18th-century abbots' house, is now a charming 14-room hotel tucked away on a little street right off Calle Mateos Gago, just a couple of blocks from the cathedral. The exterior rooms have windows onto a pedestrian street, and a few of the interior rooms have small windows that look into the inner courtyard; all rooms are neatly appointed (Sb-€50-84, Db-€50-94, Tb-€75-115, Qb-€85-135, higher rates are for weekends, no breakfast, air-con, free Wi-Fi, Calle Abades 30, tel. 954-228-324, www.yh-hoteles.com, yhgiralda@yh-hoteles.com).

$$ Hotel Alcántara offers more no-nonsense comfort than character. Well-located but strangely out of place in the midst of the Santa Cruz jumble, it rents 21 slick rooms at a good price (Sb-€71, small Db-€82, bigger Db twin-€93, fancy Db-€117; 10 percent discount or a free breakfast—your choice—if you book direct, pay cash, and show this book in 2014, offer not valid during Holy Week or April Fair; breakfast-€6, air-con, elevator, free Wi-Fi, rentable laptop and bikes, outdoor patio, Calle Ximénez de Enciso 28, tel. 954-500-595, www.hotelalcantara.net, info@hotel alcantara.net). The hotel also functions as the box office for the nightly La Casa del Flamenco show, next door.

$$ Hotel Murillo enjoys one of the most appealing locations in Santa Cruz, along one of the very narrow "kissing lanes." Above its elegant, antiques-filled lobby are 57 nondescript rooms with marble floors (Sb-€69-95, Db-€85-111, about €30 more for "superior" rooms with fancier decor, breakfast-€9, air-con, elevator, free Wi-Fi in lobby, bar across the street closes at midnight, Calle Lope de Rueda 7, tel. 954-216-095, www.hotelmurillo .com, reservas@hotelmurillo.com). They also rent apartments with kitchens (Db-€90-120, see website for details).

$$ Pensión Córdoba, a homier and cheaper option, has 12 tidy, quiet rooms, solid modern furniture, and a showpiece tiled courtyard (S-€35-45, Sb-€40-55, D-€50-65, Db-€60-75, no breakfast, cash only, air-con, guest computer, free Wi-Fi in lobby, on a tiny lane off Calle Santa María la Blanca at Calle Farnesio 12, tel. 954-227-498, www.pensioncordoba.com, reservas@pension cordoba.com, Ana and María).

$ Plaza Santa Cruz Hostal is a charming little place, with thoughtful touches that you wouldn't expect in this price range. The 17 clean, basic rooms surround a bright little courtyard that's buried deep in the Barrio Santa Cruz, just off Plaza

Santa Cruz (Sb-€55, Db-€60, Qb-€75, includes breakfast, air-con, free Wi-Fi, Calle Santa Teresa 15, tel. 954-228-808, www .hostalplazasantacruz.com, info@hostalplazasantacruz.com).

$ Samay Hostel, on a busy street a block from the edge of the Barrio Santa Cruz, is a youthful, well-run slumbermill with 90 beds in 23 rooms (bunk in 4- to 10-bed dorm-€15-20, Db-€50-64, includes linens, buffet breakfast-€2.50, shared kitchen, air-con, elevator, guest computer, free Wi-Fi, laundry service, 24-hour reception, rooftop terrace, Avenida de Menéndez Pelayo 13, tel. 955-100-160, www.samayhostels.com, Pablo).

Near the Cathedral

$$$ Hotel Alminar, plush and elegant, rents 12 fresh, slick, minimalist rooms (Sb-€60-95, Db-€95-125, superior Db with terrace-€115-155, extra bed-€25, breakfast-€6, air-con, elevator, loaner laptop-€2/hour, free Wi-Fi, just 100 yards from the cathedral at Calle Álvarez Quintero 52, tel. 954-293-913, www.hotel alminar.com, reservas@hotelalminar.com, run by well-dressed, never-stressed Francisco).

$ Hotel San Francisco may have a classy facade, but inside its 17 rooms are sparsely decorated, with metal doors. It's centrally located, clean, and quiet, except for the noisy ground-floor room next to the TV and reception (Sb-€40-55, Db-€50-68, Tb-€62-80, no breakfast, air-con, elevator, small rooftop terrace with cathedral view, free Wi-Fi in lobby with loaner netbook, located on pedestrian Calle Álvarez Quintero at #38, tel. 954-501-541, www.sanfranciscoh.com, info@sanfranciscoh.com, Carlos).

West of Avenida de la Constitución

$$$ Hotel Vincci La Rábida, part of a big, impersonal hotel chain, offers four-star comfort with its 103 rooms, huge and inviting courtyard lounge, and powerful air-conditioning. Its pricing is dictated by a computer that has it down to a science (see website for prices—rates can spike to €400 with high demand and dip to €80 during slow times, when that air-con is most welcome; elevator, pay Wi-Fi, Calle Castelar 24, tel. 954-501-280, www.vincci hoteles.com, larabida@vinccihoteles.com).

$$$ Hotel Taberna del Alabardero is unique, with only seven rooms occupying the top floor of a poet's mansion (above the classy recommended restaurant, Taberna del Alabardero). It's nicely located, a great value, and the ambience is perfectly circa-1900 (Db-€90-140, Db suite-€122-190, includes breakfast, 10 percent discount with this book in 2014, air-con, elevator, free Wi-Fi, parking-€20/day, closed in Aug, Zaragoza 20, tel. 954-502-721, www.tabernadelalabardero.es, rest.alabardero@esh.es).

$$ Hotel Maestranza, sparkling with loving care and charm, has 18 simple, small, clean rooms well-located on a street just off Plaza Nueva. It feels elegant for its price. Double-paned windows help to cut down on noise from the tapas bars below (Sb-€41-53, Db-€57-87, family suite-€105-135, extra bed-€20, 5 percent cash discount, no breakfast, air-con, elevator, free Wi-Fi, Gamazo 12, tel. 954-561-070, www.hotelmaestranza.es, sevilla@hotel maestranza.es, Antonio).

$$ Sevilla Plaza Suites rents 10 self-catering apartments with kitchenettes. Just opened in 2013, it's squeaky clean, family friendly, and well-located—and comes with an Astroturf sun terrace with a cathedral view. While service is scaled down, reception is open long hours (8:00-22:00) and rooms are cleaned daily (small Db-€75, big Db-€90, Qb apartment-€85-100, 6b apartment-€100-150, no breakfast, air-con, inside rooms are quieter, best deals though their website are nonrefundable, a block off Plaza Nueva at Calle Zaragoza 52, tel. 955-038-533, www.suites sevillaplaza.com, javier@suitessevillaplaza.com, Javier).

North of Plaza Nueva, Between Plaza de la Encarnación and Plaza de la Alfalfa

$ Oasis Backpackers Hostel is a good place for cheap beds, and perhaps Sevilla's best place to connect with young backpackers. Each of the eight rooms, with up to eight double bunks, comes with a modern bathroom and individual lockers. The rooftop terrace—with lounge chairs, a small pool, and adjacent kitchen— is well-used (€15-44/bed, includes breakfast, guest computer, free Wi-Fi, just off Plaza de la Encarnación on the tiny and quiet lane behind the church at #29 1/2, tel. 954-293-777, www.hostelsoasis .com, sevilla@hostelsoasis.com). Oasis also runs popular branches in Granada, Málaga, and Lisbon.

Eating in Sevilla

Eating in Sevilla is fun and affordable. People from Madrid and Barcelona find it a wonderful value. Make a point to get out and eat well when in Sevilla.

A clear eating trend in Sevilla is the rise of gourmet tapas bars, with spiffed-up decor and creative menus, at the expense of traditional restaurants. Even in difficult economic times, when other businesses are closing down, tapas bars are popping up all over. (Locals explain that with the collapse of the construction industry here, engineers, architects, and other professionals— eager for a business opportunity—are investing in trendy tapas bars.) Old-school places survive, but they often lack energy, and it seems that their clientele is aging with them. My quandary: I like the classic *típico* places. But the lively atmosphere and the best food are in the new places. On thing's for certain: If you want a good "restaurant" experience, your best value these days is to find a trendy tapas bar that offers good table seating, and sit down to enjoy some *raciones*.

In Triana

Crusty and colorful Triana, across the river from the city center, offers a nice range of eating options. Its covered market is home to a world of tempting lunchtime eateries—take a stroll, take in the scene, and take your pick (busiest Tue-Sat morning through afternoon). Beyond the market, the neighborhood has three main restaurant zones to consider: trendy Calle San Jacinto, the neighborhood scene behind the Church of Santa Ana, and several riverside restaurants with views of central Sevilla.

On or near Calle San Jacinto

The area's newly pedestrianized main drag is lined with tables of several easy-to-enjoy restaurants.

Taberna Miami is a reliable bet for seafood. Grab a table with a good perch right on the street (€7 half-*raciones*, €11 *raciones*, Wed-Mon 11:00-17:00 & 20:00-23:30, closed Tue, Calle San Jacinto 21, tel. 954-340-843).

Blanca Paloma Bar is an untouristy classic that's a hit with the neighborhood crowd. It offers plenty of small tables for a sit-down meal, a delightful bar, and a fine selection of good Spanish wines by the glass, listed on the blackboard (tapas at bar only, €7 half-*raciones*, €12 *raciones*, Mon-Sat 12:00-17:00 & 20:00-24:00, Sun 12:00-17:00 only, at the corner of Calle Pagés del Corro, tel. 954-333-640).

Las Golondrinas Bar ("The Little Sparrows") is the talk of the Triana tapas scene, with a wonderful list of cheap and tasty tapas. Favorites here are the pork *solomillo* (sirloin) and *champiñónes* (mushrooms). Complement your meat with a veggie plate from the *aliños* section of the menu. Though they don't post a wine list, they serve plenty of nice wines by the glass. Cling to a corner of the bar and watch the amazingly productive little kitchen jam; you'll need to be aggressive to get an order in. To make a sit-down meal of it, nab one of the tables upstairs (Tue-Sun 13:00-16:00 & 20:00-24:00, may also be open Mon; one block down Calle San Jacinto from Isobel II Bridge—take the first right onto Calle Alfarería, then the first left onto Calle Antillano Campos to #26; tel. 954-331-626). The same owners also have a modern, less atmospheric place a couple of blocks away at Calle Pagés del Corro 76.

SEVILLA

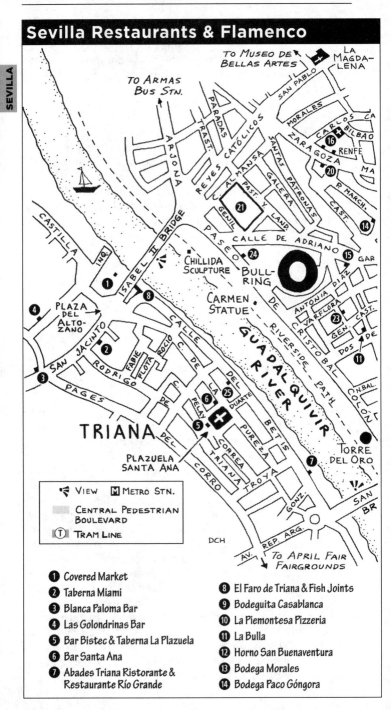

Sevilla Restaurants & Flamenco

TO MUSEO DE BELLAS ARTES
LA MAGDALENA
TO ARMAS BUS STN.
SAN PABLO
MORALES
CARLOS CA
BILBAO
16 RENFE
20 MA
ZARAGOZA
PARADAS
REYES CATÓLICOS
TRAST.
ARJONA
ALMANSA
SANTAS PATRONAS
GALERA
PAST Y LAND
GENIL
21
P. MARCH
CAST.
14
CALLE DE ADRIANO
PASEO
15
GAR
CASTILLA
ISABEL II BRIDGE
CHILLIDA SCULPTURE
24
BULL-RING
CARMEN STATUE
ANTONIA DIAZ
VARFLORA
23
GEN
CAST.
DE
4
PLAZA DEL ALTO-ZANO
8
CALLE C. DE LA
GUADALQUIVIR
DOS
DE
11
2
SAN JACINTO
RODRIGO
FABIE
FLOTA
ROCIO
DE
RIVERSIDE PATH
DE CRISTOBAL
CNBAL
COLON
3
PAGES
C.
PELAY
6 25
DUARTE
TRIANA
BETIS
5
CORREA
PUREZA
7
TORRE DEL ORO
PLAZUELA SANTA ANA
TRIANA
TROYA
GONZ
SAN BR

View   M Metro Stn.
Central Pedestrian Boulevard
T Tram Line
DCH
AV. REP. ARG.
To April Fair Fairgrounds

1 Covered Market
2 Taberna Miami
3 Blanca Paloma Bar
4 Las Golondrinas Bar
5 Bar Bistec & Taberna La Plazuela
6 Bar Santa Ana
7 Abades Triana Ristorante & Restaurante Río Grande

8 El Faro de Triana & Fish Joints
9 Bodeguita Casablanca
10 La Piemontesa Pizzeria
11 La Bulla
12 Horno San Buenaventura
13 Bodega Morales
14 Bodega Paco Góngora

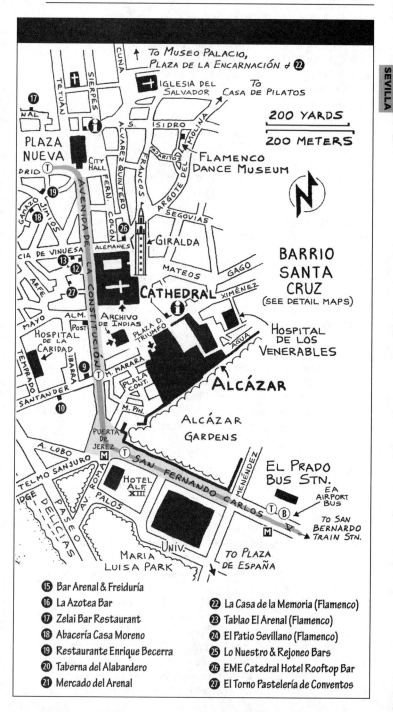

To Museo Palacio, Plaza de la Encarnación & 22

IGLESIA DEL SALVADOR

To Casa de Pilatos

200 YARDS

200 METERS

Flamenco Dance Museum

PLAZA NUEVA

City Hall

BARRIO SANTA CRUZ
(SEE DETAIL MAPS)

GIRALDA

CATHEDRAL

HOSPITAL DE LOS VENERABLES

ARCHIVO DE INDIAS

HOSPITAL DE LA CARIDAD

ALCÁZAR

ALCÁZAR GARDENS

PUERTA DE JEREZ

SAN FERNANDO

EL PRADO BUS STN.

EA AIRPORT BUS

HOTEL ALF. XIII

TO SAN BERNARDO TRAIN STN.

UNIV.

MARIA LUISA PARK

TO PLAZA DE ESPAÑA

⑮ Bar Arenal & Freiduría
⑯ La Azotea Bar
⑰ Zelai Bar Restaurant
⑱ Abacería Casa Moreno
⑲ Restaurante Enrique Becerra
⑳ Taberna del Alabardero
㉑ Mercado del Arenal
㉒ La Casa de la Memoria (Flamenco)
㉓ Tablao El Arenal (Flamenco)
㉔ El Patio Sevillano (Flamenco)
㉕ Lo Nuestro & Rejoneo Bars
㉖ EME Catedral Hotel Rooftop Bar
㉗ El Torno Pastelería de Conventos

Behind the Church of Santa Ana

This is the best place in the area to take a break from the trendy dining scene. It offers a charming setting where you can sit down under a big tree to eat dinner along with local families.

Bar Bistec, with most of the square's tables, does grilled fish with gusto. They're enthusiastic about their cod fritters and calamari, and brag about their pigeon, quail, and snails in sauce. Before taking a seat out on the square, consider the indoor seating and the fun action at the bar (€8 half-*raciones*, €14 *raciones*, daily 11:30-16:00 & 20:00-24:00, Plazuela de Santa Ana, tel. 954-274-759). **Taberna La Plazuela,** which shares the square, is simpler, doing fried fish, grilled sardines, and *caracoles* (tree snails).

Bar Santa Ana, just a block away alongside the church, is a rustic neighborhood sports-and-bull bar with great seating on the street. Peruse the interior, draped in bullfighting and Weeping Virgin memorabilia. It's always busy with the neighborhood gang, who enjoy fun tapas like *delicia de solomillo* (tenderloin) and appreciate the bar's willingness to serve even cheap tapas at the outdoor tables. If you stand at the bar, they'll keep track of your bill by chalking it directly on the counter in front of you (facing the side of the church at Pureza 82, tel. 954-272-102).

Along the River

Abades Triana Ristorante is the new hit in town for special occasions and fancy riverfront dining. It's a dressy restaurant with formal waiters serving modern Mediterranean cuisine. You'll sit in air-conditioned comfort behind a big glass wall facing the river or on a classy outdoor terrace (€3.50 cover, €15-20 starters, €20-25 fish and meat plates, daily 13:30-16:00 & 20:00-24:00, directly across from Torre del Oro at Calle Betis 69, tel. 954-286-459, www.abadestriana.com, reservations smart but they don't reserve specific tables).

Restaurante Río Grande is your stuffy, traditional, candlelit-fancy option—a good place for a restaurant dinner, with properly attired waiters, a full menu rather than tapas, and lots of seafood. Dining on the terrace (closer to the bridge) is less expensive and more casual (€3 tapas, €10-20 starters, €18-25 main dishes, daily 13:00-16:00 & 20:00-24:00, air-con, next to the San Telmo Bridge, tel. 954-273-956).

More Riverside Dining: **El Faro de Triana** charges high prices for basic food, but its fun setting—on four levels within the old yellow bridge tower overlooking the Isabel II Bridge—might make it worthwhile (€7-9 half-*raciones*, €12-18 *raciones*, open daily, tel. 954-336-192). The little fish joints fronting the river just beyond the bridge (**La Taberna del Pescador, Betis 12 La Terraza,** and **Taberna Antigua Barberia**) charge a little extra for their scenic setting, but if you want to eat reasonably on the river, they are worth considering.

In Barrio Santa Cruz
Tapas with the Tourists

For tapas, the Barrio Santa Cruz is trendy and *romántico*. Plenty of atmospheric-but-touristy restaurants fill the neighborhood near the cathedral and along Calle Santa María la Blanca. From the cathedral, walk up Calle Mateos Gago, where several classic old bars—with the day's tapas scrawled on chalkboards—keep tourists and locals well fed and watered.

Bodega Santa Cruz (a.k.a. **Las Columnas**) is a popular, user-friendly standby with cheap, unpretentious tapas. You're not coming here for the food (which is basic), but for the bustling atmosphere, as locals and tourists alike crowd the place, inside and out, for hours on end. You can keep an eye on the busy kitchen from the bar, or hang out like a cowboy at the tiny stand-up tables out front. Separate chalkboards list €2 tapas and €2 *montaditos* (little sandwiches served on a bun).

Las Teresas is a characteristic small bar draped in fun photos. It serves good tapas from a tight little menu. Prices at the bar and outside tables (for fun tourist-watching) are the same, but they serve tapas only at the bar. The hams (with little upside-down umbrellas that catch the dripping fat) are a reminder that the Spanish are enthusiastic about their cured-meat dishes (€3-4 tapas, €8-10 half-*raciones*, €14-20 *raciones*, open daily, Calle Santa Teresa 2, tel. 954-213-069).

Cervecería Giralda is a long-established meeting place for locals. With an almost genteel tiled setting and stiff waiters, it has an exclusive air. It's famous for its fine tapas, but feels particularly touristy—confirm prices, and stick with straight items on the menu rather than expensive trick specials proposed by waiters. You can order from the same menu, and at the same prices, whether you sit outside, at an inside table, or at the bar (€3-4 tapas, €10 *raciones*, daily 9:00-24:00, Calle Mateos Gago 1, tel. 954-256-162).

Restaurante San Marco serves basic, reasonably priced Italian cuisine under the arches of what was a Moorish bath in the Middle Ages (and a disco in the 1990s). The air-conditioned atmosphere may feel rather upscale, but it's also easygoing and family-friendly, with live Spanish guitar every night (€7-9 salads, pizza, and pastas; €11-12 meat dishes, daily 13:00-16:15 & 20:00-24:00, Calle Mesón del Moro 6, tel. 954-564-390, staff speaks English, welcoming Angelo).

Casa Roman Taberna has a classic bar and tavern interior, with good tables inside and a few more on a great little square outside. When they're quiet, they may serve tapas at the tables (ask); otherwise, it's your standard *raciones* (easy menu, lots of wines by the glass, Plaza de los Venerables 1, tel. 954-228-483).

On or near Calle Santa María la Blanca

This lively street, which defines the eastern boundary of the Barrio Santa Cruz, has an inviting concentration of eateries and is only slightly less touristy.

Taberna Poncio, with a well-known chef who recently downsized from a formal restaurant to a gourmet tapas bar, offers about 30 different €5-10 plates (including desserts). It's good for restaurant-type seating, both inside or on a quiet square at the edge of the Barrio Santa Cruz (Mon-Sat 13:00-16:00 & 20:00-24:00, closed Sun, just off Plaza Santa María la Blanca at Calle Ximénez de Enciso 33, tel. 954-460-717).

Tapas Restaurants on Paseo Catalina de Ribera: Three easy and good-value places located next to each other are worth considering; they have similar prices (€3-4 tapas, €8-10 plates), fine bars, good indoor seating, and wonderful tables outside on a busy sidewalk facing the Murillo Gardens at the east end of the Barrio Santa Cruz. **Modesto Tapas** is the old-fashioned place, with standard tapas and a crowd that seems averse to trendiness. The other two are more happening and creative. **Vinería San Telmo** advertises "vino and tapas" and offers lots of wine by the glass (tel. 954-410-600). **Catalina Tapas Bar** is my favorite—like me, it's more up-to-date and creative than Modesto, but less hip than San Telmo (tel. 954-412-412).

Restaurante Modesto is a local favorite serving pricey but top-notch Andalusian fare—especially fish—with a comfortable dining room and atmospheric outdoor seating in the bright, bustling square just outside the Barrio Santa Cruz. It offers creative, fun meals—look around before ordering—and a good €20 fixed-price lunch or dinner served by energetic, occasionally pushy waiters. The €9 house salad is a meal, and the €15.50 *fritura modesto* (fried seafood plate) is popular (€7-15 starters, €12-20 main dishes, daily 12:00-17:00 & 20:00-24:00, near Santa María la Blanca at Calle Cano y Cueto 5, tel. 954-416-811).

Freiduría Puerta de la Carne and **Bar Restaurante El 3 de Oro** are a two-for-one operation. Freiduría is a fried-fish-to-go place, with great outdoor seating, while El 3 de Oro is a fancier restaurant across the street that serves fine wine or beer to the fry shop's outdoor tables. First go into the fry shop and order a cheap cone of tasty fried fish with a tomato salad. Study the photos of the various kinds of seafood available; *un quarto* (250 grams, for €5-7) serves one person. Then head out front and flag down a server to order a drink (technically from the restaurant), all while enjoying a great outdoor setting—almost dining for the cost of a picnic

(Freiduría open daily in summer 20:00-24:30, also open for lunch in off-season; Santa María la Blanca 34, tel. 954-426-820).

Breakfast and Dessert on Plaza Santa María la Blanca: Several nondescript places work to keep travelers happy at breakfast time on the sunny main square near most of my recommended hotels. I like **Café Bar Carmela.** For the cost of a continental breakfast at your hotel (€5.50-7.50), you can be out on the square, with your choice of either a smaller, local-style breakfast, or a hearty American-style meal (breakfast served 9:00-13:00, easy menus, Calle Santa María la Blanca 6, tel. 954-540-590).

Villar Ice Cream is the neighborhood favorite. *Maestro Heladero* Antonino has been making ice cream in Sevilla for the past 40 years, with a focus on fresh, natural, and inventive products. They are generous with samples and creative with their offerings, so try a few wild flavors before choosing. Antonino's friendly wife, Cecilia, speaks English and doles out samples (daily 12:00-24:00, Puerto de la Carne 3, mobile 664-608-960).

Between the Cathedral and the River

I don't like the restaurants surrounding the cathedral, but many good places are nearby, just across Avenida de la Constitución. In the area between the cathedral and the river, you can find tapas, cheap eats, and fine dining. Calle García de Vinuesa leads past several colorful and cheap tapas places to a busy corner surrounded with an impressive selection of happy eateries (where Calle de Adriano meets Calle Antonia Díaz).

Bodeguita Casablanca is famously the choice of bullfighters, and even the king. Just steps from the touristy cathedral area, this classy place seems a world apart, with elegant locals, a great menu, and a dressy interior complete with a stuffed bull's head. Sit inside for a serious meal of half-*raciones*. Be bold and experiment with your order—you can't go wrong here (€2.50 tapas, Mon-Fri 13:30-24:00, closed Sat-Sun, across from Archivo de Indias at Calle Adolfo Rodríguez Jurado 12, tel. 954-224-114).

La Piemontesa Pizzeria creates its own world, with a calm, spacious, elegant interior built upon 12th-century Moorish ruins (look through the glass floor) and under historic arches of what used to be the city's treasury. It's a good, dressy Italian alternative to the tapas commotion, with mellow lighting and music (€12 salads, pastas, and pizzas; Calle Santander 1, tel. 954-503-921).

La Bulla feels like the brainchild of a gang of local foodies who, intent upon mixing traditional dishes, create an inventive international menu that's a welcome break from the usual fare. The place is bohemian-chic, with rickety tables gathered around a busy kitchen. The day's offerings are only listed on big chalkboards; insist on a stand-up English-language tour of what's available.

While risotto is their signature dish, I prefer their other offerings. You'll enjoy gourmet presentation, a hip local crowd, easy jazz ambience, and good-looking servers. There's no bar—only table seating (and only indoors)—and the €4-10 dishes are easily splittable; three will stuff two people (daily 12:00-16:30 & 20:00-24:00, midway between cathedral and Torre del Oro at Calle 2 de Mayo 26, tel. 954-219-262, no reservations).

Horno San Buenaventura, across from the cathedral on the corner of Calle García de Vinuesa and Avenida de la Constitución, is a big, venerable bakery with tables out on the *avenida* and a quiet dining room upstairs. Its slick, chrome-filled, spacious main floor is lined with long display cases of sandwiches and desserts. The tapas bar upstairs has table service only (open daily, light meals are posted by the door, avoid the frozen paella).

Bodega Morales, farther up Calle García de Vinuesa (at #11), oozes old-Sevilla ambience. The front area is more of a drinking bar; for food, go in the back section (use the separate entrance around the corner). Here, sitting among huge adobe jugs, you can munch tiny sandwiches *(montaditos)* and tapas; both are just €2 (€6 half-*raciones,* order at the bar, good wine selection, daily 13:00-16:00 & 19:30-24:00, tel. 954-221-242).

Bodega Paco Góngora is colorful and a bit classier than most tapas bars, with a tight dining area and delightful tapas. Its sit-down meals are well presented and reasonably priced (€3-4 tapas at bar only, €8 half-*raciones,* €11 *raciones* at tables, daily 12:00-16:00 & 20:00-24:00, ask for the English menu, off Plaza Nueva at Calle Padre Marchena 1, tel. 954-214-139).

Bar Arenal is a classic bull bar with tables spilling out onto a great street-corner setting. It's good for just a drink and to hang out with a crusty crowd. While they sell cheap, old-school tapas, you can complete the experience memorably by buying a load of fried fish from **El Arenal Freiduría** next door—this is perfectly permissible (€6-7 fresh-fried portions can feed two, open evenings only, bar is at Calle Arfe 2, tel. 954-223-686).

Near Plaza Nueva

La Azotea Bar is a modern place that makes up for its lack of traditional character with gourmet tapas—made with local, seasonal ingredients—that have earned it a loyal following. It's run by Juan Antonio and his partner from San Diego, Jeanine, who've taken care to make the menu easy and accessible for English speakers. You can dine elegantly, yet cheaply, on tapas at the bar, or enjoy a sit-down meal at its tables—but you'll need to arrive early. The big, €10 half-*raciones* feed two (Mon-Sat lunch starts at 13:30, dinner at 20:30, closed Sun, Calle Zaragoza 5, tel. 954-564-316).

Zelai Bar Restaurant is completely contemporary, without a hint of a historic-Sevilla feel or touristy vibe. Their pricey gourmet tapas (€5-6) and *raciones* (€10-13) are a hit with a smart local crowd, who enjoy the fusion of Basque, Andalusian, and international flavors. They also have a dressy little restaurant in back (reservations generally required) with a €40 tasting *menu* (closed Sun-Mon, just off Plaza Nueva at Calle Albareda 22, tel. 954-229-992).

Abacería Casa Moreno is a rare, classic *abacería,* a neighborhood grocery store that doubles as a standing-room-only tapas bar. Squeeze into the back room and you're slipping back in time—and behind a tall language barrier. Help yourself to the box of pork scratchings at the bar while choosing from an enticing list of €2.50 tapas. They're proud of their top-quality *jamón serrano* and *queso manchego,* and serve hot tapas only at lunch. Rubbing elbows here with local eaters, under a bull's head, surrounded by jars of peaches and cans of sardines, you feel like you're in on a secret (Mon-Fri 8:00-15:30 & 19:30-22:30, closed Sat-Sun, 3 blocks off Plaza Nueva at Calle Gamazo 7, tel. 954-228-315).

Restaurante Enrique Becerra is a fancy little 10-table place popular with local foodies. It's well-known for its gourmet Andalusian cuisine and fine wine. Muscle past the well-dressed locals at the tapas bar for gourmet snacks and wine by the glass, or head to the quieter, more elegant upstairs dining room. While the restaurant satisfies its guests with quality food, given the tight seating and its popularity with tourists, it can feel like a trap (€3-4 tapas available at the bar and ground-floor tables, €10 half-*raciones,* €20 plates upstairs, Mon-Sat 13:00-16:30 & 20:00-24:00, closed Sun, reservations essential, Gamazo 2, tel. 954-213-049, www .enriquebecerra.com).

Taberna del Alabardero, one of Sevilla's finest restaurants, serves refined Spanish cuisine in chandeliered elegance just a couple of blocks from the cathedral. If you order à la carte, it adds up to about €45 a meal, but for €48 (or €58 with wine) you can have a fun five-course fixed-price meal with lots of little surprises from the chef. Or consider their €18/person (no sharing) starter sampler, followed by an entrée. The service in the fancy upstairs dining rooms gets mixed reviews (carefully read and understand your bill)...but the setting is stunning (daily 13:00-16:30 & 20:30-24:00, closed Aug, air-con, reservations smart, Zaragoza 20, tel. 954-502-721, www.tabernadelalabardero.es).

Taberna del Alabardero Student-Served Lunch: The ground-floor dining rooms (elegant but nothing like upstairs) are popular with local office workers for a great-value, student-chef-prepared, fixed-price lunch sampler (three delightful courses-€13 Mon-Fri, €18 Sat-Sun; €20 dinner available daily, drinks not included, open daily 13:00-16:30 & 20:00-23:30). To avoid a wait at lunch, arrive before 14:00 (no reservations possible).

At the Arenal Market Hall

Mercado del Arenal, the covered fish-and-produce market, is ideal for both snapping photos and grabbing a cheap lunch. As with most markets, you'll find characteristic little diners with prices designed to lure in savvy shoppers, not to mention a crispy fresh world of picnic goodies—and a riverside promenade with benches just a block away (Mon-Sat 9:00-14:30, closed Sun, sleepy on Mon, on Calle Pastor y Landero at Calle Arenal, just beyond bullring).

Marisquería Arenal Sevilla is a popular fish restaurant that thrives in the middle of the Arenal Market, but stays open after the market closes. In the afternoon and evening, you're surrounded by the empty Industrial Age market, with workers dragging their crates to and fro. It's a great family-friendly, finger-licking-good scene that's much appreciated by its enthusiastic local following. Fish is priced by weight, so be careful when ordering, and double-check the bill (€6-18 fish plates, Tue-Sat 13:00-17:00 & 21:00-24:00, closed Sun-Mon, reservations smart for dinner, enter on Calle Pastor y Landero 9, tel. 954-220-881).

Sevilla Connections

Note that many destinations are well served by both trains and buses.

By Train

Most trains arriving and departing Sevilla, including all high-speed AVE trains, leave from the larger, more distant **Santa Justa Station**. But many *cercanías* and inter-regional trains heading south to Granada, Jerez, Cádiz, and Málaga also stop at the smaller **San Bernardo** station a few minutes away, which is connected to downtown by tram. Hourly *cercanías* trains connect both stations (about a 3-minute trip). For tips on arrival at either station, see "Arrival in Sevilla," earlier.

From Sevilla by AVE Train to Madrid: The AVE express train is expensive but fast (2.5 hours to Madrid; hourly departures 7:00-23:00). Departures between 16:00 and 19:00 can book up far in advance, but surprise holidays and long weekends can totally jam up trains as well—reserve as far ahead as possible.

From Sevilla by Train to Córdoba: There are three options for this journey: slow and cheap **regional** trains (7/day, 80 minutes), fast and cheap regional high-speed **Avant** trains (9/day, 45 minutes, requires reservation), and fast and expensive **AVE** trains en route to Madrid (2-3/hour, 45 minutes, requires reservation). Unless you must be on a particular departure, there's no reason to pay more for AVE; Avant is just as quick and a third the price. (If you have a railpass, you still must buy a reservation; Avant reservations cost about half as much as ones for AVE.)

Other Trains from Sevilla to: **Málaga** (6/day, 2 hours on Avant; 5/day, 2.5 hours on slower regional trains), **Ronda** (5/day, 3-4 hours, transfer in Bobadilla, Antequera, or Córdoba), **Granada** (4/day, 3 hours), **Jerez** (nearly hourly, 1.25 hours), **Barcelona** (11/day, 5.5-6 hours; plus one overnight train, 13 hours), **Algeciras** (3/day, 5-6 hours, transfer at Antequera or Bobadilla—bus is better). There are no direct trains to **Lisbon,** Portugal, so you'll have to take AVE to Madrid, then overnight to Lisbon; buses to Lisbon are far better (see later). Train info: Tel. 902-320-320, www.renfe .com.

By Bus

Sevilla has two bus stations: The El Prado de San Sebastián station, just south of the Alcázar, primarily serves regional destinations; the Plaza de Armas station, farther north (near the bullring), handles most long-distance buses. Bus info: Tel. 954-908-040 but rarely answered, go to TI for latest schedule info.

From Sevilla's El Prado de San Sebastián station to Andalucía and the South Coast: Regional buses are operated by Comes (www.tgcomes.es), Los Amarillos (www.losamarillos .es), and Linesur (www.linesur.com). Connections to **Jerez** are frequent, as many southbound buses head there first (7-10/day, 1.5 hours, run by all three companies; note that train is also possible— see above). Los Amarillos runs buses to some of Andalucía's hill towns, including **Ronda** (8/day, 2-2.5 hours, some via Villamartín, fewer on weekends) and **Arcos** (1-2/day, 2 hours; many more departures possible with transfer in Jerez). For the Costa del Sol, a handy Comes bus departs Sevilla four times a day and heads for **Tarifa** (2.5-3.25 hours), **Algeciras** (3-4 hours), and **La Línea/ Gibraltar** (4-4.5 hours). However, if **Algeciras** is your goal, Linesur has a much faster direct connection (8/day, fewer on weekends, 2.5-3 hours). There are also two buses a day from this station to **Granada** (2/day, 3-3.5 hours); the rest depart from the Plaza de Armas station.

From Sevilla's Plaza de Armas station to: **Madrid** (9/day, 6 hours, www.socibus.es, tel. 902-229-292), **Córdoba** (7/day, 1-2 hours), **Granada** (7/day, 3 hours *directo,* 3.5-4.5 hours *ruta*), **Málaga** (6/day direct, 2.5-3 hours), **Nerja** (2/day, 4-5 hours), **Barcelona** (2/day, 16.5 hours, including one overnight bus). Information: Tel. 902-450-550.

By Bus to Portugal: The best way to get to **Lisbon,** Portugal, is by bus (2/day, departures at 15:00 and 24:00, 7 hours, departs Plaza de Armas station, tel. 954-905-102, www.alsa.es). The midnight departure continues past Lisbon to **Coimbra** (arriving

10:30) and **Porto** (arriving 12:15). Sevilla also has direct bus service to **Lagos,** Portugal, on the Algarve (4/day in summer, 2/day off-season, about 4.5 hours, buy ticket a day or two in advance May-Oct, tel. 954-907-737, www.damas-sa.es). The bus departs from Sevilla's Plaza de Armas bus station and arrives at the Lagos bus station. If you'd like to visit Tavira on the way to Lagos, purchase a bus ticket to Tavira, have lunch there, then take the train to Lagos.

GRANADA

For a time, Granada was the grandest city in Spain. But after the tumult that came with the change from Moorish to Christian rule, it lost its power and settled into a long slumber. Today, Granada seems to specialize in evocative history and good living. Settle down in the old center and explore monuments of the Moorish civilization and its conquest. Taste the treats of a North African-flavored culture that survives here today.

Compared to other Spanish cities its size, Granada is delightfully cosmopolitan—it's worked hard to accept a range of cultures, and you'll see far more ethnic restaurants here than elsewhere in Andalucía. Its large student population (70,000 students, including more than 10,000 from abroad) also lends it a youthful zest. The Grenadine people are serious about hospitality, and have earned a reputation among travelers for being particularly friendly and eager to help you enjoy their historic city.

Granada's magnificent Alhambra fortress was the last stronghold of the Moorish kingdom in Spain. The city's exotically tangled Moorish quarter, the Albayzín, invites exploration. From its viewpoints, romantics can enjoy the sunset and evening views of the grand, floodlit Alhambra.

An old Spanish saying goes, "Give him a coin, woman, for there is nothing worse in this life than to be blind in Granada." This city has much to see, yet it reveals itself in unpredictable ways; it takes a poet to sort through and assemble the jumbled shards of Granada. Peer through the intricate lattice of a Moorish window. Hear water burbling unseen among the labyrinthine hedges of the

Generalife Gardens. Listen to a flute trilling deep in the swirl of alleys around the cathedral. Don't be blind in Granada—open all your senses.

Planning Your Time

Granada is worth two days and two nights, but you could conceivably hit its highlights in one very busy day. No matter what, reserve in advance for the Alhambra—at least several days, or, better, several weeks ahead.

If you only have one full day here, you could fit in the top sights by following this intense plan: In the morning, stroll the Pescadería market streets and follow my self-guided walk of the old town (or catch the 10:30 Cicerone walking tour), including a visit to the cathedral and its Royal Chapel. After a quick lunch, do the Alhambra in the afternoon (reservation essential). Hike the hippie lane into the Albayzín Moorish quarter (or catch minibus #31) to the San Nicolás viewpoint for the magic hour before sunset, then find the right place for a suitably late dinner. This is an extremely ambitious one-day plan; if you can spread it over two days, you'll be able to slow down and smell the incense (or make the most of one and a half days—e.g., if you're arriving in the early afternoon, do the self-guided walk before dinner).

When you're ready to move on, consider heading to nearby Nerja, the Costa del Sol's best beach town (2 hours by car or bus). You can also get to White Hill Towns such as Ronda (2.5 hours by train). Sevilla is an easy 3-hour train ride away. The Madrid-Granada train service is somewhat slow (4.5 hours), but passes through beautiful countryside.

Orientation to Granada

Modern Granada sprawls (300,000 people), but its sights are all within a 20-minute walk of Plaza Nueva, where dogs wag their tails to the rhythm of modern hippies and street musicians. Most of my recommended hotels are within a few blocks of Plaza Nueva. Make this the hub of your Granada visit.

Plaza Nueva was a main square back when kings called Granada home. This historic center is in the Darro River Valley, which separates two hills (the river now flows under the square). On one hill is the great Moorish palace, the Alhambra, and on the other is the best-preserved Moorish quarter in Spain, the Albayzín. To the southwest are the

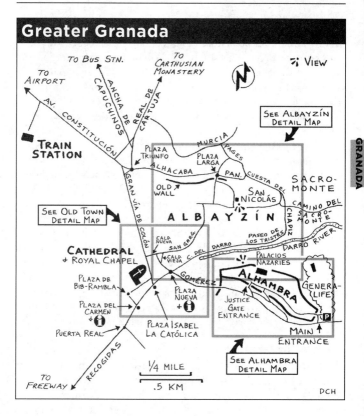

Greater Granada

TO BUS STN.

TO CARTHUSIAN MONASTERY

TO AIRPORT

↗ VIEW

N

ANCHA DE CAPUCHINOS

REAL DE CARTUJA

AV. CONSTITUCIÓN

TRAIN STATION

SEE ALBAYZÍN DETAIL MAP

PLAZA TRIUNFO

MURCIA

PAGES

PLAZA LARGA

ALHACABA

PAN.

CUESTA DEL

SACRO-MONTE

OLD WALL

SAN NICOLÁS

CAMINO DEL SACRO-MONTE

SEE OLD TOWN DETAIL MAP

GRAN VÍA DE COLÓN

A L B A Y Z Í N

CHAPIZ

CALD. NUEVA

SAN GREG.

CALD. VIEJA

C. DEL DARRO

PASEO DE LOS TRISTES

DARRO RIVER

CATHEDRAL ♦ ROYAL CHAPEL

PALACIOS NAZARÍES

PLAZA DE BIB-RAMBLA

GÓMEREZ

A L H A M B R A

GENERA-LIFE

PLAZA NUEVA ♦ ⓘ

PLAZA DEL CARMEN ♦ ⓘ

PUERTA REAL

PLAZA ISABEL LA CATÓLICA

JUSTICE GATE ENTRANCE

P

MAIN ENTRANCE

RECOGIDAS

¼ MILE

.5 KM

SEE ALHAMBRA DETAIL MAP

TO FREEWAY

DCH

cathedral, Royal Chapel, and Alcaicería (Moorish market), where the city's two main drags—Gran Vía de Colón (often just called "Gran Vía" by locals) and Calle Reyes Católicos—lead away into the modern city.

Tourist Information

The TI is tucked away just above Plaza Nueva on Santa Ana (Mon-Fri 9:00-19:30, Sat-Sun 9:30-15:00, above the church, tel. 958-575-202). Get a free city map and the *Pocket Guía* magazine in easy Spanish, and verify your Alhambra plans. To save yourself a trip to the train or bus stations, get schedule information here; the TI posts all departures on its walls. This TI covers not only Granada, but also Andalucía (pick up good, free maps for wherever else you're going in the region). A municipal TI, which covers only Granada, is inside City Hall on Plaza del Carmen, a short walk from the cathedral; they also sell the Bono Turístico city pass described later (Mon-Sat 10:00-19:00, Sun 10:00-14:00, tel. 958-248-280).

Alhambra Info: While any TI has information on the town's top sight, the very helpful info desk just inside the door of the official Alhambra bookstore (Tienda Librería de la Alhambra) is your best resource, as it's run by the Alhambra administration and is located right in the heart of town. The counter sells Alhambra tickets for future dates (no same-day sales) and has a ServiCaixa machine for printing prebooked tickets (daily 9:30-20:30, between Plaza Isabel La Católica and Plaza Nueva at Calle Reyes Católicos 40, tel. 958-227-846).

Sightseeing Pass: The **Bono Turístico** city pass covers the Alhambra, cathedral, Royal Chapel, Carthusian Monastery, and several trips on city buses, plus minor sights and discounts on others (€33/3 days, €37/5 days—this version also includes CitySightseeing bus). When you buy your pass, the vendor schedules a time for your Alhambra visit. (Because Bono Turístico Alhambra reservations occasionally book up, be sure that slots are available before you buy the pass.) Passes are sold at the TI in City Hall on Plaza del Carmen, at the Caja Granada Bank branch in Plaza Isabel La Católica, and at the "This is Granada" kiosk on Plaza Nueva; you can also book in advance online (www.bonoturisticogranada.com). Fancier hotels provide one free pass per room for stays of two or more nights; check with your hotel before buying a pass yourself.

Arrival in Granada

By Train: Granada's modest train station is connected to the center by frequent buses, a €7 taxi ride, or a 30-minute walk down Avenida de la Constitución and Gran Vía. If your itinerary is set, reserve your outbound train upon arrival. The train station does not have luggage storage, but you can store your bags at the nearby Granada iLocker (€3.50-5/day, price depends on bag size, daily 8:30-20:30, Avenida Andaluces 14, just across the parking lot in front of station, look for green door on your left).

Taxis wait out front, and it's a three-minute walk to reach the bus stop: Exiting the train station, walk straight ahead up the tree-lined Avenida Andaluces. At the first major intersection, turn right onto Avenida de la Constitución, and within a block you'll see a series of bus stops with routes marked on the signposts. Most of these buses stop at the cathedral (Gran Vía Catedral), which is four stops from the train station and the nearest stop to Plaza Nueva. Check the easy-to-read routes for the "Gran Vía Catedral" stop (your options include buses #1, #3, #4, #5, #6, #7, #8, #9, and others). An electronic board shows how long the wait is for each bus. When you board, buy a €1.20 ticket from the driver. For Plaza Nueva and most of my recommended hotels, get off at the cathedral (ask, "¿Catedral?"—kah-tay-DRAHL); cross the busy Gran Vía and walk three short blocks to Plaza Nueva.

By Bus: Located on the city outskirts, Granada's bus

station *(estación de autobuses)* has a good and cheap cafeteria, ATMs, luggage lockers (€3.50), coin-op Internet terminal, and a privately run tourist agency masquerading as a TI—all of these are downstairs, where you exit the buses. Upstairs is the main arrivals hall with ticket windows, ticket machines, and a helpful information counter in the main hall that hands out printed schedules for each route. All buses are operated by Alsa (tel. 902-422-242, www.alsa.es).

To get from the bus station to the city center, either take a 10-minute taxi ride (€8) or bus #3 or #33 (€1.20, pay driver). It's about a 20-minute bus ride; nearing the center, the bus goes up Gran Vía. For Plaza Nueva, get off at the "Gran Vía Catedral" stop near the cathedral (cathedral not visible from bus; ask, "*¿Catedral?*"—kah-tay-DRAHL), a half-block before the grand square called Plaza Isabel La Católica. From here, it's a short three-block walk to Plaza Nueva and most of my recommended hotels.

By Car: With all the one-way streets, GPS can be frustrating for tourists driving into Granada. And driving in Granada's historic center is restricted to buses, taxis, and

tourists with hotel reservations. Signs are posted to this effect, and entrances are strictly controlled. Hidden cameras snap a photo of your license plate as soon as you enter the restricted zone. If you have a reservation, simply drive past the sign, check in, and make sure your hotel registers you with the local traffic police (this is routine for them, but if they don't do it within 48 hours, you'll be stuck with a steep ticket). Hotels provide parking or have a deal with a central-zone garage (such as Parking San Agustín, just off Gran Vía del Colón, €25/day).

If you're driving and don't have a hotel reservation in the center, find a place to park outside the prohibited zone. The Alhambra, above the old town, has a huge lot where you can park for €19 per 24 hours (and walk, catch the minibus, or taxi into the center). There are also garages just outside the restricted zone: the Triunfo garage to the east (€20/day, Avenida de la Constitución 5) or the Neptune garage (Centro Comercial Neptuno) to the south (€15/day, Calle Neptuno). To reach the city center from either parking garage, catch bus #6 nearby and get off at the "Gran Vía Catedral" stop (every 10-20 minutes, €1.20, pay driver).

If, upon arrival in Granada, you're driving directly to the Alhambra, you can easily avoid the historic center.

By Plane: Granada's sleepy airport, which serves only a dozen or so planes a day, is about 10 miles west of the city center (airport code: GRX, tel. 958-245-223—press "2" for English, www.aena-aeropuertos.es). To get between the airport and downtown, you can take a taxi (€30) or, much cheaper, the airport bus, timed to leave directly outside the terminal when flights arrive and depart (€3, 12/day, 40 minutes). If you're leaving from the town center, use the bus stop at Gran Vía del Colón, nearly across from the cathedral.

Helpful Hints

Theft Alert: In general, be on guard for pickpockets, especially late at night in the Albayzín. Your biggest threat is being conned while enjoying drinks and music in Sacromonte. Down-and-out women, usually hanging out near the cathedral and Alcaicería, will accost you with sprigs of rosemary, then demand a tip—just ignore them.

Festivals and Concerts: From late June to early July, the **International Festival of Music and Dance** offers classical music, ballet, flamenco, and zarzuela (light opera) nightly in the Alhambra and other historic venues at reasonable prices. The ticket office is located in the Corral del Carbón (open mid-April-Oct). Beginning in February, you can also book tickets online at www.granadafestival.org. This festival is one of the most respected and popular in Spain, and tickets for major performers typically sell out months in advance. During the festival, flamenco is free every night at midnight; ask the ticket office or TI for the venue.

From fall through spring, the **City of Granada Orchestra** offers popular concerts—mostly on weekends— that generally sell out quickly (€6-23, late Sept-mid-May only, Auditorio Manuel de Falla, ticket office in Corral del Carbón, Mon-Sat 12:00-14:00 & 17:00-19:00, closed Sun, tel. 958-221-144, www.orquestaciudadgranada.es).

Internet Access: Almost all Granada hotels have Wi-Fi for their guests, and some have computers for use as well. Many Internet points are scattered throughout Granada, often part of *locutorios* (call centers).

Laundry: Tintorería-Lavandería Duquesa, a few blocks west of the cathedral area, offers a pricey service to wash, dry, and fold your clothes (€10/small load, same-day service possible if you bring it in the morning, no self-service, Mon-Fri 9:30-14:00 & 17:00-21:00, Sat 9:30-14:00, closed Sun, near the San Jerónimo Monastery at Duquesa 24, tel. 958-280-685).

Post Office: It's on Puerta Real (daily 8:30-20:30, tel. 958-221-138).

Travel Agencies: All travel agencies book flights, and many also sell long-distance bus and train tickets. Mega-chain **El Corte Inglés** sells plane, train, and bus tickets (Mon-Sat 10:00-22:00, closed Sun, Acera del Darro, floor 2, tel. 958-282-612).

Getting Around Granada

With cheap taxis, frisky minibuses, good city buses, and nearly all points of interest an easy walk from Plaza Nueva, you'll get around Granada easily.

Tickets for minibuses and city buses cost €1.20 per ride (buy from driver). Credibus magnetic cards save you money if you'll be riding often—or, since they're shareable, if you're part of a group (€5/7 trips, €10/16 trips, plus refundable €2 fee for each card issued). You can buy these from the driver as well. To get a €5 card, ask for "*un bono de cinco euros.*" For a €10 card, request "*un bono de diez euros.*" These are valid on minibuses and city buses (no fee for connecting bus if you transfer within 45 minutes).

By Minibus: Handy little made-for-tourists red minibuses, which cover the city center, depart every few minutes from Plaza Nueva, Plaza Isabel La Católica, and the cathedral (Gran Vía stops) until late in the evening. Here are several handy minibus routes to look for:

Bus #30 is the best for a trip up to the Alhambra, departing every 10-15 minutes from the "Gran Vía Catedral" stop, with Alhambra stops at the Generalife, Charles V's Palace, and Justice Gate (in that order).

Bus #31 departs from Plaza Nueva and winds around the Albayzín quarter (departs about every 15 minutes).

Bus #35 follows the same route as #31, but also makes a side-trip into Sacromonte. It runs less frequently (every 30-40 minutes).

By City Bus: These are handy if you're visiting the Carthusian Monastery (bus #8) or going to the bus station (#3 or #33) or train station (#1 or #3-#9).

Tours in Granada

Walking Tours

Cicerone, run by María, offers informative 2.5-hour city tours. Their excellent guides describe the fitful and fascinating changes the city underwent as it morphed from a Moorish capital to a Christian one 500 years ago. While the tour doesn't enter any actual sights, it weaves together bits of the Moorish heritage that survive around the cathedral and the Albayzín. Tours start on Plaza de Bib-Rambla and finish on Plaza Nueva. Groups are small; reservations are encouraged (though not required). Visits are generally only in English, but may be in both English and

GRANADA

Getting Tickets for the Alhambra's Palacios Nazaries

The popular Palacio Nazaries is often sold out during the day. (The Generalife Gardens and Alcazaba fort don't sell out.) If you're not prepared, you could become one of the untold number of tourists who show up in Granada...and never see its main sight. You have three main options to ensure that you get into the Palacio during your stay. The easiest is the Bono Turístico city pass, which lets you choose virtually any entry time, even the same day (get details on page 86). You can also visit the Palacio at night, when it's rarely sold out (see page 105; if you do this, you can also get a daytime ticket for the rest of the complex, which never sells out). Or you can make a reservation.

Reserving in Advance: Getting a reservation is easy, provided you do it well in advance. You reserve a specific entry time (€1.30 surcharge) and pick up your tickets in Spain. Reserve as soon as you're ready to commit to a time, as much as three months before your visit. For most of the year, book at least two weeks in advance—more for Holy Week, weekends, and major holidays. Off-season (July-Aug and winter), you can generally book a few days in advance, or even walk right in—but it's not worth the risk. When you reserve, get the "General Daytime Visit" ticket (described on page 99). For advice on timing your visit, see the sidebar on page 104.

Here are your reservation options:

• When you book your hotel room, ask if your hotelier can reserve Alhambra tickets; if so, request a time slot.

• Order online at www.alhambra-tickets.es. Select the "General Daytime Visit" ticket, then choose your date and time period—morning *(De 8:30h a 14h)* or afternoon *(De 14h a 20h)*—then the exact half-hour time window for entry. *Agotado* means "sold out." Unless you're traveling with a child under 12 *(Niños menos 12a)*, ignore the "special offers" options and simply hit "Continue."

• By phone, an English-speaking operator walks you through the process. Within Spain, dial 958-926-031 or 902-888-001. From the US, dial 011-34-958-926-031. The line is open Mon-Fri

Spanish on slow days (€15, show this book to save €3, kids under 14 free, daily March-Oct at 10:30, Nov-Feb at 11:00; to book a tour, visit the kiosk labeled *Meeting Point* on Plaza de Bib-Rambla—staffed by cheerful Rocio, or call 958-561-810 or mobile 607-691-676; www.ciceronegranada.com, reservas@ciceronegranada.com). They also offer tours of the Alhambra that include an entry time to Palacios Nazaries—handy if you have trouble getting a reservation on your own (€50, includes Alhambra ticket, ideally reserve at least 3-4 days ahead).

8:00-21:00 Spanish time, closed Sat-Sun. (While you wait for an operator, a recording tells you in Spanish the date of the next available tickets.)

Picking Up Tickets: Your reservation still needs to be converted to a printed ticket, which you pick up in Spain. To confirm your purchase, bring the same credit card you used to reserve. (To be 100 percent sure, also bring your credit card's PIN number and your passport.)

Save time by retrieving your tickets before you reach the crowded Alhambra. You can print tickets at one of Spain's many yellow, ATM-like ServiCaixa terminals (such as the one across from the cathedral at Gran Vía 16). Or go to the official Alhambra bookstore in town (a half-block from Plaza Nueva at Calle Reyes Católicos 40) and get your ticket from their ServiCaixa machine or at the information desk. Picking up your ticket in advance lets you use the Justice Gate shortcut, avoiding the mob at the main entrance (described on page 106).

You can also pick up tickets at the Alhambra's main entrance, but it can be crowded. At the entrance, follow "Bookings collection with credit card" signs to the windows marked *Retirada de Reservas*, or use their less-crowded ServiCaixa machines (beyond the bookstore and café). Allow up to an hour to wait in line to pick up tickets and walk from there to the Palacio.

If You're in Granada Without a Palace Reservation: You can generally buy a ticket good for entry later the same day if you're in line at the main entrance by 7:30 (they open at 8:00). On a slow day, you can sometimes get in right away. The entrance's ServiCaixa ticket machines (for credit cards; these are just beyond the bookstore and café) are faster than the cash-only window labeled *Venta Directa*.

Otherwise, you can try one of the following: Take a guided tour, which admits you without reservations (see "Tours," pages 89 and 106); try for a last-minute reservation online, by phone, through your hotel, or at the Alhambra bookstore (the store sells tickets for future dates, but not same-day tickets); buy a Bono Turístico pass; or visit at night.

Local Guides

Margarita Ortiz de Landazuri (tel. 958-221-406, www.alhambra tours.com, info@alhambratours.com) and **Miguel Ángel** (mobile 617-565-711, miguelangelalhambratours@gmail.com) are both good, English-speaking, licensed guides with lots of experience and a passion for teaching. Guide rates are standard (€130/2.5 hours, €260/day).

Hop-On, Hop-Off Bus Tour

CitySightseeing operates a route with 11 stops around the city. But Granada doesn't lend itself to this type of tour, and the bus concentrates on far-flung areas that are far less interesting than the easy-to-walk city center (€18/48 hours, 1.5-hour loop, 2 buses/hour, 9:30-20:00 in summer, 9:30-18:00 in winter, only stops at the Carthusian Monastery in the afternoon, tel. 958-535-028, www.granadatour.com).

This is Granada Audio Tour
You can rent an MP3 player preloaded with four different walking-tour itineraries around the city, including the Alhambra. Two people get the system for up to two days for €15 (rent from "This is Granada" kiosk on Plaza Nueva, includes map, tel. 958-210-239).

Olive Oil Tour
This company helps you explore Granada's countryside and taste some local olive oil. Choose between a three-hour tour that departs in the morning or afternoon (€38) or a six-hour tour that includes lunch (€58). Tours are in English, and a driver will pick you up at your hotel (tel. 958-559-643, mobile 651-147-504, www.oliveoiltour.com, reservas@oliveoiltour.com).

Gayle's Granada Tapas Tours
Gayle Mackie takes small groups off the beaten path to a series of four characteristic tapas bars, providing food tips, light banter, and fascinating insights into Granada along the way. For a movable feast (and what amounts to a filling meal) with good wine and beer, join their "classic walk" (2.5 hours, €35/person, €5 discount with this book, tours for 2-6 people, daily at 13:30 or 20:00, other tapa tour variations include family and group options, mobile 619-444-984, www.granadatapastours.com).

Self-Guided Walk

▲▲Granada's Old Town

This short walk covers all the essential sights beyond the Alhambra. Along the way, we'll see vivid evidence of the dramatic Moorish-to-Christian transition brought about by the Reconquista, the long and ultimately successful battle to retake Spain from the Moors and re-establish Christian rule.

• *Start at Corral del Carbón, near Plaza del Carmen.*

❶ **Corral del Carbón:** A caravanserai (of Silk Road fame) was a protected place for merchants to rest their camels, spend the night, get a bite to eat, and spin yarns. This, the only surviving caravanserai of Granada's original 14, was just a block away from the silk market (Alcaicería; the next stop on this walk). Stepping through the caravanserai's grand

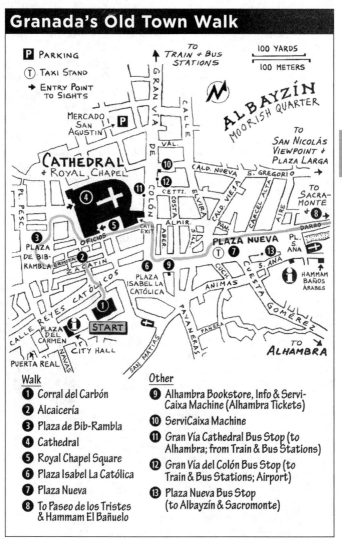

Granada's Old Town Walk

P PARKING
T TAXI STAND
→ ENTRY POINT TO SIGHTS

TO TRAIN + BUS STATIONS

100 YARDS
100 METERS

M ALBAYZÍN MOORISH QUARTER

MERCADO SAN AGUSTIN

P

TO SAN NICOLÁS VIEWPOINT + PLAZA LARGA →

GRANADA

CATHEDRAL + ROYAL CHAPEL

GRAN VIA DE COLÓN

CALLE

VAL.

10

CALD. NUEVA S. GREGORIO

TO SACRO-MONTE

CETTI. ELVIRA.

11

12

CALLE

COSTA

CALD. VIEJA

CÁRCEL ALTA

AIRE

8

4

PL. PESC.

3

PLAZA DE BIB-RAMBLA

5

OFICIOS

CATH. EXIT

ALMIR.

ABEN.

PAN.

DARRO

PLAZA NUEVA

T **7**

PL. S. ANA

HAMMAM BAÑOS ARABES

ERMITA

ZACATIN

2

6

9

PLAZA ISABEL LA CATÓLICA

ANIMAS

CUCH.

CUESTA S. ANA

GOMEREZ

CALLE REYES CATÓLICOS

1

PLAZA DEL CARMEN

START

i

CITY HALL

SAN MATIAS

PAVANERAS

PANERA

TO ALHAMBRA

NAVAS

PUERTA REAL

Walk
1 Corral del Carbón
2 Alcaicería
3 Plaza de Bib-Rambla
4 Cathedral
5 Royal Chapel Square
6 Plaza Isabel La Católica
7 Plaza Nueva
8 To Paseo de los Tristes & Hammam El Bañuelo

Other
9 Alhambra Bookstore, Info & Servi-Caixa Machine (Alhambra Tickets)
10 ServiCaixa Machine
11 Gran Vía Cathedral Bus Stop (to Alhambra; from Train & Bus Stations)
12 Gran Vía del Colón Bus Stop (to Train & Bus Stations; Airport)
13 Plaza Nueva Bus Stop (to Albayzín & Sacromonte)

Moorish door, you find a square with 14th-century Moorish brickwork surrounding a water fountain. This plain-yet-elegant structure evokes the times when traders would gather here with exotic goods and swap tales from across the Muslim world.

It's a common mistake to think of the Muslim Moors as somehow not Spanish. They lived here for seven centuries and were really just as "indigenous" as the Romans, Goths, and Celts. While the Moors were Muslim, they were no more connected to Arabia than they were to France.

After the Reconquista, this space was used as a coal storage facility (hence "del Carbón"). These days it houses two offices where you can buy tickets for musical events.

• *From the caravanserai, exit straight ahead and walk down Puente del Carbón to the big street named Calle Reyes Católicos (for the "Catholic Monarchs" Ferdinand and Isabel, who finally conquered the Moors). The street covers a river that once ran openly here, with a series of bridges (like the "Coal Bridge," Puente del Carbón) lacing together the two parts of town. Today, the modern commercial center is to your left. Continue one block farther to the yellow gate marked* Alcaicería. *The pedestrian street you're crossing, Zacatin, was the main drag, which ran parallel to the river before it was covered in the 19th century. Today it's a favorite paseo destination, busy each evening with strollers. Pass through the Alcaicería gate and walk 20 yards into the old market to the first intersection.*

❷ **Alcaicería:** Originally a Moorish silk market with 200 shops, the Alcaicería (al-kai-thay-REE-ah) was filled with precious salt, silver, spices, and silk. It had 10 armed gates and its own guards. Silk was huge in Moorish times, and silkworm-friendly mulberry trees flourished in the countryside. It was such an important product that the sultans controlled and guarded it by constructing this fine, fortified market. After the Reconquista, the Christians realized this market was good for business and didn't mess with it. Later, the more zealous Philip II had it shut down. A terrible fire in 1850 destroyed what was left. Today's Alcaicería was rebuilt in the late 1800s as a  tourist souk (marketplace) to complement the romantic image of Granada popularized by the writings of Washington Irving.

Explore the mesh of tiny shopping lanes: overpriced trinkets, popcorn machines popping, men selling balloons, leather goods spread out on streets, kids playing soccer, barking dogs, dogged shoe-shine boys, and the whirring grind of bicycle-powered knife sharpeners. You'll invariably meet obnoxious and persistent women pushing their green sprigs on innocents in order to extort money. Be strong.

• *Turn left down Ermita lane. After 50 yards, leave the market via another fortified gate and enter a big square. The Neptune fountain marks the center of the...*

❸ **Plaza de Bib-Rambla:** This exuberant square, just two blocks behind the cathedral (from the fountain you can see its blocky spire peeking above the big orange building) was once the center of Moorish Granada. While Moorish rule of Spain lasted

GRANADA

700 years, the last couple of those centuries were a period of decline as Muslim culture split under weak leadership and Christian forces grew more determined. The last remnants of the Moorish kingdom united and ruled from Granada. As Muslims fled south from reconquered lands, Granada was flooded with refugees. By 1400, Granada had an estimated 100,000 people—huge for medieval Europe. This was the main square, the focal point of market and festivals, but it was much smaller then than now, pushed in by the jam-packed city.

GRANADA

Under Christian rule, Moors and Jews were initially tolerated (as they were considered good for business), and this area became the Moorish ghetto. Then, with the Inquisition (under Philip II, c. 1550), ideology trumped pragmatism, and Jews and Muslims were evicted or forced to convert. The elegant square you see today was built, and built big. In-your-face Catholic processions started here. To assert Christian rule, all the trappings of Christian power were layered upon what had been the trappings of Moorish power. Between here and the cathedral were the Christian University (the big orange building) and the adjacent archbishop's palace.

Today Plaza de Bib-Rambla is good for coffee or a meal amid the color and fragrance of flower stalls and the burbling of its Neptune-topped fountain. It remains a multigenerational hangout, where it seems everyone is enjoying a peaceful retirement. A block away (Neptune would get there if he could just turn 180 degrees and walk 100 yards), the Pescadería square is a smaller, similarly lively version of Bib-Rambla.

• *Leave the square by walking toward the cathedral, heading down the lane between the big orange building and Bar Manolo. In a block, you come to a small square fronting a very big church.*

❹ **Cathedral:** Wow, the cathedral facade just screams triumph. That's partly because its design is based on a triumphal arch, built over a destroyed mosque. Five hundred yards away, there was once open space outside the city wall with good soil for a foundation. But the Christian conquerors said, "No way." Instead, they destroyed the mosque and built their cathedral right here on difficult, sandy soil. This was the place where the people of Granada traditionally

worshipped—and now they would worship as Christians.

The church—started in the early 1500s and not finished until the late 1700s—has a Gothic foundation and was built mostly in the Renaissance style, with its last altars done in Neoclassical style. Hometown artist Alonso Cano (1601-1667) finished the building, at the king's request, in Baroque. Accentuating the power of the Roman Catholic Church, the emphasis here is on Mary rather than Christ. The facade declares *Ave Maria*. (This was Counter-Reformation time, and the Church was threatened by Protestant Christians. Mary was also more palatable to Muslim converts, as she is revered in the Quran.)

• *To tour the cathedral now, you can enter here. You'll exit on the far side, near the Royal Chapel Square (next on this walk).*

To skip the cathedral interior for now and continue with this walk, circle around the cathedral to the right, keeping the church to your left, until you reach the small square facing the Royal Chapel.

❺ **Royal Chapel Square:** This square was once ringed by important Moorish buildings. A hammam (public bath), a madrassa (school), a caravanserai (Day's Inn), the silk market, and the leading mosque were all right here. With Christian rule, the madrassa (the faux-gray-stone building with the walls painted in 3-D Baroque style) became Granada's first City Hall. The royal coffins were moved from the Alhambra's parador here to the Royal Chapel in 1521.

• *Continue up the cobbled, stepped lane to the big street, Gran Vía de Colón. With the arrival of cars and the modern age, the people of Granada wanted a Parisian-style boulevard. In the early 20th century, they mercilessly cut through the old town and created Gran Vía and its French-style buildings—in the process destroying everything in its path, including many historic convents.*

From here you could catch minibus #30 to the Alhambra, or go left two blocks, cross the street, and walk up Calle Cárcel Baja into the Albayzín. But for now let's continue our orientation tour. Cross the busy street, turn right, and walk down Gran Vía to the big square ahead. Face the statue above the fountain from across the busy intersection.

❻ **Plaza Isabel La Católica:** Granada's two grand boulevards, Gran Vía and Calle Reyes Católicos, meet a block off Plaza Nueva at Plaza Isabel La Católica. Above the fountain, a beautiful statue shows Columbus unfurling a long contract with Isabel. It lists the terms of Columbus' *mcccclxxxxii* voyage: "For as much as you, Columbus, are

going by our command to discover and subdue some Islands and Continents in the ocean...." The two reliefs show the big events in Granada of 1492: Isabel and Ferdinand accepting Columbus' proposal and a stirring battle scene (which never happened) at the walls of the Alhambra.

Isabel was driven by her desire to spread Catholicism. Spain, needing an alternate trade route to the Orient's spices after the Ottoman Empire cut off the traditional overland routes, was driven by trade. And Columbus was driven by his desire for money. As a reward for adding territory to Spain's Catholic empire, Isabel promised Columbus the ranks of Admiral of the Oceans and Governor of the New World. To sweeten the pot, she tossed in one-eighth of all the riches he brought home. Isabel died thinking that Columbus had found India or China. Columbus died poor and disillusioned.

Calle Reyes Católicos leads from this square downhill to the busy intersection with Puerta Real. From there, Acera del Darro takes you through modern Granada to the river via the huge El Corte Inglés department store and lots of modern commerce. This area erupts with locals out strolling each night. For the best Granada paseo, wander the streets here around 19:00.

• *Follow Calle Reyes Católicos a couple of blocks uphill to the left, where you'll find another square.*

❼ Plaza Nueva: Long a leading square in Granada, Plaza Nueva is dominated by the Palace of Justice (grand Baroque facade with green Andalusian flag). The fountain is capped by a stylized pomegranate—the symbol of the city, always open and fertile. The main action here is the comings and goings of the busy little shuttle buses serving the Albayzín. The local hippie community, nicknamed the *pies negros* (black feet) for obvious reasons, hangs out here and on Calle de Elvira. They squat—with their dogs and guitars—in abandoned caves above those the Gypsies occupy in Sacromonte. Many are the children of rich Spanish families from the north, hell-bent on disappointing their high-achieving parents.

• *Our tour continues with a stroll up Paseo de los Tristes. Leave Plaza Nueva opposite where you entered (via the street to the left of the church) and walk up the Darro River Valley. This is particularly enjoyable in the cool of the evening. If you're tired, note that minibus #31 runs from Plaza Nueva into and through the Albayzín quarter.*

❽ Paseo de los Tristes: This "Walk of the Sad Ones" was once the route of funeral processions to the cemetery at the edge of town. Leaving Plaza Nueva, pass the Church of Santa Ana on your right. This was originally a mosque—the church tower replaced a minaret. Notice the ceramic brickwork. This is Mudejar art by Moorish craftsmen, whose techniques were later employed by Christians. Inside you'll see a fine Alhambra-style cedar ceiling.

Follow Carrera del Darro high above the River Darro, which flows along the base of the Alhambra (look down by the river for a glimpse of feral cats). Six miles upstream, part of the Darro is diverted to provide water for the Alhambra's many fountains—a remarkable feat of Moorish engineering that allowed the grand fortress complex to be resistant to siege.

After passing two small, picturesque bridges, you'll see the broken nub of a once-grand 11th-century bridge over the river, leading to the Alhambra. Notice two slits in the column: One held an iron portcullis to keep bad guys from entering the town via the river. The second held a solid door that was lowered to build up water, then released to flush out the riverbed and keep it clean.

• *Across from the remains of the bridge is the brick facade of an evocative Moorish bath, the Hammam El Bañuelo.*

Hammam El Bañuelo (Moorish Baths): In Moorish times, hammams were a big part of the community (working-class homes didn't have bathrooms). Baths were strictly segregated (as they are today) and functioned as more than a place to wash: Business was done here, and it was a social meeting point. In Christian times it was assumed that conspiracies brewed in these baths—therefore, only a few of them survive. This place gives you the chance to explore the stark but evocative ruins of an 11th-century Moorish public bath (free, unreliably Tue-Sat 10:00-14:30, April-Sept opens at 9:00, closed Sun-Mon year-round, English descriptions posted throughout, photos OK, Carrera del Darro 31, tel. 958-027-800).

Entering the baths, you pass the house of the keeper and the foyer, then visit the cold room, the warm room (where services like massage were offered), and finally the hot, or steam, room. Beyond that, you can see the oven that generated the heat, which flowed under the hypocaust-style floor tiles (the ones closest to the oven were the hottest). The romantic little holes in the ceiling once had stained-glass louvers that attendants opened and closed with sticks to regulate the heat and steaminess. Whereas Romans soaked in their pools, Muslims just doused. Rather than being totally immersed, people scooped and splashed water over themselves. Imagine attendants stoking the fires under the metal boiler...while people in towels and wooden slippers (to protect their feet from the heated floors) enjoyed all the spa services you can imagine as beams of light slashed through the mist.

This was a great social mixer. As all were naked, class distinctions disappeared—elites learned the latest from commoners. Mothers found matches for their kids. A popular Muslim phrase sums up the attraction of the baths: "This is where anyone would spend their last coin."

• *Continuing straight ahead, on your right is the Church of San Pedro, the parish church of Sacromonte's Gypsy community (across from the Mudejar Art Museum). Within its rich interior is an ornate oxcart used to carry the host on the annual pilgrimage to Rocio, a town near the Portuguese border. Just past this, on your left, is Santa Catalina de Zafra, a convent of cloistered nuns (they worship behind a screen that divides the church's rich interior in half).*

This walk ends at Paseo de los Tristes—with its restaurant tables spilling out under the floodlit Alhambra. From here, the road arcs up into Sacromonte. If you've worked up a hunger, you can backtrack a few blocks to Calle de Gloria where the Convento de San Bernardo sells cookies and monastic wine. Look for the Venta de Dulces *sign; goods are sold from behind a lazy Susan.*

GRANADA

Sights in Granada

▲▲▲The Alhambra

This last and greatest Moorish palace is one of Europe's top sights. Attracting up to 8,000 visitors a day, it's the reason most tourists

come to Granada. Nowhere else does the splendor of Moorish civilization shine so beautifully.

The last Moorish stronghold in Europe is, with all due respect, really a symbol of retreat. For centuries, Granada was merely a regional capital. Gradually the Christian Reconquista moved south, taking Córdoba (1237) and Sevilla (1248). The Nazarids, one of the many diverse ethnic groups of Spanish Muslims, held together the last Moorish kingdom, which they ruled from Granada until 1492. As you tour their grand palace, remember that while Europe slumbered through the Dark Ages, Moorish magnificence blossomed—ornate stucco, plaster "stalactites," colors galore, scalloped windows framing Granada views, exuberant gardens, and water, water everywhere. Water—so rare and precious in most of the Islamic world—was the purest symbol of life to the Moors. The Alhambra is decorated with water: standing still, cascading, masking secret conversations, and drip-dropping playfully.

Cost: Various tickets cover the sights of the Alhambra. The one you want is the €13 **"General Daytime Visit"** *(visita diurna*

Granada at a Glance

▲▲▲**The Alhambra** The last and greatest Moorish palace, highlighting the splendor of that civilization in the 13th and 14th centuries. Reservations are a must if you plan to visit during the day. **Hours:** The entire complex is open daily mid-March-mid-Oct 8:30-20:00, off-season 8:30-18:00. Palacios Nazaries and Generalife Gardens are open for nighttime visits mid-March-mid-Oct Tue-Sat 22:00-23:30, closed Sun-Mon; off-season Fri-Sat 20:00-21:30, closed Sun-Thu. See page 99.

▲▲**Royal Chapel** Lavish 16th-century Plateresque Gothic chapel with the tombs of Queen Isabel and King Ferdinand. **Hours:** March-Oct daily 10:15-13:30 & 16:00-19:30 except opens at 11:00 on Sun; Nov-Feb daily 10:15-13:30 & 15:30-18:30 except opens at 11:00 on Sun. See page 118.

▲▲**San Nicolás Viewpoint** Breathtaking vista over the Alhambra and the Albayzín. **Hours:** Always open; best at sunset. See page 127.

▲**Cathedral** The second-largest cathedral in Spain, unusual for its bright Renaissance interior. **Hours:** April-Oct Mon-Sat 10:30-13:15 & 16:00-20:00, Sun 16:00-20:00; Nov-March until 19:00. See page 122.

▲**The Albayzín** Spain's best old Moorish quarter. **Hours:** Always open, but use caution after dark. See page 124.

Cave Museum of Sacromonte A center with caves and displays on Roma cave-building, crafts, food, and music. **Hours:** Mid-March-mid-Oct daily 10:00-20:00, until 18:00 off-season. See page 130.

general) ticket, which covers the Alcazaba fort, Palacios Nazaries, and Generalife Gardens. This ticket is the only one that allows you to see Palacios Nazaries during the day. Note that same-day tickets are virtually never available—reservations are essential.

If you make the mistake of showing up without a reservation, get in line and look for the electric sign indicating just what's still available that day. Other, less-ideal tickets are available for people who've waited too long to get the General Daytime Visit ticket:

• Daytime ticket for just the Alcazaba and Generalife Gardens—€7

• Nighttime ticket for just Palacios Nazaries—€8

• Nighttime ticket for just Generalife Gardens—€5

Alcaicería Tiny shopping lanes filled with tacky tourist shops. **Hours:** Always open, with shops open long hours. See page 94.

Corral del Carbón Granada's only surviving caravanserai (inn for traveling merchants), with impressive Moorish door. **Hours:** Always viewable. See page 92.

Paseo de los Tristes A prime strolling strip above the Darro River lined with eateries and peppered with Moorish history. **Hours:** Always open; best in the evenings. See page 97.

Hammam El Bañuelo 11th-century ruins of Moorish baths. **Hours:** Unreliably Tue-Sat 10:00-14:30, April-Sept opens at 9:00, closed Sun-Mon year-round. See page 98.

Great Mosque of Granada Islamic house of worship featuring a minaret with a live call to prayer, an information center for the Muslim perspective on Granada history, and a courtyard with commanding views. **Hours:** Daily 11:00-14:00 & 18:00-21:00, shorter hours in winter. See page 128.

Hammam Baños Árabes Tranquil spot for soaks and massages in Arab baths. **Hours:** Daily 10:00-24:00. See page 124.

Zambra **Dance** Touristy flamenco-like dance performance in Sacromonte district. **Hours:** Shows generally daily at 22:00. See page 131.

Carthusian Monastery Lavish Baroque monastery on the outskirts of town. **Hours:** Daily April-Oct 10:00-13:00 & 16:00-20:00, Nov-March 10:00-13:00 & 15:00-18:00. See page 132.

• "Circular Azul" ticket, which allows a nighttime visit of the Palacio Nazaries, then (the next morning) the Alcazaba and Generalife Gardens—€15

The Alhambra grounds are free to visit, as is Charles V's Palace (and the Alhambra Museum inside it).

Hours: The whole Alhambra complex is open daily mid-March-mid-Oct 8:30-20:00, off-season 8:30-18:00 (ticket office opens at 8:00, last entry one hour before closing, toll tel. 902-441-221, www.alhambra-patronato.es).

Palacios Nazaries and Generalife Gardens are also open most **evenings** mid-March-mid-Oct Tue-Sat 22:00-23:30 (ticket office open 21:30-22:30), closed Sun-Mon; and off-season Fri-Sat 20:00-21:30 (ticket office open 19:30-20:30), closed Sun-Thu.

GRANADA

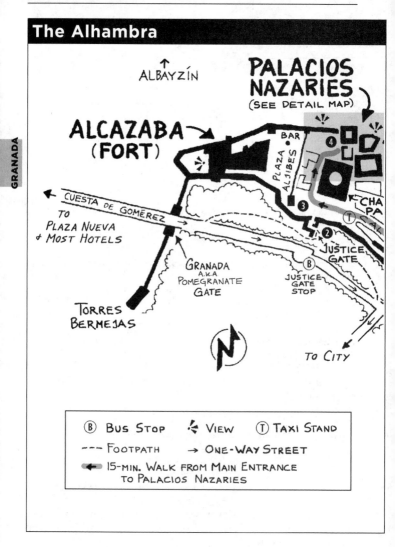

The Alhambra

↑
ALBAYZÍN

PALACIOS NAZARIES
(SEE DETAIL MAP)

ALCAZABA (FORT) →

BAR

PLAZA ALJIBES

❹

❸

CHA PA

← CUESTA DE GOMÉREZ

TO PLAZA NUEVA & MOST HOTELS

Ⓣ

❷

GRANADA A.K.A. POMEGRANATE GATE

Ⓑ

JUSTICE GATE

JUSTICE-GATE STOP

TORRES BERMEJAS

N

TO CITY

Ⓑ BUS STOP   ⅙ VIEW   Ⓣ TAXI STAND

--- FOOTPATH   → ONE-WAY STREET

⬅ 15-MIN. WALK FROM MAIN ENTRANCE TO PALACIOS NAZARIES

Getting There: You have four options for getting to the Alhambra.

On Foot: From Plaza Nueva, hike 20-25 minutes up the street called Cuesta de Gomérez. Keep going straight—you'll see the Alhambra high on your left. (Along the way, after about 10 minutes, look for the Justice Gate shortcut, described later.) The ticket pavilion is on the far side of the Alhambra, near the Generalife Gardens.

By Bus: From the "Gran Vía Catedral" bus stop near the cathedral, catch a red #30 minibus, marked *Alhambra* (€1.20, runs

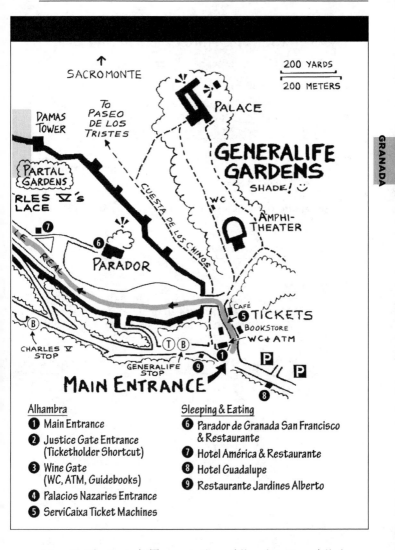

GRANADA

Alhambra
❶ Main Entrance
❷ Justice Gate Entrance (Ticketholder Shortcut)
❸ Wine Gate (WC, ATM, Guidebooks)
❹ Palacios Nazaries Entrance
❺ ServiCaixa Ticket Machines

Sleeping & Eating
❻ Parador de Granada San Francisco & Restaurante
❼ Hotel América & Restaurante
❽ Hotel Guadalupe
❾ Restaurante Jardines Alberto

every 10-15 minutes). There are three Alhambra stops (all shown on the map above): Justice Gate (best if you have a printed ticket—described later), Charles V, and Generalife (main ticket office and the gardens).

By Taxi: It's a €5 ride from the taxi stand on Plaza Nueva.

By Car: If you're coming from outside the city by car, you can drive to the Alhambra without passing through Granada's historic center. From the freeway, take the exit marked *Ronda Sur-Alhambra*. Signs will lead you to the Alhambra parking lot, conveniently located near the entrance of the Alhambra (€2/hour). Overnight

Planning Your Time at the Alhambra

The Alhambra consists of four sights clustered together atop a hill:

▲▲▲**Palacios Nazaries**—Exquisite Moorish palace, the one must-see sight. To see it during the day, advance reservations are a must.

▲▲**Charles V's Palace**—Christian Renaissance palace plopped on top of the Alhambra after the Reconquista, with the fine Alhambra Museum (free entry).

▲▲**Generalife Gardens**—Fancy, manicured gardens with small summer palace.

Alcazaba—Empty old fort with tower and views.

When to Go

Daytime tickets for Palacios Nazaries come stamped with a 30-minute time slot. Time your visit around that appointment, as your reservation is only good if you enter the palace within that 30-minute window. (Once inside the palace, you can linger as long as you like.)

How best to see the rest of the Alhambra complex depends on whether your Palacios Nazaries reservation is for a time before or after 14:00. If your entry time for Palacios Nazaries is before 14:00, you can visit the other Alhambra sights (the Alcazaba, Generalife Gardens, and Charles V's Palace) anytime in the morning, see Palacios Nazaries at your appointed time, and leave the Alhambra by 14:00 (although you can get away with staying longer in the fort, gardens, or Palacios Nazaries, you won't be allowed to *enter* any of these sites after 14:00). If your ticket is stamped for 14:00 or later, you cannot enter the Alhambra sights any earlier than 14:00. For instance, if you have a reservation to visit Palacios Nazaries at 16:30, you can enter the Alhambra sights any time after 14:00 and see the fort and Generalife Gardens before Palacios Nazaries.

Because of the time restriction on afternoon visits, morning tickets sell out the quickest. But for most travelers, an afternoon is ample time to see the site—the light is perfect, and there are fewer tour groups.

If you're picking up your tickets at the main entrance (at the top end), or just want to start with the gardens, be aware that you're a 15-minute walk away from Palacios Nazaries at the other end. Be sure to arrive at the Alhambra with enough time to make it to the palace before your allotted half-hour entry time slot ends. The ticket-checkers at Palacios Nazaries are strict.

GRANADA

Your Route

To minimize walking, see Charles V's Palace and the Alcazaba fort before your visit to Palacios Nazaries. When you finish touring the palace, you'll leave through the Partal Gardens, a pleasant 15-to-20-minute walk from the Generalife Gardens. Depending on the time, you can visit the Generalife Gardens before or after seeing Palacios Nazaries. If you have any time to kill before your palace appointment, do it luxuriously on the breezy view  terrace of the parador bar (actually within the Alhambra walls; for other options see "Eating," page 139). Drinks, WCs, and guidebooks are available at the Wine Gate, near the entrance of Palacios Nazaries, but not inside the palace.

The Alhambra by Moonlight

If you prefer doing things after dark, you can avoid the reservation hassle. Late-night visits to the Alhambra are easy (separate nighttime tickets are sold for Palacio Nazaries and the Generalife Gardens; see "Cost," page 99)—just buy your ticket upon arrival, as night-visit tickets hardly ever sell out. Keep in mind that two separate tickets (Alcazaba and Generalife Gardens by day, Palacios Nazaries by night) cost the same as the Circular Azul ticket, and offer more flexibility, as you're not locked into the Circular Azul's next-morning stipulation.

You can't see the Alcazaba fort at night, but, hey, Palacios Nazaries provides 80 percent of the Alhambra's thrills anyway. Although a few small sections of both the palace and the gardens are closed at night, you'll see most of what the daytime visitors see. While some find the Alhambra disappointing at night, others find it even more magical (less crowded and beautifully lit); either way, it's better than not seeing it at all (for exact times see "Hours," page 101).

parking here is perfectly permissible (€19/24 hours, guarded at night). When you leave, be careful to go out the same way you came in, avoiding the driving ban in Granada's historic center.

Justice Gate Shortcut Entrance: If you already have your printed ticket in hand (i.e., you picked it up from a ServiCaixa machine in town), you can take a shortcut to the core of the complex by entering through the Justice Gate, downhill from the main entrance (if you're walking, this saves about 15 minutes of uphill climbing; you can also get off the minibus here). But if you want to go to the Generalife Gardens first, or don't yet have a ticket in hand, use the upper, main entrance.

Tours: Various companies run tours for about €44-50 that include transportation to the Alhambra and a guided tour of Palacios Nazaries (for example, GranaVisión has a tour for €44, tel. 958-535-872, www.granavision.com; Cicerone also has tours for €50).

Audioguides: The €6.50 "complete" audioguide brings the palace to life, with a quality description of 50 stops throughout the complex. The €4 "garden" audioguide covers just 15 stops, mostly outside the buildings (rent it at the entrance or at Charles V's Palace, leave €40 cash deposit or your ID—you'll need to return the audioguide where you picked it up). Audioguides are not available for night visits.

Guidebooks: Consider getting a guidebook in town and reading it the night before to understand the layout and history of this remarkable sight before entering. Official Alhambra bookstores (including the one in town, and those up at the grounds) push the €18 *Official Guide,* a well-produced, scholarly tome loaded with history, photos, maps, and practical information—but it weighs a ton. Other bookstores sell additional options. Of these, I enjoy the slick and colorful *Alhambra and Generalife in Focus* (€9); the thinner *The Alhambra and the Generalife* has less information and mostly photos (€8).

Photography: Photos with flash are allowed everywhere except in the Alhambra Museum.

Eating: Within the Alhambra walls, your food options are somewhat limited. Choose between the restaurant at the **parador** (*cafetería:* €9-13 sandwiches, €12-20 light meals; restaurant—get a table on the terrace: €10-15 starters, €18-27 main dishes, €34 fixed-price meal); the courtyard of the **Hotel América** (with pricey €15-20 meals but affordable €6 sandwiches and a great peaceful ambience, Sun-Fri 12:30-16:30, closed Sat); a small **bar-café kiosk** in front of the Alcazaba fort (€3 basic sandwiches and other snacks); and **vending machines** (at the WC) next to the Wine Gate, near Charles V's Palace. You're welcome to bring in a **picnic** as long as you eat it in a public area.

For better-value (but touristy) options, head outside to the area around the parking lot and ticket booth at the top of the complex, where there's a strip of handy eateries. **Restaurante Jardines Alberto,** across from the breezy Restaurante La Mimbre, has a nice courtyard and offers a good value (€5 sandwiches, €8-12 salads, €12-22 main dishes, €14-17 fixed-price lunch, daily 9:00-23:00, until 20:00 off-season, Paseo de la Sabica 1, enter through street-level gift shop).

Nearby: If you're going to the Albayzín afterward, walk back into town along the **Cuesta de los Chinos.** (It starts near the ticket booth, by Restaurante La Mimbre and the minibus stop.) You'll walk on a desolate lane downhill along a stream, beneath the Alhambra ramparts, and past the sultan's cobbled horse lane leading up to Generalife Gardens. In 10 minutes you're back in town at Paseo de los Tristes, where you can stroll to Plaza Nueva or continue walking into the Albayzín district. Walking downhill on this trail from the Alhambra, you can't get lost.

◑ Self-Guided Tour

I've listed these sights in the order you're likely to visit them. The first three sights cluster at the bottom/far end of the complex, while the Generalife Gardens are about a 15-minute walk away, at the top (main entrance). If you have a long time to wait for your Palacios Nazaries appointment, you could do the gardens first, then head down to the other three; otherwise it makes sense to start on the lower end of the hill and finish with the gardens.

▲▲Charles V's Palace and the Alhambra Museum

While it's only natural for a conquering king to build his own palace over his foe's palace, the Christian king Charles V (called

Carlos I in Spain) respected the splendid Moorish palace. And so, to make his mark, he built a modern Renaissance palace for official functions and used the existing Palacios Nazaries as a royal residence. With a unique circle-within-a-square design by Pedro Machuca, a pupil of Michelangelo, this is Spain's most impressive Renaissance building. Stand in the circular courtyard surrounded by mottled marble columns, then climb the stairs. Perhaps Charles' palace was designed to have a dome, but it was never finished—his son, Philip II, abandoned it to build his own, much more massive palace outside Madrid, El Escorial (the final and most austere example of

Spanish Renaissance architecture). Even without the dome, acoustics are perfect in the center—stand in the middle and sing your best aria. The palace doubles as one of the venues for the popular International Festival of Music and Dance.

The Alhambra Museum (Museo de la Alhambra, on the ground floor of Charles V's Palace), worth ▲, shows off some of the Alhambra's best surviving Moorish art. The museum's beautifully displayed and well-described artifacts—including tiles, pottery, pieces of fountains, and a beautiful carved-wood door—help humanize the Alhambra (free, Tue-Sun 8:30-14:00, closed Mon). The **Fine Arts Museum** (Museo de Bellas Artes, upstairs) is of little interest to most.

• *From the front of Charles V's Palace (as you face the Alcazaba fort), the entrance to Palacios Nazaries is to the right (look for the line snaking along the outside edge of the garden), while the Alcazaba is across a moat straight ahead (to get there, bear left through the keyhole-shaped Wine Gate, then hook right and walk up to the open area in front of the fort).*

Alcazaba

This fort—the original "red castle" ("Alhambra")—is the oldest and most ruined part of the complex, offering exercise and fine city views. What you see is from the mid-13th century, but there was probably a fort here in Roman times. Once upon a time, this tower defended a medina (town) of 2,000 Muslims living within the Alhambra walls. It's a huge, sprawling complex—wind your way through passages and courtyards, over uneven terrain, to reach the biggest tower at the  tip of the complex. Then climb stairs steeply up to the very top. From there (looking north), find Plaza Nueva and the San Nicolás viewpoint (in the Albayzín). To the south are the Sierra Nevada Mountains. Is anybody skiing today? Notice the tower's four flags: the blue of the European Union, the green and white of Andalucía, the red and yellow of Spain, and the red and green of Granada.

Speaking of flags, imagine that day in 1492 when the Christian cross and the flags of Aragon and Castile were raised on this tower, and (according to a probably fanciful legend) the fleeing Moorish king Boabdil (Abu Abdullah, in Arabic) looked back and wept. His mom chewed him out, saying, "You weep like a woman for what you couldn't defend like a man." With this defeat, more than seven centuries of Muslim rule in Spain came to an end. Much later, Napoleon stationed his troops at the Alhambra, contributing substantially to its ruin when he left.

• *If you're going from the Alcazaba to Palacios Nazaries, you'll have to backtrack through the Wine Gate, then look for the people lined up along the gardens in front of Charles V's Palace.*

▲▲▲Palacios Nazaries

During the 30-minute entry time slot stamped on your ticket, enter the jewel of the Alhambra: the Moorish royal palace. Once you're

in, you can relax—you're no longer under any time constraints. You'll walk through three basic sections: royal offices, ceremonial rooms, and private quarters. Built mostly in the 14th century, this palace offers your best possible look at the refined, elegant Moorish civilization of Al-Andalus (the Arabic word for the Moorish-controlled Iberian Peninsula).

You'll visit rooms decorated from top to bottom with carved wood ceilings, stucco "stalactites," ceramic tiles, molded-plaster walls, and filigree windows. Open-air courtyards feature fountains with bubbling water, which give the palace a desert-oasis feel. A garden enlivened by lush vegetation and peaceful pools is the Quran's symbol of heaven. The palace is well-preserved, but the trick to fully appreciating it is to imagine it furnished and filled with Moorish life...sultans with hookah pipes lounging on pillows upon Persian carpets, heavy curtains on the windows, and ivory-studded wooden furniture. The whole place was painted with bright colors, many suggested by the Quran—red (blood), blue (heaven), green (oasis), and gold (wealth). Throughout the palace, walls, ceilings, vases, carpets, and tiles were covered with decorative patterns, mostly poems and verses of praise from the Quran written in calligraphy and from local poets. Much of what is known about the Alhambra is known simply from reading the inscriptions that decorate its walls.

As you wander, keep the palace themes in mind: water, a near absence of figural images (forbidden by the Quran), "stalactite" ceilings—and few signs telling you where you are. As tempting as it might be to touch the stucco, don't—it is very susceptible to the oils from your hand. Use the map on the following page to locate the essential stops listed below.

• *Begin by walking through a few administrative rooms (the* mexuar*) with a stunning Mecca-oriented prayer room (the oratorio, with a niche on the right facing Mecca) and a small courtyard with a round fountain, until you hit the big rectangular courtyard with a fish pond lined by a myrtle-bush hedge.*

GRANADA

GRANADA

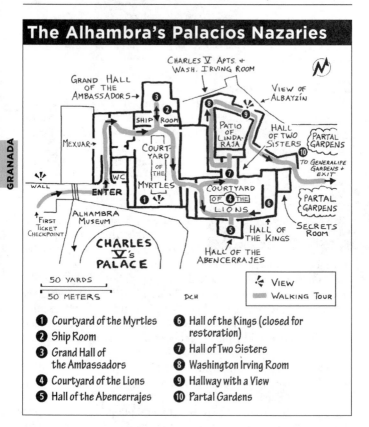

The Alhambra's Palacios Nazaries

1. Courtyard of the Myrtles
2. Ship Room
3. Grand Hall of the Ambassadors
4. Courtyard of the Lions
5. Hall of the Abencerrajes
6. Hall of the Kings (closed for restoration)
7. Hall of Two Sisters
8. Washington Irving Room
9. Hallway with a View
10. Partal Gardens

❶ Courtyard of the Myrtles (Patio de Arrayanes)

The standard palace design included a central courtyard like this. Moors loved their patios—with a garden and water, under the sky. In accordance with medieval Moorish mores, women rarely went out, so they stayed in touch with nature in courtyards like the Courtyard of the Myrtles—named for the two fragrant myrtle hedges that added to the courtyard's charm. Notice the wooden screens (erected by

jealous husbands) that allowed the cloistered women to look out without being clearly seen. The upstairs was likely for winter use, and the cooler ground level was probably used in summer.

• *Head left from the entry through gigantic wooden doors into the long narrow antechamber to the throne room, called the...*

❷ Ship Room (Sala de la Barca)

It's understandable that many think the Ship Room is named for the upside-down-hull shape of its fine cedar ceiling. But the name is actually derived from the Arab word *baraka,* meaning "divine blessing and luck" (which was corrupted to *barca,* the Spanish word for "ship" or "boat"). As you passed through this room, blessings and luck are exactly what you'd need—because in the next room, you'd be face-to-face with the sultan.

• *Oh, it's your turn. Enter the ornate throne room.*

❸ Grand Hall of the Ambassadors (Gran Salón de los Embajadores)

The palace's largest room, the Gran Salón de los Embajadores (also known as the Salón de Comares), functioned as the throne room.

It was here that the sultan, seated on a throne opposite the entrance, received foreign emissaries. Ogle the room—a perfect cube—from top to bottom. The star-studded, domed wooden ceiling (made from 8,017 inlaid pieces like a giant jigsaw puzzle) suggests the complexity of Allah's infinite universe. Wooden "stalactites" form the cornice, running around the entire base of the ceiling. The stucco walls, even without their original paint and gilding, are still glorious. The filigree windows once held stained glass and had heavy drapes to block out the heat. Some precious 16th-century tiles survive in the center of the floor.

A visitor here would have stepped from the glaring Courtyard of the Myrtles into this dim, cool, incense-filled world, to meet the silhouetted sultan. Imagine the alcoves functioning busily as work stations, and the light at sunrise or sunset, rich and warm, filling the room.

Let your eyes trace the finely carved Arabic script. Muslims avoided making images of living creatures—that was God's work. But they could carve decorative religious messages. One phrase—"only Allah is victorious"—is repeated 9,000 times throughout the palace. Find the character for "Allah"—it looks like a cursive W with a nose on its left side. The swoopy toboggan blades underneath are a kind of artistic punctuation used to set off one phrase.

In 1492, two historic events likely took place in this room. Culminating a 700-year-long battle, the Reconquista was completed here as the last Moorish king, Boabdil, signed the terms of his surrender before eventually leaving for Africa.

And it was here that Columbus made one of his final pitches

Islamic Art

Rather than making paintings and statues, Islamic artists expressed themselves with beautiful but functional objects. Ceramics (most of them blue and white, or green and white), carpets, glazed tile panels, stucco-work ceilings, and glass tableware are covered with complex patterns. The intricate interweaving, repetition, and unending lines suggest the complex, infinite nature of God, known to Muslims as Allah.

You'll see only a few pictures of humans or animals, since Islamic doctrine is wary of any "graven images" or idols forbidden by God. However, secular art by Muslims for their homes and palaces was not bound by this restriction; you'll get an occasional glimpse of realistic art featuring men and women enjoying a garden paradise, a symbol of the Muslim heaven.

Look for floral patterns (twining vines, flowers, and arabesques) and geometric designs (stars and diamonds). The decorative motifs (Arabic script, patterns, flowers, shells, and so on) that repeat countless times throughout the palace were made by pressing wet plaster into molds. The most common pattern is calligraphy—elaborate lettering of an inscription in Arabic, the language of the Quran. A quote from the Quran on a vase or lamp combines the power of the message with the beauty of the calligraphy.

to Isabel and Ferdinand to finance a sea voyage to the Orient. Imagine the scene: The king, the queen, and the greatest minds from the University of Salamanca gathered here while Columbus produced maps and pie charts to make his case that he could sail west to reach the East. Ferdinand and the professors laughed and called Columbus mad—not because they thought the world was flat (most educated people knew otherwise), but because they thought Columbus had underestimated the size of the globe, and thus the length and cost of the journey.

But Isabel said, *"Sí, señor."* Columbus fell to his knees (promising to pack light, wear a money belt, and use the most current guidebook available).

Opposite the Ship Room entrance, photographers pause for a picture-perfect view of the tower reflected in the Courtyard of the Myrtles pool. This was the original palace entrance (before Charles V's Palace was built).

• *Continue deeper into the palace, to a courtyard where, 600 years ago, only the royal family and their servants could enter. It's the much-photographed...*

❹ Courtyard of the Lions (Patio de los Leones)

This delightful courtyard is named for the famous fountain ringed with 12 lions, marble originals from the 14th century. Why did

the architect choose 12? Since the fountain was a gift from a Jewish leader celebrating good relations with the sultan (Granada had a big Jewish community), the lions probably represent the 12 tribes of Israel. (Conquering Christians disassembled the fountain to see how it worked, rendering it nonfunctional until its 2012 restoration.) From the center, four streams went out—figuratively to the corners of the earth and literally to various more private apartments of the royal family. Notice how the court, with its 124 columns, resembles the cloister of a Catholic monastery. The craftsmanship is first-class. For example, the lead fittings between the precut sections of the columns allow things to flex during an earthquake, preventing destruction during shakes.

Six hundred years ago, the Muslim Moors could read the Quranic poetry that ornaments this court, and they could understand the symbolism of this lush, enclosed garden, considered the embodiment of paradise or truth. ("How beautiful is this garden / where the flowers of Earth rival the stars of Heaven. / What can compare with this alabaster fountain, gushing crystal-clear water? / Nothing except the fullest moon, pouring light from an unclouded sky.") Imagine—they appreciated this part of the palace even more than we do today.

• *On the right, off the courtyard, the only original door still in the palace leads into a square room called the...*

❺ Hall of the Abencerrajes (Sala de los Abencerrajes)

This was the sultan's living room, with an exquisite ceiling based on the eight-sided Muslim star. The room has a sad history. The father of Boabdil took a new wife and wanted to disinherit the children of his first marriage—one of whom was Boabdil. In order to deny power to Boabdil and his siblings, the sultan killed nearly all of the pre-Boabdil

Abencerraje family members. He thought this would pave the way for the son of his new wife to be the next sultan. He stacked 36 Abencerraje heads in the pool, under the sumptuous honeycombed stucco ceiling in this hall. But his scheme failed, and Boabdil ultimately assumed the throne. Bloody power struggles like this were the norm here in the Alhambra.

• *At the end of the court opposite where you entered is the...*

❻ Hall of the Kings (Sala de los Reyes)

This hall will most likely be closed for several years during restoration. If it were open, you'd see paintings on the goat-leather ceiling depicting scenes of the sultan and his family. The center room's group portrait shows the first 10 of the Alhambra's 22 sultans. The scene is a fantasy, since these people lived over a span of many generations. The two end rooms display scenes of princely pastimes, such as hunting and shooting skeet. In a palace otherwise devoid of figures, these offer a rare look at royal life in the palace.

• *Backtrack around the fountain. As you exit, you'll pass doors leading right and left to a 14th-century WC plumbed by running water and stairs up to the harem. Next is the...*

❼ Hall of Two Sisters (Sala de Dos Hermanas)

The Sala de Dos Hermanas—nicknamed for the giant twin slabs of white marble on the floor flanking the fountain—has another oh-wow stucco ceiling lit from below by clerestory window. This is a typical royal bedroom, with alcoves for private use and a fountain. Running water helped cool and humidify the room but also added elegance and extravagance, as running water was a luxury most could only dream of.

The room features geometric patterns and stylized Arabic script quoting verses from the Quran. If the inlaid color tiles look "Escher-esque," you've got it backward: Escher is Alhambra-esque. M. C. Escher was inspired by these very patterns on his visit. Study the patterns—they remind us of the Moorish expertise in math. The sitting room (farthest from the entry) has low windows, because Moorish people sat on the floor. Some rare stained glass survives in the ceiling. From here the sultana enjoyed a grand view of the medieval city (before the 16th-century wing was added, which blocks the view today).

• *That's about it for the palace. From here, we enter the later, 16th-century Christian section, and wander past the domed roofs of the old baths down a hallway to a pair of rooms decorated with a mahogany ceiling. Marked with a large plaque is the...*

❽ Washington Irving Room

Washington Irving wrote *Tales of the Alhambra* in this room. While living in Spain in 1829, Irving stayed in the Alhambra. It was a romantic time, when the palace was home to Gypsies and donkeys. His "tales" kindled interest in the Alhambra, causing it to become recognized as a national treasure. A plaque on the wall thanks Irving, who later served as the US ambassador to Spain (1842-1846). Here's a quote from Irving's *The Alhambra by Moonlight:* "On such heavenly nights I would sit for hours at my window inhaling the sweetness of the garden, and musing on the checkered fortunes of those whose history was dimly shadowed out in the elegant memorials around."

• *As you leave, stop at the open-air...*

❾ Hallway with a View

Here you'll enjoy the best-in-the-palace view of the labyrinthine Albayzín—the old Moorish town on the opposite hillside. Find the famous San Nicolás viewpoint (below where the white San Nicolás church tower breaks the horizon). Creeping into the mountains on the right are the Gypsy neighborhoods of Sacromonte. Still circling old Granada is the Moorish wall (built in the 1400s to protect the city's population, swollen by Muslim refugees driven south by the Reconquista).

The Patio de Lindaraja (with its maze-like hedge pattern garden) marks the end of the palace visit. Before exiting, you can detour right into the adjacent "Secrets Room"—stark brick rooms of the former bath with fun acoustics. Whisper into a corner, and your friend—with an ear to the wall—can hear you in the opposite corner. Try talking in the exact center.

• *Step outside into our last stop...*

❿ The Partal Gardens (El Partal)

The Partal Gardens are built upon the ruins of the Partal Palace. Imagine a palace like the one you just toured, built around this reflecting pond. A fragment of it still stands—once the living quarters—on the cooler north side. The Alhambra was the site of seven different palaces in 150 years. You have toured parts of just two or three.

• *Leaving the palace, climb a few stairs, continue through the gardens, and follow signs directing you left to the Generalife Gardens or right to the Alcazaba (and the rest of the Alhambra grounds). If you're interested*

GRANADA

The Alhambra Grounds

As you wander the grounds, remember that the Alhambra was once a city of a thousand people fortified by a 1.5-mile rampart and 30 towers. The zone within the walls was the **medina**, a town with a general urban scene. As you stroll from the ticket booth down the garden-like Calle Real de la Alhambra to the palace, you're walking through the ruins of the medina (destroyed by the French in 1812). This path traces the wall, with its towers on your left. In the distance, notice the snow-capped Sierra Nevada peaks—the highest mountains in Iberia. The Palacios Nazaries, Alcazaba fort, and Generalife Gardens all have entry fees and turnstiles. But the medina—with Charles V's Palace, a church, a line of shops showing off traditional wood-working techniques, and the fancy Alhambra parador—is wide open to anyone.

It's especially fun to snoop around the historic **Parador de Granada San Francisco,** which—as a national monument—is legally required to be open to the public. Once a Moorish palace within the Alhambra, it was later converted into a Franciscan monastery, with a historic claim to fame: Its church is where the Catholic Monarchs (Ferdinand and Isabel) chose to be

in poking around the Alhambra grounds, exit and do it now before entering the Generalife (because you can't easily backtrack into the Alhambra grounds after leaving the gardens).

When you're ready to go from the Partal Gardens to the Generalife Gardens, it's a delightful 15-minute stroll through lesser (but still pleasant) gardens, along a row of fortified towers—just follow signs for Generalife. Just before reaching Generalife, you'll cross over a bridge and look down on the dusty lane called Cuesta de los Chinos (a handy shortcut for returning to downtown later).

▲▲Generalife Gardens

If you have a long wait before your entry to Palacios Nazaries, tour these gardens first, then the Alcazaba fort and Charles V's Palace.

The sultan's vegetable and fruit orchards and summer garden retreat, called the Generalife (heh-neh-raw-LEE-fay), was outside the protection of the Alhambra wall—and, today, a short hike uphill past the ticket office. The thousand or so residents of the Alhambra enjoyed the fresh fruit and veggies grown here. But buried. For a peek, step in through the arch leading to a small garden area and reception. Enter to see the burial place, located in the open-air ruins of the church (just before the reception desk and the "guests-only-beyond-this-point" sign; the history is described in English). The slab on the ground near the altar—a surviving bit from the mosque that was here before the church—marks the place where the greatest king and queen of Spain were buried until 1521 (when they were moved to the Royal

Chapel—described later). The next room is a delightful former cloister. Now a hotel, the parador has a restaurant and terrace café—with lush views of the Generalife—open to non-guests.

The medina's main road dead-ended at the **Wine Gate** (Puerta del Vino), which protected the fortress. When you pass through the Wine Gate, you enter a courtyard that was originally a moat, then a reservoir (in Christian times). The well—now encased in a bar-kiosk—is still a place for cold drinks. If you're done with your Alhambra visit, you can exit down to the city from the Wine Gate via the Justice Gate, immediately below.

most importantly, this little palace provided the sultan with a cool and quiet summer escape.

Follow the simple one-way path through the sprawling gardens (planted only in the 1930s—in Moorish times, there were no cypress topiaries here).

The sleek, modern theater has been renovated and continues to be an important concert venue for Granada. Its cypress-lined stage sees most activity during the International Festival of Music and Dance. Many of the world's greatest artists have performed here, including Arthur Rubenstein, Rudolf Nureyev, and Margot Fonteyn.

Head for the top of the theater, then walk through the manicured hedge gardens, along delightful ponds and fountains, to the palace.

At the small palace, pass through the dismounting room

(imagine dismounting onto the helpful stone ledge, and letting your horse drink from the trough here). Show your ticket and enter the most accurately re-created Arabian garden in Andalucía.

Here in the retreat of the Moorish kings, this garden is the closest thing on earth to the Quran's description of heaven. It was planted more than 600 years ago—that's remarkable longevity for a European garden. While there were originally only eight water jets, most of the details in today's garden closely match those lovingly described in old poems. The flowers, herbs, aromas, and water are exquisite...even for a sultan. Up the Darro River, the royal aqueduct diverted a life-giving stream of water into the Alhambra. It was channeled through this extra-long decorative fountain to irrigate the bigger garden outside, then along an aqueduct into the Alhambra for its thirsty residents. And though the splashing fountains are a delight, they are a 19th-century addition. The Moors liked a peaceful pond instead.

At the end of the pond, you enter the sultan's tiny three-room summer retreat.

From the end, climb 10 steps into the Christian Renaissance gardens (c. 1600). The ancient tree rising over the pond inspired Washington Irving, who wrote that this must be the "only surviving witness to the wonders of that age of Al-Andalus."

Climbing up and going through the turnstile, you enter the Romantic 19th-century garden. From here you have two options. If you're exhausted, just head to the right and follow *salida* signs toward the gardens' exit (next to the Alhambra's main entrance). But if you want a little more exercise (and views), turn left at the sign for *continuacion visita*, and take the half-mile loop up and around to see the staircase called Escalera del Agua, whose banisters double as little water canals. From the top, you'll have a chance to enter the "Romantic Viewpoint"—climb up the stairs for a top-floor view over the gardens (pleasant enough, but less impressive than other views at the Alhambra). Then hike back down through the garden and follow *salida* signs, through the long oleander trellis tunnel, to the exit. Remember: The most direct and scenic return to town is on the easily overlooked **Cuesta de los Chinos** pathway, which begins near the ticket booth.

Your visit to the Alhambra is complete, and you've earned your reward. "Surely Allah will make those who believe and do good deeds enter gardens beneath which rivers flow; they shall be adorned therein with bracelets of gold and pearls, and their garments therein shall be of silk" (Quran 22.23).

▲▲Royal Chapel (Capilla Real)

Without a doubt Granada's top Christian sight, this lavish chapel in the old town holds the dreams—and bodies—of Queen Isabel and King Ferdinand. The "Catholic Monarchs" were all about the Reconquista. Their marriage united the Aragon and Castile kingdoms, allowing an acceleration of the Christian and Spanish push south. In its last 10 years, the Reconquista snowballed. This last Moorish capital—symbolic of their victory—was their chosen burial place. While smaller and less architecturally striking than the cathedral (described later), the chapel is far more historically significant.

Cost and Hours: €4; March-Oct daily 10:15-13:30 & 16:00-19:30 except opens at 11:00 on Sun; Nov-Feb daily 10:15-13:30 & 15:30-18:30 except opens at 11:00 on Sun; no photos, entrance on Calle Oficios, just off Gran Vía del Colón—go through iron gate, tel. 958-227-848.

❂ Self-Guided Tour: In the lobby, before you show your ticket and enter the chapel, notice the **painting of Boabdil** (on the black horse) giving the key of Granada to the conquering King Ferdinand. Boabdil wanted to fall to his knees, but the Spanish king, who had great respect for his Moorish foe, embraced him instead. They fought a long and noble war (for instance, respectfully returning the bodies of dead soldiers). Ferdinand is in red, and Isabel is behind him wearing a crown. The painting is flanked high on the wall by portraits of Ferdinand and Isabel. Two small exhibits celebrate the 500th anniversaries of the death of Isabel in 2004 (with eight portraits) and of Philip the Fair (her son-in-law, a playboy who earned his nickname for his seductively good looks).

Isabel decided to make Granada the capital of Spain (and burial place for Spanish royalty) for three reasons: 1) With the conquest of this city, Christianity had finally overcome Islam in Europe; 2) her marriage with Ferdinand, followed by the conquest of Granada, had marked the beginning of a united Spain; and 3) in Granada, she agreed to sponsor Columbus.

Show your ticket and step into the **chapel.** It's Plateresque Gothic—light and lacy silver-filigree style, named for and inspired by the fine silverwork of the Moors. The chapel's interior was originally austere, with fancy touches added later by Ferdinand and Isabel's grandson Charles V. Five hundred years ago, this must have been the most splendid space imaginable. Because of its speedy completion (1506-1521), the Gothic architecture is unusually harmonious.

King Charles V thought it wasn't dazzling enough to honor his grandparents' importance, so he funded decorative touches like the screen and the Rogier van der Weyden painting *The Deposition* (left of the altar, one of five original versions he painted). Immediately to the right of that altar, with the hardest-working altar boys in Christendom holding up gilded Corinthian columns, is a chapel with a relic (an arm) of John the Baptist.

In the center of the chapel (in front of the main altar), the **four royal tombs** are Renaissance-style. Carved in Italy in 1521 out of Carrara marble, they were sent by ship to Spain. The faces—based on death masks—are considered accurate. If you're looking at the altar, **Ferdinand** and **Isabel** are on the right. (Isabel fans attribute the bigger dent she puts in the pillow to her larger brain.) Isabel's contemporaries described  the queen as being of medium height, with auburn hair and blue eyes, and possessing a serious, modest, and gentle personality. (Compare Ferdinand and Isabel's tomb statues with the painted and gilded wood statues of them kneeling in prayer, flanking the altarpiece.)

Philip the Fair and **Juana the Mad** (who succeeded Ferdinand and Isabel) lie on the left. Philip was so "Fair" that it drove the insanely jealous Juana "Mad." Philip died young, and for two years Juana kept his casket at her bedside, kissing his embalmed body good night. Philip and Juana's son, Charles V, was a key figure in European history, as his coronation merged the Holy Roman Empire (Philip the Fair's Habsburg domain) with Juana's Spanish empire. Europe's top king, Charles V ruled a vast empire stretching from Holland to Sicily, from Bohemia to Bolivia (1519-1556).

When Philip II, the son of Charles V, decided to build El Escorial (his palace outside Madrid) and establish Madrid as the single capital of a single Spain, Granada lost power and importance. More importantly, Spain began to decline. After the reign of Charles V, Spain squandered her vast wealth trying to maintain this impossibly huge empire. The country's rulers did it not only for material riches, but to defend the romantic, quixotic dream of a Catholic empire—ruled by one divinely ordained Catholic monarch—against an irrepressible tide of nationalism and Protestantism that was sweeping across the vast Habsburg holdings in Central and Eastern Europe. Spain's relatively poor modern history can be blamed, in part, on its people's stubborn unwillingness to accept the end of this old-regime notion. Even Franco borrowed symbols from the Catholic Monarchs to legitimize his dictatorship and keep the 500-year-old legacy alive. Today's Spaniards reflect that the momentous marriage that created their country also sucked them into centuries of European squabbling, eventually leaving Spain impoverished.

Look at the intricate carving on the Renaissance tombs. It's a humanistic statement, with these healthy, organic, realistic figures rising out of the Gothic age.

From the feet of the marble tombs, step downstairs to see the actual **coffins.** They are plain. Ferdinand and Isabel were originally buried in the Franciscan monastery (in what is today the parador, up at the Alhambra). You're standing in front of the two people who created Spain. The fifth coffin (on right, marked *Principe Miguel*) belongs to a young Prince Michael, who would have been king of a united Spain and Portugal. (A sad—but too long—story...)

The **high altar** is one of the finest Renaissance works in Spain. It's dedicated to two Johns: the Baptist and the Evangelist. In the center you can see the Baptist and the Evangelist chatting as if over tapas—an appropriately humanistic scene. Scenes from the Baptist's life are on the left: John beheaded after Salomé's fine dancing, and (below) John baptizing Jesus. Scenes from the Evangelist's life are on the right: John's martyrdom (a failed attempt to boil him alive in oil), and, below, John on Patmos (where he may have written the last book of the Bible, Revelation). John is talking to the eagle that, according to tradition, flew him to heaven. A colorful series of reliefs at the bottom level recalls the Christian conquest of the Moors (left to right): Ferdinand, Boabdil with army and key to Alhambra, Moors expelled from Alhambra (right of altar table), conversion of Muslims by tonsured monks, and Ferdinand again.

A finely carved Plateresque arch, with the gilded royal initials *F* and *Y,* leads to a small glass pyramid in the **treasury.** This

holds Queen Isabel's silver crown ringed with pomegranates (symbolizing Granada), her scepter, and King Ferdinand's sword. Do a counterclockwise spin around the room to see it all, starting to the right of the entry arch. There you'll see the devout Isabel's prayer book, in which she followed the Mass. The book and its sturdy box date from 1496. According to legend, the fancy box on the other side of the door is supposedly the one that Isabel filled with jewels and gave to bankers as collateral for the cash to pay Columbus. In the corner (and also behind glass) is the ornate silver-and-gold cross that Cardinal Mendoza, staunch supporter of Queen Isabel, carried into the Alhambra on that historic day in 1492—and used as the centerpiece for the first Christian Mass in the conquered fortress. Next, the big silver-and-gold silk tapestry is the altar banner for the mobile campaign chapel of Ferdinand and Isabel, who always traveled with their army. In the case to its left, you'll see the original Christian army flags raised over the Alhambra in 1492.

The next zone of this grand hall holds the first great art collection ever established by a woman. Queen Isabel amassed more than 200 important paintings. After Napoleon's visit, only 31 remained. Even so, this is an exquisite collection, all on wood, featuring works by Sandro Botticelli, Pietro Perugino, the Flemish master Hans Memling, and some less-famous Spanish masters.

Finally, at the end of the room, the two carved sculptures of Ferdinand and Isabel were the originals from the high altar. Charles V considered these primitive (I disagree) and replaced them with the ones you saw earlier.

To reach the cathedral (described next), exit the chapel behind Isabel, and walk around the block either way.

▲Cathedral

One of only two Renaissance churches in Spain (the other is in Córdoba), Granada's cathedral is the second-largest church in Spain after Sevilla's. While it was started as a Gothic church, it was built using Renaissance elements, and then decorated in Baroque style.

Cost and Hours: €4, audioguide-€2; April-Oct Mon-Sat 10:30-13:15 & 16:00-20:00, Sun 16:00-20:00; Nov-March until 19:00; last entrance 15 minutes before closing, tel. 958-222-959.

◉ Self-Guided Tour: Enter the church from Plaza de las Pasiegas. Stand in the back of the nave for an overview.

From the back, survey the church. It's huge. It was designed to be the national church when Granada was the capital of a newly reconquered-from-the-Muslims Spain. High above the main altar are square niches originally intended for the burial of Charles V and his family. But King Philip II changed focus and abandoned Granada for El Escorial, so the niches are now plugged with paintings, including seven from the life of Mary by hometown great Alonso Cano.

The cathedral's cool, spacious, bright interior is mostly Baroque—a refreshing break from the dark Gothic of so many Spanish churches. In a move that was modern back in the 18th century, the walls of the choir (the big, heavy wooden box that dominates the center of most Spanish churches) were taken out so that people could be involved in the worship. (Back when a choir clogged the middle of the church, regular people only heard the Mass.) At about the same time, a bishop ordered the interior painted with lime (for hygienic reasons, during a time of disease).

The people liked it, and it stayed white.

Notice that the two rear chapels (on right and left) are Neoclassical in style—a reminder that the church took 300 years to finish.

As you explore, remember that the abundance of Marys is all part of the Counter-Reformation. Most of the side chapels are decorated in Baroque style. On the outer wall, directly to the right of the high altar, is a politically incorrect version of St. James the Moor-Slayer, with his sword raised high and an armored Moor trampled under his horse's hooves.

Now, walk to the front for a closer look at the altar. You pass a fine organ with horizontal trumpet pipes, unique to Spain.

Standing before the altar, notice the abundance of gold leaf. It's from the local Dorro River, which originally attracted Romans here for its gold. As this is a seat of the local bishop, there's a fine wooden bishop's throne on the right.

Between the fine Corinthian columns flanking the altar are paintings with a strong parenting theme: In the round tondo frames are Adam and Eve, from whom came mankind. Around them are the four evangelists, who—with the New Testament—brought the Good News of salvation to believers (not Jews or Muslims). Completing the big parenting picture are Ferdinand and Isabel, who brought Catholicism to the land. Their complex coat of arms celebrates how their marriage united kingdoms to essentially create the European country with the oldest border. When Reconquista forces finally won Granada in 1492, the puzzle was complete.

To your right is the ornate carved stone Gothic door to the Royal Chapel (described earlier), with a 15th-century facade that predates the cathedral. The chapel holds the most important historic relics in town—the tombs of the Catholic Monarchs. And, because the chapel and cathedral are run by two different religious orders, this door is always closed and there are separate admission fees for each.

Strolling behind the altar, look for the giant music sheets: They're mostly 16th-century Gregorian chants. Notice the sliding C clef. Rather than a fixed G or F clef, the monks knew that this clef—which could be located wherever worked best on the staff—marked middle C, and they chanted to notes relative to that. Go ahead—try singing a few verses of the Latin.

The cathedral's little museum is tucked away back near the cathedral's entrance, filling the ground floor of the big bell tower. In it, it's worth seeking out a beautiful bust of San Pablo (Paul, with a flowing beard)—a self-portrait by Cano.

The sacristy (near the exit and the St. James altarpiece, in the right corner) is worth a look. It's lush and wide-open; its gilded ceilings, mirrors, and wooden cabinets give it a light, airy feel. Two grandfather clocks made in London (one with Asian motifs) ensured that everyone got dressed on time. The highlight of this room: Cano's small, delicate painted wood statue of the *Immaculate Conception.*

Immediately in front of the cathedral is the stop for minibus #30 to the Alhambra. And four blocks away (if you head left up the busy street, then turn right) is the Albayzín.

Near Plaza Nueva
Hammam Baños Árabes (Arab Baths)

For an intimate and subdued experience, consider some serious relaxation at the Arab Baths, where you can enjoy the three different-temperature pools and a steam room. A maximum of 35 people are allowed in the baths at one time.

Cost and Hours: If you just want a 90-minute soak in the baths, the cost is €24; it costs more to add a 15-minute massage: a regular massage is €36, a traditional scrubbing massage is €43, and to have both costs €55. Open daily 10:00-24:00, appointments scheduled every even-numbered hour, coed with mandatory swimsuits, quiet atmosphere encouraged, free lockers and towels available, no loaner swimsuits but you can buy one for €12, just off Plaza Nueva—follow signs a few doors down from the TI to Santa Ana 16, 50 percent paid reservation required, tel. 958-229-978, www.hammamalandalus.com.

▲The Albayzín

Explore Spain's best old Moorish quarter, with countless color-ful corners, flowery patios, and shady lanes. While the city center of Granada—which is pleasant enough—feels more or less like many other Spanish cities, the Albayzín is unique. You can't say you've really seen Granada until you've at least strolled a few of its twisty lanes. Climb high to the San Nicolás church for the best view of the Alhambra.

Then wander through the mysterious back streets. (I've listed these sights roughly in order from the San Nicolás viewpoint.)

Getting to the Albayzín: City **minibus** #31 threads its way around the Albayzín from Plaza Nueva (see "Albayzín Circular Bus Tour," next), getting you scenically and sweatlessly to the San Nicolás viewpoint. You can also **taxi** to the San Nicolás church and explore from there. (Consider having your cabbie take you

Albayzín Neighborhood

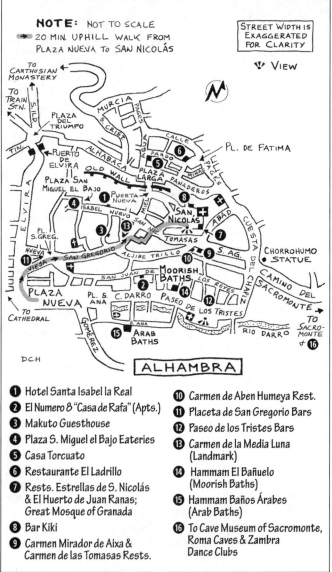

NOTE: NOT TO SCALE

➡ 20 MIN. UPHILL WALK FROM PLAZA NUEVA TO SAN NICOLÁS

STREET WIDTH IS EXAGGERATED FOR CLARITY

♥ VIEW

TO CARTHUSIAN MONASTERY

TO TRAIN STN.

PLAZA DEL TRIUMFO

MURCIA

S. CRIST.

PAGES

CALLE

PL. DE FATIMA

PUERTO DE ELVIRA

ALHABACA

OLD WALL

PARDO

PLAZA LARGA

PANADEROS

MINAS

PAGES

PLAZA SAN MIGUEL EL BAJO

ISABEL

PUERTA NUEVA

NUEVO SAN MIG.

SAN NICOLAS

ABAD

CUESTA DEL CHAPIZ

ELVIRA

PL. S. GREG.

NUEVA

SAN GREGORIO

ALJIBE TRILLO

TOMASAS

S. AG.

CHORROHUMO STATUE

CAMINO DEL SACROMONTE

VIEJA

SAN JUAN DE

MOORISH BATHS

LOS REYES

PLAZA NUEVA

PL. S. ANA

C. DARRO

PASEO DE LOS TRISTES

S. ANA

TO CATHEDRAL

GOMEREZ

RIO DARRO

TO SACRO-MONTE

DCH

ARAB BATHS

ALHAMBRA

❶ Hotel Santa Isabel la Real
❷ El Numero 8 "Casa de Rafa" (Apts.)
❸ Makuto Guesthouse
❹ Plaza S. Miguel el Bajo Eateries
❺ Casa Torcuato
❻ Restaurante El Ladrillo
❼ Rests. Estrellas de S. Nicolás & El Huerto de Juan Ranas; Great Mosque of Granada
❽ Bar Kiki
❾ Carmen Mirador de Aixa & Carmen de las Tomasas Rests.

❿ Carmen de Aben Humeya Rest.
⓫ Placeta de San Gregorio Bars
⓬ Paseo de los Tristes Bars
⓭ Carmen de la Media Luna (Landmark)
⓮ Hammam El Bañuelo (Moorish Baths)
⓯ Hammam Baños Árabes (Arab Baths)
⓰ To Cave Museum of Sacromonte, Roma Caves & Zambra Dance Clubs

Safety in the Albayzín

With tough economic times, young ruffians are hanging out in the dark back lanes of the labyrinthine Albayzín quarter.

While this charming Moorish district is certainly safe by day, it can be edgy after dark. Most of the area is fine to wander, though many streets are poorly lit, and the maze of lanes can make it easy to get lost and wind up somewhere you don't want to be. Some nervous travelers choose to avoid the neighborhood entirely after dark, but I recommend venturing into the Albayzín to enjoy its restaurants, ideal sunset views, and charming ambience. Just be sure to exercise normal precautions: Leave your valuables at your hotel, stick to better-lit streets, and take a minibus or taxi home if you're unsure of your route. Violent crime is rare, but pickpocketing is common. Keep a very close eye on your stuff. Some visitors mistakenly think that the danger in this historic "Moorish" district is from Arabs, but the real crooks can be Northern and Eastern European hippies loitering in the squares.

Locals say the biggest hazard when walking in the Albayzín are the many deposits left by its four-legged inhabitants (and not cleaned up by their poorly trained owners). If you bury your nose in a guidebook while you walk, you'll likely wind up burying your shoe in something else.

on a detour to the Sacromonte enclave of cave-dwelling Gypsies, described later.)

It's a steep but fascinating 20-minute **walk** up: Leave the west end of Plaza Nueva on Calle de Elvira. After about 50 yards, at the pharmacy and newsstand, bear right on Calle Calderería Vieja. Follow this stepped street past Moroccan eateries and pastry shops, vendors of imported North African goods, halal butchers, and *teterías* (Moorish tea rooms). The lane bears right, then passes to the left of the church (becoming Cuesta de San Gregorio), and slants, winds, and zigzags uphill. Cuesta de San Gregorio eventually curves left and is regularly signposted. When you reach the Moorish-style house, La Media Luna (with the tall trees and keyhole-style doorway), stop for a photo and a breather, then follow the wall, continuing uphill. At the next intersection (with the black cats), turn right on Aljibe del Gato. Farther on, this street takes a 90-degree turn to the right; at this point, turn left onto Calle Atarasana Vieja. It's confusing, but keep going up, up, up. At the crest (and the dead-end), turn right on Camino Nuevo de San Nicolás, then walk 200 yards to the street that curves up left (look for a bus-stop sign—this is where the minibus would have dropped you off). Continue up the curve, and soon you'll see feet hanging from the plaza wall. Steps lead up to the church's viewpoint. Whew! You made it!

Albayzín Circular Bus Tour

The handy Albayzín minibus #31 makes a 20-minute loop through the quarter, departing from Plaza Nueva about every 15 minutes (pay driver €1.20). While good for a lift to the top of the Albayzín (buzz when you want to get off), I'd stay on for an entire circle and return to the Albayzín later for dinner—either on foot or by bus again. (Note: The less frequent minibus #35, departing every 30-40 minutes, does nearly the same trip with a side-trip up into Sacromonte.)

Here's the route: The minibus leaves Plaza Nueva and heads down the city's main drag, Gran Vía del Colón, turning right at the Gardens of the Triumph, which celebrate the Immaculate Conception of the Virgin Mary (notice her statue atop a column). Just above the gardens is the old Royal Hospital—built in the 16th century for Granada's poor by the Catholic kings. (After the Reconquista, they hoped to win the favor of the city's conquered residents.) Then the bus ascends, giving you a commanding view of Granada on the right. Turning downhill, the bus plunges into the thick of the Albayzín, with stops below the San Nicolás church (famous viewpoint, and the jumping-off point for my "Exploring the Albayzín" stroll, described later; the driver generally calls out this stop for tourists) and at Plaza San Miguel el Bajo (cute square with recommended eateries and another viewpoint). From here, you can ride back through the Gran Vía to Plaza Nueva.

▲▲San Nicolás Viewpoint (Mirador de San Nicolás)

For one of Europe's most romantic viewpoints, be here at sunset, when the Alhambra glows red and the Albayzín widows share

the benches with local lovers, hippies, and tourists (free, always open). In 1997, President Clinton made a point to bring his family here—a favorite spot from a trip he made as a student. But this was hardly an original idea; generations of visitors have been drawn here. For an affordable (€3-6) drink with the same million-euro view, step into the El Huerto de Juan Ranas Bar (just below and to the left, at Calle de Atarazana 8). Enjoy the Roma (Gypsy) musicians who perform here for tips. Order a drink, tip them, settle in, and consider it a concert.

GRANADA

Great Mosque of Granada

Granada's Muslim population is on the rebound, and now numbers 8 percent of the city's residents. A striking and inviting mosque is just next to the San Nicolás viewpoint (to your left as you face the Alhambra). Local Muslims write, "The Great Mosque of Granada signals, after a hiatus of 500 years, the restoration of a missing link with a rich and fecund Islamic contribution to all spheres of human enterprise and activity." Built in 2003 (with  money from the local community and Islamic Arab nations), it has a peaceful view courtyard and a minaret that comes with a live call to prayer five times a day (printed schedule inside). It's stirring to see the muezzin holler "God is Great" from the minaret without amplification (locals didn't want it amplified). Visitors are welcome in the courtyard, which offers Alhambra views without the hedonistic ambience of the more famous San Nicolás viewpoint.

Cost and Hours: Free, daily 11:00-14:00 & 18:00-21:00, shorter hours in winter, tel. 958-202-526, www.mezquitadegranada .com.

Background: While tourists come to Granada to learn about the expulsion of the Moors in 1492, local Muslims are frustrated by what a flier at the mosque calls the "errors, nonsense, and lies local guides perpetuate without knowledge nor shame which flocks of passive tourists accept without questioning." The flier tries to set the record straight, from the Muslim perspective: Muslims were as indigenous as any other group. After living here for seven centuries, the Muslims of Granada and Andalucía were as Iberian as the modern Spaniards of today. Islam is not a religion of immigrants; Islam is not a culture of the Orient and Arabs. "Muslim" and "Arab" are not interchangeable terms. The Muslims of Al-Andalus were not hedonistic. The Reconquista did not "liberate" Spain. Harems were not just full of sexy women. (For more on the Muslim perspective, visit the info desk at the mosque.)

To Muslims, the city is a symbol of the "holocaust" of the Reconquista, when 135,000 of their people were brutally expelled and many more suffered "forced conversion" in the 16th century. Today there are about 1 million Muslims in Spain (and about 5 million in France).

Exploring the Albayzín

From the San Nicolás viewpoint and the Great Mosque, you're at the edge of a hilltop neighborhood even the people of Granada recognize as a world apart. Each of the district's 20 churches sits on a spot once occupied by a mosque. When the Reconquista arrived in Granada, the Christians attempted to coexist with the Muslims. But after seven years, this idealistic attempt ended in failure, and the Christians forced the Muslims to convert. In 1567, Muslims were expelled, leading to 200 years of economic depression for the city. Eventually, large walled noble manor houses with private gardens were built here in the depopulated Albayzín. These survive today in the form of the characteristic *carmen* restaurants so popular with visitors.

From the San Nicolás viewpoint, turn your back to the Alhambra and walk north (passing the church on your right and the Biblioteca Municipal on your left). A lane leads past a white stone arch (on your right)—now a chapel built into the old Moorish wall. You're walking past the scant remains of the pre-Alhambra fortress of Granada. At the end of the lane, step down to the right through the 11th-century "New Gate" (Puerta Nueva—older than the Alhambra) and into **Plaza Larga.** In medieval times, this tiny square (called "long," because back then it was) served as the local marketplace. It still is a busy market each morning. Casa Pasteles, at the near end of the square, serves good coffee and cakes.

Leave Plaza Larga on **Calle Agua de Albayzín** (as you face Casa Pasteles, it's to your right). The street, named for the public baths that used to line it, shows evidence of the Moorish plumbing system: gutters. Back when Europe's streets were filled with muck, Granada actually had Roman Empire-style gutters with drains leading to clay and lead pipes.

You're in the heart of the Albayzín. Explore. Poke into an old church. They're plain by design to go easy on the Muslim converts, who weren't used to being surrounded by images as they worshipped. You'll see lots of real Muslim culture living in the streets, including many recent Spanish converts. When you are finished exploring, find your way back to the San Nicolás viewpoint, where you can catch minibus #31 or #35 (just below the viewpoint) back into town. Or it's a pleasant downhill walk, following San Gregorio back to Plaza Nueva.

Sacromonte

The Sacromonte district is home to Granada's thriving Roma community. Marking the entrance to Sacromonte is a statue of Chorrohumo (literally, "exudes smoke," and a play on the slang word for "thief": *chorro*). He was a Roma from Granada, popular in the 1950s for guiding people around the city.

While the neighboring Albayzín is a sprawling zone blanketing a hilltop, Sacromonte is much smaller—very compact and very steep. Most houses are burrowed into the wall of a cliff.

Sacromonte has one main street: Camino del Sacromonte, which is lined with caves primed for tourists and restaurants ready to fight over the bill. (Don't come here expecting to get a deal on anything.) Intriguing lanes run above and below this main drag—a steep hike above Camino del Sacromonte is the cliff-hanging, parallel secondary street, Vereda de Enmedio, which is less touristy, with an authentically residential vibe.

Cave Museum of Sacromonte (Museo Cuevas del Sacromonte)

This hilltop complex, also known as the Center for the Interpretation of Sacromonte (Centro de Interpretación del  Sacromonte), is a kind of open-air folk museum about Granada's unique Roma cave-dwelling tradition (though it doesn't have much on the people themselves). The exhibits, with good English descriptions, are spread through a series of whitewashed caves along a ridge, with spectacular views to the Alhambra. As you stroll from cave to cave, you'll learn about the local geology (rocks, flora, and fauna); crafts (basket-weaving, pottery-making, metalworking, and weaving); and lifestyles (including a look into a typical home and kitchen). There's also an exhibit about other cave-dwelling cultures from around the "troglodyte world," and one about Sacromonte's vital role in the development of Granada's local brand of flamenco. As you wander, imagine this in the 1950s, when it was still a bustling community of Roma cave-dwellers. Today, hippies squat in abandoned caves higher up.

Cost and Hours: €5, mid-March–mid-Oct daily 10:00-20:00, until 18:00 in winter, Barranco de los Negros, tel. 958-215-120, www.sacromontegranada.com.

Getting There: You can ride minibus #35 from Plaza Nueva (ask driver, "*¿Museo Cuevas?*," departs only every 30-40 minutes) or a taxi. You'll get off at the "Sacromonte 2" bus stop, next to the Venta El Gallo restaurant, at the bottom of the hill along the main road. From there, it's a very steep 10-minute hike past cave dwellings up to the top of the hill—follow the signs. If you don't want to wait for minibus #35, you can ride #31 to near the entrance of Sacromonte, and walk from there—giving you a good look at the whole area.

Performances: In summer (July-Aug), the center also features flamenco shows and classical guitar concerts in its wonderfully scenic setting (prices and schedules vary—see website above for details).

Granada's Roma (Gypsies)

Both the English word "Gypsy" and its Spanish counterpart, *gitano,* come from the word "Egypt"—where Europeans once believed these nomadic people had originated. Today the preferred term is "Roma," since "Gypsy" has acquired negative connotations (though for clarity's sake, I've used both terms throughout this book).

After migrating from India in the 14th century, the Roma people settled mostly in the Muslim-occupied lands in southern Europe (such as the Balkan Peninsula, then controlled by the Ottoman Turks). Under medieval Muslims, the Roma enjoyed relative tolerance. They were traditionally good with crafts and animals.

The first Roma arrived in Granada in the 15th century—and they've remained tight-knit ever since. Today 50,000 Roma call Granada home, many of them in the district called Sacromonte. In most of Spain, Roma are more assimilated into the general population, but Sacromonte is a large, distinct Roma community. (After the difficult Spanish Civil War era, they were joined by many farmers who, like the Roma, appreciated Sacromonte's affordable, practical cave dwellings—warm in the winter and cool in the summer.)

Spaniards, who generally consider themselves to be tolerant and not racist, claim that in maintaining such a tight community, the Roma segregate themselves. The Roma call Spaniards *payos* ("whites"). Recent mixing of Roma and *payos* has given birth to the term *gallipavo* (rooster-duck), although who's who depends upon whom you ask.

Are Roma thieves? Sure, some of them are. But others are honest citizens, trying to make their way in the world just like anyone else. Because of the high incidence of theft, it's wise to be cautious when dealing with a Roma person—but it's also important to keep an open mind.

Zambra Dance

A long flamenco tradition exists in Granada, and the Roma of Sacromonte are credited with developing this city's unique flavor of this Andalusian art form. Sacromonte is a good place to see *zambra,* a flamenco variation with a more Oriental feel in which the singer also dances. A half-dozen cave-bars offering *zambra* in the evenings line Sacromonte's main drag. Hotels are happy to book you a seat and arrange the included transfer. Two well-established venues are **Zambra Cueva de la Rocío** (€30, includes a drink and bus ride from and back to hotel, €25 without transport, daily show at 22:00, 1 hour, Camino del Sacromonte 70, tel. 958-227-129) and **María la Canastera** (€26, includes drink and bus from hotel, €20 without transport, daily show at 22:00, 1 hour,

Camino del Sacromonte 89, tel. 958-121-183, www.granadainfo
.com/canastera). The biggest operation here is the restaurant
Venta El Gallo, which has performances of more straightforward
flamenco (not specifically *zambra*, €30 with bus from hotel, €25
without transport, daily shows at 21:15 and 22:45, Barranco los
Negros 5, tel. 958-228-476). Or consider the summer performances
at the **Cave Museum** (explained earlier). A final option for the
more adventurous: Just go and explore late at night on your own
(with no wallet and €30 in your pocket).

Enjoying the Paseo without the Tourists

While the old town is great for strolling, it's also fun to leave
the aura of the Alhambra and just be in workaday Granada with
everyday locals. A five-minute walk from Plaza Nueva gets you
into a delightful and untouristy urban slice of Andalucía. Carrera
de la Virgen is the town's mini-Ramblas. (From the old center,
walk south down Calle Reyes Católicos to Puerta Real de España,
and take a left.) It leads gracefully down to the Paseo del Salón
riverbank park, great for making the local scene. Carrera de la
Virgen also happens to pass the huge and practical El Corte Inglés
department store (Mon-Sat 10:00-22:00, closed Sun).

Near Granada

Carthusian Monastery (La Cartuja)

A church with an interior that looks as if it squirted out of a
can of whipped cream, La Cartuja is nicknamed the "Christian
Alhambra" for its elaborate white Baroque stucco work. In the
rooms just off the cloister, notice the gruesome paintings of
martyrs placidly meeting their grisly fates.

Cost and Hours: €4, daily April-Oct 10:00-13:00 & 16:00-
20:00, Nov-March 10:00-13:00 & 15:00-18:00, catch bus #8 from
Gran Vía del Colón, tel. 958-161-932. The monastery is a mile
north of town on the way to Madrid; drivers take the *Méndez
Núñez* exit from the A-44 expressway and follow signs.

Sleeping in Granada

In July and August, when Granada's streets are littered with
sunstroke victims, rooms are plentiful and prices soft. In the
crowded months of April, May, September, and October, prices
can spike up 20 percent. (If you see a price range below, it indicates
low- to high-season rates—though I've excluded Holy Week and
other inflated prices.) Except for the hotels in the Albayzín and
near the Alhambra, most of my listings are within a 5-to-10-
minute walk of Plaza Nueva.

If you're traveling by car, you're free to drive into the prohibited

Sleep Code

(€1 = about $1.30, country code: 34)

S = Single, **D** = Double/Twin, **T** = Triple, **Q** = Quad, **b** = bathroom, **s** = shower only. Unless otherwise noted, credit cards are accepted and English is spoken. Some hotels include the 10 percent IVA tax in the room price; others tack it onto your bill. Breakfast is not included unless specified.

To help you easily sort through these listings, I've divided the accommodations into three categories based on the price for a standard double room with bath during high season:

$$$ Higher Priced—Most rooms €110 or more.
$$ Moderately Priced—Most rooms between €60-110.
$ Lower Priced—Most rooms €60 or less.

Prices can change without notice; verify the hotel's current rates online or by email. For the best prices, always book direct.

center zone, but be sure your hotel registers you immediately with the traffic police.

On or near Plaza Nueva

Each of these (except the hostel) is big, professional, plenty comfortable, and perfectly located. Prices vary with demand.

$$$ Hotel Casa 1800 Granada, with 25 rooms around a beautiful, airy old courtyard in the lower part of the Albayzín (just steps above the Paseo de los Tristes), sets the bar for affordable class. It's tidy and well-run, and offers special extras, such as a complimentary tea and coffee bar each afternoon (standard Db-€155, pricier "superior" and "deluxe" rooms available but not much different, big buffet breakfast-€9.50, air-con, elevator, free Wi-Fi, Benalúa 11, tel. 958-210-700, www.hotelcasa1800granada.com, info@hotel casa1800granada.com).

$$$ Hotel Maciá Plaza, right on the colorful Plaza Nueva, has 44 smallish, clean, modern, and classy rooms. Choose between an on-the-square view or a quieter interior room (Sb-€60-80, Db-€140, square view-€20 extra, extra bed-€25, 15 percent discount in 2014 when you book direct by email and show this book at check-in, buffet breakfast-€8.50, air-con, elevator, free Wi-Fi, Plaza Nueva 5, tel. 958-227-536, www.maciahoteles.com, maciaplaza@maciahoteles.com).

$$ Casa del Capitel Nazarí, just off the church end of Plaza Nueva, is a restored 16th-century Renaissance palace transformed into 18 small but tastefully decorated rooms, all facing a courtyard

GRANADA

that hosts changing art exhibits. Insomniacs have a choice of five different pillows (Sb-€80-103, Db-€109-129, extra bed-€36, apartments available, 5 percent discount in 2014 when you book direct and show this book at check-in, breakfast-€10, includes afternoon tea/coffee, air-con, free guest computer, free Wi-Fi, parking-€19.50/day, Cuesta Aceituneros 6, tel. 958-215-260, www .hotelcasacapitel.com, info@hotelcasacapitel.com).

$$ Hotel Anacapri is a bright, cool marble oasis with 49 modern rooms and a quiet lounge (Sb-€59-80, Db-€79-110, Tb-€95-125, extra bed-€22, includes breakfast with direct bookings in 2014 except with promotional rates, air-con, elevator, free guest computer, free Wi-Fi in lobby with this book, parking-€15/day, 2 blocks toward Gran Vía from Plaza Nueva at Calle Joaquín Costa 7, just a block from cathedral bus stop, tel. 958-227-477, www .hotelanacapri.com, reservas@hotelanacapri.com, helpful Kathy speaks Iowan).

$$ NH Hotel Inglaterra is a modern and peaceful chain hotel, with 36 rooms offering all the comforts (Db-€70-120, extra bed-€20-30, buffet breakfast-€13, air-con, elevator to third floor only, free Wi-Fi in lobby, parking-€16/day, Cetti Merien 6, tel. 958-221-559, www.nh-hotels.com, nhinglaterra@nh-hotels.com).

$ Oasis Hostel Granada offers 90 beds in 10 coed rooms and lots of backpacker bonding, just a block above the lively Moorish-flavored tourist drag (4-10 bunks per room, €16-21 per person; includes sheets and 2-for-1 welcome drink; free guest computer, free Wi-Fi, shared kitchen, laundry service-€7, Placeta Correo Viejo 3, tel. 958-215-848, www.hostelsoasis.com, oasisgranada @gmail.com).

Cheap Sleeps on Cuesta de Gomérez

These are inexpensive and ramshackle lodgings on this street leading from Plaza Nueva up to the Alhambra.

$$ Hotel Puerta de las Granadas has 16 rooms with a sterile business-class vibe, an inviting cafeteria courtyard, and a handy location (basic patio-view Db-€59-89, €5-10 more for street view, €15 more for cathedral view, €25 more for Alhambra view, book direct and ask for 10 percent Rick Steves discount, breakfast-€8 or included during slow times, air-con, elevator, free guest computer, free Wi-Fi, free tea and coffee in cafeteria all day, Cuesta de Gomérez 14, tel. 958-216-230, www.hotelpuertadelasgranadas .com, reservas@hotelpuertadelasgranadas.com).

$ Pensión Landazuri is run by friendly English-speaking Matilde Landazuri, her son Manolo, and daughters Margarita and Elisa. Their characteristic old house has 18 rooms—some are well-worn, while others are renovated. It boasts hardworking, helpful management and a great roof garden with an Alhambra view

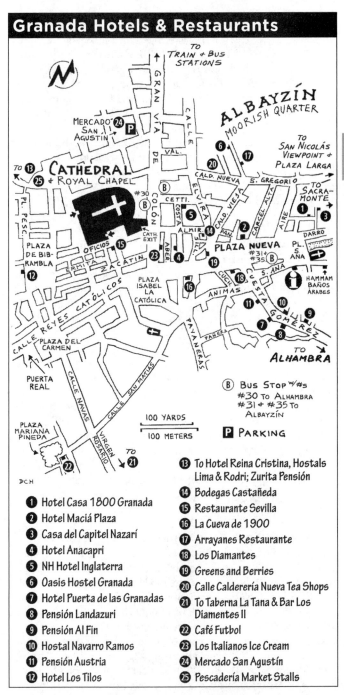

Granada Hotels & Restaurants

GRANADA

TO TRAIN & BUS STATIONS

GRAN VIA

CALLE

CALLE DE

VAL.

ALBAYZÍN

MOORISH QUARTER

TO SAN NICOLÁS VIEWPOINT & PLAZA LARGA

MERCADO SAN AGUSTÍN **24** P

6

20

17

CALD. NUEVA

S. GREGORIO

TO SACRAMONTE

13

25 CATHEDRAL & ROYAL CHAPEL

#30 **B**

COLÓN

CETTI.

COSTA

B

5

ALMIR.

CALD. VIEJA

CÁRCEL ALTA

AIRE

DARRO

1

3

2

PL. PESC.

CATH. EXIT

14

RAM.

23

ABEN.

4

OFICIOS

15

ZACATÍN

ERMITA

PLAZA NUEVA

#31 #35 **B**

PL. S. ANA

19

CUCH.

18

S. ANA

HAMMAM BAÑOS ÁRABES

PLAZA DE BIB-RAMBLA

12

PLAZA ISABEL LA CATÓLICA

16

ÁNIMAS

11

CUESTA

GOMEREZ

10

9

7

8

CALLE REYES CATÓLICOS

PAVANERAS

PANERA

TO ALHAMBRA

CALLE

PLAZA DEL CARMEN

PUERTA REAL

CALLE NAVAS

CALLE SAN MATÍAS

100 YARDS

100 METERS

B BUS STOP w/#s
#30 TO ALHAMBRA
#31 & #35 TO ALBAYZÍN

P PARKING

PLAZA MARIANA PINEDA

VIRGEN ROSARIO

TO **21**

22

DCH

13 To Hotel Reina Cristina, Hostals Lima & Rodri; Zurita Pensión

14 Bodegas Castañeda

15 Restaurante Sevilla

16 La Cueva de 1900

17 Arrayanes Restaurante

18 Los Diamantes

19 Greens and Berries

20 Calle Calderería Nueva Tea Shops

21 To Taberna La Tana & Bar Los Diamantes II

22 Café Futbol

23 Los Italianos Ice Cream

24 Mercado San Agustín

25 Pescadería Market Stalls

1 Hotel Casa 1800 Granada

2 Hotel Maciá Plaza

3 Casa del Capitel Nazarí

4 Hotel Anacapri

5 NH Hotel Inglaterra

6 Oasis Hostel Granada

7 Hotel Puerta de las Granadas

8 Pensión Landazuri

9 Pensión Al Fin

10 Hostal Navarro Ramos

11 Pensión Austria

12 Hotel Los Tilos

(S-€29, Sb-€39, D-€39, Db-€49, Tb-€69, Qb-€79, eggs-and-bacon breakfast-€3.50, free Wi-Fi, parking-€12/day, Cuesta de Gomérez 24, tel. 958-221-406, www.hostallandazuri.com, info@hostal landazuri.com). The Landazuris also run a good, cheap café.

$ Pensión Al Fin is located just up the street from Pensión Landazuri and run by the same family. Its five rooms feature antique wooden beams and marble columns with sultry, Moorish-style decor. A glass floor in the lobby lets you peer into a well from an ancient house (Db-€49, Tb-€69, some with balconies, breakfast-€3.50, Wi-Fi, parking-€12/day, reception at Pensión Landazuri, Cuesta de Gomérez 31, tel. 958-228-172, www .pensionalfin.com, info@pensionalfin.com).

$ Hostal Navarro Ramos is a little cash-only cheapie, renting seven rooms (five with private baths) facing an interior airshaft (S-€20, D-€30, Db-€37, free Wi-Fi, Cuesta de Gomérez 21, tel. 958-250-555, www.pensionnavarroramos.com, Carmen).

$ Pensión Austria, run by English-speaking Austrian Irene (ee-RAY-nay), rents 15 basic but tidy backpacker-type rooms (Sb-€25-30, Db-€35-40, Tb-€50-60, Qb-€65-75, Quint/b-€80-90, family rooms, air-con, free Wi-Fi, Cuesta de Gomérez 4, tel. 958-227-075, www.pensionaustria.com, pensionaustria@pension austria.com).

Near the Cathedral

$$ Hotel Los Tilos offers 30 comfortable, business-like rooms (some with balconies) on the charming traffic-free Plaza de Bib-Rambla behind the cathedral. Guests are welcome to use the fourth-floor terrace with views of the cathedral and the Alhambra (Sb-€45-55, Db-€55-80, Tb-€77-100, prices may be cheaper if you reserve online, free breakfast when you book direct and show the 2014 edition of this book at check-in, air-con, free Wi-Fi, parking-€26/day, Plaza de Bib-Rambla 4, tel. 958-266-712, www .hotellostilos.com, clientes@hotellostilos.com, friendly José María).

On or near Plaza de la Trinidad

The charming, park-like square called Plaza de la Trinidad is just a short walk west of the cathedral area (Pescadería and Bib-Rambla squares). It's also home to several good accommodations.

$$$ Hotel Reina Cristina has 55 quiet, elegant rooms a few steps off Plaza de la Trinidad. Check out the great Mudejar ceiling and the painting at the entrance of this house, where the famous Spanish poet Federico García Lorca hid until he was captured and executed by the Guardia Civil during the Spanish Civil War (Sb-€46-90, Db-€66-139, Tb-€81-169, includes breakfast—skip it to save €13 per person, air-con, elevator, Wi-Fi-€2/day, parking-€18/

day, near Plaza de la Trinidad at Tablas 4, tel. 958-253-211, www.hotelreinacristina.com, clientes@hotelreinacristina.com).

$ Hostal Lima, run with class by Manolo and Carmen, has 25 small but well-appointed rooms in two buildings a block off the square. The public areas and rooms are decorated with flamboyant medieval flair—colorful tiles, wood-carved life-sized figures, and so on (Sb-€33, Db-€48, Tb-€67, breakfast-€7, home-cooked dinner available if booked in advance, air-con, elevator in one building only, free Wi-Fi, parking-€14/day, Laurel de las Tablas 17, tel. 958-295-029, www.hostallimagranada.com, info @hostallimagranada.eu).

$ Hostal Rodri, run by Manolo's brother José, has 10 similarly good rooms a few doors down that feel new and classy for their price range (Sb-€32, Db-€45, air-con, elevator, free cable Internet and Wi-Fi, parking-€14/day, Laurel de las Tablas 9, tel. 958-288-043, www.hostalrodri.com, info@hostalrodri.com).

$ Zurita Pensión, well-run by Francisco and Loli, faces Plaza de la Trinidad. Eight of the 14 rooms have small balconies, but even with their double-paned windows, they may come with night noise (S-€21, D-€34, Db-€42, Tb-€63, air-con, free Wi-Fi, parking-€14-16/day, Plaza de la Trinidad 7, tel. 958-275-020, www .pensionzurita.com, pensionzurita@gmail.com).

In the Albayzín

Note that some consider this area sketchy after dark.

$$ Hotel Santa Isabel la Real, an elegant medieval mansion, has 11 rooms ringing a noble courtyard. Each room is a bit different; basic rooms look to the patio, while various pricier rooms have better exterior views. Buried deep in the Albayzín and furnished in a way that gives you the old Moorish Granada ambience, it offers a warm welcome and rich memories (Db-€85-105 with breakfast, air-con, elevator, free guest computer, free Wi-Fi, parking-€14/ day, midway between San Nicolás viewpoint and Plaza San Miguel el Bajo on Calle Santa Isabel la Real, immediately at a bus stop, tel. 958-294-658, www.hotelsantaisabellareal.com, info@hotel santaisabellareal.com).

$$ El Numero 8 "Casa de Rafa" is a traditional house in the heart of the Albayzín that's been converted into four small, funky kitchenette apartments with an eclectic, ever-evolving artistic feel. Chicago-raised, easygoing owner Rafa lives on-site. You'll share two tiny patios and a rooftop terrace with a spectacular, in-your-face view of the Alhambra. Contact Rafa in advance to set up a time to check in. He'll ease your arrival by meeting you at a taxi or bus drop-off point and walking you back to the apartment (Sb-€35-60, Db-€40-70, extra person-€10, 2-night minimum, fans but no air-con, free Wi-Fi, 5-minute walk from Plaza Nueva at tiny Plaza

Virgen del Carmen, tel. 958-220-682, mobile 610-322-216, www. elnumero8.com, casaocho@gmail.com).

$$ Tournights Granada is run by Frederick, an American who rents 15 renovated and fully furnished duplexes and apartments in traditional Moorish houses situated in the Albayzín district, many with grand Alhambra views (Db-€80-100 plus €40 cleaning fee, prices vary with size—see photos and videos on website, 2-night minimum—longer during holidays, 20 percent deposit required to reserve online, pay the balance in cash after you arrive, air-con, free Wi-Fi, some units have private terraces and swimming pools, mobile 620-585-594, www.tournights.com, info@tournights.com).

$ Makuto Guesthouse, a hostel tucked deep in the Albayzín, feels like a hippie commune you can pay to join for a couple of days. With 42 beds in seven rooms clustered around a lush garden courtyard that feels made for hanging out—including several hammock-and-lounge-sofa "hang-out zones"—it exudes an easygoing Albayzín vibe (Db-€55-70, bunk in 4- to 6-bed room-€14-20, includes breakfast, dinners available, free guest computer, free Wi-Fi, Calle Tiña 18, tel. 958-805-876, www.makutoguesthouse .com, info@makutoguesthouse.com).

In or near the Alhambra

If you want to stay on the Alhambra grounds, you have two popular options (famous, overpriced, and generally booked up long in advance) and one practical and economic place above the parking lot. All are a half-mile up the hill from Plaza Nueva.

$$$ Parador de Granada San Francisco offers 40 designer rooms in a former Moorish palace that was later transformed into a 15th-century Franciscan monastery. It's considered Spain's premier parador...and that's saying something (standard Db-€336, breakfast-€20, air-con, free Wi-Fi, free parking, Calle Real de la Alhambra, tel. 958-221-440, www.parador.es, granada@parador .es). You must book months ahead to spend the night in this lavishly located, stodgy, and historic palace. Any peasant, however, can drop in for a coffee, drink, snack, or meal.

$$ Hotel América is classy and cozy, with 17 rooms in an early-19th-century house next to the parador (Sb-€60-80, Db-€90-120, €25 more for bigger room with terrace, breakfast-€8.50, free Wi-Fi, parking-€15/day, closed Dec-Feb, Calle Real de la Alhambra 53, tel. 958-227-471, www.hotelamericagranada.com, reservas@hotelamericagranada.com, friendly Isabel).

$$ Hotel Guadalupe, big and modern with 58 sleek rooms, is quietly and conveniently located overlooking the Alhambra parking lot. While a 30-minute hike above the town, many (especially drivers) find this to be a practical option (Sb-€50-75,

Db-€58-124, Tb-€75-135, "superior" rooms with Jacuzzis and balconies aren't worth the extra cost, continental breakfast-€13, breakfast buffet-€23, air-con, elevator, free Wi-Fi in lobby, parking in Alhambra lot-€14/day, Paseo de la Sabica 30, tel. 958-225-730, www.hotelguadalupe.es, info@hotelguadalupe.es).

Eating in Granada

Restaurants generally serve lunch from 13:00 to 16:00 and dinner from 20:00 until very late (remember, Spaniards don't start dinner until about 21:00). Many

of Granada's bars still serve a small tapas plate free with any beer or wine—a tradition that's dying out in most of Spain. Save on your food expenses by doing a tapas crawl (especially good along Calle Navas, right off Plaza del Carmen) and claim your "right" to a free tapa with every drink. (It helps to order your drink and wait for the free tapa before ordering food. If you order food with your drink, you likely won't get the freebie.) For more budget-eating thrills, buy picnic supplies near Plaza Nueva, and schlep them up into the Albayzín. This makes for a great cheap date at the San Nicolás viewpoint or on one of the scattered squares and lookout points.

In search of an edible memory? A local specialty, *tortilla Sacromonte*, is a spicy omelet with pig's brain and other organs. *Berenjenas fritas* (fried eggplant) and *habas con jamón* (small green fava beans cooked with cured ham) are worth seeking out. *Tinto de verano*—a red-wine spritzer with lemon and ice—is refreshing on a hot evening.

In the Albayzín
Many interesting meals hide out deep in the Albayzín (Moorish quarter). To find a particular square, ask any local, or follow my directions and the full-color Granada map at the front of this book. If dining late, take the minibus or a taxi back to your hotel; Albayzín back streets can be poorly lit, confusing to follow, and plagued by pickpockets. Part of the charm of the quarter is the lazy ambience on its squares. My two favorites are Plaza Larga and Plaza San Miguel el Bajo.

Plaza Larga is extremely characteristic, with tapas bar tables spilling out onto the square, a morning market, and a much-loved pastry shop.

Plaza San Miguel el Bajo, the farthest hike into the

Albayzín, boasts my favorite funky local scene—kids kicking soccer balls, old-timers warming benches, and women gossiping under the facade of a humble church. It's circled by half a dozen inviting little bars and restaurants—each very competitive with €10 lunch deals, more expensive à la carte and evening meals, and good seating right on the square. Drop by for lunch or dinner and spend a few minutes surveying your options: **El Acebuche,** run with pride by friendly María, promises "Andalusian flavor with a light dash of the Orient" (open daily). **Rincón de la Aurora** feels more comfortable and has tapas (closed Wed and Sun afternoon). **El Ají** is a sit-down restaurant with a mod vibe and a bit of Argentinian flair (closed Tue). And just down the street (beyond El Ají) is a little hole-in-the-wall **takeaway shop** selling cheap empanadas and pizza by the slice to munch out on the square (closed Tue). This square is a great spot to end your Albayzín visit, as there's a viewpoint overlooking the modern city a block away. Minibus #31 rumbles by every few minutes, ready to zip you back to Plaza Nueva. Or just walk five minutes down from the viewpoint.

Casa Torcuato is a hardworking eatery serving straight-forward yet creative food in a smart upstairs dining room. They serve a good fixed-price lunch (€9.50), plates of fresh fish (€11-15), and prizewinning, thick, *salmorejo*—style gazpacho (closed Sun-Mon, 2 blocks beyond Plaza Larga at Calle Aqua 20, tel. 958-202-039).

Restaurante El Ladrillo, a tiny and humble joint with out-door tables on a peaceful square (and no indoor seating), is *the* place for piles of fish. Their popular €12 *barco* ("boatload" of mixed fried fish) is a fishy feast that stuffs two to the gills. Even their €8.50 half-*barco* can be split (daily 12:00-17:00 & 19:00-23:00, on Placeta de Fátima, just off Calle Pagés, tel. 958-286-123).

Near the San Nicolás Viewpoint

This area is thoroughly touristy, so don't expect any local hangouts here. But these options are suitable for a good meal with a view you'll never forget.

Restaurante Estrellas de San Nicolás, in the former home of a well-loved Albayzín bigwig, immediately next to the view terrace, features dreamy Alhambra views from its two floors of indoor seating. Serving a mix of French and Spanish cuisine, this splurge keeps its mostly tourist clientele very happy (€10-22 starters, €20-29 main dishes, €31 fixed-price dinner, €20 or €27 fixed-price lunch, smart to reserve a view table, Atrazana Vieja 1, tel. 958-288-739, www.estrellasdesannicolas.es).

El Huerto de Juan Ranas Restaurante has a simple terrace bar immediately below the San Nicolás viewpoint, with amazing

Alhambra views and a simple menu at half the price of their restaurant (€9 dish of the day, €15 *raciones*, Calle de Atarazana 8, tel. 958-286-925).

Bar Kiki, a laid-back and popular bar-restaurant on an unpretentious square with no view, serves simple tapas. Try their tasty fried eggplant (random hours, closed Wed, just behind viewpoint at Plaza de San Nicolás 9, tel. 958-276-715).

Carmens in the Albayzín

For a more memorable but pricey experience, consider fine dining with Alhambra views in a *carmen*, a typical Albayzín house with a garden (buzz to get in). After the Reconquista, the Albayzín became depopulated. Wealthy families took larger tracts of land and built fortified mansions with terraced gardens within their walls. Today, rather than growing produce, the gardens of many of these *carmens* host dining tables and romantic restaurants.

Carmen Mirador de Aixa, small and elegant, has the dreamiest Alhambra views among the *carmens*. You'll pay a little more, but the food is exquisitely presented and the view makes the splurge worthwhile. Try the codfish or ox (€13-23 starters, €20-27 main dishes, 13:30-15:30 & 20:30-23:00, closed Sun dinner, all day Mon, and Tue lunch; next to Carmen de las Tomasas at Carril de San Agustín 2, tel. 958-223-616).

Carmen de las Tomasas serves gourmet traditional Andalusian cuisine with killer views in a dressy/stuffy atmosphere (expect to spend €40 with wine, Tue-Sat 13:30-16:00 & 20:15-23:30, closed Sun-Mon, reservations required, Carril de San Agustín 4, tel. 958-224-108, Joaquim and Cristina).

Carmen de Aben Humeya is the least expensive, least stuffy, and least romantic. Its outdoor-only seating lets you enjoy a meal or just a long cup of coffee while gazing at the Alhambra. This is a rare place enthusiastic about dinner salads (€10-20 starters and nicely presented main dishes, Mon-Tue and Thu-Fri 13:00-17:00 & 20:00-24:00, Sat-Sun 13:00-24:00, closed Wed, Cuesta de las Tomasas 12, tel. 958-226-665).

Near Plaza Nueva

For people-watching, consider the many restaurants on Plaza Nueva or Plaza de Bib-Rambla (south of cathedral). For a happening scene, check out the bars on and around Calle de Elvira. It's best to wander and see where the biggest crowds are.

Bodegas Castañeda, just a block off Plaza Nueva, is the best mix of lively, central, and cheap among the tapas bars I visited. When it's crowded, you need to power your way to the bar to order. When it's quiet, you can order at the bar and grab a little table (same budget prices). Consider their *tablas combinadas—*

variety plates of cheese, meat, and *ahumados* (four different varieties of smoked fish)—and tasty *croquetas* (breaded and fried mashed potatoes and ham). Order a glass of their gazpacho. Their €12 *plato Casteñeda* feeds two. The big kegs tempt you with different local vermouths, and the €1.70 glasses of wine come with a free tapa (€2-3 tapas, €6-13 half-*raciones*, €8-17 *raciones*, daily 11:30-16:30 & 19:00-24:00, Calle Almireceros 1, tel. 958-215-464). Don't be confused by the neighboring, similar "Antigua Bodega Castañeda" restaurant (run by a relative and not as good).

Restaurante Sevilla, with its tight and charming little dining room behind a high-energy tapas bar, has been a favorite of well-dressed natives for 75 years. Specialties include paella, other rice dishes (€24 for two), soups, and salads. You'll eat surrounded by old photos of local big shots who've dined here. On hot nights, tables pour out onto the little square facing the Royal Chapel. It's a local-feeling, elegant, urban scene. In the evenings, the bar displays a yummy spread of tapas—you get one free with any drink you buy, then pay €2 for each additional one (€10-15 starters, €14-20 main dishes, €11.50 fixed-price meal, daily from 12:00 and from 20:00, closed Sun; across from Royal Chapel at Calle Oficios 12, tel. 958-221-223, Danny).

La Cueva de 1900 is a fresh, family-friendly deli-like place on the main drag appreciated for its simple dishes and quality ingredients. Though it lacks character, it's reliable and low-stress. They're proud of their homemade hams, sausages, and cheeses—sold in 100-gram lots. Their fixed-price lunch is €10, but if you've had enough meat, try one of their good €5-7 salads (€3-4 *bocadillo* sandwiches, €8-17 meaty meals, open long hours daily, Calle Reyes Católicos 42, tel. 958-229-327).

Arrayanes is a good Moroccan restaurant a world apart from anything else listed here. Mostafa will help you choose among the many salads, the *briwat* (a chicken-and-cinnamon pastry appetizer), the *pastela* (a first-course version of *briwat*), the couscous, or *tajin* dishes. He treats his guests like old friends... especially the ladies (€4-10 starters, €10-16 main dishes, Wed-Mon 13:30-16:30 & 19:30-23:30, closed Tue, Cuesta Marañas 4, where Calles Calderería Nueva and Vieja meet, tel. 958-228-401, mobile 619-076-862).

Los Diamantes is a modern, high-energy local favorite for fresh seafood (free tapa with drink, only *raciones* and half-*raciones* on the menu, prices the same at outside table as at the bar, Mon-Fri 12:00-18:00 & 20:00-24:00, Sat-Sun 11:00-24:00, facing Plaza Nueva at #13, tel. 958-075-313).

Greens and Berries anchors Plaza Nueva, serving fresh salads, sandwiches, and real fruit smoothies to go (no seating). Try one of their €7 combos—such as the *queso de cabra y tomate* sandwich (goat cheese and tomato with caramelized onions) paired with a Caribbean smoothie—and enjoy it on a sunny plaza bench (€3-6 salads and sandwiches, daily 9:00-23:00, Plaza Nueva 1, tel. 633-895-086).

Hippie Options on Calle Calderería Nueva: From Plaza Nueva, walk two long blocks down Calle de Elvira and turn right onto the wonderfully hip and Arabic-feeling Calle Calderería Nueva, which leads uphill into the Albayzín. The street is lined with trendy *teterías.* These small tea shops, open all day, are good places to linger, chat, and imagine you're in Morocco. Many also offer the opportunity to rent a hookah (water pipe) to smoke some fruit-flavored tobacco with friends. Some are conservative and unmemorable, and others are achingly romantic, filled with incense, beaded cushions, live African music, and effervescent young hippies. They sell light meals such as crêpes, and a worldwide range of teas, all marinated in a candlelit snake-charmer ambience.

Placeta de San Gregorio: This tiny junction at the top of Calle Calderería Nueva has a special laid-back character. Grab a rickety seat here (at **Taverna 22** or **Bar las Cuevas**), under the classic church facade with potted plants and a commotion of tiled roofs, and enjoy the steady stream of hippies (and people who wish they were hippies) flowing by.

Paseo de los Tristes: This spot is like a stage set of outdoor bars on a terrace over the river gorge. While it lacks a serious restaurant and the food values are mediocre at best, the scene—cool, along a stream under trees, with the floodlit Alhambra high above and a happy crowd of locals enjoying a meal or drink out—is a winner. As this is at the base of the Albayzín, there's no issue of danger after dark here. It's a simple, level, five-minute walk back to Plaza Nueva.

Tapas Beyond Plaza del Carmen, Away from the Tourist Zone: Granada is a wonderland of happening little tapas bars. As the scene changes from night to night, it's best to simply wander and see what appeals. You'll be amazed at how the vibe changes when you venture just five minutes from the historic and touristic center. From Plaza del Carmen, wander down Calle Navas, consider a side-trip down Calle San Matías, and don't miss my favorite stretch, where Calle Navas becomes Calle Virgen del Rosario. On Virgen del Rosario, consider **Taberna La Tana** (for fine wine) and **Bar Los Diamentes II** (across the street, for seafood). And, remember, you can always wrap things up with a sit on the square at Café Fútbol for chocolate and *churros* (described later).

Gayle's Granada Tapas Tours: Seventeen years ago, Gayle Mackie moved from Scotland to Granada, and for the last decade or so she's brought visitors on tapas tours of her new city. For details, see "Tours in Granada," earlier.

Chocolate and Churros: **Café Fútbol** is the best place in town for the local coffee and doughnut-dunking ritual—but with thick hot chocolate and greasy, freshly made *churros* instead. While Café Alhambra on Plaza de Bib-Rambla is another favorite for *chocolate con churros,* I prefer Café Fútbol, with its great scene on a lazy square (€3.30 for hot chocolate and *churros,* Plaza Mariana Pineda 6, tel. 958-226-662).

Ice Cream: **Los Italianos,** Italian-run and teeming with locals, is popular for its ice cream, *horchata* (*chufa*-nut drink), and shakes. When Michelle Obama visited Granada in 2010, this is where she got her ice-cream fix. For something special, try their *cassata,* a slice (not scoop) of mixed flavors with frozen fruit in a cone (mid-March-mid-Oct daily 9:00-24:00, closed off-season, across the street from cathedral and Royal Chapel at Gran Vía 4, tel. 958-224-034).

Markets: Though heavy on meat, **Mercado San Agustín** also sells fruits and veggies. Throughout the EU, locals lament the loss of the authentic old market halls as they are replaced with new hygienic versions. If nothing else, it's as refreshingly cool as a meat locker (Mon-Sat 9:00-15:00, closed Sun, very quiet on Mon, a block north of cathedral and a half-block off Gran Vía on Calle Cristo San Agustín). Tucked away in the back of the market is a very cheap and colorful little eatery: **Cafetería San Agustín.** They make their own *churros* and give a small tapa free with each drink (menu on wall). If you are waiting for the cathedral or Royal Chapel to open, kill time in the market. The stalls around the market and the **Pescadería** square, downhill from the actual market and a block from Plaza de Bib-Rambla, are actually more popular with locals looking to buy produce.

Granada Connections

From Granada by Train to: Barcelona (1/day, 9.5 hours on Altaria and AVE, transfer in Madrid; also 1 night daily, 10.5 hours), **Madrid** (2/day on Altaria, 4.5 hours), **Toledo** (all service is via Madrid, with nearly hourly AVE connections to Toledo), **Algeciras** (3/day, 4.25-5 hours), **Ronda** (3/day, 2.5 hours), **Sevilla** (4/day, 3 hours), **Córdoba** (2/day, 2.5 hours), **Málaga** (6/day, 2.5 hours with 1 transfer—bus is better). Train info: toll tel. 902-320-320, www.renfe.com. Many of these connections have a more frequent (and sometimes much faster) bus option—see below.

By Bus to: Nerja (8/day, 2-2.5 hours, more with transfer in Motril), **Sevilla** (to Plaza de Armas Station: 7/day, 3 hours *directo,* 3.5-4.5 hours *ruta;* to El Prado Station: 2/day, 3-3.5 hours), **Córdoba** (9/day, 2.5-4 hours), **Madrid** (roughly hourly, 5-5.75 hours; most to Estación Sur, a few to Avenida de América, one

direct to Barajas Airport), **Málaga** (hourly, 1.5-2 hours), **Algeciras** (3/day *directo*, 4 hours; 1/day *ruta*, 5.5 hours), **La Línea de la Concepción/Gibraltar** (3/day, 6-7 hours, change in Algeciras), Jerez (1/day, 4.75 hours), **Barcelona** (4/day, 13-14.75 hours, often at odd times, only one fully daytime connection departs Granada at 10:00 and arrives Barcelona at 24:15). To reach **Ronda,** change in Málaga or Antequera; to reach **Tarifa,** change in Algeciras or Málaga. Bus info: Main bus station tel. 913-270-540; all of these routes are run by Alsa (tel. 902-422-242, www.alsa.es). If there's a long line at the ticket windows, you can use the machines (press the flag for English)—but these only sell tickets for some major routes (such as Málaga), and sometimes eat credit cards like a Spaniard eats *jamón.*

GRANADA

CÓRDOBA

Straddling a sharp bend of the Guadalquivir River, Córdoba has a glorious Roman and Moorish past, once serving as a regional capital for both empires. It's home to Europe's best Islamic sight after Granada's Alhambra: the Mezquita, a splendid and remarkably well-preserved mosque that dates from A.D. 784. When you step inside the mosque, which is magical in its grandeur, you can imagine Córdoba as the center of a thriving and sophisticated culture. During the Dark Ages, when much of Europe was barbaric and illiterate, Córdoba was a haven of enlightened thought—famous for religious tolerance, artistic expression, and dedication to philosophy and the sciences. To this day, you'll still hear the Muslim call to prayer in Córdoba.

Beyond the magnificent Mezquita, the city of Córdoba has two sides: the extremely touristy maze of streets immediately surrounding the giant main attraction, lined with trinket shops, hotels, and restaurants; and the workaday part of town (centered on Plaza de las Tendillas). While the over-commercialized vibe of the touristy area can be off-putting, a quick walk takes you to real-life Córdoba.

Planning Your Time

Ideally, Córdoba is worth two nights and a day. Don't rush the magnificent Mezquita, but also consider sticking around to experience the city's other pleasures: Wander the evocative Jewish Quarter, enjoy the tapas scene, and explore the modern part of town.

However, if you're tight on time, it's possible to do Córdoba more quickly—especially since it's conveniently located on the AVE bullet-train line (and because, frankly, Córdoba is less interesting than the other two big Andalusian cities, Sevilla and Granada). To see Córdoba as an efficient stopover between Madrid and Sevilla (or as a side-trip from Sevilla—frequent trains, 45-minute trip), focus on the Mezquita: Taxi from the station, spend two hours there, explore the old town for an hour...and then scram.

Orientation to Córdoba

Córdoba's big draw is the mosque-turned-cathedral called the Mezquita (for pronunciation ease, think female mosquito). Most of the town's major sights are nearby, including the Alcázar, a former royal castle. And though the town seems to ignore its marshy Guadalquivir River (a prime bird-watching area), the riverbank sports a Renaissance triumphal arch next to a stout "Roman Bridge." The bridge leads to the town's old fortified gate (which now houses a museum on Moorish culture, the Museum of Al-Andalus Life). The Mezquita is buried in the characteristic medieval town. Around that stretches the Jewish Quarter, then the modern city—which feels much like any other in Spain, but with some striking Art Deco buildings at Plaza de las Tendillas and lots of Art Nouveau lining Avenida del Gran Capitán.

Tourist Information

Córdoba has helpful TIs at the train station, Alcázar, and Plaza de las Tendillas (all open daily 9:00-14:00 & 17:00-19:30, tel. 902-201-774, www.turismodecordoba.org). Another TI, near the Mezquita, is run separately and covers all of Andalucía (Mon-Fri 9:00-19:30, Sat-Sun 9:00-15:00, Torrijos 10, tel. 957-355-179).

Arrival in Córdoba

By Train or Bus: Córdoba's train station is located on Avenida de América. Built in 1991 to accommodate the high-speed AVE train line, the slick train station has ATMs, restaurants, a variety of shops, a TI booth (on the concourse above the track), an information counter, and a small lounge for first-class AVE passengers. Taxis and local buses are just outside, to the left as you come up the escalators from the platforms.

The bus station is across the street from the train station (on Avenida Vía Augusta, to the north). There's no luggage storage at the train station, but the bus station has lockers (€4, look for *consigna* sign and buy token at machine).

To get to the old town, hop a **taxi** (€7 to the Mezquita) or catch **bus** #3 (buy €1.20 ticket on board, ask driver for "*mezquita*," get off at Calle San Fernando, and take Calle del Portillo, following the

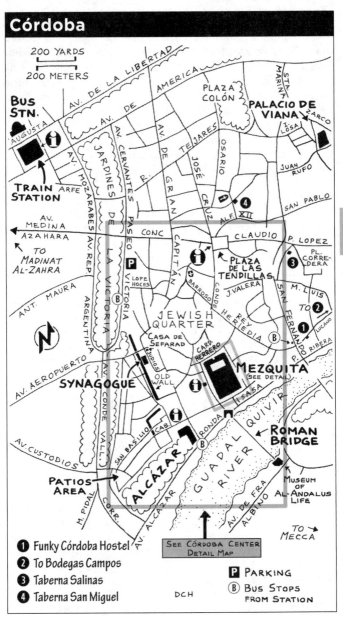

Córdoba

200 YARDS
200 METERS

CÓRDOBA

1 Funky Córdoba Hostel
2 To Bodegas Campos
3 Taberna Salinas
4 Taberna San Miguel

P PARKING
B BUS STOPS FROM STATION

DCH

twists and turns—and occasional signs—to the Mezquita).

It's about a 25-minute **walk** from either station to the old town. To walk from the train station to the Mezquita, turn left onto Avenida de América, then right through the Jardines de la Victoria park. Near the end of the park, on the left, you'll see a section of the old city walls. The Puerta de Almodóvar gate marks the start of Calle Cairuan—follow this street downhill, with the wall still on your left, until you reach Plaza Campo de los Martires. Consider popping in to the TI on this square for a city map. Then head left, past the Alcázar, down Calle Amador de los Reyes, which leads directly to the Mezquita.

Helpful Hints

Closed Days: The synagogue, Alcázar, Madinat Al-Zahra, and Palacio de Viana are closed on Monday. The Mezquita is open daily.

Festivals: May is busy with festivals. During the first half of May, Córdoba hosts the Concurso Popular de Patios Cordobeses—a patio contest.

Local Guides: Isabel Martinez Richter is a charming archaeologist who loves to make the city come to life for curious Americans (€130/3 hours, mobile 669-369-645, isabmr@gmail .com). **Angel Lucena** is also a good teacher and a joy to be with (€100/3 hours, mobile 607-898-079, lucenaangel@hot mail.com).

Sights in Córdoba

▲▲▲Mezquita

This massive former mosque—now with a 16th-century church rising up from the middle—was once the center of Western Islam and the heart of a cultural capital that rivaled Baghdad and Constantinople. A wonder of the medieval world, it's remarkably well-preserved, giving today's visitors a chance to soak up the ambience of Islamic Córdoba in its 10th-century prime.

Cost and Hours: €8, ticket kiosk inside the Patio de los Naranjos, Mon-Sat free entry until 10:00 (because they don't want to charge a fee to attend the 9:30 Mass), dry €3.50 audioguide; open March-Oct Mon-Sat 8:30-19:00, Sun 8:30-11:30 & 15:00-19:00; Nov-Feb Mon-Sat 8:30-18:00, Sun 8:30-11:30 & 15:00-18:00; last entry 30 minutes before closing, Christian altar accessible only after 11:00 unless you attend Mass, try to avoid midday crowds (11:00-15:00) by coming early or late; tel. 957-470-512, www.catedraldecordoba.es. You can also enjoy the Mezquita on a sound-and-light tour on some summer evenings.

The Mezquita

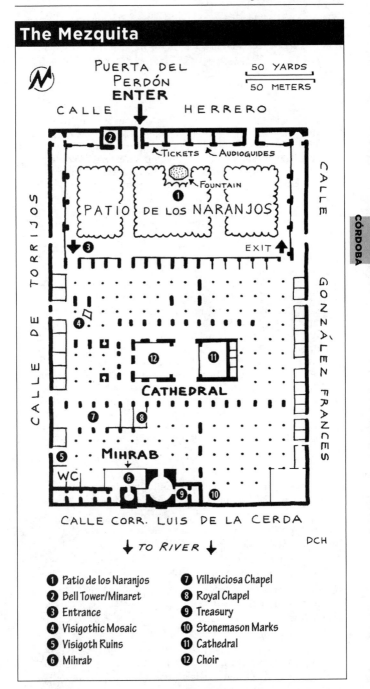

CÓRDOBA

① Patio de los Naranjos
② Bell Tower/Minaret
③ Entrance
④ Visigothic Mosaic
⑤ Visigoth Ruins
⑥ Mihrab
⑦ Villaviciosa Chapel
⑧ Royal Chapel
⑨ Treasury
⑩ Stonemason Marks
⑪ Cathedral
⑫ Choir

Islamic Córdoba (756-1236): Medieval Europe's Cultural Capital

After his family was slaughtered by political rivals (A.D. 750), 20-year-old Prince Abd Al-Rahman fled the royal palace at Damascus, headed west across North Africa, and went undercover among the Berber tribesmen of Morocco. For six years he avoided assassination while building a power base among his fellow Arab expatriates and the local Muslim Berbers. As an heir to the title of "caliph" (akin to an emperor-pope), he sailed north and claimed Moorish Spain as his own, confirming his power by decapitating his enemies and sending their salted heads to the rival caliph in Baghdad. This split in Islam was somewhat like the papal schism that stirred up medieval Christian Europe, when the Church split into factions over who was the rightful pope.

Thus began an Islamic flowering in southern Spain under Abd Al-Rahman's family, the Umayyads. They dominated Sevilla and Granada, ruling the independent state of "Al-Andalus," with their capital at Córdoba.

By the year 950—when the rest of Europe was mired in poverty, ignorance, and superstition—Córdoba was Europe's greatest city, rivaling Constantinople and Baghdad. It had well over 100,000 people (Paris had a third that many), with hundreds of mosques, palaces, and public baths. The streets were paved and lighted at night with oil lamps, and running water was piped in from the outskirts of the city. Medieval visitors marveled at the size and luxury of its mosque (the Mezquita), a symbol that the Umayyads of Spain were the equal of the caliphs of Baghdad.

This Golden Age was marked by a remarkable spirit of tolerance and cooperation in this region among the three great monotheistic religions: Islam, Judaism, and Christianity. As a proudly Andalusian guide once explained to me, "Umayyad

◐ **Self-Guided Tour:** Before entering the patio, take in the exterior of the Mezquita. The mosque's massive footprint is clear when you survey its sprawling walls from outside. At 600 feet by 400 feet, it seems to dominate the higgledy-piggledy medieval town that surrounds it.

❶ **Patio de los Naranjos:** The Mezquita's big, welcoming courtyard is free to enter. When this was a mosque, the Muslim faithful would gather in this courtyard to perform ablution—ritual washing before prayer, as directed by Muslim law. The courtyard walls display many of the mosque's carved ceiling panels and beams, which date from the 10th century.

Al-Andalus was not one country with three cultures. It was one culture with three religions...its people shared the same food, dress, art, music, and language. Different religious rituals within the community were practiced in private. But clearly, Muslims ruled. No church spire could be taller than a minaret, and while the call to prayer rang out five times daily, there was no ringing of church bells."

The university rang with voices in Arabic, Hebrew, and Latin, sharing their knowledge of medicine, law, literature, and *al-jibra*. The city fell under the enlightened spell of the ancient Greeks, and Córdoba's 70 libraries bulged with translated manuscripts of Plato and Aristotle, works that would later inspire medieval Christians.

Ruling over the Golden Age were two energetic leaders—Abd Al-Rahman III (912-961) and Al-Hakam II (961-976)—who conquered territory, expanded the Mezquita, and boldly proclaimed themselves caliphs.

Córdoba's Y1K crisis brought civil wars that toppled the caliph (1031), splintering Al-Andalus into several kingdoms. Córdoba came under the control of the Almoravids (Berbers from North Africa), who were less sophisticated than the Arab-based Umayyads. Then a wave of even stricter Islam swept through Spain, bringing the Almohads to power (1147) and driving Córdoba's best and brightest into exile. The city's glory days were over, and it was replaced by Sevilla and Granada as the centers of Spanish Islam. On June 29, 1236, Christians conquered the city. That morning Muslims said their last prayers in the great mosque. That afternoon, the Christians set up their portable road altar and celebrated the church's first Mass. Córdoba's days as a political and cultural superpower were over.

❷ **Bell Tower/Minaret:** Gaze up through the trees for views of the bell tower (c. 1600), built over the remains of the original Muslim minaret. For four centuries, five times a day, a singing cleric (the muezzin) would ride a donkey up the ramp of the minaret, then call to all Muslims in earshot that it was time to face Mecca and pray.

• *Buy your ticket (and, if you wish, rent an audioguide at a separate kiosk to the right). Enter the building by passing through the keyhole gate at the far-right corner (pick up an English map-brochure as you enter).*

❸ **Entrance:** Walking into the former mosque from the patio, you pass from an orchard of orange trees into a forest of delicate columns (erected here in the eighth century). The more than 800 red-and-blue columns are topped with double arches—a round Romanesque arch above a Visigothic horseshoe arch—made from alternating red brick and white stone. The columns and capitals

(built of marble, granite, and alabaster) were recycled from ancient
Roman ruins and conquered
Visigothic churches. (Golden Age
Arabs excelled at absorbing both
the technology and the building
materials of the people they conquered—no surprise, considering
the culture's nomadic roots; cen-

turies of tentmaking didn't lend much stoneworking expertise.)
The columns seem to recede to infinity, as if reflecting the immensity and complexity of Allah's creation.

Although it's a vast room, the low ceilings and dense columns
create an intimate and worshipful atmosphere. The original mosque
was brighter, before Christians renovated the place for their use
and closed in the arched entrances from the patio and street. The
giant cathedral sits in the center of the mosque. For now, pretend it
doesn't exist. We'll visit it after exploring the mosque.

• *From the entrance, walk along the side wall five columns in and find a
glass floor over a section of mosaic floor below. Look in.*

❹ Visigothic Mosaic: The mosque stands on the site of the
early-Christian Church of San Vicente, built during the Visigothic
period (sixth century). Peering down, you can see a mosaic that
remains from that original church. This is important to Catholic
locals, as it proves there was a church here before the mosque—
thereby giving credence to those who see the modern-day church
on this spot as a return to the site's original purpose, rather than a
violation of the mosque.

• *Walk straight ahead to the far right corner (opposite the entrance),
where you'll find more...*

❺ Visigothic Ruins: On display in the corner are rare bits of
carved stone from that same sixth-century church. (Most other
stonework here had been scrubbed of its Christian symbolism
by Muslims seeking to reuse them for the mosque.) Prince Abd
Al-Rahman bought the church from his Christian subjects before
leveling it to build his mosque. From here, pan to the right to
take in the sheer vastness of the mosque. (Keep panning to find a
hidden WC and drinking fountain in the corner.)

• *Walk to your left until you come to the mosque's focal point, the...*

❻ Mihrab: The mosque equivalent of a church's high altar,
this was the focus of the mosque and remains a highlight of the
Mezquita today. Picture the original mosque at prayer time, with a
dirt floor covered by a patchwork of big carpets...more than 20,000
people could pray at once here. Imagine the multitude kneeling in
prayer, facing the mihrab, rocking forward to touch their heads to
the ground, and saying, *"Allahu Akbar, la illa a il Allah, Muhammad*

razul Allah"—"Allah is great, there is no god but Allah, and Muhammad is his prophet."

The mihrab, a feature in all mosques, is a decorated "niche"—in this case, more like a small room with a golden-arch entrance. During a service, the imam (prayer leader) would stand here to read scripture and give sermons. He spoke loudly into the niche, his back to the assembled crowd, and the architecture worked to amplify his voice so all could hear. Built in the mid-10th century by Al-Hakam II, the exquisite room reflects the wealth of Córdoba in its prime. Three thousand pounds of multicolored glass-and-enamel cubes panel the walls and domes in mosaics designed by Byzantine craftsmen, depicting flowers and quotes from the Quran. Gape up. Overhead rises a colorful, starry dome with skylights and interlocking lobe-shaped arches.

• *Now turn around so that you're facing away from the mihrab. Ahead of you, and a bit to the left, is a roped-off open area. Step up, and gaze into the first chapel built within the mosque after the Christian Reconquista.*

❼ **Villaviciosa Chapel:** In 1236, Saint-King Ferdinand III conquered the city and turned the mosque into a church. The

higher ceiling allowed for clerestory windows and more light, which were key to making it feel more church-like. Still, the locals continued to call it "la Mezquita," and left the structure virtually unchanged (70 percent of the original mosque structure survives to this day). Sixteen columns were removed and replaced by Gothic arches to make this first chapel. It feels as if the church architects appreciated the opportunity to incorporate the sublime architecture of the pre-existing mosque into their church. Notice how the floor was once almost entirely covered with the tombs of nobles and big shots eager to make this their final resting place.

• *Immediately to your right (as you face the main entrance of the Mezquita), you'll see the...*

❽ **Royal Chapel:** The chapel—designed for the tombs of Christian kings—is completely closed off. While it was never open to the public, the tall, well-preserved Mudejar walls and dome are easily visible. Notice the elaborate stucco work. The lavish Arabic-style decor dates from the 1370s, done by Muslim artisans after the

Reconquista. The floor is a bit higher here to accommodate tombs buried beneath it. The fact that a Christian king chose to be buried in a tomb so clearly Moorish in design indicates the mutual respect between the cultures (before the Inquisition changed all that).

• *Return to the mihrab, then go through the big door to your immediate left, which leads into the Baroque...*

❾ **Treasury (Tesoro):** The treasury is filled with display cases of religious artifacts and the enormous monstrance that is paraded through the streets of Córdoba each Corpus Christi, 60 days after Easter (notice the handles).

The monstrance was an attempt by 16th-century Christians to create something exquisite enough to merit being the holder of the Holy Communion wafer. As they believed the wafer actually was the body of Christ, this trumped any relics. The monstrance is designed like a seven-scoop ice-cream cone, held together by gravity. While the bottom is silver-plated 18th-century Baroque, the top is late Gothic—solid silver with gold plating courtesy of 16th-century conquistadors.

The big canvas nearest the entrance shows Saint-King Ferdinand III, who conquered Córdoba in 1236, accepting the keys to the city's fortified gate from the vanquished Muslims. The victory ended a six-month siege and resulted in a negotiated settlement: The losers' lives were spared, providing they evacuated. Most went to Granada, which remained Muslim for another 250 years. The same day, the Spaniards celebrated Mass in a makeshift chapel right here in the great mosque.

Among the other Catholic treasures, don't miss the ivory crucifix (next room, body carved from one tusk, arms carefully fitted on) from 1665. Get close to study Jesus' mouth—it's incredibly realistic. The artist? No one knows.

• *Just outside the treasury exit, a glass case holds casts that show many...*

❿ **Stonemason Marks:** These stones still bear the marks and signatures left by those who cut them to build the original Visigothic church. Try to locate the actual ones on nearby columns. (I went five for six.) This part of the mosque has the best light for photography, thanks to skylights put in by 18th-century Christians.

The mosque grew over several centuries under a series of rulers. Remarkably, each ruler kept to the original vision—rows and rows of multicolored columns topped by double arches. Then came the Christians.

• *Find the towering church in the center of the mosque and step in.*

⓫ **Cathedral:** Rising up in the middle of the forest of columns is the bright and newly restored cathedral, oriented in the Christian tradition, with its altar at the east end. Gazing up at the rich decoration, it's easy to forget that you were in a former mosque

just seconds ago. While the mosque is about 30 feet high, the cathedral's space soars 130 feet up. Look at the glorious ceiling.

In 1523 Córdoba's bishop proposed building this grand church in the Mezquita's center. The town council opposed it, but Charles V (called Carlos I in Spain) ordered it done. If that seems like a travesty to you, consider what some locals will point out: Though it would have been quicker and less expensive for the Christian builders to destroy the mosque entirely, they respected its beauty and built their church into it instead.

As you take in the styles of these two great places of worship, ponder how they reflect the differences between Catholic and Islamic aesthetics and psychology: horizontal versus vertical, intimate versus powerful, fear-inspiring versus loving, dark versus bright, simple versus elaborate, feeling close to God versus feeling small before God.

The basic structure is late Gothic, with fancy Isabelline-style columns. The nave's towering Renaissance arches and dome emphasize the triumph of Christianity over Islam in Córdoba. The twin pulpits feature a marble bull, eagle, angel, and lion—symbols of the four evangelists. The modern *cátedra* (the seat of the bishop) is made of Carrara marble.

While churches and mosques normally both face east (to Jerusalem or Mecca), this space holds worship areas aimed 90 degrees from each other, since the mihrab faces south. Perhaps it's because from here you have to go south (via Gibraltar) to get to Mecca. Or maybe it's because this mosque was designed by the Umayyad branch of Islam, whose ancestral home was Damascus—from where Mecca lies to the south.

• *Facing the high altar is a big, finely decorated wooden enclosure.*

❿ **Choir:** The Baroque-era choir stalls were added much later—made in 1750 of New World mahogany. While cluttering up a previously open Gothic space, the choir is considered one of the masterpieces of 18th-century Andalusian Baroque. Each of the 109 stalls (108 plus the throne of the bishop) features a scene from the Bible: Mary's life on one side facing Jesus' life on the other. The lower chairs feature carved reliefs of the 49 martyrs of Córdoba (from Roman, Visigothic, and Moorish times), each with a palm frond symbolizing martyrdom and the scene of their death in the background.

The medieval church strayed from the inclusiveness taught by Jesus: Choirs (which were standard throughout Spain) were for clerics (canons, priests, and the bishop). The pews in the nave were for nobles. And the peasants listened in from outside. (Lay people didn't understand what they were hearing anyway, as Mass was held in Latin until the 1960s.) Those days are long over. Today, a public Mass is said—in Spanish—right here most mornings (Mon-Sat at 9:30).

Near the Mezquita
All of these sights are within a few minutes' walk of the Mezquita.

On and near the River
Just downhill from the Mezquita is the Guadalquivir River, which flows on to Sevilla and eventually out to the Atlantic. While silted up today, it was once navigable from here. The town now seems to turn its back on the Guadalquivir, but the arch next to the Roman Bridge (with its ancient foundation surviving) and the fortified gate on the far bank (now housing a museum, described later) evoke a day when the river was key to the city's existence.

Triumphal Arch and Plague Monument
The unfinished Renaissance arch was designed to give King Philip II a royal welcome, but he arrived before its completion—so the job was canceled. ("Very Andalusian," according to a local friend.) The adjacent monument with the single column is an 18th-century plague monument dedicated to St. Raphael (he was in charge of protecting the region's population from its main scourges: plague, hunger, and floods).

The modern visitors center behind the arch is unlikely to be open during your visit—like so many other projects affected by Spain's economic crisis, the completion of the building's interior has been abandoned for the time being.

Roman Bridge
The bridge, which sits on its first-century-A.D. foundations and retains its 16th-century arches, was poorly restored in 2009. It feels like so much other modern work along this riverbank—done on the cheap. As it was the first bridge over this river, it established Córdoba as a strategic place. Walk across the bridge for a fine view of the city—especially the huge mosque with its cathedral busting through the center. You'll be steps away from the museum described next.

▲Museum of Al-Andalus Life
The Museo Vivo de Al-Andalus fills the fortified gate (built in the 14th century to protect the Christian city) at the far side of the

Central Córdoba

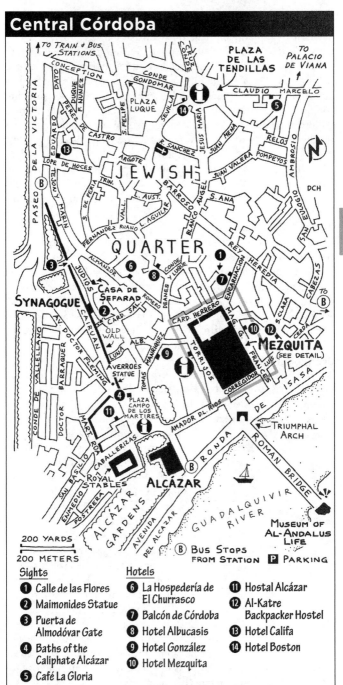

CÓRDOBA

Sights

1. Calle de las Flores
2. Maimonides Statue
3. Puerta de Almodóvar Gate
4. Baths of the Caliphate Alcázar
5. Café La Gloria

Hotels

6. La Hospedería de El Churrasco
7. Balcón de Córdoba
8. Hotel Albucasis
9. Hotel González
10. Hotel Mezquita
11. Hostal Alcázar
12. Al-Katre Backpacker Hostel
13. Hotel Califa
14. Hotel Boston

Ⓑ Bus Stops from Station Ⓟ Parking

Roman Bridge. It is a velvety, philosophical, almost evangelical attempt to explain the Muslim Moorish culture, and is funded by a foundation started by Roger Garaudy, a former French politician and writer. Don a headset and wander through simple displays as the clear and engrossing (if gauzy) commentary lets you sit at the feet of the great poets and poke into Moorish living rooms. It's worth the climb up to the rooftop terrace for the best panoramic view of Córdoba. Garaudy's flowery audiotour focuses on the formation of the great monotheistic religions...the greatest of which—in his opinion—is Islam.

Cost and Hours: €4.50, includes one-hour audio tour, daily May-Sept 10:00-14:00 & 16:30-20:30, Oct-April 10:00-18:00, Torre de la Calahorra, tel. 957-293-929, www.torrecalahorra.com.

Jewish Córdoba

Córdoba's Jewish Quarter dates from the late Middle Ages, after Muslim rule and during the Christian era. Now little remains. For a sense of the neighborhood in its thriving heyday, visit the synagogue and the cultural center located a few steps away (both described in this section). For a pretty picture, find **Calle de las Flores** (a.k.a. "Blossom Lane"). This narrow flower-bedecked street frames the cathedral's bell tower as it hovers in the distance (the view is a favorite for local guidebook covers).

Synagogue (Sinagoga)

The small yet beautifully preserved synagogue was built in 1315, under Christian rule, but the Islamic decoration has roots way back to Abd Al-Rahman I. During Muslim times, Córdoba's siz-

able Jewish community was welcomed, though its members paid substantial taxes to the city—money that enlarged the Mezquita and generated goodwill. That goodwill came in handy when Córdoba's era of prosperity and mutual respect ended with the arrival of the intolerant Almohad Berbers. Christians and Jews were repressed, and brilliant minds—such as the philosopher Maimonides—fled for their own safety.

The Christian Reconquista of Córdoba (1236) brought another brief period of religious tolerance. That's when this synagogue was built—the result of a joint effort by Christians, Jews, and Muslim (Mudejar) craftsmen. By the end of the 14th century, however, Spain's Jews were again persecuted. They were finally expelled or forced to convert in 1492; this is one of only three surviving synagogues in Spain built before that year.

Córdoba's Jewish Quarter: A Ten-Point Scavenger Hunt

Whereas most of the area around the Mezquita is commercial and touristy, the neighborhood to the east seems somehow almost untouched by tourism and the modern world (as you leave the Mezquita, turn right and exit the orange-grove patio, then wander into the lanes immediately behind Hotel Mezquita). To catch a whiff of Córdoba as it was before the onslaught of tourism and the affluence of the 21st century, explore this district. Just meander and observe. Here are a few characteristics to look for:

1. **Narrow streets.** Skinny streets make sense in hot climates, as they provide much-appreciated shade. The ones in this area are remnants from the old Moorish bazaar, crammed in to fit within the protective city walls.

2. **Thick, whitewashed walls.** Both features serve as a kind of natural air-conditioning—and the chalk ingredient in the whitewash "bugs" bugs.

3. **Colorful doors and windows.** In this famously white city, what little color there is—mostly added in modern times—helps counter the boring whitewash.

4. **Iron grilles.** Historically, these were more artistic, but modern ones are more practical. Their continued presence is a reminder of the persistent gap through the ages between rich and poor. The wooden latticework covering many windows is a holdover from days when women, held to extreme standards of modesty, wanted to be able to see out while still keeping their privacy.

5. **Stone bumpers on corners.** These protected buildings against reckless drivers. Scavenged secondhand ancient Roman pillars worked well.

6. **Scuff guards.** Made of harder materials, these guards sit at the base of the whitewashed walls—and, from the looks of it, are serving their purpose.

7. **Riverstone cobbles.** These stones were cheap and local, and provided drains down the middle of a lane. They were flanked by smooth stones that stayed dry for walking (and now aid the rolling suitcases of modern-day tourists).

8. **Pretty patios.** Cordovans are proud of their patios. Walk up to the inner iron gates of the wide-open front doors and peek in (see "Patios" sidebar, later).

9. **Remnants of old towers from minarets.** Muslim Córdoba peaked in the 10th century with an estimated 600,000 people, which meant lots of neighborhood mosques.

10. **A real neighborhood.** People really live here. There are no tacky shops, and just about the only tourist is… you.

Rich Mudejar decorations of intertwined flowers, arabesques, and Stars of David plaster the walls. What appear to be quotes from the Quran in Arabic are actually quotes from the Bible in Hebrew. On the east wall (the symbolic direction of Jerusalem), find the niche for the Ark, which held the scrolls of the Torah (the Jewish scriptures). The upstairs gallery was reserved for women. This synagogue, the only one that survives in Córdoba, was left undisturbed because it was used as a church until the 19th century (look for the cross painted into a niche).

Cost and Hours: Free, Tue-Sun 9:30-14:00 & 15:30-17:30, closed Mon, Calle de los Judíos 20, tel. 957-202-928. To learn more about the synagogue and its community, head next to the Casa de Sefarad, just 10 steps uphill.

Casa de Sefarad

Set inside a restored 14th-century home directly across from the synagogue, this interpretive museum brings to life Córdoba's rich Jewish past. Eight rooms around a central patio are themed to help you understand different aspects of daily life for Spain's former Jewish community. The rooms focus on themes such as contributions from women in the community, Jewish holidays, and musical traditions. Upstairs is an interpretive center for the synagogue, along with rooms dedicated to Maimonides, the Inquisition, and the synagogue. The Casa de Sefarad is a cultural center for Sephardic (the Hebrew word for "Spanish") Jewish heritage. Jaime and his staff stress that the center's purpose is not political or religious, but cultural. Along with running this small museum, they teach courses, offer a library, and promote an appreciation of Córdoba's Jewish heritage.

Cost and Hours: €4, Mon-Sat 11:00-18:00, Sun 11:00-14:00, 30-minute guided tours in English available by request if guide is available, next to synagogue at the corner of Calle de los Judíos and Calle Averroes, tel. 957-421-404, www.casadesefarad.es. The Casa de Sefarad hosts occasional concerts—acoustic, Sephardic, Andalusian, and flamenco—on its patio (€15, some Sat in season, usually at 19:00).

City Walls

Built upon the foundation of Córdoba's Roman walls, these fortifications date mostly from the 12th century. While the city stretched beyond the walls in Moorish times, these walls protected its political, religious, and commercial center. Of the seven original gates, the Puerta de Almodóvar (near the synagogue) is best preserved today. Just outside this gate, you'll find statues of Córdoba's great thinkers: Seneca (the Roman philosopher and adviser to Nero), Maimonides, and Averroes.

Statues of Maimonides and Averroes

Statues honor two of Córdoba's deepest-thinking homeboys—one Jewish, one Muslim, both driven out during the wave of intolerance after the fall of the Umayyad caliphate. (Maimonides is 30 yards downhill from the synagogue; Averroes is at the end of the old wall, where Cairuán and Doctor Fleming streets meet.)

Moses Maimonides (1135-1204), "the Jewish Aquinas," was born in Córdoba and raised on both Jewish scripture and the philosophy of Aristotle. Like many tolerant Cordovans, he saw no con-flict between the two. An influential Talmudic scholar, astronomer, and med-ical doctor, Maimonides left his biggest mark as the author of *The Guide for the Perplexed*, in which he asserted that sec-ular knowledge and religious faith could go hand-in-hand (thereby inspiring the philosophy of St. Thomas Aquinas). In 1148, Córdoba was transformed when the fundamentalist Almohads assumed power, and young Maimonides and his

family were driven out. Today tourists, Jewish scholars, and fans of Aquinas rub the statue's foot in the hope that some of Maimonides' genius and wisdom will rub off on them.

The story of **Averroes** (1126-1198) is a near match of Maimonides', except that Averroes was a Muslim lawyer, not a Jewish physician. He became the medieval world's number-one authority on Aristotle, also influencing Aquinas. Averroes' biting tract *The Incoherence of the Incoherence* attacked narrow-mindedness, asserting that secular philosophy (for the elite) and religious faith (for the masses) both led to truth. The Almohads banished him from the city and burned his books, ending four centuries of Cordovan enlightenment.

Alcázar
Alcázar de los Reyes Cristianos

Tourists line up to visit Córdoba's overrated fortress, the "Castle of the Christian Monarchs," which sits strategically next to the Guadalquivir River. (I think they confuse it with the much more worthy Alcázar in Sevilla.) Upon entering, look to the right to see a big, beautiful garden rich with flowers and fountains. To the left is a modern-feeling, unimpressive fort. While it was built along the Roman walls in Visigothic times, constant reuse and recycling has left it sparse and barren (with the exception of a few interesting Roman mosaics on the walls). Crowds squeeze up and down the congested spiral staircases of "Las Torres" for meager views. Ferdinand and Isabel donated the castle to the Inquisition in 1482, and it became central in the church's effort to discover "false converts to Christianity"—mostly Jews who had decided not to flee Spain in 1492.

Cost and Hours: €4.50, free Tue-Fri 8:30-10:30; open mid-June-mid-Sept Tue-Sun 8:30-14:30; off-season Tue-Fri 8:30-19:30, Sat 9:30-16:30, Sun 9:30-14:30; closed Mon year-round. On Fridays and Saturdays, you're likely to see people celebrating civil weddings here.

Baths of the Caliphate Alcázar (Baños Califales)

The scant but evocative remains of these 10th-century royal baths are all that's left from the caliph's palace complex. They date from a time when the city had hundreds of baths to serve a population of several hundred thousand. The exhibit teaches about Arabic baths in general and the caliph's in particular. A 10-minute video (normally in Spanish, English on request) tells the story well.

Cost and Hours: €2.50, free Tue-Fri 8:30-10:30, open same hours as Alcázar, just outside the wall—near the Alcázar.

Away from the Mezquita

Plaza de las Tendillas

While most tourists leave Córdoba having seen only the Mezquita and the cute medieval quarter that surrounds it, the modern city offers a good peek at urban Andalucía. Perhaps the best way to sample this is to browse Plaza de las Tendillas and the surrounding streets. The square, with an Art Deco charm, acts like there is no tourism in Córdoba. On the hour, a clock here chimes the guitar chords of Juan Serrano—a Cordovan classic.

Characteristic cafés and shops abound. For example, **Café La Gloria** provides an earthy Art Nouveau experience. Located just down the street from Plaza de las Tendillas, it has an unassuming entrance, but a sumptuous interior. Carved floral designs wind around the bar, mixing with *feria* posters and bullfighting memories. Pop in for a quick beer or coffee (daily from 8:00 until late, quiet after the lunch crowd clears out, Calle Claudio Marcelo 15, tel. 957-477-780).

Palacio de Viana

Decidedly off the beaten path, this former palatial estate is a 25-minute walk northeast from the cluster of sights near the Mezquita. A guided tour whisks you through each room of an exuberant 16th-century estate, while an English handout drudges through the dates and origin of each important piece. But the house is best enjoyed by

ignoring the guide and gasping at the massive collection of—for lack of a better word—stuff. Decorative-art fans will have a field day. The sight is known as the "patio museum" for its 12 connecting patios, each with a different theme.

Cost and Hours: House-€8, patios only-€5, July-Aug Tue-Sun 9:00-15:00, Sept-June Tue-Sun 10:00-19:00 closed Mon year-round, last entry one hour before closing, no photos inside, Plaza Don Gome 2, tel. 957-496-741.

Near Córdoba
Madinat Al-Zahra (Medina Azahara)

Five miles northwest of Córdoba, these ruins of a once-fabulous

palace of the caliph were completely forgotten until excavations began in the early 20th century. Built in A.D. 929 as a power center to replace Córdoba, Madinat Al-Zahra was both a palace and an entirely new capital city—the "City of the Flower"—covering nearly half a square mile (only about 10 percent has been uncovered). Extensively planned with an orderly design, Madinat Al-Zahra was meant to symbolize and project a new discipline on an increasingly unstable Moorish empire in Spain. It failed. Only 75 years later, the city was looted and destroyed.

The site is underwhelming—a jigsaw puzzle waiting to be reassembled by patient archaeologists. Upper terrace excava-

tions have uncovered stables and servants' quarters. Farther downhill, the house of a high-ranking official has been partially reconstructed. At the lowest level, you'll come to the remains of the mosque—placed at a diagonal, facing true east. The highlight of the visit is an elaborate reconstruction of the caliph's throne room, capturing a moody world of horseshoe arches and delicate stucco. Legendary accounts say the palace featured waterfall walls, lions in cages, and—in the center of the throne room—a basin filled with mercury, reflecting the colorful walls. The effect likely humbled anyone fortunate enough to see the caliph.

Cost and Hours: €1.50, Tue-Sat 10:00-20:00, Sun 10:00-17:00, closed Mon, tel. 957-352-860.

Getting There: Madinat Al-Zahra is located on a back road

Patios

In Córdoba, patios are taken very seriously, as shown by the fiercely fought contest, the Concurso Popular de Patios Cordobeses, which takes place the first half of every May to pick the city's most picturesque. Patios, a common feature of houses throughout Andalucía, have a long history here. The Romans used them to cool off, and the Moors added lush, decorative touches. The patio functioned as a quiet outdoor living  room, an oasis from the heat. Inside elaborate ironwork gates, roses, geraniums, and jasmine spill down whitewashed walls, while fountains play and caged birds sing. Some patios are owned by individuals, some are communal courtyards for several homes, and some grace public buildings like museums or convents.

Today homeowners take pride in these mini-paradises, and have no problem sharing them with tourists. Keep an eye out for square metal signs that indicate historic homes. As you wander Córdoba's back streets, pop your head into any wooden door that's open. The proud owners (who keep inner gates locked) enjoy showing off their picture-perfect patios. A concentration of patio-contest award-winners runs along Calle de San Basilio and Calle Martín Roa, just across from the Alcázar gardens. Some of these winners have banded together to keep their patios open to the public on a daily basis (€5, daily Sept-May 11:00-14:00 & 17:00-20:00, June 11:00-14:00 & 19:00-22:00, closed July-Aug, get tickets at at their office on Calle de San Basilio, tel. 957-043-325, www.patiosdelalcazarviejo.com). Many other nearby patios, however, are open and free to visit.

five miles from Córdoba. By **car,** head to Avenida de Medina Azahara (one block south of the train station), following signs for *A-431;* the site is well-signposted from the highway. Though the ruins aren't accessible by regular public transportation, the TI runs a **shuttle bus** that leaves twice a day and returns 2.5 hours later (€7, must buy ticket at any of the city TIs; runs year-round Tue-Sun at 9:30 and 10:15, no buses on Mon; informative English booklet provided). Catch the bus near the Cruz Roja Hospital at Paseo de la Victoria.

Entertainment in Córdoba

Caballerizas Reales de Córdoba

This equestrian show at the royal stables (just beyond the Alcázar) combines an artful demonstration of different riding styles with flamenco dance (€15; 1-hour shows generally Wed, Fri, and Sat at 21:00; Sun at 12:00, no shows Mon-Tue, outside in summer, inside in winter, mobile 671-949-514, tel. 957-497-843, www.caballerizasreales.com). During the day, you can tour the stables for free (Tue-Sat 11:00-13:30 & 17:00-20:00, Sun 10:00-11:30, closed Mon).

Flamenco

While flamenco is better in nearby Sevilla, you can see it in Córdoba, too. **Tablao Flamenco El Cardenal** is the city's most popular show, with 200 seats in a former archbishop's palace, just across the street from the Mezquita (€23, includes one drink, 1.5-hour shows nightly at 22:30, Calle de Torrijos 10, tel. 957-483-320).

El Alma de Córdoba

To experience "the soul of Córdoba"—or at least the Mezquita by night—you can take this pricey one-hour audiotour, joining about 80 people to be shepherded around the complex listening via headset to an obviously Christian-produced sound-and-light show (€18, at least four nights a week most of year, Fri-Sat in winter, 1-2 shows a night, book at TI or at Mezquita, www.elalmadecordoba.com).

Sleeping in Córdoba

I've listed prices for the high season; most of these are cheaper outside peak times. If it's hot and you've got a lot of luggage, don't bother with the inconvenient city buses; just hop in a taxi.

Near the Mezquita

These are all within a five-minute stroll of the Mezquita.

$$$ **La Hospedería de El Churrasco** is a nine-room jewel box of an inn, featuring plush furniture, tasteful traditional decor, and hardwood floors. Quiet and romantic, it's tucked in the old quarter just far enough away from the tourist storm, yet still handy for sightseeing (Sb-€135, Db-€155, superior Db-€199, €20 more per room in April-May and Oct, website shows each distinct room, no twin rooms, includes breakfast, air-con, guest computer, free Wi-Fi, parking-€21/day, midway between Puerta de Almodóvar and the Mezquita at Calle Romero 38, tel. 957-294-808, www.elchurrasco.com, hospederia@elchurrasco.com).

$$$ **Balcón de Córdoba** is an elegant little boutique hotel buried in the old town, just steps away from the Mezquita. With

Sleep Code

(€1 = about $1.30, country code: 34)

S = Single, **D** = Double/Twin, **T** = Triple, **Q** = Quad, **b** = bathroom, **s** = shower only. Unless otherwise noted, credit cards are accepted, English is spoken, and breakfast costs extra. Some hotels include the 10 percent IVA tax in the room price; others tack it onto your bill.

To help you easily sort through these listings, I've divided the accommodations into three categories based on the price for a standard double room with bath during high season:

$$$ Higher Priced—Most rooms €100 or more.
  $$ Moderately Priced—Most rooms between €60-100.
    $ Lower Priced—Most rooms €60 or less.

Prices can change without notice; verify the hotel's current rates online or by email. For the best prices, always book direct.

10 stylish rooms, generous public spaces, plenty of thoughtful touches, and a magnificent rooftop terrace, it's a lot of luxury for the price. It feels both new and steeped in tradition (Db-€140—though prices fluctuate depending on room and season, includes breakfast, check website for special promotions, Calle Encarnación 8, tel. 957-498-478, www.balcondecordoba.com, reservas@balcondecordoba.com).

$$ Hotel Albucasis, at the edge of the tourist zone, features 15 basic, clean rooms, all of which face quiet interior patios. The friendly, accommodating staff and cozy setting make you feel right at home (Sb-€55, Db-€85, breakfast-€7, air-con, elevator, free Wi-Fi in lobby, parking-€14/day but free in off-season, Buen Pastor 11, tel. 957-478-625, www.hotelalbucasis.com, hotelalbucasis @hotmail.com).

$$ Hotel González, with many of its 29 basic rooms facing its cool and peaceful patio, is sparse but sleepable. It's clean and well-run, with a good location and price (Sb-€42, Db-€75, Tb-€110, higher prices for busy times—especially weekends, breakfast-€5, air-con, elevator, free Wi-Fi in lobby, Calle de los Man ríquez 3, tel. 957-479-819, www.hotelgonzalez.com, recepcion @hotelgonzalez.com).

$$ Hotel Mezquita, just across from the main entrance of the Mezquita, rents 31 modern and comfortable rooms. The grand entrance lobby elegantly recycles an upper-class mansion (Sb-€45, Db-€89, Tb-€135, breakfast-€6, air-con, elevator, free Wi-Fi in lobby, Plaza Santa Catalina 1, tel. 957-475-585, www.hotel

mezquita.com, recepcion@hotelmezquita.com).

$ Hostal Alcázar is your best cheapie option. Run-down and budget-priced, without a real reception desk, this friendly place is just outside the old city wall on a quiet, cobbled, traffic-free street known for its prizewinning patios. Its 16 rooms are split between 2 homes on opposite sides of the lane, conveniently located 50 yards from a taxi and bus stop (Sb-€20, D-€30, small Db-€36, bigger Db-€50, Tb-€60, 2-room apartment-€60 for 3 or €80 for 4, rooms with air-con cost more, breakfast-€4, free Wi-Fi on patio, parking-€6/day, near Alcázar at Calle de San Basilio 2, tel. 957-202-561, www.hostalalcazar.com, hostalalcazar@hotmail.com, ladies' man Fernando and family, son Demitrio speaks English).

$ Al-Katre Backpacker is a fun new hostel run in a homey way by three energetic girlfriends. Its 13 rooms, with 32 beds total, gather around a cool courtyard (about €20 per person in 2-, 4-, and 6-bed rooms, D-€45-50, includes breakfast, lockers, free Wi-Fi, guest kitchen, Calle Martinez Rucker 14, tel. 957-487-539, www.alkatre.com, alkatre@alkatre.com).

In the Modern City

While still within easy walking distance of the Mezquita, these places are outside of the main tourist zone—not buried in all that tangled medieval cuteness.

$$ Hotel Califa, a modern 65-room business-class hotel belonging to the NH chain, sits on a quiet street a block off busy Paseo Victoria, on the edge of the jumbled old quarter. Still close enough to the sights, its slick modern rooms can be a great value if you get a deal (vast price range depending on demand but Db generally €80-90 during the week, €120 weekends, around €70 in heat of summer, Tb generally €20-25 more, air-con, elevator, guest computer, pay Wi-Fi in rooms, free Wi-Fi in lobby, parking-€15/day, Lope de Hoces 14, tel. 957-299-400, www.nh-hotels.com, nhcalifa@nh-hotels.com).

$$ Hotel Boston, with 39 rooms, is a decent budget bet if you want a reliable, basic hotel away from the touristy Mezquita zone. It's a taste of workaday Córdoba (Sb-€45-55, Db-€60-85, Tb-€75-110, check website for best price, breakfast-€5, air-con, elevator, pay guest computer, free Wi-Fi, parking-€12/day, Calle Málaga 2, just off Plaza de las Tendillas, tel. 957-474-176, www.hotel-boston.com, info@hotel-boston.com).

$ Funky Córdoba Hostel rents dorm beds and simple doubles in a great neighborhood (dorm beds-€13-22, Sb-€22, Db-€40-56, air-con, free Wi-Fi, terrace, kitchen, self-service laundry, lots of hostel-type info and help, right by Potro bus stop—take #3 from station—at Calle Lucano 12, tel. 957-492-966, www.funkycordoba.com, funkycordoba@funkyhostels.es).

Eating in Córdoba

Córdoba is a great dining town, with options ranging from obvious touristy bars in the old center to enticing, locals-only hangouts a few blocks away. Specialties include *salmorejo,* Córdoba's version of gazpacho. It's creamier, with more bread and olive oil and generally served with pieces of ham and hard-boiled egg. Most places serve white wines from the nearby Montilla-Moriles region; these *finos* are slightly less dry but more aromatic than the sherry produced in Jerez de la Frontera.

Near the Mezquita

Touristy options abound near the Mezquita. By walking a couple of blocks north or east of the Mezquita, you'll find plenty of cheap, accessible little places offering a better value.

Bodegas Mezquita is one of the touristy places, but it's easy and handy—a good bet for a bright, air-conditioned place a block from the mosque. They have a good *menú del día,* or you can order from their menu of €3-4 tapas, €4-10 half-*raciones,* and €8-16 *raciones* (long hours daily, one block above the Mezquita garden at Céspedes 12, tel. 957-490-004).

La Abacería is another good option on a touristy street in the old center. They have a fun and accessible menu with good €3 tapas and €8 *raciones* (open daily, Calle de los Deanes 1, tel. 957-487-050, Blanca).

Bar Santos, facing the Mezquita, supplies the *tortillas de patatas* (potato omelettes) that you see locals happily munching on the steps of the mosque. All of their food is served "to go" in disposable containers. A hearty €2 *tortilla* and a €2 beer makes for a very cheap meal; add a €3 *salmorejo* and it feels complete (daily 10:00-24:00, Calle Magistral González Francés 3, tel. 957-484-975).

Barrio San Basilio

This delightful little quarter outside the town wall, just a couple of minutes' walk west of the Mezquita and behind the royal stables, is famous for its patios. It's traffic-free, quaint as can be, and feels perfectly Cordovan without the crush of tourists around the Mezquita.

La Posada del Caballo Andaluz is a fresh, modern place with tables delightfully scattered around a courtyard. Enjoy tasty traditional Cordovan cuisine at great prices (all half-*raciones* are €5, all *raciones* €8) while sitting amid flowers and under the stars (closed Sun, Calle de San Basilio 16, tel. 957-290-374).

Mesón San Basilio, just across the street, is the longtime neighborhood favorite, with no tourists and no pretense. Although

Central Córdoba Restaurants

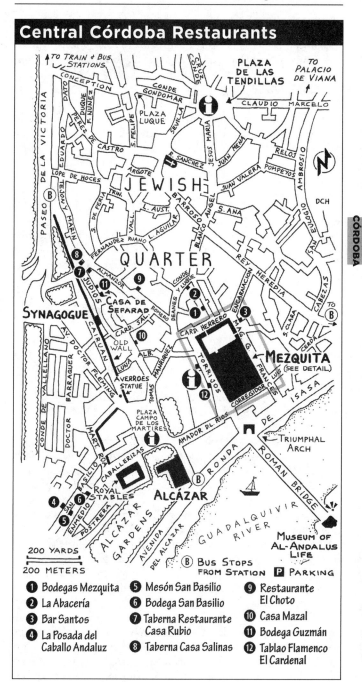

B Bus Stops from Station   **P** Parking

1 Bodegas Mezquita
2 La Abacería
3 Bar Santos
4 La Posada del Caballo Andaluz
5 Mesón San Basilio
6 Bodega San Basilio
7 Taberna Restaurante Casa Rubio
8 Taberna Casa Salinas
9 Restaurante El Choto
10 Casa Mazal
11 Bodega Guzmán
12 Tablao Flamenco El Cardenal

there's no outside seating, it still offers a certain patio ambience, with a view of the kitchen action (classic €16 fixed-priced meal, €9 lunch special weekdays, lots of €9-15 fish and meat dishes, Mon-Sat 13:00-16:00 & 20:00-24:00, closed Sun, Calle de San Basilio 19, tel. 957-297-007).

Bodega San Basilio, around the corner, is rougher, serving rustic tapas and good meals to workaday crowds. The bullfight decor gives the place a crusty character—and you won't find a word of English here (€5 half-*raciones*, €8 *raciones*, €9 fixed-price meal, closed Tue, on the corner of Calle de Enmedio and small street leading to Calle de San Basilio at #29, tel. 957-297-832).

Between Puerta de Almodóvar and the Jewish Quarter

The evocative Puerta de Almodóvar gate connects a park-like scene outside the wall with a delightfully jumbled Jewish quarter just inside it, where cafés and restaurants take advantage of the neighborhood's pools, shady trees, and dramatic face of the wall. The first two recommendations are immediately inside the gate; the others are on or near Calle de los Judíos, which runs south from there.

Taberna Restaurante Casa Rubio serves reliably good traditional dishes with smart service and several zones to chose from: on the sidewalk, with classic people-watching; inside, with a timeless interior; or on the rooftop, with dressy white tablecloths and a view of the old wall (€2 tapas, €4 half-*raciones*, €6 *raciones*, open daily, easy English menu, Calle Puerta de Almodóvar 5, tel. 957-420-853).

Taberna Casa Salinas is a more basic place with a fine reputation for quality food at a good price (run by the same people who run the highly recommended Taberna Salinas in the modern town, at Puerta de Almodóvar gate at Calle Puerta de Almodóvar 2, tel. 957-290-846).

Restaurante El Choto is bright, formal, and dressy steak house buried deep in the Jewish Quarter. With a small leafy patio, it's touristy yet intimate, serving well-presented international dishes with an emphasis on grilled meat. The favorite is kid goat with garlic—*choto al ajillo* (€22 fixed-price meal, €15-28 main dishes, closed Sun evening year-round and all day Mon in summer, Calle de Almanzor 10, tel. 957-760-115).

Casa Mazal, run by the nearby Casa de Sefarad Jewish cultural center, serves updated, modern Jewish cuisine. Small dining rooms sprawl around the charming medieval courtyard of a former house. With a seasonal menu that includes several vegetarian options, it offers a welcome dose of variety from the typical Spanish standards (€6-12 starters, €10-18 main dishes, daily 12:30-

17:00 & 20:00-24:00, Calle de Tomás Conde 3, tel. 957-941-888).

Bodega Guzmán could hardly care less about attracting tourists. This rough, dark holdover from a long-gone age proudly displays the heads of brave-but-unlucky bulls, while serving cold, very basic tapas to locals who burst into song when they feel the flamenco groove. Notice how everyone seems to be on a first-name basis with the waiters. It may feel like a drinks-only place, but they do serve rustic €2-3 tapas and €6 *raciones* (ask for the list in English). Choose a table or belly up to the bar and try a €1 glass of local white wine, either dry *(blanco seco)* or sweet *(blanco dulce)*. If it's grape juice you want, ask for *mosto* (closed Thu; if entering the old town through Puerta de Almodóvar take the first right—it's 100 yards from the gate at Calle de los Judíos 7, tel. 957-290-960).

Just East of the Mezquita Zone

Bodegas Campos, my favorite place in town, is a historic and venerable house of eating, attracting so many locals it comes with its own garage. It's worth the 10-minute walk from the tourist zone. They have a stuffy and expensive formal restaurant upstairs (€12-20 starters, €17-27 main dishes), but I'd eat in the more relaxed and affordable tavern on the ground floor (€6-11 half-*raciones*). The service is great and the menu is inviting. In two visits I nearly ate my way through the offerings, a half-*ración* at a time, and enjoyed each dish. Experiment—you can't go wrong. House specialties are bull-tail stew *(rabo de toro*—rich, tasty, and a good splurge) and anything with *pisto,* the local ratatouille-like vegetable stew. Don't leave without exploring the sprawling complex, which fills 14 old houses that have been connected to create a network of dining rooms and patios, small and large. The place is a virtual town history museum: Look for the wine barrels signed by celebrities and VIPs, the old refectory from a convent, and a huge collection of classic, original *feria* posters and great photos (Mon-Sat 12:00-17:00 & 20:00-24:00, Sun 12:00-17:00 only; from river end of Mezquita walk east along Calle Cardenal González, then continue 10 minutes straight to Calle de Lineros 32; tel. 957-497-500). Its trendy annex, called **Pick and Go,** serves dishes from the same fine kitchen, but with livelier music and a hipper crowd.

In the Modern City

These are worth the 10-to-15-minute walk from the main tourist zone—walking here, you feel a world apart from the touristy scene. Combine a meal here with a paseo through the Plaza de las Tendillas area to get a good look at modern Córdoba. If Taberna Salinas is full, as is likely, there are plenty of characteristic bars nearby in the lanes around Plaza de la Corredera.

Taberna Salinas seems like a movie set designed to give you the classic Córdoba scene. Though all the seating is indoors, it's still pleasantly patio-esque, and popular with locals for its traditional cuisine and exuberant bustle. The seating fills a big courtyard and sprawls through several smaller, semi-private rooms. The fun menu features a slew of enticing €6-7 plates (spinach with chickpeas is a house specialty). Study what locals are eating before ordering. There's no drinks menu—just basic beer or inexpensive wine. If there's a line (as there often is later in the evening), leave your name and throw yourself into the adjacent tapas-bar mosh pit for a drink (Mon-Sat 12:30-16:00 & 20:00-23:30, closed Sun and Aug; from Plaza de las Tendillas walk 3 blocks to the Roman temple, then go 1 more block and turn right to Tundidores 3; tel. 957-480-135).

Taberna San Miguel is nicknamed "Casa el Pisto" for its famous vegetable stew *(pisto)*. Well-respected, it's packed with locals who appreciate regional cuisine, a good value, and a place with a long Cordovan history. There's great seating in its charming interior or on the lively square (€2-3 tapas at bar only, €6-10 half-*raciones*, €7-14 *raciones*, closed Sun and Aug, 2 blocks north of Plaza de las Tendillas at Plaza San Miguel 1, tel. 957-478-328).

Córdoba Connections

From Córdoba by Train: Córdoba is on the slick **AVE** train line (reservations required), making it an easy stopover between **Madrid** (2-3/hour, 1.75 hours) and **Sevilla** (2-3/hour, 45 minutes). The **Avant** train connects Córdoba to Sevilla just as fast for nearly half the price (9/day, 45 minutes; railpass reservations also about half-price). The slow **regional** train to Sevilla takes about twice as long, but doesn't require a reservation and is even cheaper (7/day, 80 minutes).

Other trains go to **Granada** (2/day on Altaria, 2.5 hours—bus is more frequent, cheaper, and nearly as fast), **Ronda** (2/day direct on Altaria, 1.75 hours, 1/day cheaper but much longer with transfer in Bobadilla, 3.75 hours), **Jerez** (to transfer to Arcos; 8/day, 2-2.5 hours), **Málaga** (fast and cheap Avant train, 6/day, 1 hour; fast and expensive AVE train, 10/day, 1 hour), and **Algeciras** (2/day direct, 3.25 hours, more with transfer, 5-5.5 hours). **Train info:** Toll tel. 902-320-320.

By Bus to: Granada (7/day *directo*, 2.75 hours; 2/day *ruta*, 4 hours), **Sevilla** (7/day, 1-2 hours), **Madrid** (6/day, 4.75 hours), **Málaga** (4/day, 2.5-3.5 hours *directo*), **Barcelona** (2/day, 10 hours). The efficient staff at the information desk prints bus schedules for you—or you can check all schedules at www.estacionautobuses cordoba.es. **Bus info:** Tel. 957-404-040.

ANDALUCÍA'S WHITE HILL TOWNS

*Arcos de la Frontera • Ronda • Zahara
and Grazalema • Jerez*

Just as the American image of Germany is Bavaria, the Yankee dream of Spain is Andalucía. This is the home of bullfights, flamenco, gazpacho, pristine whitewashed hill towns, and glamorous Mediterranean resorts. This chapter explores Andalucía's hill-town highlights.

The Route of the White Hill Towns (Ruta de los Pueblos Blancos), Andalucía's charm bracelet of cute towns perched in the sierras, gives you wonderfully untouched Spanish culture. Spend a night in the romantic queen of the white towns, Arcos de la Frontera. (Towns with "de la Frontera" in their names were established on the front line of the centuries-long fight to recapture Spain from the Muslims, who were slowly pushed back into Africa.) Farther east, the larger town of Ronda stuns visitors with its breathtaking setting—straddling a gorge that thrusts deep into the Andalusian bedrock. Ronda's venerable old bullring, smattering of enjoyable sights, and thriving tapas scene round out its charms. Smaller hill towns, such as Zahara and Grazalema, offer plenty of beauty. As a whole, the hill towns—no longer strategic, no longer on any frontier—are now just passing time peacefully. Join them.

Between Sevilla and the hill towns, the city of Jerez—teeming with traffic and lacking in charm—is worth a peek for its famous Horse Symphony and a glass of sherry on a sherry bodega tour.

To study ahead, visit www.andalucia.com for information on hotels, festivals, museums, nightlife, and sports in the region.

Planning Your Time

On a three-week vacation in Spain, Andalucía's hill towns are worth two nights and up to two days sandwiched between visits

Southern Andalucía

WHITE HILL TOWNS

to Sevilla and Tarifa. Arcos makes the best home base, as it's close to interesting smaller towns, near Jerez, and conveniently situated halfway between Sevilla and Tarifa. The towns can also be accessed from the Costa del Sol resorts via Ronda.

See Jerez on your way in or out, spend a day hopping from town to town in the more remote interior (including Grazalema and Zahara), and enjoy Arcos early and late in the day. For more details on exploring this region by car, see "Route Tips for Drivers" at the end of this chapter.

Without a car, keep things simple and focus only on Arcos and Jerez (both well-served by frequent-enough public buses from Sevilla). Ronda, however, is also easy to visit—right on a train line.

Spring and fall are high season throughout this area. In summer you'll encounter intense heat, but empty hotels, lower prices, and no crowds.

Arcos de la Frontera

Arcos smothers its long, narrow hilltop and tumbles down the back of the ridge like the train of a wedding dress. It's larger than most other Andalusian hill towns, but equally atmospheric. Arcos consists of two towns: the fairy-tale old town on top of the hill and the fun-loving lower, or new, town. The old center is a labyrinthine wonderland, a photographer's feast. Viewpoint-hop through town. Feel the wind funnel through the narrow streets as cars inch around tight corners. Join the kids' soccer game on the churchyard patio. Enjoy the moonlit view from the main square.

Though it tries, Arcos doesn't have much to offer other than its basic whitewashed self. The locally produced English guidebook on Arcos waxes poetic and at length about very little. You can arrive late and leave early and still see it all.

Orientation to Arcos

Tourist Information

The **main TI,** on the road leading up into the old town, is helpful and loaded with information, including bus schedules (Mon-Sat 9:30-14:00 & 15:00-19:30, Sun 10:00-14:00; Cuesta de Belén 5, tel. 956-702-264, www.turismoarcos.es). On the floors above the TI is a skippable local history museum called Centro de Interpretación Ciudad de Arcos (CICA), with sparse exhibits described only in Spanish.

The TI organizes a one-hour **walking tour** through the old town, covering Arcos' history, lifestyles, and Moorish influences. It includes the history museum and gives you a peek at a private courtyard patio (€4; Mon-Sat at 11:00; also at 18:00 but only if you reserve ahead, 5-person minimum—off-season at 17:00; none on Sun, meet at main TI, in Spanish and/or English; for private tours, call TI).

There's also a small **TI kiosk** at the top of Plaza de España, handy for those parking in the pay lot there (Mon-Sat 10:30-13:30 & 16:30-19:30, Sun 10:30-13:30).

WHITE HILL TOWNS

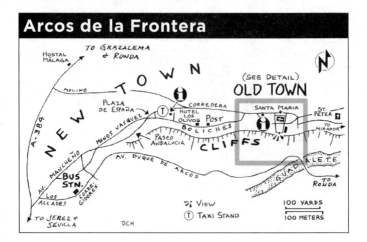

WHITE HILL TOWNS

Arrival in Arcos

By Bus: The bus station is on Calle Corregidores, at the foot of the hill. To get up to the old town, catch the shuttle bus marked *Centro* from inside the station (€1, pay driver, 2/hour, runs roughly Mon-Fri 7:00-22:00, Sat 9:00-14:30, none on Sun), hop a taxi (€5 fixed rate; if there are no taxis waiting, call 956-704-640), or hike 20 uphill minutes (see map).

By Car: The old town is a tight squeeze with a one-way traffic flow from west to east (coming from the east, circle south under town). The TI and my recommended hotels are in the west. If you miss your target, you must drive out the other end, double back, and try again. Driving in Arcos is like threading needles (many drivers pull in their side-view mirrors to buy a few extra precious inches). Turns are tight, parking is frustrating, and congestion can lead to long jams.

Small cars can park in the main square of the old town at the top of the hill (Plaza del Cabildo). Buy a ticket from the machine (€0.70/hour, 2-hour maximum, only necessary Mon-Fri 9:00-14:00 & 17:00-21:00 and Sat 9:00-14:00—confirm times on machine).

It's less stressful (and better exercise) to park in the modern underground pay lot at Plaza de España in the new town (€15/day). From this lot, hike 15 minutes, or catch a taxi or the shuttle bus up to the old town (2/hour; as you're looking uphill, the bus stop is to the right of the traffic circle).

Getting Around Arcos

The old town is easily walkable, but it's fun and relaxing to take a circular **minibus** joyride. The little shuttle bus (also mentioned in "Arrival in Arcos," above) constantly circles through the town's one-way system and around the valley (€1, 2/hour, runs roughly

Mon-Fri 7:00-22:00, Sat 9:00-14:30, none on Sun). For a 30-minute tour, hop on. You can catch it just below the main church in the old town near the mystical stone circle (generally departs roughly at :20 and :50 past the hour). Sit in the front seat for the best view of the tight squeezes and the school kids hanging out in the plazas as you wind through the old town. After passing under a Moorish gate, you enter a modern residential neighborhood, circle under the eroding cliff, and return to the old town by way of the bus station and Plaza de España.

Helpful Hints

Internet Access: Most hotels have Wi-Fi for guests, and some also have guest computers. There's no real Internet café in Arcos' old town, but the TI has a terminal where you can pay to get online (€0.40 for 15 minutes, €1 for first hour, €0.20/ hour after that).

Post Office: It's at the lower end of the old town at Paseo de los Boliches 24, a few doors up from Hotel Los Olivos (Mon-Fri 8:30-14:30, Sat 9:30-13:00, closed Sun).

Money: There are no ATMs in the old town. To reach one, take the main street past the Church of Santa María toward Plaza de España; you'll find several ATMs along Calle Corredera.

Viewpoint: For drivers, the best town overlook is from a tiny park just beyond the new bridge on the El Bosque road. In town, there are some fine viewpoints (for instance, from the main square), but the  church towers are no longer open to the public.

Arcos Old-Town Walk

This walk will introduce you to virtually everything worth seeing in Arcos.

• *Start at the top of the hill, in the main square dominated by the church. (Avoid this walk during the hot midday siesta.)*

Plaza del Cabildo: Stand at the viewpoint opposite the church on the town's main square. Survey the square, which in the old days doubled as a bullring. On your right is the parador, a former palace of the governor. It flies three flags: green for Andalucía, red-and-yellow for Spain, and blue-and-yellow for the European Union. On your left are City Hall, below the 11th-century Moorish castle where Ferdinand and Isabel held Reconquista strategy meetings

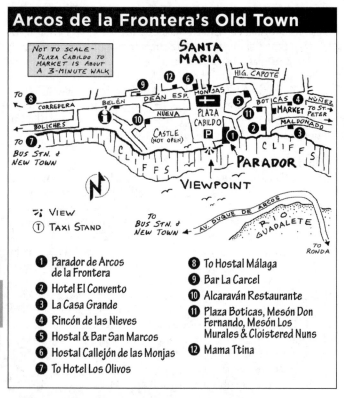

Arcos de la Frontera's Old Town

NOT TO SCALE— PLAZA CABILDO TO MARKET IS ABOUT A 3-MINUTE WALK

SANTA MARIA

HIG. CAPOTE

CORREDERA · BELÉN · DEAN ESP. · MONJAS · BOTICAS · NÚÑEZ

TO ST. PETER

MARKET

NUEVA

PLAZA CABILDO

MALDONADO

BOLICHES

CASTLE (NOT OPEN)

TO BUS STN. & NEW TOWN

CLIFFS

CLIFFS

PARADOR

VIEWPOINT

TO BUS STN. & NEW TOWN ← AV. DUQUE DE ARCOS

RIO GUADALETE

TO RONDA

🐦 VIEW
Ⓣ TAXI STAND

❶ Parador de Arcos de la Frontera
❷ Hotel El Convento
❸ La Casa Grande
❹ Rincón de las Nieves
❺ Hostal & Bar San Marcos
❻ Hostal Callejón de las Monjas
❼ To Hotel Los Olivos

❽ To Hostal Málaga
❾ Bar La Carcel
❿ Alcaraván Restaurante
⓫ Plaza Boticas, Mesón Don Fernando, Mesón Los Murales & Cloistered Nuns
⓬ Mama Ttina

(castle privately owned and closed to the public).

Now belly up to the railing and look down. The people of Arcos boast that only they see the backs of the birds as they fly. Ponder the parador's erosion concerns (it lost part of its lounge in the 1990s when it dropped right off), the orderly orange groves, and fine views toward Morocco. The city council considered building an underground parking lot to clear up the square, but nixed it because of the land's fragility. You're 330 feet above the Guadalete River. This is the town's suicide departure point for men (women jump from the other side).

• *Looming over the square is the...*

Church of Santa María: After Arcos was retaken from the Moors in the 13th century, this church was built atop a mosque. Notice the church's fine but chopped-off bell tower. The old one

fell in the earthquake of 1755 (famous for destroying Lisbon). The replacement was intended to be the tallest in Andalucía after Sevilla's—but money ran out. It looks like someone lives on an upper floor. Someone does—the church guardian resides there in a room strewn with bell-ringing ropes.

Buy a ticket (€2, Mon-Fri 10:00-13:00 & 16:00-19:00, Sat 10:00-14:00, shorter hours in winter, closed Sun and Jan-Feb), and step into the center, where you can see the beautifully carved choir. The organ was built in 1789 with that many pipes. At the very front of the church, the nice Renaissance high altar—carved in wood—covers up a Muslim prayer niche that survived from the older mosque. The altar shows God with a globe in his hand (on top), and scenes from the life of Jesus (on the right) and Mary (left). Circle the church counterclockwise and notice the elaborate chapels. Although most of the architecture is Gothic, the chapels are decorated in Baroque and Rococo styles. The ornate statues are used in Holy Week processions. Sniff out the "incorruptible body" (miraculously never rotting) of St. Felix—a third-century martyr (directly across from the entry). Felix may be nicknamed "the incorruptible," but take a close look at his knee. He's no longer skin and bones...just bones and the fine silver mesh that once covered his skin. Rome sent his body here in 1764, after recognizing this church as the most important in Arcos. In the back of the church, under a huge fresco of St. Christopher (carrying his staff and Baby Jesus), is a gnarly Easter candle from 1767.

• *Back outside, examine the...*

Church Exterior: Circle clockwise around the church, down four steps, to find the third-century Roman votive altar with a carving of the palm tree of life directly in front of you. Though the Romans didn't build this high in the mountains, they did have a town and temple at the foot of Arcos. This carved stone was discovered in the foundation of the original Moorish mosque, which stood here before the first church was built.

Head down a few more steps and come to the main entrance (west portal) of the church (closed for restoration). This is a good example of Plateresque Gothic—Spain's last and most ornate kind of Gothic.

In the pavement, notice the 15th-century magic circle with 12 red and 12 white stones—the white ones have various "constellations" marked (though they don't resemble any of today's star charts). When a child would come to the church to be baptized, the parents stopped here first for a good Christian

exorcism. The exorcist would stand inside the protective circle and cleanse the baby of any evil spirits. While locals no longer do this (and a modern rain drain now marks the center), many Sufi Muslims still come here in a kind of pilgrimage every November. (Down a few more steps and 10 yards to the left, you can catch the public bus for a circular minibus joyride through Arcos; see "Getting Around Arcos," earlier.)

Continuing along under the **flying buttresses,** notice the scratches of innumerable car mirrors on each wall (and be glad you're walking). The buttresses were built to shore up the church when it was damaged by an earthquake in 1699. (Thanks to these supports, the church survived the bigger earthquake of 1755.) The security grille (over the window above) protected cloistered nuns when this building was a convent. Look at the arches that prop up the houses downhill on the left; all over town, arches support earthquake-damaged structures.

• *Now make your way...*

From the Church to the Market: Completing your circle around the church (huffing back uphill), turn left under more arches built to repair earthquake damage and walk east down the bright, white Calle Escribanos. From now to the end of this walk, you'll basically follow this lane until you come to the town's second big church (St. Peter's). After a block, you hit Plaza Boticas.

On your right is the last remaining **convent** in Arcos. Notice the no-nunsense, spiky window grilles high above, with tiny peepholes in the latticework for the cloistered nuns to see through. Step into the lobby under the fine portico to find their one-way mirror and a spinning cupboard that hides the nuns from view. Push the buzzer, and one of the eight sisters (several are from Kenya and speak English well) will spin out some boxes of excellent, freshly baked cookies—made from pine nuts, peanuts, almonds, and other nuts—for you to consider buying (€6-7, open daily but not reliably 8:30-14:30 & 17:00-19:00; be careful—if you stand big and tall to block out the light, you can actually see the sister through the glass). If you ask for *magdalenas*, bags of cupcakes will swing around (€2.50). These are traditional goodies made from natural ingredients. Buy some goodies to support their church work, and give them to kids as you complete your walk.

The **covered market** *(mercado)* at the bottom of the plaza (down from the convent) resides in an unfinished church. At the entry, notice what is half of a church wall. The church was being built for the Jesuits, but construction stopped in 1767 when King Charles III, tired of the Jesuit appetite for politics, expelled the order from Spain. The market is closed on Sunday and Monday— they rest on Sunday, so there's no produce, fish, or meat ready for Monday. Poke inside. It's tiny but has everything you need. Pop into the *servicio público* (public WC)—no gender bias here.

• *As you exit the market, turn right and continue straight down Calle Botica...*

From the Market to the Church of St. Peter: As you walk, peek discreetly into private patios. These wonderful, cool-tiled courtyards filled with plants, pools, furniture, and happy family activities are typical of Arcos. Except in the mansions, these patios are generally shared by several families. Originally, each courtyard served as a catchment system, funneling rainwater to a drain in the middle, which filled the well. You can still see tiny wells in wall niches with now-decorative pulleys for the bucket.

At the next corner (Calle Platera), look back and up at the corner of the tiled rooftop on the right. The tiny stone—where the corner hits the sky—is a very eroded mask, placed here to scare evil spirits from the house. This is Arcos' last surviving mask from a tradition that lasted until the mid-19th century.

Also notice the ancient columns on each corner. All over town, these columns—many actually Roman, appropriated from their original ancient settlement at the foot of the hill—were put up to protect buildings from reckless donkey carts and tourists in rental cars.

As you continue straight, notice that the walls are scooped out on either side of the windows. These are a reminder of the days when women stayed inside but wanted the best possible view of any people action in the streets. These "window ears" also enabled boys in a more modest age to lean inconspicuously against the wall to chat up eligible young ladies.

Across from the old facade ahead, find the **Association of San Miguel.** Duck right, past a bar, into the oldest courtyards in town—you can still see the graceful Neo-Gothic lines of this noble home from 1850. The bar is a club for retired men—always busy when a bullfight's on TV or during card games. The guys are friendly, and drinks are cheap. You're welcome to flip on the light and explore the old-town photos in the back room.

Just beyond, facing the elegant front door of that noble house, is Arcos' second church, **St. Peter's** (€1 donation, Mon-Fri 9:00-14:00 & 15:30-18:30, Sat 10:00-14:00, closed Sun). You know it's St. Peter's because St. Peter, mother of God, is the centerpiece of the facade. Let me explain. It really is the second church, having had an extended battle with Santa María for papal recognition as the leading church in Arcos. When the pope finally favored Santa

WHITE HILL TOWNS

María, St. Peter's parishioners changed their prayers. Rather than honoring "María," they wouldn't even say her name. They prayed "St. Peter, mother of God." Like Santa María, it's a Gothic structure, filled with Baroque decor, many Holy Week procession statues, humble English descriptions, and relic skeletons in glass caskets (two from the third century A.D.).

In the cool of the evening, the tiny square in front of the church—about the only flat piece of pavement around—serves as the old-town soccer field for neighborhood kids. Until a few years ago, this church also had a resident bellman—notice the cozy balcony halfway up. He was a basket-maker and a colorful character, famous for bringing a donkey into his quarters, which grew too big to get back out. Finally, he had no choice but to kill and eat the donkey.

Twenty yards beyond the church, step into the nice **Galería de Arte San Pedro,** featuring artisans in action and their reasonably priced paintings and pottery. Walk inside. Find the water drain and the well.

Across the street, a sign directs you to **Mirador**—a tiny square 100 yards downhill that affords a commanding view of Arcos. The reservoir you see to the east of town is used for water sports in the summertime, and forms part of a power plant that local residents protested—to no avail—based on environmental concerns.

From the Church of St. Peter, circle down and around back to the main square, wandering the tiny neighborhood lanes. Just below St. Peter's (on Calle Maldonado), is a delightful little Andalusian garden (formal Arabic style, with aromatic plants such as jasmine, rose, and lavender, and water in the center). A bit farther along on Maldonado, peek into **Belén Artístico,** a quirky, little cave-like museum, featuring miniatures of favorite Nativity scenes (free, but donations accepted). The lane called Higinio Capote, below the Church of Santa María, is particularly picturesque with its many geraniums. Peek into patios, kick a few soccer balls, and savor the views.

Nightlife in Arcos

Evening Action in the New Town

The newer part of Arcos has a modern charm. In the cool of the evening, all generations enjoy life out around Plaza de España (10-minute walk from the old town). Several good tapas bars border the square or are nearby.

The big park (Recinto Ferial) below Plaza de España is the late-night fun zone in the summer (June-Aug) when *carpas* (restaurant tents) fill with merrymakers, especially on weekends. The scene includes open-air tapas bars, disco music, and dancing.

Sleeping in Arcos

Hotels in Arcos consider April, May, August, September, and October to be high season. Note that some hotels double their rates during the motorbike races in nearby Jerez (usually April or May, varies yearly, call TI or ask your hotel) and during Holy Week (the week leading up to Easter); these spikes are not reflected in the prices below.

In the Old Town

For an overnight stay, avoid the parking lot on the main square, which has a two-hour daytime limit. Instead, park in the lot at Plaza de España, and catch a taxi or the shuttle bus up to the old town (see "Arrival in Arcos," earlier).

$$$ **Parador de Arcos de la Frontera** is royally located, with 24 elegant, recently refurbished and reasonably priced rooms (8 have balconies). If you're going to experience a parador, this is a good one (Sb-€80-137, Db-€95-171, Db with terrace-€130-206, cheaper rates are for Nov-Feb, breakfast-€16, air-con, elevator, Wi-Fi, free parking, Plaza del Cabildo, tel. 956-700-500, www .parador.es, arcos@parador.es).

$$ **Hotel El Convento,** deep in the old town just beyond the parador, is the best value in town. Run by a hardworking family and their wonderful staff, this cozy hotel offers 13 fine rooms—all with great views, most with balconies. In 1998 I enjoyed a big party with most of Arcos' big shots as they dedicated a fine room with a grand-view balcony to "Rick Steves, Periodista Turístico." Guess where I sleep when in Arcos...(Sb with balcony-€62, Sb with terrace-€78, Db with balcony-€82, Db with terrace-€97, extra person-€18; 10 percent discount in 2014 when you book direct, pay in cash, and show this book; usually closed Nov-Feb; Wi-Fi, Maldonado 2, tel. 956-702-333, www.hotelelconvento.es, reservas @hotelelconvento.es). Over an à la carte breakfast, bird-watch on their view terrace, with all of Andalucía spreading beyond your *café con leche.*

Sleep Code

(€1 = about $1.30, country code: 34)
S = Single, **D** = Double/Twin, **T** = Triple, **Q** = Quad, **b** = bathroom,
s = shower only. Unless otherwise noted, credit cards are
accepted, and English is spoken, but breakfast is not included.
Some hotels include the 10 percent IVA tax in the room price;
others tack it onto your bill.

To help you easily sort through these listings, I've divided
the accommodations into three categories based on the price
for a standard double room with bath during high season:

$$$ Higher Priced—Most rooms €100 or more.
$$ Moderately Priced—Most rooms between €50-100.
$ Lower Priced—Most rooms €50 or less.

Prices can change without notice; verify the hotel's current rates online or by email. For the best prices, always book
direct.

WHITE HILL TOWNS

$$ La Casa Grande is a lovingly appointed *Better Homes and Moroccan Tiles* kind of place that rents eight rooms with big-view windows. As in a lavish yet very authentic old-style B&B, you're free to enjoy its fine view terrace, homey library, and atrium-like patio, where you'll be served a traditional breakfast. They also offer guided visits and massage services (Db-€73-89; junior suites: Db-€89-119, Tb-€109-119, Qb-€123-140; breakfast-€9, air-con, Wi-Fi in public areas, Maldonado 10, tel. 956-703-930, www .lacasagrande.net, info@lacasagrande.net, Elena).

$$ Rincón de las Nieves, with simple Andalusian style, has a cool inner courtyard surrounded by three rooms and a sprawling apartment that can accommodate up to seven people. Two of the rooms have their own outdoor terraces with obstructed views, and all have access to the rooftop terrace (Db-€50-65, higher for Holy Week and Aug, apartment-€20-24/person, air-con, Boticas 10, tel. 956-701-528, mobile 656-886-256, www.rincondelasnieves.com, info@rincondelasnieves.com).

$ Hostal San Marcos, above a neat little bar in the heart of the old town, offers four air-conditioned rooms and a great sun terrace with views of the reservoir (Sb-€25, Db-€35, Tb-€45, air-con, Wi-Fi, Marqués de Torresoto 6, best to reserve by phone, tel. 956-105-429, mobile 664-118-052, sanmarcosdearcos@hotmail .com, José speaks some English).

$ Hostal Callejón de las Monjas (a.k.a. Hostal El Patio) offers the best cheap beds in the old town. With a tangled floor plan and nine simple rooms, it's on a sometimes-noisy street behind the Church of Santa María (Sb-€20, D-€27, Db-€35, Db with terrace-€45, Tb-€50, Qb apartment-€70, air-con, Wi-Fi, Calle Callejón de las Monjas 4, tel. 956-702-302, mobile 605-839-995, www.mesonelpatio.com, padua@mesonelpatio.com, staff speak no English). The bar-restaurant with bullfighting posters in the cellar serves breakfast, tapas, and several fixed-priced meals.

In the New Town
$$ Hotel Los Olivos is a bright, cool, and airy place with 19 rooms, an impressive courtyard, roof garden, generous public spaces, bar, view, friendly folks, and easy parking. The five view rooms can be a bit noisy in the afternoon, but—with double-paned windows—are usually fine at night (Sb-€46-51, Db-€72-87, Tb-€87-102, extra bed-€15, breakfast-€9; 10 percent discount when you book direct, pay in cash, and show this book; Wi-Fi, Paseo de Boliches 30, tel. 956-700-811, www.hotel-losolivos.es, reservas@hotel-losolivos.es, Raquel and Miguel Ángel).

$ Hostal Málaga is surprisingly nice, if for some reason you want to stay on the big, noisy road at the Jerez edge of town. Nestled on a quiet lane between truck stops on A-382, it offers 17 clean, attractive rooms and a breezy two-level roof garden (Sb-€20-25, Db-€35-38, Qb apartment-€50, air-con, Wi-Fi, easy parking, Ponce de León 5, tel. 956-702-010, www.hostalmalaga.com, hostalmalagaarcos@hotmail.com, Josefa speaks German and a *leetle* English).

Eating in Arcos

Restaurants generally serve lunch from 13:00 to 16:00 and dinner from 20:00 until very late (Spaniards don't start dinner until about 21:00).

View Dining
The **Parador** (described earlier, under "Sleeping in Arcos") has a restaurant with a cliff-edge setting. Its tapas and *raciones* are reasonably priced but mediocre; still, a drink and a snack on the million-dollar-view terrace at sunset is a nice experience (€2.50-4 tapas, €6-14 *raciones*, €22 three-course fixed-price meal at lunch or dinner, daily 13:30-16:00 & 20:30-23:00, shorter hours off-season, on main square).

Cheaper Eating in the Old Town
Several decent, rustic bar-restaurants are in the old town, within a block or two of the main square and church. Most serve tapas at the bar and *raciones* at their tables. Prices are fairly consistent (€2 tapas, €5 *media-raciones*, €8 *raciones*).

Bar La Carcel ("The Prison") is run by a hardworking family that brags about its exquisite tapas and small open-faced sandwiches. I would, too. The menu is accessible; prices are the same at the bar or at the tables; and the place has a winning energy, giving the traveler a fun peek at this community (Tue-Sun 12:00-16:00 & 20:00-24:00, closed Mon; July-Aug it's open Mon and closed Sun; Calle Deán Espinosa 18, tel. 956-700-410).

Alcaraván tries to be a bit trendier yet *típico*, with a hibachi hard at work out front. A flamenco ambience fills its medieval vault in the castle's former dungeon. This place attracts French and German tourists who give it a cool vibe. Francisco and his wife cook from 13:00 and again starting at 21:00 (closed Mon, Calle Nueva 1, tel. 956-703-397).

Bar San Marcos is a tiny, homey bar with five tables, an easy-to-understand menu offering hearty, simple home cooking, and cheap €5 plates and a variety of €7 fixed-price meals (kitchen open long hours Mon-Sat, closed Sun, Marqués de Torresoto 6).

Mesón Don Fernando gives rustic a feminine twist with an inviting bar and both indoor and great outdoor seating on the square just across from the little market (Tue-Thu 13:30-16:00 & 20:15-23:00 for food, closed Wed, longer hours for drinks on the square, on Plaza Boticas).

Mesón Los Murales serves tasty, affordable tapas, *raciones*, and fixed-price meals in their rustic bar or at tables in the square outside (€2.50 tapas and *montaditos*, €6-12 *raciones*, fixed-price meals from €9, Fri-Wed 10:00-24:00, closed Thu, at Plaza Boticas 1, tel. 685-809-661).

Mama Ttina gives you an Italian break from Andalucía, with pizza and pastas to go along with the Italian pop music and international Italian/Andaluz/Moroccan/British staff (€6-12 pizzas and pastas, Thu-Mon 13:00-16:00 & 18:30-24:00, Tue-Wed 18:30-24:00 only, Deán Espinosa 10, tel. 956-703-937).

Tapas in the New Town

Plaza de España, in the lower new town, is lined with tapas bars and restaurants. For a great perch while enjoying the local family scene, consider the busy **Restaurante Bar Terraza** (€12 plates) at the end of Plaza de España.

Arcos Connections

By Bus

Leaving Arcos by bus can be frustrating (especially if you're going to Ronda)—buses generally leave late, the schedule information boards are often inaccurate, and the ticket window usually isn't open (luckily, you can buy your tickets on the bus). But local buses do give you a glimpse at *España profunda* ("deep Spain"), where everyone seems to know each other, no one's in a hurry, and despite any language barriers, people are quite helpful when approached.

Two bus companies—Los Amarillos and Comes—share the Arcos bus station. Call the Jerez offices for departure times, or ask your hotelier for help. If you want to find out about the Arcos-Jerez schedule, make it clear you're coming from Arcos (Los Amarillos tel. 902-210-317, www.losamarillos.es; Comes tel. 956-291-168, www.tgcomes.es). Also try the privately run www.movelia.es for bus schedules and routes.

From Arcos by Bus to: Jerez (hourly, 30 minutes), **Ronda** (1-2/day, 2 hours), **Cádiz** (4-5/day, 1.25 hours), **Sevilla** (2/day, 2 hours, more departures with transfer in Jerez). Buses run less frequently on weekends. The closest train station to Arcos is Jerez.

Route Tips for Drivers

The trip to **Sevilla** takes about 1.5 hours if you pay €7 for the toll road. To reach **southern Portugal,** follow the freeway to Sevilla, skirt the city by turning west on C-30 in the direction of Huelva, and it's a straight shot from there.

For more driving tips for the region, see the end of this chapter.

WHITE HILL TOWNS

Ronda

With more than 35,000 people, Ronda is one of the largest white hill towns. It's also one of the most spectacular, thanks to its gorge-

straddling setting. Approaching the town from the train or bus station, it seems flat... until you reach the New Bridge and realize that it's clinging to the walls of a canyon.

While day-trippers from the touristy Costa del Sol clog Ronda's streets during the day, locals retake the town in the early evening, making nights peaceful. If you liked Toledo at night, you'll love the local feeling of evenings in Ronda. Since it's served by train and bus, Ronda makes a relaxing break for non-drivers traveling between Granada, Sevilla, and Córdoba. Drivers can use Ronda as a convenient base from which to explore many of the other *pueblos blancos.*

Ronda's main attractions are its gorge-spanning bridges, the oldest bullring in Spain, and an intriguing old town. The cliffside setting, dramatic today, was practical back in its day. For the Moors, it provided a tough bastion, taken by the Spaniards only in 1485, seven years before Granada fell. Spaniards know Ronda as the cradle of modern bullfighting and the romantic home of 19th-century *bandoleros*. The real joy of Ronda these days lies in exploring its back streets and taking in its beautiful balconies, exuberant flowerpots, and panoramic views. Walking the streets, you feel a strong local pride and a community where everyone seems to know everyone.

Orientation to Ronda

Ronda's breathtaking ravine divides the town's labyrinthine Moorish quarter and its new, noisier, and more sprawling Mercadillo quarter. A massive-yet-graceful 18th-century bridge connects these two neighborhoods. Most things of touristic importance (TI, post office, hotels, bullring) are clustered within a few blocks of the bridge. The paseo (early evening stroll) happens in the new town, on Ronda's major pedestrian and shopping street, Carrera Espinel.

Tourist Information

Ronda's **TI,** across the square from the bullring, covers not only the town but all of Andalucía. It gives out good, free maps of the town, Andalusia's roads, Granada, Sevilla, and the Route of the White Towns. It also sells the Bono Turístico city pass, has listings of the latest museum hours, and organizes walking tours—see details under "Tours in Ronda," later (TI open Mon-Fri 10:00-19:30, until 18:00 late-Oct-late March; Sat-Sun 10:00-14:00 & 15:00-17:00; Paseo Blas Infante, tel. 952-187-119, www.turismoderonda.es).

Sightseeing Pass: If you're an avid sightseer, consider getting the €10 **Bono Turístico** city pass, which gets you into five sights (including the Arab Baths, Museo Joaquín Peinado, and Mondragón Palace). It's valid for one week and sold at the TI and a few participating sights (including the Arab Baths and Museo Joaquín Peinado).

Arrival in Ronda

By Train: The small station has ticket windows, a train information desk, and a café, but no baggage storage (there are lockers at the nearby bus station).

From the station, it's a 15-to-20-minute **walk** to the center: Turn right out of the station on Avenida de Andalucía, and go through the roundabout (you'll see the bus station on your right). Continue straight down the street (now called San José) until you

Ronda

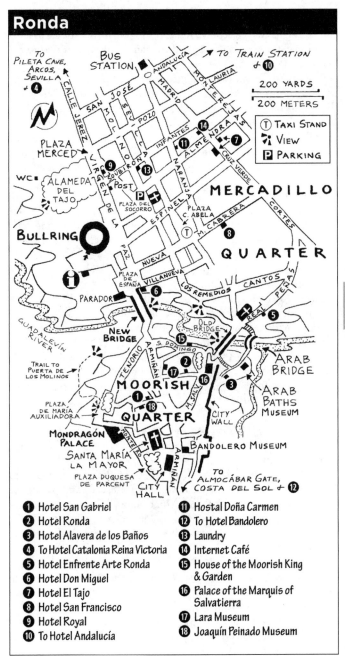

- **1** Hotel San Gabriel
- **2** Hotel Ronda
- **3** Hotel Alavera de los Baños
- **4** To Hotel Catalonia Reina Victoria
- **5** Hotel Enfrente Arte Ronda
- **6** Hotel Don Miguel
- **7** Hotel El Tajo
- **8** Hotel San Francisco
- **9** Hotel Royal
- **10** To Hotel Andalucía
- **11** Hostal Doña Carmen
- **12** To Hotel Bandolero
- **13** Laundry
- **14** Internet Café
- **15** House of the Moorish King & Garden
- **16** Palace of the Marquis of Salvatierra
- **17** Lara Museum
- **18** Joaquín Peinado Museum

WHITE HILL TOWNS

reach Calle Jerez. Turn left and walk downhill past a church and the Alameda del Tajo park. Keep going down this street, passing the bullring, to get to the TI and the famous bridge. A **taxi** to the center costs about €6.50.

By Bus: To get to the center from the bus station, leave the station walking to the right of the roundabout, then follow the directions for train travelers (described earlier). To use the station's baggage lockers, buy a token *(ficha)* at the kiosk by the exit (€3.50).

By Car: Street parking away from the center is often free. The handiest place to park in the center of Ronda is the underground lot at Plaza del Socorro (one block from bullring, €18/24 hours).

Helpful Hints

Laundry: HigienSec has one machine for self-service. For twice the cost, they will wash, dry, and fold your clothes, and offer same-day service if you drop off early enough (€6/load wash-and-dry, €12/load drop-off service, Mon-Fri 10:00-14:00 & 17:00-20:30, Sat 10:00-14:00, closed Sun, 2 blocks east of the bullring at Calle Molino 6, tel. 952-875-249).

Internet Access: Almost every hotel in town has Wi-Fi, and many also have computers for guest use. You can get online, make international phone calls, print, and fax at **Internet Mundi@1** (€0.50/15 minutes, Mon-Sat 10:00-14:00 & 16:00-22:00, Sun 16:00-22:00, near the recommended Hotel El Tajo at Calle Cruz Verde 21, tel. 952-161-588).

Baggage Storage: Use the lockers at the bus station (see "Arrival in Ronda," earlier).

Tours in Ronda

Walking Tours

The TI offers two-hour guided walks of the city (Sat-Sun at 13:00; in summer also Thu-Sat at 20:00). Reserve and pay at the TI (€18 daytime tour includes Mondragón Palace and bullring; €15 evening tour includes Mondragón Palace and Arab Baths; sometimes in two languages). Tours can be canceled if there aren't enough sign-ups.

Local Guide

Energetic and knowledgeable **Antonio Jesús Naranjo** will take you on a two-hour walking tour of the city's sights. He showed Michelle Obama around when she was in town (from €120/day, reserve early, tel. 952-870-614, mobile 639-073-763, www .guiaoficialderonda.com, guiajesus@yahoo.es). The TI has a list of other local guides.

Sights in Ronda

Ronda's New Town

▲▲▲The Gorge and New Bridge (Puente Nuevo)

The ravine, called El Tajo—360 feet down and 200 feet wide—divides Ronda into the whitewashed old Moorish town (La Ciudad) and the new town (El Mercadillo) that was built after the Christian reconquest in 1485. The New Bridge mightily spans the gorge. A different bridge was built here in 1735, but fell after six years. This one was built from 1751 to 1793. Look down...carefully.

You can see the foundations of the original bridge (and a super view of the New Bridge) from the Jardines de Cuenca park (daily in summer 9:30-21:30, winter 9:30-18:30): From Plaza de España, walk down Calle Rosario, turn right on Calle Los Remedios, and then take another right at the sign for the park. There are also good views from the parador, which overlooks the gorge and bridge from the new-town side.

From the new-town side of the bridge, on the right, you'll see the entrance to the **New Bridge Interpretive Center,** where you can pay to climb down and enter the structure of the bridge itself (€2; Mon-Fri 10:00-19:00, late Oct-late March until 18:00; Sat-Sun 10:00-15:00 year-round; mobile 649-965-338). Inside the mostly empty-feeling hall are modest audiovisual displays about the bridge's construction and famous visitors to Ronda. But the views of the bridge and gorge from the outside are far more thrilling than anything you'll find within.

▲▲▲Bullring (Real Maestranza de Caballería de Ronda)

Ronda is the birthplace of modern bullfighting, and this was the first great Spanish bullring. Philip II initiated bullfighting as war training for knights in the 16th century. Back then, there were two kinds of bullfighting: the type with noble knights on horseback,

and the coarser, man-versus-beast entertainment for the commoners (with no rules...much like when the WWF wrestlers bring out the folding chairs). Ronda practically worships Francisco Romero, who melded the noble and chaotic kinds of bullfighting with rules to establish modern bullfighting

WHITE HILL TOWNS

right here in the early 1700s. He introduced the scarlet cape, held unfurled with a stick. His son Juan further developed the ritual (local aficionados would never call it a "sport"—you'll read newspaper coverage of fights not on the sports pages but in the culture section), and his grandson Pedro was one of the first great matadors (killing nearly 6,000 bulls in his career).

Ronda's bullring and museum are Spain's most interesting (even better than Sevilla's). To tour the ring, stables, chapel, and museum, buy a ticket at the back of the bullring, the farthest point from the main drag.

Cost and Hours: €6.50, daily April-Sept 10:00-20:00, March and Oct 10:00-20:00, Nov-Feb 10:00-18:00, no photography in museum, tel. 952-874-132, www.rmcr.org. The excellent €2 audioguide describes everything and is essential to fully enjoy your visit.

Bullfights: Bullfights are scheduled only for the first weekend of September during the *feria* (fair) and occur very rarely in the spring. Whereas every other *feria* in Andalucía celebrates a patron saint, the Ronda fair glorifies legendary bullfighter Pedro Romero. For September bullfights, tickets go on sale the preceding July. (As these sell out immediately, Sevilla and Madrid are more practical places for a tourist to see a bullfight.)

Visiting the Bullring: I'd visit in this order. Directly to the right as you enter is the bullfighters' **chapel.** Before going into the ring, every matador would stop here to pray to Mary for safety—and hope to see her again.

• *Just beyond the chapel are the doors to the museum exhibits: horse gear and weapons on the left, and the story of bullfighting on the right, with some English translations.*

The **horse gear and guns exhibit** makes the connection with bullfighting and the equestrian upper class. As throughout Europe, "chivalry" began as a code among the sophisticated, horse-riding gentry. (In Spanish, the word for "gentleman" is the same as the word for "horseman" or "cowboy"—*caballero*.) And, of course, nobles are into hunting and dueling, hence the fancy guns. Don't miss the well-described  dueling section with gun cases for two, as charming as a picnic basket with matching wine glasses.

Backtrack past the chapel to see Spain's best **bullfighting exhibit.** It's a shrine to bullfighting and the historic Romero family. First it traces the long history of bullfighting, going all the way back to the ancient Minoans on Crete. Historically, there were only two arenas built solely for bullfighting: in Ronda and Sevilla. Elsewhere, bullfights were held in town squares—you'll see a painting of Madrid's Plaza Mayor filled with spectators for a bullfight. (For this reason, to this day, even a purpose-built bullring is generally called *plaza de toros*—"square of bulls.") You'll also see stuffed bull heads, photos, "suits of light" worn by bullfighters, and capes (bulls are actually colorblind, but the traditional red cape was designed to disguise all the blood). One section explains some of the big "dynasties" of fighters. At the end of the hall are historic posters from Ronda's bullfights (all originals except the Picasso). Running along the left wall are various examples of artwork glorifying bullfighting, including original Goya engravings.

• *From the museum, take advantage of the opportunity to walk in the actual arena.*

Here's your chance to play *toro*, surrounded by 5,000 empty seats. The two-tiered **arena** was built in 1785—on the 300th anni-

versary of the defeat of the Moors in Ronda. Notice the 136 classy Tuscan columns, creating a kind of 18th-century Italian theater. Lovers of the "art" of bullfighting will explain that the event is much more than the actual killing of the bull. It celebrates the noble heritage and the Andalusian horse culture. When you leave the museum and walk out on the sand, look across to see the ornamental columns and painted door-way where the dignitaries sit (over the gate where the bull enters). On the right is the place for the band (marked *música*), which, in the case of a small town like Ronda, is most likely a high school band.

• *Just beyond the arena are more parts of the complex.*

From the arena, walk through the bulls' entry into the bullpen and the **stables.** There are six bulls per fight (plus two backups)—and three matadors. The bulls are penned up here beforehand, and ropes and pulleys safely open the right door at the right time. Climb upstairs and find the indoor arena (Picadero) and see Spanish thoroughbred horses training from the **Equestrian School** of the Real Maestranza (Mon-Fri).

Alameda del Tajo Park
One block away from the bullring, the town's main park is a great place for a picnic lunch, people-watching, a snooze in the shade, or practicing your Spanish with seniors from the old folks' home.

Ronda's Old Town
▲Church of Santa María la Mayor (Iglesia de Santa María)

This 15th-century church with a fine Mudejar bell tower shares a park-like square with orange trees and City Hall. It was built on and around the remains of Moorish Ronda's main mosque (which was itself built on the site of a temple to Julius Caesar). With a pleasantly eclectic interior that features some art with unusually modern flair, and a good audioguide to explain it all, it's worth a visit.

Cost and Hours: €4, includes audioguide, daily April-Sept 10:00-20:00, March and Oct 10:00-19:00, Nov-Feb 10:00-18:00, closed Sun 12:30-14:00 for Mass, Plaza Duquesa de Parcent in the old town.

Visiting the Church: In the room where you purchase your ticket, look for the only surviving mosque **prayer niche** (that's a mirror; look back at the actual mihrab, which faces not Mecca, but Gibraltar—where you'd travel to get to Mecca). Partially destroyed by an earthquake, the reconstruction of the church resulted in the Moorish/Gothic/Renaissance/Baroque fusion (or confusion) you see today.

The front of the church interior is dominated by a magnificent Baroque **high altar** with the standard statue of the *Immaculate Conception* in the center. The even more ornate chapel directly to the right is a good example of Churrigueresque architecture, a kind of Spanish Rococo in which decoration obliterates the architecture—notice that you can hardly make out the souped-up columns. This chapel's fancy decor provides a frame for an artistic highlight of the town, the "Virgin of the Ultimate Sorrow." The big fresco of St. Christopher with Baby Jesus on his shoulders (on the left, where you entered) shows the patron saint both of Ronda and of travelers.

Facing the altar is an elaborately carved **choir** with a wall of modern bronze reliefs depicting scenes from the life of the Virgin Mary. Similar to the Via Crucis (Way of the Cross), this is the Via Lucis (Way of the Light), with 14 stations (such as #13—the Immaculate Conception, and #14—Mary's assumption into heaven) that serve as a worship  aid to devout Catholics. The centerpiece is Mary as the light of the world (with the moon, stars, and sun around her).

Head to the left around the choir, noticing the bright **paintings** along the wall by French artist Raymonde Pagegie, who gave sacred scenes a fresh twist—like the Last Supper attended by female servants, or the scene of Judgment Day, when the four horsemen of the apocalypse pause to adore the Lamb of God.

The **treasury** (at the far-right corner, with your back to the high altar) displays vestments that look curiously like matadors' brocaded outfits—appropriate for this bullfight-crazy town.

Mondragón Palace (Palacio de Mondragón)

This beautiful, originally Moorish building was erected in the 14th century, and is the legendary (but not actual) residence of Moorish kings. The building was restored in the 16th century (notice the late Gothic courtyard), and its facade dates only from the 18th century. At the entrance (free to view without a ticket) is a topographic model of Ronda, which helps you envision the fortified old town apart from the grid-like new one. The rest of the building houses Ronda's Municipal Museum, focusing on prehistory and geology. Wander through its many rooms to find the kid-friendly prehistory section, with exhibits on Neolithic toolmaking and early metallurgy (described in English). If you plan to visit the Pileta Cave, find the panels that describe the cave's formation and shape. Even if you have no interest in your ancestors or speleology, the building's architecture is impressive; linger in the two small gardens, especially the shaded one.

Cost and Hours: €3; Mon-Fri 10:00-19:00, late Oct-late March until 18:00; Sat-Sun 10:00-15:00; on Plaza Mondragón in old town, tel. 952-870-818.

Nearby: Leaving the palace, wander left a few short blocks to the nearby Plaza de María Auxiliadora for more views and a look at the two rare *pinsapos* (resembling extra-large Christmas trees) in the middle of the park; this part of Andalucía is the only region in Europe where these ancient trees still grow. For an intense workout but a picture-perfect view, find the *Puerta de los Molinos* sign and head down, down, down. (Just remember you have to walk back up, up, up.) Not for the faint of heart or in the heat of the afternoon sun, this pathway leads down to the viewpoint where windmills once stood. Photographers go crazy reproducing the most famous postcard view of Ronda—the entirety of the New Bridge. Wait until just before sunset for the best light and cooler temperatures.

Lara Museum (Museo Lara)

This discombobulated collection of Ronda's history in dusty glass cases displays everything from sewing machines to fans to old movie projectors to matador outfits (with decent English explanations). The highlight for many is the basement, with juvenile displays showing torture devices from the Inquisition and local witchcraft.

Cost and Hours: €4, audioguide-€1, daily 11:00-20:00, mid-Oct-mid-March until 19:00, Calle Arminan 29, tel. 952-871-263, www.museolara.org.

Bandit Museum (Museo del Bandolero)

This tiny museum, while not as intriguing as it sounds, has an interesting assembly of *bandolero* photos, guns, clothing, knickknacks, and old documents and newspaper clippings. The Jesse Jameses and Billy el Niños of Andalucía called this remote area home. One brand of romantic bandits fought Napoleon's army—often more effectively than the regular Spanish troops. The exhibits profile specific *bandoleros* and display books (from comics to pulp fiction) that helped romanticize these heroes of Spain's "Old West." The museum feels a bit like a tourist trap (with a well-stocked gift shop), but brief but helpful English descriptions make this a fun stop. Next door is a free 22-minute movie about *bandoleros*, (only in Spanish).

Cost and Hours: €3.75, daily May-Sept 11:00-20:00, Oct-April until 18:30, across main street below Church of Santa María la Mayor at Calle Armiñan 65, tel. 952-877-785, www.museobandolero.com.

▲Joaquín Peinado Museum (Museo Joaquín Peinado)

Housed in an old palace, this fresh museum features an impressively large professional overview of the life's work of

Joaquín Peinado (1898-1975), a Ronda native and pal of Picasso. Because Franco killed creativity in Spain for much of the last century, nearly all of Peinado's creative work was done in Paris. His style evolved through the big "isms" of the 20th century, ranging from Expressionist to Cubist, and even to erotic. While Peinado's works seem a bit derivative, perhaps that's understandable as he was friends with one of the art world's biggest talents. The nine-minute movie that kicks it off is only in Spanish, though there are good English explanations throughout the museum. You'll have an interesting modern-art experience here, without the crowds of Madrid's museums. It's fun to be exposed to a lesser-known but very talented artist in his hometown.

Cost and Hours: €4, Mon-Fri 10:00-17:00, Sat 10:00-15:00, closed Sun, Plaza del Gigante, tel. 952-871-585, www.museojoaquinpeinado.com.

Walk Through Old Town to Bottom of Gorge

From the New Bridge you can descend down Cuesta de Santo Domingo (crossing the bridge from the new town into the old, take the first left at the former Dominican Church, once the headquarters of the Inquisition in Ronda) into a world of

whitewashed houses, tiny grilled balconies, and winding lanes—
the old town.

A couple of blocks steeply downhill (on the left), you'll see the
House of the Moorish King (Casa del Rey Moro). It was never the
home of any king; it was given its fictitious name by the grandson
of President McKinley, who once lived here. It offers visitors entry
to the fine "Moorish-Hispanic" belle époque garden, designed in
1912 by a French landscape architect (the house interior is not open
to visitors). Follow signs to the "Mine," an exhausting series of 280
slick, dark, and narrow stairs (like climbing down and then up a
20-story building) leading to the floor of the gorge. The Moors cut
this zigzag staircase into the wall of the gorge in the 14th century
to access water when under siege, then used Spanish slaves to haul
water up to the thirsty town (€4, generally daily 10:00-20:00).

Fifty yards downhill from the garden is the **Palace of the
Marquis of Salvatierra** (Palacio del Marqués de Salvatierra,
closed to public). As part of the "distribution" following the
Reconquista here in 1485, the Spanish king gave this grand house
to the Salvatierra family (who live here to this day). The facade is
rich in colonial symbolism from Spanish America—note the pre-
Columbian-looking characters (four Peruvian Indians) flanking
the balcony above the door and below the family coat of arms.

Just below the palace, stop to enjoy the view terrace. Look
below. A series of square vats are all that remains of the old
tanneries. There are two old bridges, with the Arab Baths just to
the right, and at the edge of town is a rectangular horse-training
area.

Twenty steps farther down, you'll pass through the Philip V
gate, for centuries the main gate to the fortified city of Ronda.

Continuing downhill, you come
to the **Old Bridge** (Puente
Viejo), rebuilt in 1616 upon
the ruins of an Arabic bridge.
Enjoy the views from the bridge
(but don't cross it yet), then
continue down the old stairs.
From the base of the staircase,
look back up to glimpse some
of the surviving highly fortified Moorish city walls. You've now
reached the oldest bridge in Ronda, the Arab Bridge (also called
the San Miguel Bridge). Sometimes given the misnomer of Puente
Romano (Roman Bridge), it was more likely built long after the
Romans left. For centuries, this was the main gate to the fortified
city. In Moorish times, you'd purify both your body and your soul
here before entering the city, so just outside the gate was a little

mosque (now the ruined chapel) and the Arab Baths.

The **Arab Baths** (Baños Árabes), worth ▲, are evocative ruins that warrant a quick look. They were located half underground to

maintain the temperature and served by a horse-powered water tower. You can still see the top of the shaft (30 yards beyond the bath rooftops, near a cyprus tree, connected to the baths by an aqueduct). Water was hoisted from the river below to the aqueduct by ceramic containers that were attached to a belt powered by a horse walking in circles. Inside, two of the original eight columns scavenged from the Roman ruins still support brick vaulting. A delightful 10-minute video brings the entire complex to life—Spanish and English versions run alternately (€3, free on Mon; open Mon-Fri 10:00-19:00, Nov-April until 18:00; Sat-Sun 10:00-15:00 year-round; sometimes open later in summer, call ahead before making the trip, mobile 656-950-937).

From here, hike back to the new town along the other side of the gorge: Return to the bridge just uphill. Cross it and take the stairs immediately on the left, which lead scenically along the gorge up to the New Bridge.

Near Ronda: Pileta Cave

The Pileta Cave (Cueva de la Pileta) offers Spain's most intimate look at Neolithic and Paleolithic paintings that are up to 25,000 years old. Set in a dramatic, rocky limestone ridge at the eastern edge of Sierra de Grazalema Natural Park, Pileta Cave is 14 miles from Ronda, past the town of Benaoján, at the end of an access road. It's particularly handy if you're driving between Ronda and Grazalema.

Cost and Hours: €8, one-hour tours generally depart daily at 13:00 & 16:00, additional tours go between 10:00-13:00 and 16:00-18:00 if enough people gather (Nov-mid-April until 17:00), closing times indicate last tour, €10 guidebook, no photos, tel. 952-167-343, www.cuevadelapileta.org.

Getting There: It's possible to get here without wheels, but I wouldn't bother (you'd have to take the Ronda-Benaoján bus—2/day, departs at 8:30 and 13:00, 30 minutes—and then it's a 2-hour, 3-mile uphill hike). You can get from Ronda to the cave by taxi—it's about a half-hour drive on twisty roads—and have the driver wait (€60 round-trip). If you're driving, it's easy: Leave Ronda through the new part of town, and take A-374. After a few miles, passing Cueva del Gato, exit left toward Benaoján on MA-555. Go through Benaoján and follow the numerous signs to the cave. Leave nothing of value in your car.

Visiting the Cave: Farmer José Bullón and his family live down the hill from the cave, and because they strictly limit the number of visitors, Pileta's rare paintings are among the best-preserved in the world. Señor Bullón and his son lead up to 25 people at a time through the cave, which was discovered by Bullón's grandfather in 1905. Call the night before to see if there's a tour and space available at the time you want. Note that if you simply show up for the 13:00 tour, you'll risk not getting a spot—and it'll be another three hours before the next one starts. Bring a sweater and good shoes. You need a good sense of balance to take the tour. The 10-minute hike, from the parking lot up a trail with stone steps to the cave entrance, is moderately steep. Inside the cave, there are no handrails, and it can be difficult to keep your footing on the slippery, uneven floor while being led single-file, with only a lantern light illuminating the way.

Señor Bullón is a master at hurdling the language barrier. As you walk the cool half-mile, he'll spend an hour pointing out lots of black, ochre, and red drawings, which are five times as old as the Egyptian pyramids. Mostly it's just lines or patterns, but there are also horses, goats, cattle, and a rare giant fish, made from a mixture of clay and fat by finger-painting prehistoric *hombres*. The 200-foot main cavern is impressive, as are some weirdly recognizable natural formations such as the Michelin man and a Christmas tree.

Eating near the Cave: Nearby Montejaque has several good restaurants clustered around the central square.

Sleeping near the Cave: A good base for visiting Ronda and the Pileta Cave (as well as Grazalema) is **$$ Cortijo las Piletas.** Nestled at the edge of Sierra de Grazalema Natural Park (just a 15-minute drive from Ronda, with easy access from the main highway), this spacious family-run country estate has nine rooms and plenty of opportunities for swimming, hiking, bird-watching, and exploring the surrounding area. They can also arrange for biking and horseback riding (Sb-€71-76, Db-€86-92, extra bed-€15-18, includes breakfast but not tax, dinner offered some days—book in advance, mobile 605-080-295, www.cortijolaspiletas.com, info @cortijolaspiletas.com, Pablo and Elisenda). Another countryside option is **$$ Finca La Guzmana,** run by expat Brit Peter. Six beautifully appointed pastel rooms surround an open patio at this renovated estate house. Bird-watching, swimming, and trekking are possible (Db-€75-80, includes breakfast, mobile 600-006-305, www.laguzmana.com, info@laguzmana.com).

Sleeping in Ronda

Ronda has plenty of reasonably priced, decent-value accommodations. It's crowded only during Holy Week (the week leading up to Easter) and the first week of September (for bullfighting season). Most of my recommendations are in the new town, a short stroll from the New Bridge and about a 10-minute walk from the train station. In the cheaper places, ask for a room with a *ventana* (window) to avoid the few interior rooms. Breakfast is usually not included.

In the Old Town

Clearly the best options in town, these hotels are worth reserving early. The first two are right in the heart of the Old Town, while the Alavera de los Baños is a steep 15-to-20-minute hike below, but still easily walkable to all the sights (if you're in good shape) and in a bucolic setting.

$$ Hotel San Gabriel has 22 pleasant rooms, a kind staff, public rooms filled with art and poetry books, a cozy wine cellar, and a fine garden terrace. It's a large 1736 townhouse, once the family's home, that's been converted to a characteristic hotel, marinated in history. If you're a cinephile, kick back in the charming TV room—with seats from Ronda's old theater and a collection of DVD classics—then head to the breakfast room to check out photos of big movie stars (and, ahem, bespectacled travel writers) who have stayed here (Sb-€66, Db-€88, bigger superior Db-€98, Db junior suite-€115, lavish honeymoon suite-€150, breakfast-€5, air-con, incognito elevator, guest computer, Wi-Fi, double-park in front and they'll direct you to a €9/day parking spot, follow signs on the main street of old town to Calle Marqués de Moctezuma 19, tel. 952-190-392, www.hotelsangabriel.com, info@hotelsangabriel.com, family-run by José Manuel and Ana).

$$ Hotel Ronda provides an interesting mix of minimalist and traditional Spanish decor in this refurbished mansion, which is both quiet and homey. Although its five rooms are without views, the small, lovely rooftop deck overlooks the town (Sb-€55, Db-€70, additional bed-€22, no breakfast, air-con, Wi-Fi, Ruedo Doña Elvira 12, tel. 952-872-232, www.hotelronda.net, laraln@telefonica.net, some English spoken).

$$ Alavera de los Baños, a delightful oasis located next to ancient Moorish baths at the bottom of the hill, has nine small rooms and big inviting public places, with appropriately Moorish decor. This hotel offers a swimming pool, a peaceful Arabic garden, and a selection of sandwiches for lunch. The artistic ambience urges, "Relax!" You're literally in the countryside, with sheep and horses outside near the garden (Sb-€60-70, Db-€85-

97, Db with terrace-€95-107, includes breakfast, Wi-Fi in some rooms and lobby, free and easy parking, closed Jan, steeply below the heart of town at Calle Molino de Alarcón, tel. 952-879-143, www.alaveradelosbanos.com, alavera@telefonica.net, well-run by personable Christian and Inma).

In the New Town

More convenient than charming (except the Hotel Enfrente Arte Ronda—in a class all its own), these hotels put you in the thriving new town.

$$$ Hotel Catalonia Reina Victoria hangs royally over the gorge at the edge of town and has a marvelous view—Hemingway loved it. Its 89 renovated rooms are sleek and modern but lack character. Rooms with a gorge view cost €15 more—and they're worth it (Sb-€97-117, Db-€115-156, breakfast-€13, air-con, elevator, Wi-Fi in lobby, pool, parking-€15/day, 10-minute walk from city center; easy to miss—look for intersection of Avenida Victoria and Calle Jerez, Jerez 25; tel. 952-871-240, www.hoteles-catalonia.com, reinavictoria@hoteles-catalonia.com).

$$ Hotel Enfrente Arte Ronda, on the edge of things a steep 10-to-15-minute walk below the heart of the new town, is relaxed, funky, and friendly. The 12 rooms are spacious and exotically decorated, but dimly lit. It features a sprawling maze of exuberantly decorated public spaces, including a peaceful bamboo garden, game and reading room, small swimming pool, sauna, and terraces with sweeping countryside views. Guests can help themselves to free drinks from the self-service bar. This one-of-a-kind place is in all the guidebooks, so reserve early—Madonna even stayed here once (Db-€80-105, extra bed-€28-40, includes buffet breakfast, air-con, elevator, Wi-Fi in lobby, Real 40, tel. 952-879-088, www.enfrentearte.com, reservations@enfrentearte.com).

$$ Hotel Don Miguel, facing the gorge just left of the bridge, has disinterested staff and all the charm of a tour-group hotel, but it couldn't be more central. Of its 30 sparse but comfortable rooms, 20 have gorgeous views at no extra cost. Street rooms come with a little noise (Sb-€59-70, Db-€91-108, Tb-€110-135, free buffet breakfast, 10 percent discount if you book direct via email and mention this book, air-con, elevator, Wi-Fi in lobby, parking garage a block away-€12/day, Plaza de España 4, tel. 952-877-722, www.dmiguel.com, reservas@dmiguel.com).

$$ Hotel El Tajo has 33 decent, quiet rooms—once you get past the tacky faux-stone Moorish decoration in the foyer (Sb-€39, Db-€55, breakfast-€6, air-con, elevator, Wi-Fi in some rooms, parking-€10/day, Calle Cruz Verde 7, a half-block off the pedestrian street, tel. 952-874-040, www.hoteleltajo.com, reservas@hoteleltajo.com).

$$ Hotel San Francisco offers 27 small, nicely decorated rooms a block off the main pedestrian street in the town center (Sb-€35-40, Db-€50-65, Tb-€70-80, breakfast-€3.50, air-con, elevator, parking-€8.50/day, María Cabrera 20, tel. 952-873-299, hotelronda@terra.es).

$ Hotel Royal has a dreary reception and 29 clean, spacious, simple rooms—many on the main street that runs between the bullring and bridge. Thick glass keeps out most of the noise, while the tree-lined Alameda del Tajo park across the street is a treat. Some rooms and hallways are dimly lit (Sb-€30-38, Db-€40-50, Tb-€55-60, breakfast-€4, air-con, Wi-Fi, parking-€10/day, 3 blocks off Plaza de España at Calle Virgen de la Paz 42, tel. 952-871-141, www.ronda.net/usuar/hotelroyal, hroyal@ronda.net).

$ Hotel Andalucía has 12 clean, comfortable, and recently renovated rooms immediately across the street from the train station (Sb-€25, Db-€35, Tb-€50, breakfast-€2, air-con and TV in all rooms, Wi-Fi, easy street parking or €6/day in nearby garage, Martínez Astein 19, tel. 952-875-450, www.hotel-andalucia.net, info@hotel-andalucia.net).

$ Hostal Doña Carmen, a basic cheapie, rents 32 bare-bones rooms in two sections. The rooms sharing a shower down the hall, with no air-con or TV, are especially reasonable (S-€17, Sb-€25, D-€28, Db-€45, T-€40, Tb-€55, no breakfast, air-con and TV only in rooms with bath, Wi-Fi in lobby, Calle Naranja 28, tel. 952-871-994, www.hostaldonacarmen.com, mturrillo@yahoo.es).

Near Ronda, in Júzcar

The village of Júzcar is about 15 miles south of Ronda. In 2011 Júzcar's white facades were painted "Smurf blue" to promote a Smurfs movie. When it came time to restore the buildings to their normal white color, the villagers realized they weren't eager to lose the tourist traffic the stunt had brought in—and voted to leave their town blue (for the time being, at least).

$$ Hotel Bandolero is for nature lovers. Settle into the rustic rooms, go hiking and bird-watching, or take a dip in the pool (Sb-€35-49, standard Db-€59-96, superior Db-€69-106, Db suite-€80-117, higher prices are for half-board, Wi-Fi, restaurant with Cordon Bleu chef, Avenida Havaral 43, Júzcar, tel. 952-183-660, www.hotelbandolero.com, reservas@hotelbandolero.com, David).

Eating in Ronda

Plaza del Socorro, a block in front of the bullring, is an energetic scene, bustling with tourists and local families enjoying the square and its restaurants. The pedestrian-only **Calle Nueva** is lined with hardworking eateries. To enjoy a drink or a light meal with the

Ronda Restaurants

TO
PILETA CAVE,
ARCOS &
SEVILLA

BUS
STATION

TO TRAIN STATION

200 YARDS
200 METERS

Ⓣ Taxi Stand
View
Ⓟ Parking

CALLE JEREZ

SAN JOSÉ

POZO

ANDALUCÍA

MADRID

MONTE LAURIA

PLAZA
MERCED

INFANTES

NARANJA

ALMENDRA

CRUZ VERDE

❸

WC

ALAMEDA
DEL
TAJO

Post

❶

CRZ DE LA PAZ

ESPINEL

Ⓟ

PLAZA DEL
SOCORRO

PLAZA
C. ABELA

M. CABRERA

MERCADILLO

CORTES

❷

BULLRING

❿

❶

NUEVA

❼

❻

QUARTER

PEÑAS

ⓘ

❾

PLAZA
DE
ESPAÑA

❹
VILLANUEVA

❺

LOS REMEDIOS

CANTOS

REAL

PARADOR

NEW
BRIDGE

❶❶

OLD
BRIDGE

GUADALEVÍN RIVER

TRAIL TO
PUERTA DE
LOS MOLINOS

TENORIO

ARMIÑÁN

S. DOMINGO

M. SALV.

ARAB
BRIDGE

ARAB
BATHS
MUSEUM

MOORISH

PLAZA
DE MARÍA
AUXILIADORA

QUARTER

CITY
WALL

MONDRAGÓN
PALACE

SANTA MARÍA
LA MAYOR

ARMIÑÁN

ⓘ

BANDOLERO MUSEUM

PLAZA DUQUESA
DE PARCENT

CITY
HALL

TO
ALMOCÁBAR GATE,
COSTA DEL SOL &

❽

WHITE HILL TOWNS

❶ Confitería Daver (2)
❷ Alameda Market
❸ Día Supermarket
❹ Tragatapas
❺ Bar Lechuguita
❻ Café & Bar Faustino
❼ La Tradicional

❽ To Bar-Restaurante Almocábar,
   La Cepa & Bodega San Francisco
❾ Restaurante Mirador de la
   Espinela
❿ Restaurante Pedro Romero
❶❶ Restaurante Casa Santa Pola

best view in town, consider the terraces of Hotel Don Miguel just under the bridge. For coffee and pastries, locals like the elegant little **Confiteria Daver** (café open daily 8:00-20:30, take-away until 21:00, two locations—Calle Virgen de los Remedios 6 and Calle Padre Mariano Soubiron 8). Picnic shoppers find the **Alameda Market** (Mon-Sat 8:30-21:00, Sun 9:00-15:00, Calle Virgen de La Paz 23) conveniently located next to Alameda del Tajo park, which has benches and a WC. The **Día** supermarket, opposite Hotel El Tajo, is also very central (Mon-Sat 9:15-21:15, closed Sun, Calle Cruz Verde 18).

Tapas in the City Center

Ronda has a fine tapas scene. You won't get a free tapa with your drink as in some other Spanish towns, but these bars have accessible tapas lists, and they serve bigger plates. Each of the following places could make a fine solo destination for a meal, but they're close enough that you can easily try more than one.

Tragatapas, the accessible little brother of the acclaimed gourmet Restaurante Tragabuches, serves super-creative and always-tasty tapas in a stainless-steel minimalist bar. There's just a handful of tall tiny tables and stools inside, with patio seating on the pedestrian street, and an enticing blackboard of the day's specials. If you want to sample Andalusian gourmet (e.g., a handful of €1.70-3 tapas such as asparagus on a stick sprinkled with manchego cheese grated coconut-style) without going broke, this is the place to do it (also €6-12 larger plates, daily 12:00-17:00 & 20:00-24:00, Calle Nueva 4, tel. 952-877-209).

Bar Lechuguita, a hit with older locals early and younger ones later, serves a long and tasty list of tapas for a good price. Rip off a tapas inventory sheet and mark which ones you want (most cost €0.80; €5 plates also available). Be adventurous and don't miss the bar's namesake, *Lechuguita* (#15, a wedge of lettuce with vinegar, garlic, and a secret ingredient). The order-form routine makes it easy to communicate and get exactly what you like, plus you know the exact price (Mon-Sat 13:00-15:15 & 20:15-23:30, closed Sun, no chairs or tables, just a bar and tiny stand-up ledges, Calle Virgen de los Remedios 35).

Café & Bar Faustino is a place Brueghel would paint—a festival of eating with a fun and accessible menu that works both at the bar and at tables. The atmosphere makes you want to stay, and the selection makes you wish your appetite was even bigger (lots of €1 tapas, €3 sandwiches, €5-8 *raciones,* Tue-Sun 12:00-24:00, closed Mon, just off Plaza Carmen Abela at Santa Cecilia 4, tel. 952-190-307).

La Tradicional, run by Elias (from Casa María—described below), serves up €1.20 tapas and €4-11 *raciones* with an emphasis

WHITE HILL TOWNS

on meats (Thu-Tue 12:00-17:00 & 18:30-24:00, closed Wed, Las Tiendas 2, tel. 952-875-683).

Outside the Almocábar Gate

To entirely leave the quaint old town and bustling city center with all of its tourists and grand gorge views, hike 10 minutes out to the far end of the old town, past City Hall, to a big workaday square that goes about life as if the world didn't exist outside Andalucía.

Bar-Restaurante Almocábar is a favorite eatery for many Ronda locals. Its restaurant—a cozy eight-table room with Moorish tiles and a window to the kitchen—serves up tasty, creative, well-presented meals from a menu that's well-described in English (plus a handwritten list of the day's specials). Many opt for the good €8-15 salads—rare in Spain. At the busy bar up front, you can order anything from the dining room menu, or choose from the list of €1.50-2 tapas (€5-15 starters, €12-20 main dishes, closed Tue, Calle Ruedo Alameda 5, tel. 952-875-977).

La Cepa (formerly Casa María) is a small tapas bar offering typical Andalusian fare in a homey setting. In summer, their tables spill out onto the plaza (€1-3 tapas, €7-9 *raciones*, Wed-Mon 12:30-24:00, closed Tue, facing Plaza Ruedo Alameda at #27, tel. 676-126-822).

Bodega San Francisco is a rustic bar with tables upstairs and a homey restaurant across the street, offering an accessible list of €4-9 *raciones* and €1 tapas, as well as serious plates and big splittable portions (same menu in bar and restaurant). This place is understandably a neighborhood favorite (closed Thu, Ruedo de Alameda 32, tel. 952-878-162).

Dining in the City Center

Ronda is littered with upscale-seeming restaurants that toe the delicate line between a good dinner spot and a tourist trap. While (admittedly) none of the following could be called "untouristy," they each offer decent food with either a striking setting, a venerable ambience, or both. For a more authentic dining experience, do a tapas crawl through town, or head for the far more characteristic eateries just outside the Almocábar Gate (both described above).

Restaurante Mirador de la Espinela (locals often refer to it by its former name, El Escudero) serves lovingly presented Spanish food with a posh modern touch in a crystal- and cream-colored dining room or on a terrace overlooking the gorge (€12-18.50 fixed-price meals, €29 gourmet tasting meals, €7-13 starters, €16-20 main dishes, daily 12:00-22:30 except closed Sun eve in summer, behind bullring at Paseo Blas Infante 1, tel. 952-871-367).

Restaurante Pedro Romero, though touristy and overpriced, is a venerable institution in Ronda. Assuming a shrine to bullfighting draped in *el toro* memorabilia doesn't ruin your appetite, it gets good reviews. Rub elbows with the local bullfighters or dine with the likes (well, photographic likenesses) of Orson Welles, Ernest Hemingway, and Francisco Franco (€16 and 25 fixed-price meals, €7-12 starters, €16-20 main dishes, daily 12:00-16:00 & 19:30-23:00, air-con, across the street from bullring at Calle Virgen de la Paz 18, tel. 952-871-110).

Restaurante Casa Santa Pola offers gourmet versions of traditional food with friendly, professional service, with several small dining rooms and a delightful terrace perched on the side of the gorge—worth reserving ahead (€12-14 starters, €16-24 main dishes; good oxtail stew, roasted lamb, and honey-tempura eggplant; daily 12:30-16:30 & 19:00-22:30; after crossing New Bridge from the bullring, take the first left downhill and you'll see the sign, Calle Santo Domingo 3; tel. 952-879-208, www .rsantapola.com).

Ronda Connections

Note that some destinations are linked with Ronda by both bus and train. Direct bus service to other hill towns can be sparse (as few as one per day), and train service usually involves a transfer in Bobadilla. It's worth spending a few minutes in the bus or train station on arrival to plan your departure. Your options improve from major transportation hubs such as Málaga.

From Ronda by Bus to: Algeciras (1/day, 2.75 hours, Comes), **La Línea/Gibraltar** (no direct bus, transfer in Algeciras; Algeciras to Gibraltar—2/hour, 45 minutes, can buy ticket on bus), **Arcos** (1-2/day, 2 hours, Comes), **Jerez** (2/day, 2.5-3 hours, Comes), **Grazalema** (2/day, 45 minutes, Los Amarillos), **Zahara** (2/day, Mon-Fri only, 45 minutes, Comes), **Sevilla** (8/day, 2-2.5 hours, fewer on weekends, some via Villamartín, Los Amarillos; also see trains, next page), **Málaga** (*directo* 10/day Mon-Fri, 6/day Sat-Sun, 1.75-2 hours, Los Amarillos; *ruta* 2/day, 4 hours, Portillo; access other Costa del Sol points from Málaga), **Marbella** (2/day, 1.25 hours, Los Amarillos), **Fuengirola** (2/day, 1.75 hours, Los Amarillos), **Nerja** (4 hours, transfer in Málaga; can take train or bus from Ronda to Málaga, bus is better). If traveling to **Córdoba,** it's easiest to take the train since there are no direct buses (see below). **Bus info:** Los Amarillos (tel. 902-210-317, www.losamarillos.es), Portillo (tel. 902-450-550, http://portillo .avanzabus.com), and Comes (tel. 956-291-168, www.tgcomes .es). It's best to just drop by and compare schedules (at the station on Plaza Concepción García Redondo, several blocks from train station), or pick up a bus timetable from the city TI.

By Train to: **Algeciras** (5-6/day, 1.5-2 hours), **Bobadilla** (4/day, 1 hour), **Málaga** (1/day, 2 hours, more with transfer in Bobadilla), **Sevilla** (5/day, 3-4 hours, transfer in Bobadilla, Antequera, or Cordboa), **Granada** (3/day, 2.5 hours), **Córdoba** (2/day direct, 1.75 hours; more with transfer in Bobadilla or Antequera, 3.75 hours), **Madrid** (2/day, 4 hours). Transfers are a snap and time-coordinated in Bobadilla; with four trains arriving and departing simultaneously, double-check that you're jumping on the right one. **Train info:** tel. 902-320-320, www.renfe.com.

Zahara and Grazalema

There are plenty of interesting hill towns to explore. Public transportation is frustrating, so I'd do these towns only by car. Useful information on the area is rare. Fortunately, a good map, the tourist brochure (pick it up in Sevilla or Ronda), and a spirit of adventure work fine.

Along with Arcos, Zahara de la Sierra and Grazalema are my favorite white villages. While Grazalema is a better overnight stop, Zahara is a delight for those who want to hear only the sounds of the wind, birds, and elderly footsteps on ancient cobbles.

Zahara de la Sierra

This tiny town in a tingly setting under a Moorish castle (worth ▲ and the climb) has a spectacular view over a turquoise lake. While the big church facing the town square is considered one of the richest in the area, the smaller church has the most-loved statue. The Virgin of Dolores is Zahara's answer to Sevilla's Virgin of Macarena (and is similarly paraded through town during Holy Week).

The **TI** is located in the main plaza (Mon-Fri 9:00-14:00 & 16:00-19:00, Sat-Sun 10:00-12:30, gift shop, Plaza del Rey 3, tel. 956-123-114). It has a single computer with very slow Internet access (€1.50, one-hour limit). Upstairs from the TI are Spanish-only displays about the flora and fauna of nearby Sierra de Grazalema Natural Park.

Drivers can park for free in the main plaza, or continue up the hill to the parking lot at the base of the castle, just past the cliffside **$$ Hotel Arco de la Villa,** the town's only real hotel (16 small modern rooms, Sb-€36, Db-€60, breakfast-€3, tel. 956-123-230,

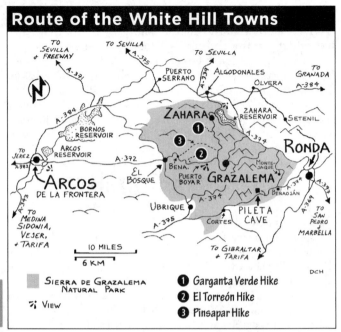

Route of the White Hill Towns

TO SEVILLA & FREEWAY

TO SEVILLA

TO SEVILLA

TO GRANADA

A-371

A-375

A-384

PUERTO SERRANO

ALGODONALES

OLVERA

A-384

ZAHARA

ZAHARA RESERVOIR

SETENIL

BORNOS RESERVOIR

ARCOS RESERVOIR

TO JEREZ

A-382

A-384

A-372

A-374

RONDA

MONTE-JAQUE

A-374

A-373

A-369

TO SAN PEDRO & MARBELLA

EL BOSQUE

BENA.

PUERTO BOYAR

GRAZALEMA

BENAOJÁN

ARCOS DE LA FRONTERA

TO MEDINA SIDONIA, VEJER, & TARIFA

UBRIQUE

CORTES

PILETA CAVE

A-375

A-374

TO GIBRALTAR & TARIFA

10 MILES

6 KM

SIERRA DE GRAZALEMA NATURAL PARK

VIEW

❶ Garganta Verde Hike
❷ El Torreón Hike
❸ Pinsapar Hike

DCH

www.tugasa.com, arco-de-la-villa@tugasa.com). The street that connects both churches, Calle de San Juan, is lined with busy tapas bars and restaurants.

Sights in Zahara: During Moorish times, Zahara lay within the fortified castle walls above today's town. It was considered the gateway to Granada and a stra- tegic stronghold for the Moors by the Christian forces of the Reconquista. Locals tell of the Spanish conquest of the Moors' castle (in 1482) as if it happened yesterday: After the Spanish failed several times to seize the castle, a clever Spanish soldier

noticed that the Moorish sentinel would check if any attackers were hiding behind a particular section of the wall by tossing a rock and setting the pigeons in flight. If they flew, the sentinel figured there was no danger. One night a Spaniard hid there with a bag of pigeons and let them fly when the sentinel tossed his rock. Upon seeing the birds, the guard assumed he was clear to enjoy a snooze. The clever Spaniard then scaled the wall and opened the door to let in his troops, who conquered the castle. Ten years later Granada fell, the Muslims were back in Africa, and the Reconquista was complete.

It's a fun climb up to the remains of the **castle** (free, tower always open). Start at the paved path across from the town's upper parking lot. It's a moderately easy 15-minute hike past some Roman ruins and along a cactus-rimmed ridge to the top, where you can enter the tower. Use your penlight or feel along the stairway to reach the roof, and enjoy spectacular views from this almost impossibly high perch far above the town. As you pretend you're defending the tower, realize that what you see is quite different from what the Moors saw: The huge lake dominating the valley is a reservoir—before 1991, the valley had only a tiny stream.

Grazalema

A beautiful postcard-pretty hill town, Grazalema offers a royal balcony for a memorable picnic, a square where you can watch old-

timers playing cards, and plenty of quiet whitewashed streets and shops to explore. Situated within Sierra de Grazalema Natural Park, Grazalema is graced with lots of scenery and greenery. Driving here from Ronda on A-372, you pass through a beautiful park-like grove of cork trees. While the park is known as the rainiest place in Spain, the clouds seem to wring themselves out before they reach the town—I've only ever had blue skies. If you want to sleep in a small Andalusian hill town, this is a good choice.

The **TI** is located at the car park at the cliffside viewpoint, Plaza de los Asomaderos. It has WCs and a small gift shop featuring locally produced products (daily 10:00-14:00 & 15:30-19:00, tel. 956-132-052, www.grazalemaguide.com). Enjoy the view, then wander into the town.

A tiny lane leads a block from the center rear of the square to Plaza de Andalucía (filled by the tables of a commotion of tapas bars). Shops sell the town's beautiful and famous handmade wool blankets and good-quality leather items from nearby Ubrique. A block farther uphill takes you to the main square with the church, Plaza de España. A coffee on the square here is a joy. Small lanes stretch from here into the rest of the town.

Popular with Spaniards, the town makes a good home base for exploring Sierra de Grazalema Natural Park—famous for its spectacularly rugged limestone landscape of cliffs, caves, and gorges (see sidebar). For outdoor gear and adventures, including hiking, caving, and canoeing, contact **Horizon** (summer

Sierra de Grazalema Natural Park

Sierra de Grazalema Natural Park is unique for its rugged mountain landscape and its relatively rainy climate, which support a wide variety of animals and plant life.  One-third of Spain's flowers bloom here, wild ibex (mountain goats) climb the steep slopes, and Europe's largest colony of griffon vultures soars high above. The park's plant poster child is the *pinsapo,* a type of fir tree left over from the last Ice Age (the park is one of the few places in Europe where these trees still grow). About a fifth of the 200-square-mile park is a special reserve area, where access is limited, largely to protect these rare trees from forest fires. Hikers need to get (free) permits for most trails in the reserve.

Zahara, Grazalema, and the Pileta Cave all fall within the park boundaries. Drivers will get an eyeful of scenery just passing through the park on their way to these sights.

If you want to more fully experience the park—by hiking, caving, canoeing, kayaking, or horseback riding—the easiest way is to take a tour from Zahara Catur (in Zahara, www.zahara catur.com) or Horizon (in Grazalema, www.horizonaventura .com). They also handle the permit procedure for you.

If you want to hike in the park on your own, you'll need a park map, a permit for most hikes within the reserve area (see hiking permit procedure), and a car to get to the trailhead. From July through September, you may have to go with a guided

Tue-Sat 9:00-14:00 & 17:00-20:00, rest of year Tue-Sat 9:00-14:00 & 16:00-19:00, closed Sun-Mon year-round, off Plaza de España at Corrales Terceros 29, tel. 956-132-363, mobile 655-934-565, www.horizonaventura.com).

Sleeping in Grazalema: **$$ La Mejorana Guesthouse** is the best bet in town—if you can manage to get one of its six rooms. You won't want to leave this beautifully perched garden villa, with its royal public rooms overlooking the valley from the upper part of town (Db-€58, includes breakfast, Wi-Fi, pool, located at top of town on tiny lane below Guardia Civil headquarters at Santa Clara 6, tel. 956-132-327, mobile 649-613-272, www.lamejorana .net, info@lamejorana.net, Ana and Andres can help with local hiking options).

$$ Hotel Peñón Grande, named for a nearby mountain, is just off the main square and rents 16 comfortable business-class rooms (Sb-€38, Db-€56, extra bed-€14, air-con, Plaza group anyway, if you want to hike in the reserve (about €13/person for a half-day hike, offered by Zahara Catur and Horizon).

Popular hikes in the reserve (all requiring permits) include:

Garganta Verde: Explore a canyon with a huge open cave near vulture breeding grounds (1.5 miles each way, initially gentle hike then very steep descent, allow 4-5 hours).

El Torreón: Climb the park's highest mountain, at 5,427 feet (1.75 miles each way, steep incline to summit, allow 4-5 hours).

Pinsapar: Hike on mountain slopes forested with *pinsapo* trees (8.5 miles each way, steep climb for first third of trail then downhill, allow 6 hours).

Information: The TIs in Grazalema and Zahara sell a Spanish-only park guide with descriptions and trail maps (€15).

Getting a Hiking Permit: A permit is free but required; a ranger will fine you if you don't have one. To get a permit, email, call, or visit the park office in the town of El Bosque, a gateway to the park. You can request a permit for a specific hike up to 30 days in advance. Pick up the permit in El Bosque, or have them fax it to the TI in Grazalema or Zahara (El Bosque park office hours generally Mon-Sat 10:00-14:00 & 17:00-19:00, Sun 9:00-14:00, Avenida de la Diputación, tel. 956-727-029 or 956-709-733, cv_elbosque@egmasa.es). Include the date, the number of people in your group, the hike you want to do, and your passport number (allow plenty of time for this process).

Hikes from Grazalema (No Permit Required): If you'd rather not hassle with getting a permit, or if you don't have a car to reach the trailheads, try one of several hikes that start from the town of Grazalema. You'll find descriptions in pamphlets available at the Grazalema TI or Horizon (€1).

Pequeña 7, tel. 956-132-434, www.hotelgrazalema.com, hotel@hotelgrazalema.com).

$ Casa de Las Piedras, just a block from the main square, has 16 comfortable rooms with private baths (Sb-€35, Db-€48); 2 other rooms that share a single bathroom and have access to a kitchen and washing machine (D-€42); and 14 super-cheap basic rooms that share 5 bathrooms (D-€28, no access to kitchen or washing machine). The beds feature the town's locally made wool blankets (10 percent discount with this book and two-night minimum stay, buffet breakfast-€6, Calle Las Piedras 32, tel. 956-132-014, mobile 627-415-047, www.casadelaspiedras.es, reservas@casadelaspiedras.net, Caty and Rafi.

Eating in Grazalema: Grazalema offers many restaurants and bars. Tiny Plaza de Andalucía has several good bars for tapas with umbrella-flecked tables spilling across the square, including **Zulema** (big salads), **La Posadilla,** and **La Cidulia.**

WHITE HILL TOWNS

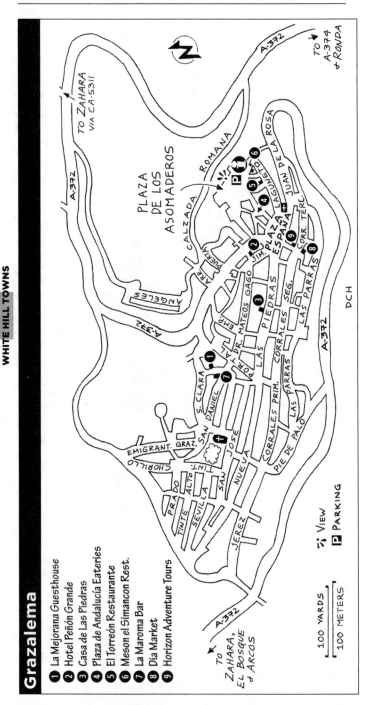

Grazalema

1. La Mejorana Guesthouse
2. Hotel Peñón Grande
3. Casa de Las Piedras
4. Plaza de Andalucía Eateries
5. El Torreón Restaurante
6. Meson el Simancon Rest.
7. La Maroma Bar
8. Dia Market
9. Horizon Adventure Tours

The recommended **Casa de Las Piedras** (earlier) has an adjacent restaurant (same name) that offers tapas, fixed-price meals, and several vegetarian options. To pick up picnic supplies, head to the **Día** supermarket (Mon-Sat 9:00-14:00 & 17:00-21:00, Sun 9:00-14:00, on Calle Corrales Terceros 3).

El Torreón specializes in local lamb and game dishes, and also has many vegetarian options (closed Wed, Calle Agua 44, tel. 956-132-313).

Meson el Simancon serves well-presented cuisine typical of the region in a romantic setting. While a bit more expensive, it's considered the best restaurant in town (closed Tue, facing Plaza de los Asomaderos and the car park, tel. 956-132-421).

La Maroma Bar serves home-cooked regional specialties, three meals a day, at affordable prices (€1.20-3 tapas, €4-8 meat and fish plates, daily 8:00 until late, Calle Santa Clara, near La Mejorana Guesthouse, tel. 617-543-756, José & María).

Grazalema Connections: **From Grazalema by Bus to: Ronda** (2/day, 45 minutes), **El Bosque** (2/day, 45 minutes). Bus service is provided by Los Amarillos (www.losamarillos.es).

Jerez

With more than 200,000 people, Jerez (officially Jerez de la Frontera) is your typical big-city mix of industry and dusty concrete suburbs, but it has a lively old center and two claims to touristic fame: horses and sherry. Jerez is ideal for a noontime visit on a weekday. See the famous horses, sip some sherry, wander through the old quarter, and swagger out.

Orientation to Jerez

Thanks to its complicated, medieval street plan, there is no easy way to feel oriented in Jerez—so ask for directions liberally.

Tourist Information

The helpful TI, on Plaza del Arenal, gives out free maps and info on the sights (June-Sept Mon-Fri 9:00-15:00 & 17:00-19:00, Sat-Sun 9:30-14:30; Oct-May Mon-Fri 8:30-15:00 & 16:00-18:30, Sat-Sun 9:00-15:00; tel. 956-338-874, www.turismojerez.com). If you're walking to see the horses, ask here for detailed directions, as the route is a bit confusing.

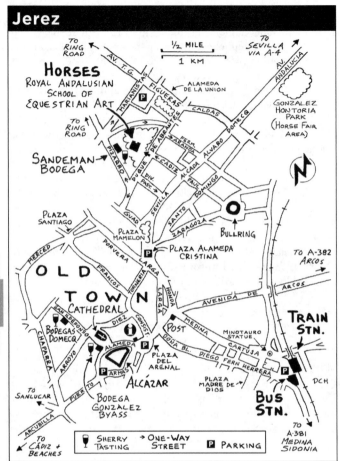

WHITE HILL TOWNS

Arrival in Jerez

By Bus or Train: The bus and train stations are located side by side, near the Plaza del Minotauro (with enormous headless statue). Unfortunately, you can't store luggage at either one. You can stow bags for free in the Royal Andalusian School's *guardaropa* (coat room) if you attend their Horse Symphony show, but only for the duration of the performance.

Cheap and easy **taxis** wait in front of the train station (€4 to TI; about €5 to the horses). It's a 20-minute **walk** from the stations to the center of town and the TI: Angle to the left across the brick plaza (in front of train station, with two black smokestacks) to find Calle Diego Fernández de Herrera. Go right, following this street faithfully for several blocks until you reach Plaza de las Angustias. Head left toward the church and continue in the same direction, straight down Calle Corredera, until you arrive at Plaza del Arenal (ringed with palm trees, with a large fountain in the center)—the TI is across the plaza on your left.

By Car from Arcos: Driving in Jerez can be frustrating. The outskirts are filled with an almost endless series of roundabouts. Continuing straight through each one will eventually bring a rail bridge into sight. Continue to follow traffic and signs to *centro ciudad*. The route may seem circuitous (it is), but it will ultimately take you into Plaza Alameda Cristina. From here, it's best to park in one of the many underground garages (at Plaza Alameda Cristina or Plaza Arenal, €1.30/hour) and catch a cab or walk. For street parking, blue-line zones require prepaid parking tickets on your dashboard (Mon-Fri 9:00-13:30 & 17:00-20:00, Sat 9:00-14:00, free on Sun and July-Aug afternoons).

Sights in Jerez

▲▲Royal Andalusian School of Equestrian Art

If you're into horses, a performance of the Royal Andalusian School of Equestrian Art (Fundación Real Escuela Andaluza del

Arte Ecuestre) is a must. Even if you're not, this is art like you've never seen.

Getting There: On **foot**, from the TI at Plaza del Arenal, it's about a half-hour walk down mostly pedestrianized shopping streets to the horses. Leave the plaza on Calle Lanceria, heading to the left of the rounded Tino La Ina Fundador building to Calle Larga. Turn right into Plaza Alameda Christina, which leads into Plaza Memelon. From here, follow the *Real Escuela de Arte Ecuestre* signs.

From the bus or train stations to the horses, it's about a €5 **taxi** ride. Taxis wait in Plaza Mamelon for the return trip.

One-way streets mean there is only one way to arrive by **car.** Follow signs to *Real Escuela de Arte Ecuestre*. Expect to make at least one wrong turn, so allow a little extra time. You'll find parking behind the school.

Horse Symphony Show

This is an equestrian ballet with choreography, purely Spanish music, and costumes from the 19th century. The stern riders and their talented, obedient steeds prance, jump, hop on their hind legs, and do-si-do in time to the music, all to the delight of an arena filled with mostly tourists and local horse aficionados.

The riders cue the horses with subtle dressage commands,

either verbally or with body movements. You'll see both purebred Spanish horses (of various colors, with long tails, calm personalities, and good jumping ability) and the larger mixed breeds (with short tails and a walking—not prancing—gait). The horses must be three years old before their three-year training begins, and most performing horses are male (stallions or geldings), since mixing the sexes brings problems.

The equestrian school is a university, open to all students in the EU, and with all coursework in Spanish. Although still a male-dominated activity, there have recently been a few female graduates. Tight-fitted mushroom hats are decorated with different stripes to show each rider's level. Professors often team with students and evaluate their performance during the show.

Cost and Hours: General seating-€21, "preference" seating-€27; 1.5-hour show runs Tue and Thu at 12:00 most of the year (also on Fri in Aug, Nov-Feb Thu only); no photos allowed in show, stables, or museum; tel. 956-318-008, tickets available online at www.realescuela.org. General seating is fine; some "preference" seats are too close for good overall views. The show explanations are in Spanish.

Training Sessions

The public can get a sneak preview at training sessions on non-performance days. Sessions can be exciting or dull, depending

on what the trainers are working on. Afterward, you can take a 1.5-hour guided tour of the stables, horses, multimedia and carriage museums, tack room, gardens, and horse health center. Sip sherry in the arena's bar to complete this Jerez experience.

Cost and Hours: €11; Mon, Wed, and Fri—except no Fri in Aug, also on Tue in Nov-Feb; arrive anytime between 10:00 and 14:00—they'll start the tour when they have a large-enough group. Tour groups crowd in at 11:00

and schedules may vary, so it's wise to call ahead.

▲▲Sherry Bodega Tours

Spain produces more than 10 million gallons per year of the fortified wine known as sherry. The name comes from English attempts to pronounce Jerez. Although sherry was traditionally the drink of England's aristocracy, today's producers are leaving the drawing-room vibe behind. Your tourist map of Jerez is speckled with *venencia* symbols, each representing a sherry bodega that offers tours and tasting. *Venencias* are specially designed ladles for

Sherry

Spanish sherry is not the sweet dessert wine sold in the States as sherry. In Spain, sherry is (most commonly) a chilled very dry fortified white wine, often served with appetizers such as tapas, seafood, and cured meats.

British traders invented the sherry-making process as a way of transporting wines so they wouldn't go bad on a long sea voyage. Some of the most popular brands (such as Sandeman and Osbourne) were begun by Brits, and for years it was a foreigners' drink. But today, sherry is typically Spanish.

Sherry is made by blending wines from different grapes and vintages, all aged together. Start with a strong, acidic wine (from grapes that grow well in the hot, chalky soil around Jerez). Mature it in large vats until a yeast crust *(flor)* forms on the surface, protecting the wine from the air. Then fortify it with distilled alcohol.

Next comes sherry-making's distinct *solera* process. Pour the young fortified wine into the top barrel of a unique contraption—a stack of oak barrels called a *criadera*. Every year, one-third of the oldest sherry (in the barrels on the ground level) is bottled. To replace it, one-third of the sherry in the barrel above is poured in, and so on. This continues until the top barrel is one-third empty, waiting to be filled with the new year's vintage.

Fino is the most popular type of sherry (and the most different from Americans' expectations)—white, dry, and chilled. The best-selling commercial brand of *fino* is Tío Pepe; *manzanilla* is a regional variation of *fino,* as is *montilla* from Córdoba. Darker-colored and sometimes sweeter varieties of sherry include *amontillado* and *oloroso.* And yes, Spain also produces the thick, sweet cream sherries served as dessert wines. A good raisin-y, syrupy-sweet variety is Pedro Ximénez, made from sun-dried grapes of the same name.

dipping inside the sherry barrel, breaking through the yeast layer, and getting to the good stuff.

Sandeman

Just around the corner from the horse school is the venerable Sandeman winery, founded in 1790 and the longtime choice of English royalty. This tour is the aficionado's choice for its knowledgeable guides and their quality explanations of the process. Each stage is explained in detail, with visual examples of *flor* (the yeast crust) in backlit barrels, graphs of how different blends are made,

and a quick walk-through of the bottling plant. The finale is a chance to taste three varieties. For efficiency, first see the Horse Symphony, which ends at 13:30, then walk to Sandeman's for the next English tour.

Cost and Hours: €7 for regular sherries, up to €21 for rare sherries, €7.50 adds tapas to the tasting, tour/tasting lasts 1-1.5 hours; English tours Mon, Wed, and Fri at 11:30, 12:30, and 13:30 plus April-Oct also at 14:30; Tue and Thu at 10:30, 12:00, 13:00, and 14:00; Sat by appointment only, closed Sun; reservations not required, tel. 665-655-318, mobile 675-647-177, www.sandeman.eu.

González Byass

The makers of the famous Tío Pepe offer a tourist-friendly tour, with more pretense and less actual sherry-making on display (that's done in a new, enormous plant outside town). The tourist train through fake vineyards and a video presentation are forgettable, but the grand circle of sherry casks signed by a *Who's Who* of sherry drinkers is worthwhile. Taste two sherries at the end of the 1.5-hour tour.

Cost and Hours: €12.50, light tapas lunch with tour-€17; tours run Mon-Sat at 12:00, 13:00, 14:00, and 17:00; Sun at 13:00 and 14:00; Manuel María González 12, tel. 956-357-017, www.bodegastiopepe.com.

Other Sherry Bodegas

You'll come across many other sherry bodegas in town, including **Fundador Pedro Domecq,** located near the cathedral. This bodega is the oldest in Jerez, and the birthplace of the city's brandy. Tastings here are generous (€8, April-Oct tours run Mon-Fri hourly between 10:00-13:00 & 17:00-19:00, July-Sept also Mon-Fri at 20:00; €13 tastings with tapas are offered Tue-Wed and Sat at 14:00—call to confirm times, Calle San Ildefonso 3, tel. 956-151-152, www.bodegasfundadorpedrodomecq.com).

Alcázar

This gutted castle looks tempting, but don't bother. The €5 entry fee doesn't even include the Camera Obscura (€7 combo-ticket covers both, Mon-Fri 9:00-18:00—or until 20:00 in mid-July-mid-Sept, Sat-Sun 9:00-15:00). Its underground parking is convenient for those touring González Byass (€1.30/hour).

Jerez Connections

Jerez's bus station is shared by six bus companies, each with its own schedule. The big ones serving most southern Spain destinations are Los Amarillos (tel. 902-210-317, www.losamarillos.es), Comes (tel. 956-291-168, www.tgcomes.es), and Linesur (tel. 956-341-063, www.linesur.com). Shop around for the best departure time and most direct route. While here, clarify routes for any further bus travel you may be doing in Andalucía—especially if you're going through Arcos de la Frontera, where the ticket office is often closed. Also try the privately run www.movelia.es for bus schedules and routes.

From Jerez by Bus to: Tarifa (1/day on Algeciras route, 2 hours, more frequent with transfer in Cádiz, Comes), **Algeciras** (2/day, 2.5 hours, Comes; 6/day, fewer on weekends, 1.5 hours, Linesur), **Arcos** (hourly, 30 minutes), **Ronda** (2/day, 2.5-3 hours), **La Línea/Gibraltar** (1/day, 2.5 hours), **Sevilla** (hourly, 1-1.5 hours), **Granada** (1/day, 4.75 hours).

By Train to: Sevilla (nearly hourly, 1 hour), **Madrid** (3-4/day direct, 3.75 hours; nearly hourly with change in Sevilla, 4 hours), **Barcelona** (nearly hourly, 7-9 hours, all with change in Sevilla and/or Madrid). **Train info:** tel. 902-320-320, www.renfe.com.

Near the Hill Towns

If you're driving between Arcos and Tarifa, here are several sights to explore.

Yeguada de la Cartuja

This breeding farm, which raises Hispanic Arab horses according to traditions dating back to the 15th century, offers shows on Saturday at 11:00 (€21.50 for best seats in *tribuna* section, €15.50 for seats in the stands, Finca Fuente del Suero, Carretera Medina-El Portal, km 6.5, Jerez de la Frontera, tel. 956-162-809, www.yeguadacartuja.com). From Jerez, take the road to Medina Sidonia, then turn right in the direction of El Portal—you'll see a cement factory on your right. Drive for five minutes until you see the farm. A taxi from Jerez will cost about €15 one-way.

Medina Sidonia

This town is as whitewashed as can be, surrounding its church and hill, which is topped with castle ruins. I never drive through here without a coffee break and a quick stroll. Signs to *centro urbano* route you through the middle to Plaza de España (lazy cafés, bakery, plenty of free parking just beyond the square out the gate). If it's lunchtime, consider buying a picnic, as all the necessary shops are nearby and the plaza benches afford a solid workaday view of a perfectly untouristy Andalusian town. According to its own TI, the town is "much appreciated for its vast gastronomy." Small lanes lead from the main square up to Plaza Iglesia Mayor (church and TI open daily 10:30-14:00 & 16:30-18:30, tel. 956-412-404, www.medinasidonia.com). At the church, a man will show you around for a tip. Even without giving a tip, you can climb yet another belfry for yet another vast Andalusian view. The castle ruins just aren't worth the trouble.

Vejer de la Frontera

Vejer, south of Jerez and just 30 miles north of Tarifa, will lure all but the very jaded off the highway. Vejer's strong Moorish roots give it a distinct Moroccan (or Greek Island) flavor—you know, black-clad women whitewashing their homes, and lanes that can't decide if they're roads or stairways. The town has no real sights—other than its women's faces—and very little tourism, making it a pleasant stop. The TI is at Calle de los Remedios 2 (tel. 956-451-736, www.turismovejer.es).

The coast near Vejer has a lonely feel, but its pretty, windswept beaches are popular with windsurfers and sand flies. The Battle of Trafalgar was fought just off Cabo de Trafalgar (a nondescript lighthouse today). I drove the circle so you don't have to.

Sleeping in Vejer: A newcomer on Andalucía's tourist map, the old town of Vejer has just a few hotels.

$$ Hotel Convento San Francisco is a poor man's parador in a refurbished convent with pristine, spacious rooms and elegant public lounges (Sb-€52, Db-€74, breakfast-€3.35, air-con, Wi-Fi in lobby, La Plazuela, tel. 956-451-001, www.tugasa.com, convento -san-francisco@tugasa.com).

$ Hostal La Posada's 10 clean and charming rooms, in a modern apartment flat, are cheap and funky. This family-run place has no reception (S-€20-25, Db-€35-40, higher prices are for mid-July-Aug, Calle de los Remedios 21, tel. 956-450-258, www.hostal -laposada.com, no English spoken).

Route Tips for Drivers

The road-numbering system from the coast into Sevilla was changed a few years back—don't rely on an old driving map.

Sevilla to Arcos (55 miles): The remote hill towns of Andalucía are a joy to tour by car with Michelin map 578 or any other good map. Drivers can zip south on N-IV from Sevilla along the river, following signs to *Cádiz*. Take the fast toll expressway (blue signs, E-5, A-4); the toll-free N-IV is curvy and dangerous. About halfway to Jerez, at Las Cabezas, take CA-403 to Villamartín. From there, circle scenically (and clockwise) through the thick of the Pueblos Blancos—Zahara and Grazalema—to Arcos.

It's about two hours from Sevilla to Zahara. You'll find decent but winding roads and sparse traffic. It gets worse (but very scenic) if you take the tortuous series of switchbacks over the 4,500-foot summit of Puerto de Las Palomas (Pass of the Pigeons, climb to the viewpoint) on the direct but difficult road from Zahara to Grazalema (you'll see several hiking trailheads into Sierra de Grazalema Natural Park, though most require free permits).

Another scenic option through the park from Grazalema to Arcos is the road that goes up over Puerto del Boyar (Pass of the Boyar), past the pretty little valley town of Benamahoma, and down to El Bosque. The road from Ronda to El Gastor, Setenil (cave houses and great olive oil), and Olvera is another picturesque alternative.

Arcos to Tarifa (80 miles): You can drive from Arcos to Jerez in about 40 minutes. If you're going to Tarifa, take the tiny C-343 road at the Jerez edge of Arcos toward Paterna and Vejer. Later, you'll pick up signs to *Medina Sidonia*, and then to *Vejer* and *Tarifa*.

Costa del Sol to Ronda and Beyond: Drivers coming up from the coast catch A-397 at San Pedro de Alcántara and climb about 20 miles into the mountains. The much longer, winding A-369 offers a scenic alternative that takes you through a series of whitewashed villages.

WHITE HILL TOWNS

COSTA DEL SOL

Nerja • Gibraltar • Tarifa

Spain's south coast—the famous Costa del Sol—is so bad, it's interesting. To northern Europeans, the sun is a drug, and this is their needle. Anything resembling a quaint fishing village has been bikini-strangled and Nivea-creamed. Oblivious to the concrete, pollution, ridiculous prices, and traffic jams, tourists lie on the beach like game hens on skewers—cooking, rolling, and sweating under the sun.

Where Europe's most popular beach isn't crowded by high-rise hotels, most of it's in a freeway choke hold. Wonderfully undeveloped beaches between Tarifa and Cádiz, and east of Almería, are ignored, while human lemmings make the scene where the coastal waters are so polluted that hotels are required to provide swimming pools. It's a fascinating study in human nature. The Costa del Sol has suffered through the recent economic crisis: Real estate, construction, and tourism had powered the economy, and the effects of its decline are still apparent. Crime and racial tension have risen, as many once-busy individuals are now without work.

Particularly in the resorts west of Málaga, most of the foreigners are British—you'll find beans on your breakfast plate and Tom Jones for Muzak. Spanish visitors complain that some restaurants have only English menus, and indeed, the typical expats here actually try *not* to integrate. I've heard locals say of the British, "If they could, they'd take the sun back home with them—but they can't, so they stay here." They enjoy English TV and radio, and many barely learn a word of Spanish. (Special school buses take British children to private English-language schools that connect with Britain's higher-education system.) For

Costa del Sol

```
☺  DELIGHTFUL
☺  TOLERABLE
☹  AWFUL
```

TO SEVILLA

50 MILES
50 KM

S P A I N

GRANADA

LANJARÓN

CAVES

PUEBLOS BLANCOS

RONDA ☺

FRIGI-LIANA ☺ ALM. ☺ MOTRIL

ARCOS ☺

S. PEDRO ☺

MÁLAGA ☹ NERJA ☺ SALO-BREÑA ☺

TORREMOLINOS ☹

CÁDIZ ☺

VEJER ☺
D.L.F.

FUENGIROLA ☹

MARBELLA ☺

ESTEPONA ☹

COSTA DE LA LUZ

ALGE-CIRAS ☺

LA LÍNEA ☹

GIBRALTAR ☺
(U.K.)

C O S T A D E L S O L

☺ TARIFA ☺

CEUTA ☺
(SP.)

ATLANTIC OCEAN

TANGIER MED

TANGIER ☺

MOROCCO

M E D I T E R R A N E A N

S E A

DCH

an insight into this British community, read the free local expat magazines.

Laugh with Ronald McDonald at the car-jammed resorts. But if you want a place to stay and play in the sun, unroll your

beach towel at Nerja, the most appealing beach-resort town on the coast. And don't forget that you're surprisingly close to jolly olde England: The land of tea and scones, fish-and-chips, pubs and bobbies awaits you—in Gibraltar. Although a British territory, Gibraltar has a unique cultural mix that makes it far more interesting than the anonymous resorts that line the coast. Beyond "The Rock," the whitewashed port of Tarifa—the least-developed piece of Spain's generally overdeveloped southern coast—is a workaday town with a historic center, broad beaches, and good hotels and restaurants. Most importantly, Tarifa is the perfect springboard for a quick trip to Tangier, Morocco. These three places alone— Nerja, Gibraltar, and Tarifa—make the Costa del Sol worth a trip.

Planning Your Time

My negative opinions on the "Costa del Turismo" are valid for peak season (mid-July–mid-Sept). If you're there during a quieter time and you like the ambience of a beach resort, it can be a pleasant stop. Off-season it can be neutron-bomb quiet.

The whole 150 miles of coastline takes six hours by bus or three hours to drive with no traffic jams. You can resort-hop by bus across the entire Costa del Sol and reach Nerja for dinner. If you want to party on the beach, it can take as much time as Mazatlán.

To day-trip to Tangier, Morocco, head for Tarifa.

Nerja

While cashing in on the fun-in-the-sun culture, Nerja has actually kept much of its quiet Old World charm. It has good beaches, a fun evening paseo (strolling scene) that culminates in the proud Balcony of Europe terrace, enough pastry shops and nightlife, and locals who get more excited about their many festivals than the tourists do.

Although Nerja's population swells from about 22,000 in winter to about 90,000 in the summer, it's more of a year-round destination and a real town than many other resorts. Thanks to cheap airfares and the completion of the expressway, real estate boomed here in the last decade (property values doubled in six years). The bubble collapsed to some extent with the recent financial crisis, but Nerja has remained hardier than other parts of the Costa del Sol. New restaurants and hotels open here all the time.

Nerja is more diverse than many of the rival resorts—in addition to British accents, you'll overhear French, German, Dutch, and Scandinavian languages being spoken on the beaches. There's also a long tradition of Spanish people retiring and vacationing here. Pensioners from northern Spain move here—enjoying long life spans, thanks in part to the low blood pressure that comes from a diet of fish and wine. While they could afford to travel elsewhere, an inertia remains from Franco's day, when people generally vacationed within the country. In summer, to escape the brutal heat of inland Spain, many Spanish moms take the kids to condos on the south coast while dads stay home to work. This is a time when husbands get to "be Rodriguez" *(estar de Rodríguez)*, an idiom whose meaning ranges from "temporary bachelor" to "when the cat's away, the mouse will play."

Orientation to Nerja

The tourist center of Nerja is right along the water and crowds close to its famous bluff, the "Balcony of Europe" (Balcón de Europa). Fine strings of beaches flank the bluff, stretching in either direction. The old town is just inland from the Balcony, while the more modern section slopes up and away from the water.

Tourist Information

The helpful English-speaking TI has bus schedules, tips on beaches and side-trips, and brochures for nearby destinations, such as the Caves of Nerja, Frigiliana, Málaga, and Ronda (July-Aug Mon-Sat 10:00-14:00 & 18:00-22:00, Sun 18:00-22:00; April-June and Sept-Oct Mon-Sat 10:00-14:00 & 17:00-21:00, Sun 10:00-14:00; Nov-March daily 10:00-14:00; 100 yards from the Balcony of Europe and half a block inland from the big church, tel. 952-521-531, www.nerja.org). Ask for a free city map and the *Leisure Guide,* which has a comprehensive listing of activities. Their *Hiking the Sierra of Nerja and Cliffs of Maro* booklet describes good local walks.

Arrival in Nerja

By Bus: The Nerja bus station is actually just a bus stop with an info kiosk on Avenida de Pescia (Mon-Tue and Fri 6:00-20:15, Wed-Thu and Sat-Sun 7:00-12:00 & 14:45-19:15, schedules posted, Alsa tel. 902-422-242, www.alsa.es). To travel from Nerja, buy tickets at the kiosk—don't assume they're available on the bus. Because many buses leave at the same times, arrive at least 15 minutes before departure to avoid having to elbow other tourists.

By Car: For the most central parking, follow *Balcón de Europa* signs, and then pull into the big underground parking lot beneath the Plaza de España (which deposits you 200 yards from the Balcony of Europe; €2.10/hour, €22.25/24 hours). The enormous Parking Carabeo, just east of the Balcony, is slightly cheaper (€1.80/hour, €18/24 hours). The handiest free parking is about a 10-minute walk farther out, next to the bridge over the dry riverbed (near the town bus stop, just off N-340). Street parking in Nerja is free and unlimited, but it's very tight. If you do find a space, avoid parking next to yellow lines, and read signs carefully—on certain days of the month you're required to move your car.

Helpful Hints

Internet Access: Nerja's scenically situated Internet café, **Europ@ Web,** is on a square overlooking Playa la Torrecilla, where Calle de Castilla Pérez meets Calle Málaga (€2.50/30 minutes, daily 10:00-21:00, until 24:00 in summer, tel. 952-526-147).

Nerja

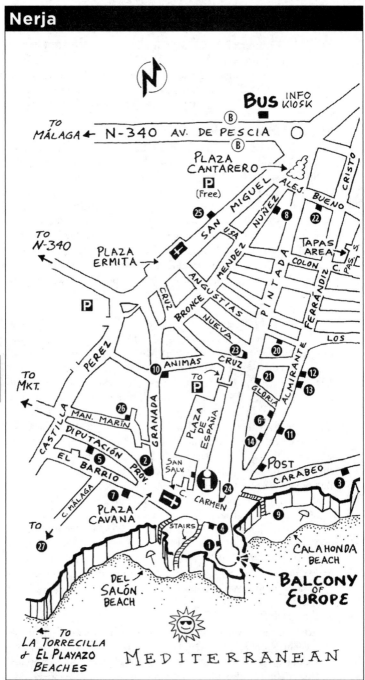

COSTA DEL SOL

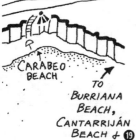

1 Hotel Balcón de Europa
2 Hotel Plaza Cavana
3 Hotel Carabeo & Restaurant 34
4 Hostal Marissal & Cochran's Terrace
5 Hostal Don Peque
6 Hostal Miguel
7 Pensión Mena
8 Hostal Lorca
9 Papagayo Beach Rest.
10 Nerja Museum
11 Pepe Rico & El Pulguilla Restaurante
12 Pinocchio Restaurante
13 Haveli Restaurante
14 Coach & Horses Pub
15 El Chispa/Bar Dolores
16 La Puntilla Bar Restaurante
17 Los Cuñaos
18 La Taberna de Pepe
19 To Ayo's Café
20 Bar El Molino
21 El Burro Blanco
22 Bodega Los Bilbainos
23 Black & White Bar
24 El Valenciano Helados Ice Cream
25 Mercadona Supermarket
26 Launderette
27 To Internet Café

TO NERJA CAVES, CANTARRIJÁN BEACH & GRANADA

Carabeo P

CARABEO BEACH
TO BURRIANA BEACH, CANTARRIJÁN BEACH & 19

SEA

*NOT TO SCALE - BUS INFO KIOSK TO BALCONY OF EUROPE IS A 10 MIN. WALK

B BUS STOP
VIEW
P PARKING

COSTA DEL SOL

Laundry: Bubbles Burbujas is a full-service launderette run by friendly Jo from England (€6/small load, same-day service if you drop off in the morning, no self-service, Mon-Fri 9:00-17:00, Sat 9:00-13:00, closed Sun; a few blocks north of Plaza de Cavana at Calle Manuel Marín 1, just off Calle Granada—look for Pasaje Granada pedestrian passage on left, just past the Irish-Nordic Properties building, tel. 665-539-256).

British Media: For a taste of the British expat scene, pick up the monthly magazines *Street Wise* or *Soltalk*, or tune in to Coastline Radio at 97.6 FM.

Local Guide: Carmen Fernandez is good, with knowledge of the entire region (€125/5-hour day, mobile 610-038-437, mfeyus @yahoo.es).

Massage: Tiny yet muscular Marie, who moved here from France, runs a massage parlor out of her apartment. She does an excellent one-hour massage for €40 (€10 more on weekends)—just give her a call (**Amarilys Masaje,** Calle de Castilla Perez 10, mobile 667-825-828).

Getting Around Nerja

You can easily **walk** anywhere you need to go.

Nerja's **taxis** are pricey—the in-town minimum is €6-7, even for a short trip. They don't use meters—instead, most journeys have a set fee (e.g., €7 to Burriana Beach, €12 to Frigiliana, tel. 952-524-519 or 952-520-537).

To clip-clop in a **horse-drawn buggy** through town, it's €35 for about 25 minutes (you'll usually find these at the Plaza de los Cangrejos above Playa la Torrecilla).

Sights in Nerja

▲▲Balcony of Europe (Balcón de Europa)

The bluff, jutting happily into the sea, is completely pedestrianized. It's the center of Nerja's paseo and a magnet for street performers. The mimes, music, and puppets can draw bigger crowds than the Balcony itself, which overlooks the Mediterranean, miles of coastline, and little coves and caves below. A castle, and later a fort, occupied this spot from the ninth century until the earthquake of 1884. Now it's a people-friendly view terrace.

Built in the early 1800s to defend against Napoleon, the English-Spanish fort here protected the harbor with the help of seven cannons. When the 1884 earthquake destroyed the castle

COSTA DEL SOL

Costa del Sol History

Many Costa del Sol towns come in pairs: the famous beach town with little history, and its smaller yet much more historic partner established a few miles inland—safely out of reach of the Barbary pirate raids that plagued this coastline for centuries. Nerja is a good example of this pattern. Whereas it has almost no history and was just an insignificant fishing village until tourism hit, its more historic sister, Frigiliana, hides out in the nearby hills. The Barbary pirate raids were a constant threat. In fact, the Spanish slang for "the coast is clear" is *"no hay moros en la costa"* (there are no Moors on the coast).

Nerja was overlooked by the tourism scene until about 1980, when the phenomenal Spanish TV show *Verano Azul (Blue Summer)* was set here. This post-Franco program featured the until-then off-limits topics of sexual intimacy, marital problems, adolescence, and so on in a beach-town scene (imagine combining *All in the Family*, *Baywatch*, and *The Hills*). To this day, when Spaniards hear the word "Nerja," they think of this TV hit.

Despite the fame, development didn't really hit until about 2000, when the expressway finally and conveniently connected Nerja with the rest of Spain. Thankfully, a building code prohibits any new buildings higher than three stories in the old town.

and fort, it sent the cannons into the sea. A century later, two were salvaged, cleaned up, and placed here. Study the beautifully aged metal work.

The cute statue of King Alfonso XII reminds locals of how this popular sovereign—the great-grandfather of today's King Juan Carlos—came here after the devastating earthquake (a huge number of locals had died). He mobilized the local rich to dig out the community and put things back together. Standing on this promontory amid the ruins of the earthquake-devastated castle, he marveled at the view and coined its now-famous name, Balcón de Europa.

The Nerja castle was part of a 16th-century lookout system. After the Christian Reconquista in 1492 drove Muslim Moors into exile, pirate action from Muslim countries in North Africa picked up. Lookout towers were stationed within sight of one another all along the coast. Warnings were sent whenever pirates threatened (smoke by day, flames by night). Look to the east—you can see three towers crowning bluffs in the distance.

Also to the east you can just see the tip of Burriana Beach. Spaniards love their *chiringuitos*, as local beach restaurants are called. The *chiringuito* immediately below you, Papagayo, is understandably popular.

Scan the horizon. Until recently this was a favored landing spot (just beyond the tighter security zone near Gibraltar) for illegal immigrants and drug runners coming in from Africa. Many Moroccan teens try to sneak into Europe here, as local laws prohibit turning away undocumented children (the police use DNA tests to determine the age of recent arrivals—if they're under 18, they stay). Laws also grant automatic EU citizenship to anyone born in Europe, so many pregnant women try to slip in (once the baby's born, the mother's legal, too). However, illegal immigration is down: With the help of a new high-tech satellite-scanning system, the Guardia Civil can now detect floating objects as small as makeshift rafts and intercept them before they reach land.

Walk beneath the Balcony for views of the scant remains (bricks and stones) of the ninth-century Moorish castle. Locals claim an underground passage connected the Moorish fortress with the mosque that stood where the Church of San Salvador stands today.

Church of San Salvador

Just a block inland from the Balcony, this church was likely built upon the ruins of a mosque (c. 1600). Its wooden ceiling is Mudejar—made by Moorish artisans working in Christian times. The woodworking technique is similar to that featured in the Alhambra in Granada. The modern fresco of the *Annunciation* (in the rear of the nave) is by Paco Hernandez, the top local artist of this generation. In front, on the right, is a niche featuring Jesus with San Isidoro (as a little boy). Isidoro is the patron saint of Madrid, Nerja, and farmers (sugarcane farming was the leading industry here before tourism hit). From the porch of the church, look inland to see City Hall, marked by four flags (Andalucía's is green for olive trees and white for the color of the houses in this part of Spain).

Nerja Museum (Museo de Nerja)

This mildly interesting and slightly disjointed museum is a good option on a rainy day or if you've just had too much sun. It's run in association with the Nerja Caves, with exhibits focusing on the history of Nerja and the surrounding region, from prehistoric to modern times. Each of its four floors contains interactive exhibits and displays, including prehistoric tools, weapons, and a skeleton found within the Nerja Caves.

Cost and Hours: €4, €2 if also getting Nerja Caves ticket;

July-Aug Tue-Sun 10:00-14:00 & 18:00-22:00, Sept-June Tue-Sun 10:00-14:00 & 16:00-18:30, closed Mon year-round; Plaza de España 4, tel. 952-527-224, www.cuevadenerja.es.

Town Strolls

Nerja was essentially destroyed after the 1884 earthquake—and at the time there was little more here beyond the castle anyway—so there's not much to see in the town itself. However, a few of its main streets are worth a quick look. From the Balcony of Europe head inland. Consider first grabbing some ice cream at El Valenciano Helados, a local favorite run by a Valencia family. Try the refreshing *chufa*-nut Valencian specialty called *horchata*.

A block farther inland, the old town's three main streets come together. The oldest street, Calle Carabeo, heads off to your right (notice how buildings around here are wired on the outside). On the left, Calle Pintada heads inland. Its name means "the painted street," as it was spiffed up in 1885 for the king's visit. Today it's the town's best shopping street. And between those streets runs Calle Almirante Ferrándiz, Nerja's restaurant row, which is particularly lively in the evenings.

Beaches

The single best thing to do on a sunny day in Nerja is to hit the beach: swim, sunbathe, sip a drink, go for a hearty hike along the rocky coves...or all of the above.

Nerja's many beaches are well-equipped, with bars and restaurants, free showers, and rentable lounge chairs and umbrellas (about €4/person for chair and umbrella, same cost for 10 minutes or all day). Nearby restaurants rent umbrellas, and you're welcome to take drinks and snacks out to your spot. Spanish law requires that all beaches are open to the public (except the one in Rota, which is reserved for American soldiers). While there are some nudist beaches (such as Cantarriján), keep in mind that in Europe, any beach can be topless. During the summer, Spanish sun worshippers pack the beach from about 11:00 until around 13:30, when they move into the beach restaurants for relief from the brutal rays. Watch out for red flags on the beach, which indicate when the seas are too rough for safe swimming (blue = safe, orange = caution, red = swimming prohibited). Don't take valuables to the beach, as thieves have fast fingers.

Beaches lie east and west of the Balcony of Europe. For each area, I've listed beaches from nearest to farthest. Even if you're not

COSTA DEL SOL

swimming or sunbathing, walking along these beaches (and the trails that connect them, if open) is a delightful pastime.

East of the Balcony of Europe
Coastal Promenade (Paseo de los Carabineros)

One of Nerja's most appealing draws has been the walkway called the Paseo de los Carabineros, which scampers up and down cliffs, just above the pebbles and sand, to connect the enticing beaches east of the Balcony. Unfortunately, due to erosion concerns and a lack of funds (and municipal motivation), the path has been closed for the past few years. For now, only the first little bit, to Calahonda Beach (described next), is completely open. To reach the other beaches east of the Balcony of Europe, you'll have to walk through the modern town above the beaches...less fun.

To discourage people from using the Paseo de los Carabineros, city officials have erected concrete barriers in a few places along the walkway, removed guardrails (so in some cases you're walking precariously along the cliffs), and allowed the path to become overgrown with plants. While it's possible to follow this pathway at your own risk, it's quite treacherous—in a couple of places you have to actually scale a wall. (Because the path closure is well-advertised at both ends, you're completely liable if anything happens.) Gung-ho travelers still make this walk (I did...carefully), and in summer and at low tide, you can likely walk along the sand and pebbles around the giant rocks (slow going)—but it's not recommended if a pleasant stroll is what you want. The good news is that plans are afoot to restore and reopen the Paseo de los Carabineros. Ask locally, but don't be disappointed if this often-delayed project fails to materialize.

Calahonda Beach (Playa Calahonda)

Directly beneath the Balcony of Europe (to the left as you face the sea) is one of Nerja's most characteristic little patches of sun. This pebbly beach is full of fun pathways, crags, and crannies, and its humble Papagayo restaurant—one of my recommended eateries—is open all day. Antonio can be seen each morning working with his nets and sorting through his fish. His little pre-tourism beach hut—a stuccoed-and-whitewashed marshmallow bulge with blue trim burrowed into the cliff—is wonderfully photogenic. To get here from the Balcony, simply head down through the arch across from the El Valenciano Helados ice-cream stand...you'll be on the beach in seconds.

Carabeo Beach (Playa Carabeo)

Less developed than the others listed here, Carabeo is wedged into a cove between the bustling Calahonda and Burriana beaches. For many, its lack of big restaurants is a plus. If the Paseo de los Carabineros is closed, you can reach the beach by walking along

Calle Carabeo and taking the stairs down from the viewpoint at the park.

Burriana Beach (Playa de Burriana)
Nerja's leading beach is a 20-minute walk east from the Balcony of Europe. Big, bustling, crowded, and fun, it's understandably a top attraction. Burriana is fun for families, with paddleboats, play-

grounds, volleyball courts, and other entertainment options. The beach is also lined with a wide range of cafés and restaurants—but the best is the recommended Ayo's, whose paella feast is a destination in itself.

Getting There: Assuming the Paseo de los Carabineros is closed, walk along Calle Carabeo. You'll pass the viewpoint park with the stairs leading down to Carabeo Beach; keep going until you're forced to jog left (up Cómpeta) into a dull modern part of town. You'll see the boxy parador on your right; circle around behind it, following the low-profile signs for *Playa Burriana* (near the parador entrance) to the right. Curl around to the right, then twist down the switchback road to the beach. Or take a taxi for €7.

Cantarriján Beach (Playa del Cantarriján)
The only beach listed here not within easy walking distance of Nerja, this is the place if you're craving a more desolate beach (and have a car). Drive about 4.5 miles (15 minutes) east (toward Herradura) to the Cerro Gordo exit, and follow *Playa Cantarriján* signs (paved road, just before the tunnel). Park at the viewpoint and hike 30 minutes down to the beach (or, in mid-June-Sept, ride the shuttle bus down). Down below, rocks and two restaurants separate two pristine beaches—one for people with bathing suits (or not); the other, more secluded, more strictly for nudists. As this beach is in a natural park and requires a long hike, it provides a fine—and rare—chance to experience the Costa del Sol in some isolation.

West of the Balcony of Europe
Unlike the walkways east of the Balcony, the promenades to the west are open for business—making this a delightful place to stroll.

Del Salón Beach (Playa del Salón)
The sandiest (and most crowded) beach in Nerja is down the walkway to the right of Cafetería Marissal, just west of the Balcony of Europe (to the right as you look out to sea). For great drinks with a view, stop by the recommended Cochran's Terrace on the way down. Continuing farther west, you'll reach another

COSTA DEL SOL

sandy beach, **Playa la Torrecilla,** at the end of Calle Málaga.

El Playazo ("Big Beach")

A short hike on a promenade west of Playa la Torrecilla, this beach is preferred by locals, as it's less developed than the more central ones, offering a couple of miles of wide-open spaces that allow for fine walks and a chance to "breathe in the beach."

Sights near Nerja

▲Nerja Caves (Cuevas de Nerja)

These caves (2.5 miles east of Nerja, exit 295), with an impressive array of stalactites and stalagmites, are a classic roadside attraction. The huge caverns, filled with backlit formations, are a big hit with cruise-ship groups and Spanish families. The visit involves a 30-minute unguided ramble deep into the mountain, up and down 400 dark stairs. At the end you reach the Hall of the Cataclysm, where you'll circle the world's largest stalactite column (certified by *Guinness Book of World Records*). Someone figured out that it took one trillion drops to make the column.

The free exhibit in the Centro de Interpretación explains the cave's history and geology (in house next to bus parking; exhibit in Spanish, but includes free English brochure).

Cost and Hours: €8.50, €6.50 if also getting Nerja Museum ticket, daily 10:00-14:00 & 16:00-18:30, July-Aug until 19:30, easy parking-€1/day, tel. 952-529-520, www.cuevadenerja.es.

Concerts: During the festival held here the third week of July, the caves provide a cool venue for hot flamenco and classical concerts (tickets sold out long in advance).

Services: The restaurant offers a view and three-course fixed-price meals for €10, and the picnic spot (behind the ticket office) offers pine trees, benches, and a kids' play area.

Getting There: To reach the caves, catch a bus across the street from Nerja's main bus stop (€1.05, 13/day, 10 minutes) or a taxi (€8 one-way).

Frigiliana

The picturesque whitewashed village of Frigiliana (free-*h*ee-lee-AH-nah), only four miles inland from Nerja, is easily reached by bus (€1, 9/day, none on Sun, 15 minutes) or taxi (€12 one-way). While it doesn't match up to the striking white hill towns, its proximity to Nerja makes it an enticing side-trip if this is the nearest you'll get to hill towns on your trip.

The bus stop is in the middle of town, on Plaza del Ingenio. This is also the point that separates the new town from the old town (the steep old Moorish quarter climbing the hill up ahead). The **TI** is a 100-yard walk uphill, in the new town (Mon-Fri 10:00-17:30, Sat-Sun 10:00-14:00 & 16:00-20:00, tel. 952-534-261, www

.frigiliana.es). Pick up a map and the translations of the tile you'll see displayed around town. The TI shares a building with the archaeological museum, with artifacts unearthed near Frigiliana; their prized piece is the fifth-century B.C. skull of a 10-year-old child (free, same hours as TI).

Focus your visit on the old town. Begin by climbing up to the terrace in front of the factory *(ingenio)*—the blocky, un-whitewashed, double-smokestack building that dominates the town. Dating from the 16th century, this still produces sugarcane honey. From the end of the terrace, hike up the steep street, bearing right at the fork up Calle Hernando el Darra. At #10 (on the right), notice the tile in the wall—the first in a series of a dozen around town that describe, in poetic Spanish, the story of the 1568 Battle of Peñón. At the next

fork, bear right (uphill) on Calle Amargura and walk steeply uphill, enjoying the flowerpot-lined lane. Notice the distinctive traditional door-knockers, shaped like a woman's hand. More common in Morocco, these are the "hand of Fatima"—the daughter of the Prophet Muhammad—and are intended to ward off evil.

After turning the corner, take the left/downhill road at the next fork, than head right up Calle Sta. Teresa de Ávila. Then head left down the steep, stepped Calle del Garral. You'll pop out just below the main church. Before going there, detour a few steps to the right, then head left to Plaza de la Fuente Vieja—home of a 17th-century fountain that's one of the town's trademarks. Then head back up the way you came to find your way to the inviting café-lined plaza in front of the Church of San Antonio of Padua (with a stark interior). From here, you can follow the main drag back to where you entered town, or enjoy exploring Frigiliana's back lanes.

Hiking
Europeans visiting the region for a longer stay generally use Nerja as a base from which to hike. The TI can describe a variety of hikes. One of the most popular is a refreshing two-to-three-hour walk up a river (at first through a dry riverbed, and later up to your shins in water; 7.5 miles one-way). Another, more demanding hike takes you to the 5,000-foot summit of El Cielo for the most memorable king-of-the-mountain feeling this region offers.

COSTA DEL SOL

Nightlife in Nerja

Bar El Molino offers live Spanish folk singing nightly in a rustic cavern that's actually an old mill—the musicians perform where the mules once tread. It's touristy but fun (starts at 22:00 but pretty dead before 23:00, no cover—just buy a drink, Calle San José 4). The local sweet white wine, *vino del terreno*—made up the hill in Frigiliana—is popular here (€3/glass).

El Burro Blanco is a touristy flamenco bar that's enjoyable and intimate, with shows nightly from 22:30. Keeping expectations pretty low, they advertise "The Best One in Nerja" (no cover—just buy a drink, live music Fri-Sat after flamenco, fewer shows off-season, on corner of Calle Pintada and Calle de la Gloria).

Bodega Los Bilbainos is a classic dreary old dive—a favorite with local men and communists (tapas and drinks, Calle Alejandro Bueno 8).

For more trendy and noisy nightlife, check out the **Black and White Bar,** with karaoke nightly, on Pintada (near El Burro Blanco at Calle Pintada 35) and the bars and dance clubs on Antonio Millón and Plaza Tutti Frutti.

Sleeping in Nerja

COSTA DEL SOL

The entire Costa del Sol is crowded during August and Holy Week (the week leading up to Easter), when prices are at their highest. Reserve in advance for peak season—basically mid-July through mid-September—which is prime time for Spanish workers to hit the beaches. Any other time of year, you'll find that Nerja has plenty of comfy, easygoing low-rise resort-type hotels and rooms. Room rates are generally three-tiered: low season (Nov-March), middle season (April-June and Oct), and high season (July-Sept).

Compared to the pricier hotels, the better *hostales* are an excellent value. Hostal Don Peque, Hostal Miguel, and Pensión Mena are all within a few blocks of the Balcony of Europe.

Breakfast: Some hotels here overcharge for breakfast. Don't hesitate to go elsewhere, as many places serve breakfast for more reasonable prices. For a cheap breakfast with a front-row view of the promenade action on the Balcony of Europe, head to **Cafetería Marissal** (in the recommended *hostal* of the same name) and grab a wicker seat under the palm trees (€4.50-5.50 options include English breakfasts, daily from 9:00). The recommended **Papagayo** serves breakfast on the beach, just below the Balcony of Europe, to those who don't mind a little sand in their coffee (from 10:00). If you're up for a short hike before breakfast, consider the recommended **Ayo's** on Burriana Beach (daily from 9:00).

Sleep Code

(€1 = about $1.30, country code: 34)
S = Single, **D** = Double/Twin, **T** = Triple, **Q** = Quad, **b** = bathroom, **s** = shower only. Unless otherwise noted, credit cards are accepted and English is spoken, but breakfast is not included. Some hotels include the 10 percent IVA tax in the room price; others tack it onto your bill.

To help you easily sort through these listings, I've divided the accommodations into three categories based on the price for a standard double room with bath during high season:

$$$ **Higher Priced**—Most rooms €100 or more.
$$ **Moderately Priced**—Most rooms between €60-100.
$ **Lower Priced**—Most rooms €60 or less.

Prices can change without notice; verify the hotel's current rates online or by email. For the best prices, always book direct.

Close to the Balcony of Europe

$$$ Hotel Balcón de Europa is the most central place in town. It's right on the water and the square, with the prestigious address Balcón de Europa 1. It has 110 rooms with modern style, plus all the comforts—including a pool and an elevator down to the beach. It's popular with groups. All the suites have seaview balconies, and most regular rooms also come with views (Sb-€84/96/125, standard Db-€115/135/165, about €30 extra for sea view and balcony, breakfast-€13.50, air-con, elevator, Wi-Fi, parking-€12/day, tel. 952-520-800, www.hotelbalconeuropa.com, reservas @hotelbalconeuropa.com).

$$$ Hotel Plaza Cavana, with 39 rooms, overlooks a plaza lily-padded with cafés. It feels a bit institutional, but if you'd like a central location, marble floors, modern furnishings, an elevator, and a small unheated rooftop swimming pool, dive in (Sb-€35-100, Db-€50-125, bigger superior Db-€10 more, Tb-20 percent more, Qb-30 percent more; 10 percent discount for Rick Steves readers for 1-to-2-night stays, 15 percent for stays of 3 nights or more, and free breakfast for those booking direct with this guidebook in 2014; some view rooms, air-con, elevator, pay guest computer, free Wi-Fi in lobby, second small unheated pool in basement, parking-€10-15/day, 2 blocks from Balcony of Europe at Plaza de Cavana 10, tel. 952-524-000, www.hotelplazacavana.es, info@hotelplazacavana.com).

$$$ Hotel Carabeo, a boutique-hotel splurge, has seven classy rooms on the cliff east of downtown—less than a 10-minute

COSTA DEL SOL

walk away, but removed from the bustle of the Balcony of Europe (non-view Db-€85-100; seaview Db-€160-205, price range depends on type of room, air-con, free Wi-Fi in lobby, Calle Carabeo 34, tel. 952-525-444, www.hotelcarabeo.com, info@hotelcarabeo .com). This is also home to the recommended Restaurant 34.

$$ Hostal Marissal has an unbeatable location next door to the fancy Balcón de Europa hotel, and 23 modern, spacious rooms with old-fashioned furniture and clever gadgets on the doors to prevent them from slamming. Some rooms have small view balconies overlooking the Balcony of Europe action. Their cafeteria and bar, run by helpful staff, make the Marissal even more welcoming (Sb-€30/35/45, Db-€40/50-60/60-70, apartment for up to 4 people-€80-160, breakfast-€4.50-5.50, double-paned windows, air-con, elevator, Wi-Fi, Balcón de Europa 3, reception at Marissal café, tel. 952-520-199, www.hostalmarissal.com, reservas @hostalmarissal.com).

$$ Hostal Don Peque sits in a dull urban zone an easy couple of blocks' walk from the Balcony of Europe—but it compensates with 10 bright, colorful, and cheery rooms (8 with balconies—a few with sea views). Owners Roberto and Clara moved here from France and have infused the place with their personality. They rent beach equipment at reasonable prices, but their bar-terrace with rooftops-and-sea views may be more enticing (Sb-€35/55/75, Db-€40/65/85, Tb-€55/75/100, bunk-bed family room for up to 4-€15 more than Tb, breakfast-€6, air-con, thin walls, Wi-Fi, Diputación 13, tel. 952-521-318, www.hostaldonpeque.com, info @hostaldonpeque.com).

$ Hostal Miguel offers nine sunny and airy rooms in the heart of "Restaurant Row" (some street noise in front rooms). Breakfast is served on the pretty green terrace with mountain views. The owners—British expats Ian, Jane, and Hannah— are long-time Nerja devotees (Sb-€30-38, Db-€40-58, book direct for these prices, 4 percent more if paying with credit card, breakfast-€5, family suite, no air-con but fans and fridges, Wi-Fi in most rooms, laundry service-€5, beach equipment available on request, Almirante Ferrándiz 31, tel. 952-521-523, mobile 696-799-218, www.hostalmiguel.com, hostalmiguel@gmail.com).

$ Pensión Mena rents 11 nice rooms—four with seaview terraces (€7 extra and worth it)—and offers a quiet, breezy garden (Sb-€20-30, Db-€29-45, no breakfast, some street noise, Wi-Fi in lobby, El Barrio 15, tel. 952-520-541, www.hostalmena.es, info @hostalmena.es, María). The reception has limited hours (daily 9:30-13:30 & 17:00-20:30); if they're closed when you arrive to check in, report to their sister hotel, Hotel Mena Plaza, a few blocks away at Plaza de España 2.

In a Residential Neighborhood

$ Hostal Lorca is located in a quiet residential area a five-minute walk from the center, three blocks from the bus stop, and close to a small, handy grocery store. Run by a friendly young Dutch couple, Femma and Rick, this *hostal* has nine modern, comfortable rooms and an inviting compact backyard with a terrace, a palm tree, and a small pool. You can use the microwave and take drinks (on the honor system) from the well-stocked fridge. This quiet, homey place is a winner (Sb-€25-34, Db-€29-55, extra bed-€12, no air-con but fans, Wi-Fi, look for yellow house at Mendez Nuñez 20, tel. 952-523-426, www.hostallorca.com, info@hostallorca.com).

Eating in Nerja

There are three Nerjas: the private domain of the giant beachside hotels; the central zone, packed with fun-loving (and often tipsy) expats and tourists eating and drinking from trilingual menus; and the back streets, where local life goes on as if there were no tourists. The whole old town (around the Balcony of Europe) is busy with lively restaurants. Wander around and see who's eating best.

To pick up picnic supplies, head to the **Mercadona** supermarket (Mon-Sat 9:15-21:15, closed Sun, inland from Plaza Ermita on Calle San Miguel).

Near the Balcony of Europe

Papagayo, a classic *chiringuito* (beach restaurant), lounges in the sand a few steps below the Balcony of Europe. You may be paying for the location, but it's quite a location. They serve drinks and snacks to those enjoying their beach umbrellas (€2-8 breakfasts, €4-12 snacks and meals, open with demand, daily breakfast from 10:00, lunch 12:00-17:00, tel. 952-523-816, "moon beach parties" on summer evenings).

Cochran's Terrace serves mediocre meals in a wonderful seaview setting, overlooking Del Salón Beach (€7-12 main dishes, open daily all day for drinks, 12:00-15:00 & 19:00-23:00 for meals, shorter hours off-season, just behind Hostal Marissal).

Restaurant 34, in Hotel Carabeo, manages white-tablecloth elegance in a relaxed atmosphere that successfully mixes eclectic antiques with modern accents. More tables sprawl outside, along the swimming pool and toward sweeping sea views (call ahead to reserve a seaview table). They offer inexpensive *raciones*—and a free tapa if you buy a drink in the bar. The staff is friendly, and the cuisine features seasonal local produce (€9-15 starters, €17-24 main dishes, €25 three-course fixed-price meal, Tue-Sun 12:30-15:30 & 19:00-late, closed Mon, Calle Carabeo 34, tel. 952-525-444).

COSTA DEL SOL

Along Restaurant Row

Strolling up Calle Almirante Ferrándiz (which changes its name farther uphill to "Cristo"), you'll find a good variety of eateries, albeit filled with tourists. On the upside, the presence of expats means you'll find places serving food earlier in the evening than the Spanish norm.

Pepe Rico is the most romantic (in a schlocky adult-contemporary way) along this street, with a big terrace and a cozy dining room (€6-12 starters, €16-22 main dishes, €28 four-course meals, Mon-Sat 12:30-15:00 & 19:00-23:00, closed Sun, Calle Almirante Ferrándiz 28, tel. 952-520-247).

Pinocchio is the local family-friendly favorite for Italian (€7-9 pizzas and pastas, €12-18 fish and meat plates, daily 12:00-late, Calle Almirante Ferrándiz 51, tel. 952-527-248).

Haveli, run by Amit and his Swedish wife, Eva, serves good Indian food in an informal atmosphere. For more than two decades, it's been a hit with Brits, who know their Indian food (€10-18 plates, daily 19:00-24:00 in summer, closed Mon off-season, Calle Almirante Ferrándiz 42, tel. 952-524-297).

Coach and Horses is a British pub run by no-nonsense expat Catherine. Although she serves the only real Irish steaks in town, she also caters to vegetarians, with daily specials that go beyond the usual omelet (€7-17 meals, daily 10:30-15:00 & 18:30-late, closed Mon off-season, Calle Almirante Ferrándiz 19, tel. 952-520-071).

El Pulguilla is a great, high-energy place for Spanish cuisine, fish, and tapas. Its two distinct zones (tapas bar up front and more formal restaurant out back) are both jammed with enthusiastic locals and tourists. The lively no-nonsense stainless-steel tapas bar doubles as a local pick-up joint later in the evening. Drinks come with a free small plate of clams, mussels, shrimp, chorizo sausage, or seafood salad. For a sit-down meal, head back to the gigantic terrace. Though not listed on the menu, half-portions *(media-raciones)* are available for many items, allowing you to easily sample different dishes (€10-16 dinners, Tue-Sun 12:30-16:00 & 18:30-23:30, closed Mon, Calle Almirante Ferrándiz 26, tel. 952-521-384).

Tapas Bars near Herrera Oria

A 10-minute gently uphill hike from the water takes you into the residential thick of things, where the sea views come thumbtacked to the walls, prices are lower, and locals fill the tables. The first three are tapas bars within a few blocks of one another. Each is a colorful local hangout with different energy levels on different nights. Survey all three before choosing one, or have a drink and tapa at each. These places are generally open all day for tapas and drinks, and serve table-service meals during normal dining hours. If you prefer a restaurant setting to a bar, try the last listing, La Taberna de Pepe.

Remember that in Nerja, tapas are snack-size portions, generally not for sale but free with each drink. To turn them into more of a meal, ask for the menu and order a full-size *ración,* or half-size *media-ración.* The half-portions are generally bigger than you'd expect.

El Chispa (a.k.a. Bar Dolores) is big on seafood, which locals enjoy on an informal terrace. Their *tomate ajo* (garlic tomato) is tasty, and their piping-hot *berenjena* (fried and salted eggplant) is worth considering—try it topped with molasses-like sugarcane syrup. They serve huge portions—*media-raciones* are enough for two (€5-12 *raciones,* daily, San Pedro 12, tel. 952-523-697).

La Puntilla Bar Restaurante is a boisterous little place, with rickety plastic furniture spilling out onto the cobbles on hot summer nights (generous €4-6 splittable salads, €3-6 half-*raciones*, €5-13 *raciones,* show this book and get a free *digestivo,* daily 12:00-24:00, a block in front of Los Cuñaos at Calle Bolivia 1, tel. 952-528-951).

Los Cuñaos hangs the banners of the entire soccer league on the walls. Local women hang out to chat, and kids wander around like it's home. Although it has the least interesting menu, it has the most interesting business card (€6.50 meals, €16-17 two-person meals, €8 and €12 tapas plates come with a bottle of wine, closed Mon, Herrera Oria 19, tel. 678-663-997).

La Taberna de Pepe is more of a sit-down restaurant, though it does have a small bar with tapas. The tight, cozy (almost cluttered) eight-table interior is decorated with old farm tools and crammed with happy eaters choosing from a short menu of well-executed seafood. It feels classier than the rough-and-tumble tapas bars listed above, but isn't pretentious (€6-15 dishes, Fri-Wed 12:15-16:00 & 19:00-24:00, closed Thu, Herrera Oria 30, tel. 952-522-195).

Paella Feast on Burriana Beach

Ayo's is famous for its character of an owner and its €6.50 beachside all-you-can-eat paella feast at lunchtime. For 30 years, Ayo—a lovable ponytailed bohemian who promises to be here until he dies—has been feeding locals. Ayo is a very big personality—one of the five kids who discovered the Nerja Caves, formerly a well-known athlete, and now someone who makes it a point to hire hard-to-employ people as a community service. The paella fires get stoked up at about noon and continue through mid-afternoon. Grab one of a hundred tables under the canopy next to the rustic open-fire cooking zone, and enjoy the beach setting in the shade with a jug of sangria. For €6.50, you can fill your plate as many times as you like. It's a 20-minute walk from the Balcony of Europe, at the east end of Burriana Beach—look for Ayo's rooftop pyramid (daily "sun to sun," for breakfast—see below, paella served only at lunch, Playa de Burriana, tel. 952-522-289).

Breakfast at Ayo's: Consider arriving at Ayo's at 9:00. Locals order the *tostada con aceite de oliva* (toast with olive oil and salt-€0.50). Ayo also serves toasted ham-and-cheese sandwiches and good coffee.

Nerja Connections

While there are some handy direct bus connections from Nerja to major destinations, many others require a transfer in the town of **Málaga.** The closest train station to Nerja is in Málaga. Fortunately, connections between Nerja and Málaga are easy, and the train and bus stations in Málaga are right next to each other.

Nerja

Almost all buses from Nerja are operated by Alsa (tel. 902-422-242, www.alsa.es), except the local bus to Frigiliana, which is run by Autocares Nerja (tel. 952-520-984). Remember to double-check the codes on bus schedules—for example, 12:00*S* means 12:00 daily except Saturday.

From Nerja by Bus to: Málaga (1-2/hour, 1 hour *directo,* 1.5 hours *ruta,* €4.30), **Nerja Caves** (13/day, 10 minutes), **Frigiliana** (9/day, none on Sun, 15 minutes), **Granada** (8/day, 2-2.5 hours, more with transfer in Motril), **Córdoba** (2/day, 4-5.5 hours), **Sevilla** (2/day, 4-5 hours), **Algeciras** (with connections to La Línea de la Concepción/Gibraltar and Tarifa; 1/day direct, 3.5 hours, more with transfer in Málaga; there are also connections to La Línea de la Concepción/Gibraltar and Tarifa via Málaga). To reach **Ronda,** you'll transfer in Málaga.

To Málaga Airport (about 40 miles west): First catch the bus to Málaga (see above). To reach the airport from Málaga, take a local bus (about 2/hour, 30 minutes, €2, buy ticket on board) or train (2/hour, 30 minutes, €2.20; Málaga's train station is a quick 5-minute walk across the street from the bus station). If you'd rather take a taxi from Nerja to the airport, figure on paying about €65, or ask your Nerja hotelier about airport shuttle transfers (airport code: AGP, tel. 952-048-804).

Málaga

This seaside city's busy airport is the gateway to the Costa del Sol. Málaga's bus and train stations—a block apart at the western edge of Málaga's town center—both have pickpockets and lockers (the train station's lockers are more modern).

Málaga's big, airy U-shaped **bus station,** on Paseo de los Tilos, has long rows of counters for the various bus companies. In the center of the building is a helpful info desk that can print out schedules for any destination and point you to the right ticket window (daily 7:00-22:00, tel. 952-350-061, www.estabus .emtsam.es). Flanking the information desk on either side are old-fashioned lockers (buy a €3.20 token, or *ficha,* from the automated machine). The station also has several basic eateries, newsstands, and WCs. The train station is just a five-minute walk away: Exit at the far corner of the bus station, cross the street, and enter the big shopping mall labeled *Estación María Zambrano*—walk a few minutes through the mall to the train station.

The **train station** (Estación María Zambrano) is slick and modern, inside a big shopping mall (with a food court upstairs). Modern lockers are by the entrance to tracks 10-11 (€3-5 depending on size, security checkpoint), and car-rental offices are by the entrance to tracks 1-9 (Hertz, Avis, Europcar, and National/ Atesa). A **TI** kiosk is in the main hall, just before the shopping mall. To reach the bus station (5 minutes away on foot), enter the mall by the TI kiosk and follow signs to *estación de autobuses.*

From Málaga by Bus to: Nerja (1-2/hour, 1 hour *directo,* 1.5 hours *ruta,* Alsa), **Ronda** (*directo* buses by Los Amarillos: 10/day Mon-Fri, 6/day Sat-Sun, 1.75-2 hours; avoid the *ruta* buses by Portillo: 2/day, 4 hours), **Algeciras** (hourly, 2.25 hours *directo,* 3 hours *ruta,* Portillo), **La Línea de Concepción/Gibraltar** (5/day, 3 hours, Portillo), **Tarifa** (2-3/day, 2.5-4 hours, Portillo), **Sevilla** (6/day direct, 2.5-3 hours, Alsa), **Granada** (hourly, 1.5-2 hours, Alsa), **Córdoba** (4/day, 2.5-3.5 hours *directo,* Alsa), **Madrid** (5/ day, 6 hours, Daibus), **Marbella** (hourly, 55 minutes *directo,* 1.25 hours *ruta,* Portillo). **Bus info:** Alsa (tel. 902-422-242, www.alsa .es), Los Amarillos (tel. 902-210-317, www.losamarillos.es), Daibus (tel. 902-277-999, www.daibus.es), Portillo (tel. 902-450-550, http: //portillo.avanzabus.com).

From Málaga by Train to: Ronda (1/day, 2 hours, more with transfer in Bobadilla), **Algeciras** (4/day, 4 hours, transfer in Bobadilla—same as Ronda train, above), **Madrid** (12/day, 2.5-3 hours on AVE), **Córdoba** (best option: 6/day on Avant, 1 hour; more expensive but no faster on AVE: 10/day, 1 hour), **Granada** (6/ day, 2.5 hours, 1 transfer—bus is better), **Sevilla** (6/day, 2 hours on Avant; 5/day, 2.5 hours on slower regional trains), **Jerez** (3/day on AVE and Avant, 3-3.5 hours, transfer in Córdoba), **Barcelona** (2/ day direct on AVE, 5.75 hours; more with transfer). **Train info:** tel. 902-320-320, www.renfe.com.

Between Nerja and Gibraltar

Buses take five hours to make the Nerja-Gibraltar trip, including a transfer in Málaga, where you may have to change bus companies. Along the way, buses stop at each of the following towns.

Fuengirola and Torremolinos

The most built-up part of the region, where those most determined to be envied settle down, is a bizarre world of Scandinavian package tours, flashing lights, pink flamenco, multilingual menus, and all-night happiness. Fuengirola is like a Spanish Mazatlán with a few older, less-pretentious budget hotels between the main drag and the beach. The water here is clean and the nightlife fun and easy. James Michener's idyllic Torremolinos has been strip-malled and parking-metered.

Marbella

This is the most polished and posh town on the Costa del Sol. High-priced boutiques, immaculate streets set with intricate pebble designs, and beautifully landscaped squares testify to Marbella's arrival on the world-class-resort scene. Have a *café con leche* on the beautiful Plaza de Naranjos in the old city's pedestrian section. Wander down to new Marbella and the high-rise beachfront apartment buildings to walk along the wide promenade lined with restaurants. Check out the beach scene. Marbella is an easy stop on the Algeciras-Málaga bus route (as you exit the bus station, take a left to reach the center of town). You can also catch a handy direct bus here from the Málaga airport (roughly every 1-2 hours, fewer off-season, 45 minutes, http://portillo.avanzabus .com).

San Pedro de Alcántara

This town's relatively undeveloped sandy beach is popular with young travelers. San Pedro's neighbor, Puerto Banús, is "where the world casts anchor." This luxurious, Monaco-esque jet-set port, complete with casino, is a strange mix of Rolls-Royces, yuppies, boutiques, rich Arabs, and budget browsers.

Gibraltar

One of the last bits of the empire upon which the sun never set, Gibraltar is a quirky mix of Anglican propriety, "God Save the  Queen" tattoos, English bookstores, military memories, and tourist shops. It's understandably famous for its dramatic Rock of Gibraltar, which rockets improbably into the air from an otherwise flat terrain, dwarfing everything around it. If the Rock didn't exist, some clever military tactician would have tried to build it to keep an eye on the Strait of Gibraltar.

Britain has controlled this highly strategic spit of land since they took it by force in 1704, in the War of Spanish Succession. In 1779, while Britain was preoccupied with its troublesome overseas colonies, Spain (later allied with France) declared war and tried to retake Gibraltar; a series of 14 sieges became a way of life, and the already imposing natural features of the Rock were used for defensive purposes. During World War II, the Rock was further fortified and dug through with more and more strategic tunnels. In the mid- to late-20th century, during the Franco period, tensions ran high—and Britain's grasp on the Rock was tenuous.

Strolling Gibraltar, you can see that it was designed as a modern military town (which means it's not particularly charming). But over the last 20 years the economy has gone from one dominated by the military to one based on tourism (as, it seems, happens to many empires). On summer days and weekends, the tiny colony is inundated by holiday-goers, primarily the Spanish (who come here for tax-free cigarettes and booze) and British (who want a change in weather but not in culture). As more and more glitzy high-rise resorts squeeze between the stout fortresses and ramparts—as if trying to create a mini-Monaco—there's a sense that this is a town in transition.

Though it may be hard to imagine a community of 30,000 that feels like its own nation, real Gibraltarians, as you'll learn when you visit, are a proud bunch. They were evacuated during World War II, and it's said that after their return, a national spirit was forged. If you doubt that, be here on Gibraltar's national holiday—September 10—when everyone's decked out in red and white, the national colors.

Gibraltarians have a mixed and interesting heritage. Spaniards call them Llanitos (yah-NEE-tohs), meaning "flat" in Spanish, though the residents live on a rock. The locals—a

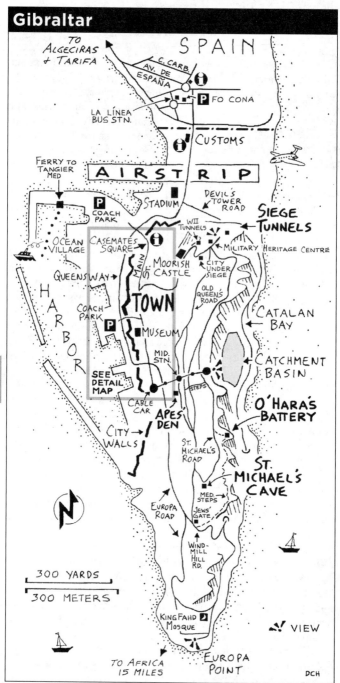

Gibraltar

COSTA DEL SOL

fun-loving and tolerant mix of British, Spanish, and Moroccan, virtually all of whom speak the Queen's English—call their place "Gib."

From a traveler's perspective, Gibraltar—with its quirky combination of Brits, monkeys, and that breathtaking Rock—is an offbeat detour that adds some variety to a Spanish itinerary. If you're heading to Gibraltar from Spain (as you almost certainly are), be aware most Spaniards still aren't thrilled with this enclave of the Commonwealth on their sunny shores. They basically ignore the place—so, for example, if you're inquiring about bus schedules, don't ask how to get to Gibraltar, but rather to La Línea de la Concepción, the neighboring Spanish town. A passport is required to cross the border.

Planning Your Time

Make Gibraltar a day trip (or just one overnight); rooms are expensive compared to Spain.

For the best day trip to Gibraltar, consider this plan: Walk across the border, catch the red bus #5, and ride it to the Market Square stop near Casemates Square. From there, catch blue bus #2 or walk through town to the cable-car station and ride to the peak for Gibraltar's ultimate top-of-the-rock view. Then, either walk down or take the cable car back into town. From the cable-car station, follow my self-guided town walk all the way back to Casemates Square. Spend your remaining free time in town before returning to Spain. Note that, with all the old walls and fortresses, Gibraltar can be tricky to navigate. Ask for directions: Locals speak English.

Tourists who stay overnight find Gibraltar a peaceful place in the evening, when the town can just be itself. No one's in a hurry. Families stroll, kids play, seniors window-shop, and everyone chats...but the food is still pretty bad.

There's no reason to take a ferry from Gibraltar to visit Morocco—for many reasons, it's a better side-trip from Tarifa.

Orientation to Gibraltar

Gibraltar is a narrow peninsula (three miles by one mile) jutting into the Mediterranean. Virtually the entire peninsula is dominated by the steep-faced Rock itself. The locals live down below in the long, skinny town at the western base of the mountain (much of it on reclaimed land).

For information on all the

Spain vs. Gibraltar

Spain has been annoyed about Gibraltar ever since Great Britain nabbed this prime 2.5-square-mile territory in 1704 (during the War of Spanish Succession) and was granted it through the Treaty of Utrecht in 1713. Although Spain long ago abandoned efforts to reassert its sovereignty by force, it still tries to make Gibraltarians see the error of their British ways. Over the years Spain has limited

Gibraltar's air and sea connections, choked traffic at the three-quarter-mile border, and even messed with the local phone system in efforts to convince Britain to give back the Rock. Still, given the choice—which they got in referenda in 1967 and 2002—Gibraltar's residents steadfastly remain Queen Elizabeth's loyal subjects, voting overwhelmingly (99 percent in the last election) to continue as a self-governing British dependency. Gibraltar's governor is popular for dealing force-fully and effectively with Spain on these issues.

COSTA DEL SOL

little differences between Gibraltar and Spain—from area codes to electricity—see "Helpful Hints," later.

Tourist Information

Gibraltar's helpful TI is at Casemates Square, the grand square at the Spain end of town. Pick up a free map and—if it's windy—confirm that the cable car is running (Mon-Fri 9:00-17:30, Sat 10:00-15:00, Sun 10:00-13:00, tel. 74982, www.visitgibraltar.gi). There's also a TI window at the border in the customs building (Mon-Fri 9:00-16:30, closed Sat-Sun).

Arrival in Gibraltar

No matter how you arrive, you'll need your passport to cross the border. These directions will get you as far as the border; from there, see "Getting from the Border into Town," later.

By Bus: Spain's La Línea de la Concepción bus station is a five-minute walk from the Gibraltar border. To reach the border, exit the station and bear left toward the Rock (you can't miss it). If you need to store your bags, you can do so at the Gibraltar Airport (see "Helpful Hints," later).

By Car: Customs checks at the border create a bit of a bottleneck for drivers. But at worst there's a 15-minute wait during the morning rush hour into Gibraltar and the evening rush hour back out. Parking in town is free and easy except for weekday working hours, when it's tight and frustrating. It's simpler to park in La Línea (explained below) and just walk across the border.

Freeway signs in Spain say *Algeciras* and *La Línea,* pretending that Gibraltar doesn't exist until you're very close. After taking the La Línea-Gibraltar exit off the main Costa del Sol road, continue as the road curves left (with the Rock to your right). Enter the left-hand lane at the traffic circle before the border and you'll end up in La Línea. The Fo-Cona underground parking lot is handy (€2.40/hour, €16.50/day, on Avenida 20 de Abril, near the bus station). You'll also find blue-lined parking spots in this area (€1.25/hour from meter, 6-hour limit 9:00-20:00, free before and after that, bring coins, leave ticket on dashboard). From La Línea, it's a five-minute stroll to the border, where you can catch a bus or taxi into town (see "Getting from the Border into Town," below).

If driving into Gibraltar, drive along the sea side of the ramparts (on Queensway—but you'll see no street name). There are big parking lots here and at the cable-car terminal. Parking is generally free—if you can find a spot. By the way, while you'll still find English-style roundabouts, cars here stopped driving on the British side of the road in the 1920s.

Getting from the Border into Town

The "frontier" (as the border is called) is a chaotic hubbub of travel agencies, confused tourists, crafty pickpockets, and duty-free shops (you may see people standing in long lines, waiting to buy cheap cigarettes). The guards barely even look up as you flash your passport. Before exiting the customs building, pick up a map at the TI window on your left (Mon-Fri 9:00-16:30, closed Sat-Sun). Note that as soon as you cross the border, the currency changes from euros to pounds (see "Helpful Hints," next).

To reach downtown, you can walk (30 minutes), catch a bus, or take a taxi. To get into town by **foot,** walk straight across the runway (look left, right, and up), then head down Winston Churchill Avenue, angling right at the Shell station on Smith Dorrien Avenue.

From the border, you can ride the red **bus** #5 (regular or London-style double-decker, runs every 15 minutes) three stops to Market Square (just outside Casemates Square, with the TI), or stay on to Cathedral Square, at the center of town. From Market Square, blue Gibraltar city buses head various points on the peninsula—the most useful route for most tourists is blue bus #2, which goes to the cable-car station and Europa Point (Gibraltar's southernmost point). Tickets are the same price on the privately run red border buses and the blue city buses (€1.30/£1 one-way, €2/£1.50 for an all-day "hoppa" ticket)—although frustratingly, tickets are not transferable between the two systems.

A **taxi** from the border is pricey (€9/£6 to the cable-car station). If you plan to join a taxi tour up to the Rock, note that you can book one right at the border.

Helpful Hints

Gibraltar Isn't Spain: Gibraltar, a British colony, uses different coins, currency (see below), stamps, and phone cards than those used in Spain. Note that British holidays such as the Queen's (official) Birthday (June 9 in 2014) and Bank Holidays (May 5, May 26, and Aug 25 in 2014) are observed, along with local holidays such as Gibraltar's National Day (Sept 10).

Use Pounds, not Euros: Gibraltar uses the British pound sterling (£1 = about $1.60). A pound is broken into 100 pence (abbreviated p). Like other parts of the UK (such as Scotland, Wales, and Northern Ireland), Gibraltar mints its own Gibraltar-specific banknotes and coins featuring local landmarks, people, and historical events—offering a colorful history lesson. Gibraltar's pounds are interchangeable with other British pounds.

Merchants in Gibraltar also accept euros...but at about a 20 percent extra cost to you. Gibraltar is expensive even at fair exchange rates. You'll save money by hitting up an ATM and taking out what you'll need. But before you leave, stop at an exchange desk and change back what you don't spend (at about a 5 percent loss), since Gibraltar currency is hard to change in Spain. (If you'll be making only a few purchases, you can try to avoid this problem by skipping the ATM and buying things with your credit card.) Be aware that if you pay for anything in euros, you may get pounds back in change.

Hours: This may be the United Kingdom, but Gibraltar follows a siesta schedule, with some businesses closing from 13:00 to 15:00 on weekdays, and shutting down at 14:00 on Saturdays until Monday morning.

Electricity: If you have electrical gadgets, note that Gibraltar uses the British three-pronged plugs (not the European two-pronged ones). Your hotel may be able to loan you an adapter.

Phoning: To telephone Gibraltar from anywhere in Europe, dial 00-350-200 and the five-digit local number. To call Gibraltar from the US or Canada, dial 011-350-200-local number.

Internet Access: The **King's Bastion Leisure Centre** has free Wi-Fi, but no terminals (see "Activities," next page). **Café Cyberworld** has several computers (£0.10/minute, £2.50/30 minutes, £4.50/hour, daily 12:00-24:00, Queensway 14, in Ocean Heights Gallery, an arcade 100 yards toward the water from Casemates Square, tel. 51416). There's also Internet access at the cultural center, listed below.

Baggage Storage: You can't store your luggage at the bus station, but there is a bag check at the Gibraltar Airport, which is right across the border (£8/day, go to airport information desk in departures hall).

John Mackintosh Cultural Centre: This is your classic British effort to provide a cozy community center. Without a hint of tourism, the upstairs library welcomes drop-ins to enjoy local newspapers and publications, and to check their email (Mon-Fri 9:30-19:30, closed Sat-Sun, 308 Main Street, tel. 75669).

Activities: The **King's Bastion Leisure Centre** fills an old fortification (the namesake bastion) with a modern entertainment complex. On the ground floor is a huge bowling alley; upstairs are an ice-skating rink and a three-screen cinema (www.leisure cinemas.com). Rounding out the complex are bars, restaurants, discos, and lounges. Many of the activities are geared for families, especially tweens and teens. It's easy to find, just outside Cathedral Square (daily 10:00-24:00, air-con, free Wi-Fi, tel. 44777).

Side-Trip to Tangier, Morocco: While a very sporadic ferry does run from Gibraltar directly to Tangier, it's designed for Moroccan workers (returning home to Tangier for the weekend) and doesn't work for a same-day round-trip. Instead, either go via Tarifa or via Algeciras (closer to Gibraltar, but ferries drop you at a port farther from downtown Tangier). Various travel agencies in town sell package tours that include a bus transfer to the boat in Algeciras.

COSTA DEL SOL

Self-Guided Walk

Welcome to Gibraltar

Gibraltar town is long and skinny, with one main street (called Main Street). Stroll the length of it from the cable-car station to Casemates Square, following this little tour. A good British pub and a room-temperature pint of beer await you at the end.

From the cable-car terminal, turn right (as you face the sea) and head into town. Soon you'll come to the **Trafalgar cemetery,** a reminder of the colony's English military heritage. Next you come to the **Charles V wall**—a reminder of its Spanish military heritage—built in 1552 by the Spanish to defend against marauding pirates. Gibraltar was controlled by Moors (711-1462), Spain (1462-1704), and then the British (since 1704). Passing through the Southport Gates, you'll see one of the many red history plaques posted about town.

Heading into town, you pass the tax office, then the **John Mackintosh Cultural Centre,** which has Internet access and a copy of today's *Gibraltar Chronicle* upstairs in its library. The *Chronicle* comes out Monday through Friday and has covered the local news since 1801. The Methodist church sponsors the recommended **Carpenter's Arms** tearoom.

The pedestrian portion of Main Street begins near the **Governor's Residence.** The British governor of Gibraltar took over a Franciscan convent, hence the name of the local white house: The Convent. The **Convent Guard Room,** facing the Governor's Residence, is good for photos.

Gibraltar's courthouse stands behind a **small tropical garden,** where John and Yoko got married back in 1969 (as the ballad goes, they "got married in Gibraltar near Spain"). Sean Connery did, too. Actually, many Brits like to get married here because weddings are cheap, fast (only 48 hours' notice required), and legally recognized as British.

Main Street now becomes a **shopping drag.** You'll notice lots of colorful price tags advertising tax-free booze, cigarettes, and

sugar (highly taxed in Spain). Lladró porcelain, while made in Valencia, is popular here (because it's sold without the hefty Spanish VAT—Value-Added Tax). The Catholic cathedral retains a whiff of Arabia (as it was built upon the remains of a mosque), while the big **Marks & Spencer department store** helps vacationing Brits feel at home.

Continue several more blocks through the bustling heart of Gibraltar. If you enjoy British products, this is your chance to stock up on Cadbury chocolates, digestive biscuits, wine gums, and Weetabix—but you'll pay a premium, since it's all "imported" from the UK.

The town (and this walk) ends at **Casemates Square.** While a lowbrow food circus today, it originated as a barracks and place for ammunition storage. When Franco closed the border with Spain in 1969, Gibraltar suffered a labor shortage, as Spanish guest workers could no longer commute into Gibraltar. The colony countered by inviting Moroccan workers to take their place—ending a nearly 500-year Moroccan absence, which began when the Moors fled in 1462. As a result, today's Moroccan community dates only from the 1970s. Whereas the previous Spanish labor force simply commuted into work, the Moroccans needed apartments, so Gibraltar converted the Casemates barracks for that purpose. Cheap Spanish labor has crept back in, causing many locals to

Gibraltar Town

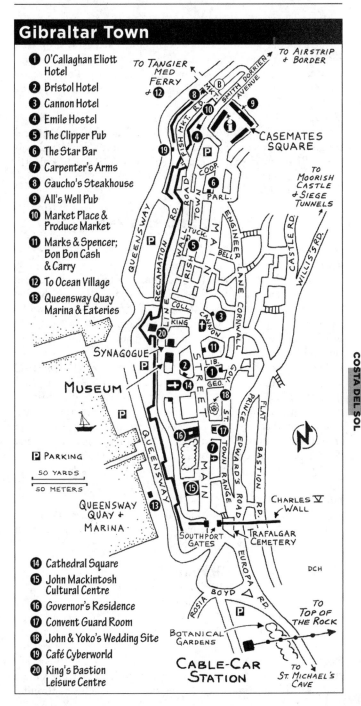

1. O'Callaghan Eliott Hotel
2. Bristol Hotel
3. Cannon Hotel
4. Emile Hostel
5. The Clipper Pub
6. The Star Bar
7. Carpenter's Arms
8. Gaucho's Steakhouse
9. All's Well Pub
10. Market Place & Produce Market
11. Marks & Spencer; Bon Bon Cash & Carry
12. To Ocean Village
13. Queensway Quay Marina & Eateries

🅟 PARKING

50 YARDS

50 METERS

14. Cathedral Square
15. John Mackintosh Cultural Centre
16. Governor's Residence
17. Convent Guard Room
18. John & Yoko's Wedding Site
19. Café Cyberworld
20. King's Bastion Leisure Centre

resent store clerks who can't speak proper English.

At the far end of Casemates Square is a **crystal shop** that makes its own crystal right there (you can watch). They claim it's the only thing actually "made in Gibraltar." But just upstairs, on the upper floor of the barracks, you'll find a string of local crafts shops.

If you go through the triple arches at the end of the square (behind the TI), you'll reach the covered **produce market** and food stalls. Across the busy road a few minutes' walk farther is the well-marked entrance to the **Ocean Village** boardwalk and entertainment complex (described later, under "Eating in Gibraltar").

Sights in Gibraltar

In Town
▲Gibraltar Museum
Built atop a Moorish bath, this museum tells the story of a chunk of land that has been fought over for centuries. Start with the fine 15-minute video overview of the story of the Rock—a worthwhile prep for the artifacts (such as ancient Roman anchors made of lead) you'll see in the museum. Then wander through the scant remains of the 14th-century Moorish baths. Upstairs you'll see military memorabilia, a 15-foot-long model of the Rock, wonderful century-old photos of old Gibraltar, paintings by local artists, and, in a cave-like room off the art gallery, a collection of prehistoric remains and artifacts. The famous skull of a Neanderthal woman found in Forbes' Quarry is a copy (the original is in the British Museum in London). Found in Gibraltar in 1848, this was the first Neanderthal skull ever discovered. No one realized its significance until a similar skull found years later in Germany's Neanderthal Valley was correctly identified—stealing the name, claim, and fame from Gibraltar.

Cost and Hours: £2, Mon-Fri 10:00-18:00, Sat 10:00-14:00, closed Sun, last entry 30 minutes before closing, no photos, on Bomb House Lane near the cathedral.

On the Rock of Gibraltar
The actual Rock of Gibraltar is the colony's best sight. Its attractions include the stupendous view from the very top, quirky apes, a hokey cave (St. Michael's), and the impressive Siege Tunnels drilled through the rock face for military purposes. Frankly, the sights that charge admission aren't that exciting; the Rock's best attractions—enjoying views from the top and seeing the monkeys—are free. Hikers can ride the lift up and take a long, steep, scenic walk down, connecting the various sights by strolling

along paved military lanes.

Cost: There's a £0.50 fee to enter the grounds of the Rock, technically called the Upper Rock Nature Reserve—that's just to walk around and enjoy the views and the monkeys. A £10 nature reserve ticket is required to visit any or all of these major sights within the reserve: St. Michael's Cave, Siege Tunnels, Moorish Castle, Military Heritage Centre, and City Under Siege exhibit (includes the £0.50 nature reserve entrance fee). If you take a taxi tour, entry to the nature reserve and sights is included; if you ride the cable car, the nature reserve grounds entry fee is included, but you'll have to buy the £10 ticket to go in the sights. (Both options are explained below.)

Hours: Daily 9:30-19:15, until 18:15 late Oct-late March, last entry 30 minutes before closing.

Additional Sights at the Rock: Two attractions at the Rock are not part of the official £10 nature reserve ticket, and have their own separate tickets and hours: O'Hara's Battery and the World War II Tunnels (both described later).

Visiting the Rock: You have two options for touring the Rock—take a taxi tour or ride the cable car. The **taxi tour** includes entry to St. Michael's Cave and the Siege Tunnels, a couple of extra stops, and running commentary from your licensed cabbie/guide. Because the cable car doesn't get you very close to the cave and tunnels (and doesn't cover cave and tunnel admission), take the taxi tour if you'll be visiting these sights and don't want to walk. On the other hand, the **cable car** takes you to the very top of the Rock (which the taxi tours don't). You can still see the sights, but you'll have to pay for an entry ticket and connect them by foot (not a bad thing—it's a pleasant walk down). Both options are explained in more detail below.

There's no reason to take a big-bus tour (advertised and sold all over town) considering how fun and easy the taxi tours are. Private cars are not allowed high on the Rock.

By Taxi Tour: Minibuses driven by cabbies trained and licensed to lead these 1.5-hour trips are standing by at the border and at various points in town (including Cathedral Square, John Mackintosh Square, Casemates Square, and Trafalgar

Cemetery near the cable-car station). They charge £22/person (4-person minimum, or £65 for only 2 people in one taxi, includes reserve sights ticket, tel. 70027). Taxi tours and big buses do the same 1.5-hour loop tour with four stops: a Mediterranean viewpoint (called the Pillar of Hercules), St.

Michael's Cave (15-minute visit), a viewpoint near the top of the Rock where you can get up close to the monkeys, and the Siege Tunnels (20-minute visit). Buddy up with other travelers and share the cost.

By Cable Car to the Summit: A ticket for just the cable car is £8.50 one-way and £10.50 round-trip. The £18.50 Nature Reserve ticket (combining a one-way cable-car ride and the £10 ticket to the sights) doesn't save any money over buying the tickets separately. You'll probably want to skip the €20.50 round-trip option, as I recommend walking downhill to the sights rather than taking the cable car down.

The cable car runs every 10-15 minutes, or continuously in busy times (daily from 9:30; April-Oct last ascent at 19:15, last descent at 19:45; Nov-March last ascent at 17:15, last descent at 17:45). Lines can be long if a cruise ship is in town. The cable car won't run if it's windy or rainy; if the weather is questionable, ask at the TI before heading to the station. The cable-car ride includes a handheld videoguide that explains what you're seeing from the spectacular viewpoints (pick it up at the well-marked booth when you disembark at the top—must leave ID as a deposit—and return it before leaving the summit). In winter (Nov-March), the cable car stops halfway down for those who want to get out, gawk at the monkeys, and take a later car down—but you'll probably see monkeys at the top anyway.

To take in all the sights, you'll want to **hike down,** rather than take the cable car back (be sure to specify that you want a one-way ticket up). Simply hiking down without visiting the sights is enjoyable, too. Approximate hiking times: from the top of the cable car to St. Michael's Cave—25 minutes; from the cave to the Apes' Den—20 minutes; from the Apes' Den to the Siege Tunnels—30 minutes; from the tunnels back into town, passing the Moorish Castle—20 minutes. Total walking time, from top to bottom: about 1.5 hours (on paved roads with almost no traffic), not including sightseeing. For hikers, I've connected the dots with directions below.

▲▲▲The Summit of the Rock

The cable car takes you to the real highlight of Gibraltar: the summit of the spectacular Rock itself. (Taxi tours don't go here; they stop on a ridge below the summit, where you enjoy a commanding view—but one that's nowhere near as good.) The limestone massif, or large rock mass, is nearly a mile long, rising 1,400 feet high with very sheer faces. According to legend, this was one of the Pillars of Hercules (paired with Djebel

Musa, another mountain across the strait in Morocco), marking the edge of the known world in ancient times. Local guides say that these pillars are the only places on the planet where you can see two seas and two continents at the same time.

In A.D. 711, the Muslim chieftain Tarik ibn Ziyad crossed over from Africa and landed on the Rock, beginning the Moorish conquest of Spain and naming the Rock after himself—Djebel-Tarik ("Rock of Tarik"), which became "Gibraltar."

At the top of the Rock (the cable-car terminal) there's a view terrace and a restaurant. From here you can explore old ramparts and drool at the 360-degree view of Morocco (including the Rif Mountains and Djebel Musa), the Strait of Gibraltar, the bay stretching west toward Algeciras, and the twinkling Costa del Sol arcing eastward. The views are especially crisp on brisk off-season days. Below you (to the east) stretches the giant catchment system that the British built to collect rainwater in the not-so-distant past, when Spain allowed neither water nor tourists to cross its disputed border. Broad sheets catch the rain, sending it through channels to reservoirs located inside the rock.

• *Up at the summit, you'll likely see some of the famed...*

▲▲Apes of Gibraltar

The Rock is home to about 200 "apes" (actually, tailless Barbary macaques—a type of monkey). Taxi tours come with great monkey

fun, but if you're on your own, you'll probably see them at the top and at various points on the walk back down (basically, the monkeys congregate anywhere that tourists do—hoping to get food). The males are bigger, females have beards, and newborns are black. They live about 15-20 years. Legend has it that as long as the monkeys remain here, so will the Brits. (According to a plausible local legend, when word came a few decades back that the ape population was waning, Winston Churchill made a point to import reinforcements.) Keep your distance from the monkeys. (Guides say that for safety reasons, "They can touch you, but you can't touch them." And while guides feed them, you shouldn't—it disrupts their diet.) Beware of the monkeys' kleptomaniac tendencies; they'll ignore the peanut in your hand and claw after the full bag in your pocket. Because the monkeys associate plastic bags with food, keep your bag close to your body: Tourists who wander by absentmindedly, loosely clutching a bag, are apt to have it stolen by a purse-snatching simian. If there's no ape action, wait for a banana-toting taxi tour to stop by and stir some up. Guides love to get the

COSTA DEL SOL

monkeys to actually climb onto the backs and shoulders of their tour members—always a crowd-pleaser.

• *If you're hiking down, you'll find that your options are clearly marked at most forks. I'll narrate the longest route down, which passes all the sights en route.*

From the top cable-car station, exit and head downhill on the well-paved path (toward Africa). You'll pass the viewpoint for taxi tours (with monkeys hanging around, waiting for tour groups to come feed them), pass under a ruined observation tower, and eventually reach a wide part of the road. Most visitors will want to continue to St. Michael's Cave (skip down to that section), but you also have an opportunity to hike (or ride a shuttle bus) steeply up to...

O'Hara's Battery

At 1,400 feet, this is the actual highest point on the Rock. A massive 9.2-inch gun sits on the summit, where a Moorish lookout post once stood. The battery was built after World War I, and the last test shot was fired in 1974. Locals are glad it's been mothballed—during test firings, they had to open their windows, which might otherwise have shattered from the pressurized air blasted from this gun. The battery was recently opened to the public; you can go inside to see not only the gun, but also the powerful engines underneath that were used to move and aim it. The iron rings you see every 30 yards or so along the military lanes around the Rock once anchored pulleys used to haul up guns like the huge one at O'Hara's Battery.

Cost and Hours: £3.50, not covered by the £10 nature reserve ticket, shuttle runs up every 20 minutes when open, Mon-Fri 10:30-17:00, closed Sat-Sun.

• *From the crossroads below O'Hara's Battery, taking the right (downhill) fork leads you down to a restaurant and shop, then the entrance to...*

▲St. Michael's Cave

Studded with stalagmites and stalactites, eerily lit, and echoing with classical music, this cave is dramatic, corny, and slippery when wet. Considered a one-star sight since Neolithic times, these caves were alluded to in ancient Greek legends—when the caves were believed to be the Gates of Hades (or the entrance of a tunnel to Africa). All taxi tours stop here (entry included in cost of taxi tour). This sight requires a long walk for cable-car riders (who must have the £10 nature reserve ticket to enter; same hours as other nature reserve sights). Walking through takes about 15 minutes; you'll pop out at the gift shop.

• *From here, most will head down to the Apes' Den (see next paragraph), but serious hikers have the opportunity to curl around to Jews' Gate at the tip of the Rock, then circle around the back of the Rock on the strenuous* **Mediterranean Steps** *(leading back up to O'Hara's Battery).*

To do this, turn sharply left after St. Michael's Cave and head for Jews' Gate. Since it's on the opposite side from the town, it's the closest thing in Gibraltar to "wilderness." If this challenging 1.5-to-2-hour hike sounds enjoyable, ask for details at the TI.

*The more standard route is to continue downhill. At the three-way fork, you can take either the middle fork (more level) or the left fork (hillier, but you'll see monkeys at the Apes' Den) to the Siege Tunnels. The **Apes' Den**, at the middle station for the cable car, is a scenic terrace where monkeys tend to gather, and where taxi tours stop to do some monkeying around.*

Continue on either fork (they converge), following signs for Siege Tunnels, *for about 30 more minutes. Eventually you'll reach a terrace with three flags (from highest to lowest: United Kingdom, Gibraltar, EU) and a fantastic view of Gibraltar's airport, "frontier" with Spain, and the Spanish city of La Línea de la Concepción. From here, the Military Heritage Centre is beneath your feet (described later), and it's a short but steep hike up to the...*

▲Siege Tunnels

Also called the Upper Galleries, these chilly tunnels were blasted out of the rock by the Brits during the Great Siege by Spanish

and French forces (1779-1783). The clever British, safe inside the Rock, wanted to chip and dig to a highly strategic outcrop called "The Notch," ideal for mounting a big gun. After blasting out some ventilation holes for the miners, they had an even better idea: Use gunpowder to carve out a whole network of tunnels with shafts that would be ideal for aiming artillery. Eventually they excavated St. George's Hall, a huge cavern that housed seven guns. These were the first tunnels inside the Rock; more than a century and a half later, during World War II, 30 more miles of tunnels were blasted out. Hokey but fun dioramas help recapture a time when Brits were known more for conquests than for crumpets. All taxi tours stop here (entry included in cost of taxi tour); hikers must have the £10 nature reserve ticket to enter (same hours as other nature reserve sights).

• *Hiding out in the bunker below the three flags (go down the stairs and open the heavy metal door—it's unlocked) is the...*

Military Heritage Centre

This small one-room collection features old military photographs from Gibraltar. The second room features a poignant memorial to the people who "have made the supreme sacrifice in defence of Gibraltar" (covered by nature reserve ticket—but tickets rarely checked, same hours as other nature reserve sights).

• *From here, the road switchbacks down into town. At each bend in the road you'll find one of the next three sights.*

City Under Siege

This hokey exhibit is worth a quick walk-through if you've been fascinated by all this Gibraltar military history. Displayed in some of the first British structures built on Gibraltar soil, it re-creates the days of the Great Siege, which lasted for more than three and a half years (1779-1783)—one of 14 sieges that attempted but failed to drive the Brits off the Rock. With evocative descriptions, some original "graffiti" scratched into the wall by besieged Gibraltarians, and some borderline-hokey dioramas, the exhibit explains what it was like to live on the Rock, cut off from the outside world, during those challenging times (covered by nature reserve ticket—but tickets rarely checked, same hours as other nature reserve sights).

World War II Tunnels

This privately run operation takes you on a tour through some of the tunnels carved out of the Rock during a much later conflict than the others described here. You'll emerge back up at the Military Heritage Centre.

Cost and Hours: £8, not covered by £10 nature reserve ticket, daily 10:00-16:30.

Moorish Castle

Actually more a tower than a castle, this recently restored building is basically an empty shell. (In the interest of political correctness, the tourist board recently tried to change the name to "Medieval Castle"...but it *is* Moorish, so the name didn't stick.) It was constructed on top of the original castle built in A.D. 711 by the Moor Tarik ibn Ziyad, who gave his name to Gibraltar.

• *The tower marks the end of the Upper Rock Nature Reserve. Heading downhill, you begin to enter the upper part of modern Gibraltar. While you could keep on twisting down the road, keep an eye out for staircase shortcuts into town (most direct are the well-marked Castle Steps).*

Nightlife in Gibraltar

If you're coming from the late-night bustle of Spain, where you'll see young parents out strolling with their toddlers at midnight, you'll find Gibraltar extremely quiet after-hours. Main Street is completely dead (with the exception of a few lively pubs, mostly a block or two off the main drag). Head instead to the **Ocean Village** complex, a five-minute walk from Casemates Square, where the boardwalk is lined with bars, restaurants, and a casino. Another waterfront locale—a bit more sedate—is the **Queensway Quay Marina.** (Both areas are described later, under "Eating in Gibraltar.") Kids love the **King's Bastion Leisure Centre** (described earlier, under "Helpful Hints").

Some pubs, lounges, and discos—especially on Casemates Square—offer live music (look around for signs, or ask at the TI). **O'Callaghan Eliott Hotel** hosts free live jazz on Thursday evenings.

Sleeping in and near Gibraltar

Gibraltar is not a good value for accommodations. There are only a handful of hotels and (disappointingly) no British-style B&Bs. As a general rule, the beds are either bad or overpriced. Remember, you'll pay a 20 percent premium if paying with euros—pay with pounds or by credit card. As an alternative, consider staying at one of my recommended accommodations in La Línea de la Concepción, across the border from Gibraltar in Spain, where hotels are a much better value.

In Gibraltar Town

$$$ O'Callaghan Eliott Hotel, with four stars, boasts a rooftop pool with a view, a fine restaurant, bar, terrace, inviting sit-a-bit public spaces, and 122 modern, mildly stylish business-class rooms—all with balconies (sky-high rack rates of Db-£240-270, but often around Db-£100 with online booking for non-peak days, breakfast-£15, non-smoking, air-con, elevator, pay Wi-Fi,

COSTA DEL SOL

Sleep Code

(£1 = about \$1.60, €1 = about \$1.30, tel. code: 350-200)
S = Single, **D** = Double/Twin, **T** = Triple, **Q** = Quad, **b** = bathroom, **s** = shower only. All of these places accept credit cards, and their staffs speak English. Unless otherwise noted, breakfast is not included. Prices in Gibraltar are in pounds, while prices in La Línea de la Concepción are in euros. Some La Línea hotels include the 10 percent IVA tax in the room price; others tack it onto your bill.

To help you easily sort through these listings, I've divided the accommodations into three categories, based on the price for a standard double room with bath during high season:

$$$ Higher Priced—Most rooms £85/€105 or more.
$$ Moderately Priced—Most rooms between £50-85/€60-105.
$ Lower Priced—Most rooms £50/€60 or less.

Prices can change without notice; verify the hotel's current rates online or by email. For the best prices, always book direct.

parking-£12/day, centrally located at Governor's Parade 2, up Library Street from main drag, tel. 70500, www.ocallaghanhotels .com, eliott@ocallaghanhotels.com).

$$$ Bristol Hotel offers 60 basic, slightly worn English rooms in the heart of Gibraltar (Sb-£69-74, Db-£86-93, Tb-£99-103, higher prices for exterior rooms, breakfast-£6, air-con, elevator, free Wi-Fi in lobby, swimming pool; limited free parking—first come, first served; Cathedral Square 10, tel. 76800, www.bristolhotel.gi, reservations@bristolhotel.gi).

$$ Cannon Hotel is a run-down dive. But it's also well-located and has the only cheap hotel rooms in town. Its 18 rooms (most with wobbly cots and no private bathrooms) look treacherously down on a little patio (S-£30, D-£42, Db-£53, T-£52.50, Tb-£60, includes full English breakfast, free Wi-Fi, behind cathedral at Cannon Lane 9, tel. 51711, www.cannonhotel .gi, cannon@sapphirenet.gi).

$ Emile Hostel, simple and the cheapest place in town, welcomes people of any age (42 beds, bunk in 6-bed dorm-£18, S-£25, D-£40, à la carte breakfast—full English is £3.95, cash only, free Wi-Fi, on Montagu Bastion diagonally across the street from Shell station, ramped entrance on Line Wall Road, tel. 51106, www.emilehostel.net, emilehostel@yahoo.co.uk).

Across the Border, in La Línea

Staying in Spain—in the border town of La Línea de la Concepción—offers an affordable, albeit less glamorous alternative to sleeping in Gibraltar. The streets north of the bus station are lined with inexpensive *hostales* and restaurants. These options are just a few blocks from the La Línea bus station and an easy 10-15 minute walk to the border—get directions when you book. All but Asur Campo are basic, family-run *hostales,* offering simple, no-frills rooms at a good price.

$$ Asur Campo de Gibraltar is a huge blocky building, with 227 cookie-cutter rooms spread over seven floors. It's a big, impersonal, business-class hotel, but it's the closest hotel to the border—just a 10-minute walk and easy to find if you have a car, as it's right on the main road as you drive in (Sb-€59/64/89, Db-€66/71/96, check website for deals, includes breakfast, air-con, elevator, pay Wi-Fi, pool, large patio, underground parking-€6/day, located at the intersection of Avenida Príncipe de Asturias and Avenida del Ejército, tel. 956-691-211, www.campodegibraltarhotel.com, lalinea@asurhoteles.com).

$ Hostal La Campana has 17 recently remodeled rooms at budget prices. Run by Ivan and his dad Andreas, this place is simple, clean, and friendly, but lacks indoor public areas except for its recommended restaurant (Sb-€27-42, Db-€36-48, Tb-€45-

56, Qb-€52-64, air-con, elevator, free Wi-Fi, limited free street parking, pay parking in nearby underground garage-€18/day, just off Plaza de la Constitución at Calle Carboneros 3, tel. 956-173-059, www.hostalcampana.es, info@hostalcampana.es).

$ Hostal Margarita is a bit farther from the border, but its fresh, modern rooms are a step above the other *hostales* in the area (Sb-€41-46, Db-€53-60, air-con, elevator, free Wi-Fi, parking-€6.60/day, Avenida de España 38, tel. 856-225-211, www.hostalmargarita.com, info@hostalmargarita.com).

Eating in and near Gibraltar

In Gibraltar Town

Take a break from *jamón* and sample some English pub grub: fish-and-chips, meat pies, jacket potatoes (baked potatoes with fillings),

or a good old greasy English breakfast. English-style beers include chilled lagers and room-temperature ales, bitters, and stouts. In general, the farther you venture away from Main Street, the cheaper and more local the places become. Since budget-priced English food isn't exactly high cuisine, the best plan may be to stroll the streets and look for the pub with the ambience you like best (various options: lots of chatting, sports fans riveted to a football match, noisy casino machines, or whatever). I've listed a few of my favorites below. Or venture to one of Gibraltar's more upscale recent developments at either end of the old town: Ocean Village or Queensway Quay.

Downtown, near Main Street

The Clipper pub offers filling £7 meals and Murphy's stout on tap (English breakfast-£5, Mon-Fri 9:30-22:00, Sat 9:30-16:00, Sun 10:00-22:30, on Irish Town Lane, tel. 79791).

The Star Bar, which brags that it's "Gibraltar's Oldest Bar," is on a quiet street with a pubby interior and good £6-9 plates (Mon-Sat 7:00-23:30, Sun 7:00-22:00, food served daily until 22:00, on Parliament Lane off Main Street, across from Corner House Restaurant, tel. 75924).

Carpenter's Arms is a fast, cheap-and-cheery café run by the Methodist church, serving snacks and meals starting at £3 with a missionary's smile. It's upstairs in the Methodist church on Main Street (Mon-Fri 9:30-14:00, closed Sat-Sun and Aug, volunteer-run, 100 yards past the Governor's Residence at 297 Main Street).

Gaucho's is a classy, atmospheric steakhouse actually inside the casemates, just outside Casemates Square (£5-8 starters, £16-24 steaks, daily 12:00-16:00 & 19:00-23:00, Waterport Casemates, tel. 59700).

Casemates Square Food Circus: The big square at the entrance of Gibraltar contains a variety of restaurants, ranging from fast food (fish-and-chips joint, Burger King, and Pizza Hut) to inviting pubs spilling out onto the square. The **All's Well** pub serves £8-10 meals (Moroccan *tajine,* salads, burgers, fish-and-chips, and more) and offers pleasant tables with umbrellas under leafy trees (daily 10:00-19:00, tel. 72987). Fruit stands and cheap take-out food stalls bustle just outside the entry to the square at the **Market Place** (Mon-Sat 9:00-14:00, closed Sun).

Groceries: The **Bon Bon Cash & Carry** minimarket is on the main drag, off Cathedral Square (daily 9:30-19:00, Main Street 239). Nearby, **Marks & Spencer** has a small food market on the ground floor, with pre-made meals and fresh-baked cookies (Mon-Thu 9:00-19:00, Fri 11:00-18:00, Sat 9:30-17:00, closed Sun).

Ocean Village

This development is the best place to get a look at the bold new face of Gibraltar. Formerly a dumpy port, it's been turned into a swanky marina fronted by glassy high-rise condo buildings. The boardwalk arcing around the marina is packed with shops, restaurants, and bars—Indian, Mexican, sports bar, pizza parlor, Irish pub, fast food, wine bar, and more. Anchoring everything is Gibraltar's casino. While the

whole thing can feel a bit corporate, it offers an enjoyable 21st-century contrast to the "English village" vibe of Main Street (which can be extremely sleepy after-hours).

Queensway Quay Marina

To dine in yacht-club ambience, stroll the marina and choose from a string of restaurants serving the boat-owning crowd. When the sun sets, the quay-side tables at each of these places are prime dining real estate. **Waterfront Restaurant** has a lounge-lizard interior and great marina-side tables outside (£5-8 starters, £10-16 main dishes, daily specials, Indian and classic British, daily 9:00-24:00, last orders at 22:45, tel. 45666). Other options include Indian, Italian, trendy lounges, and (oh, yeah) Spanish.

In La Línea

These places are close to my recommended accommodations in La Línea, on the Spanish side of the border.

Restaurante La Campana, attached to the recommended *hostal* of the same name, is particularly good. It's popular with locals for its traditional Spanish dishes made using quality ingredients and offered at affordable prices (€9 fixed-price lunch and dinner *menus* daily, Calle Carboneros 3).

Tahj Mahal, an Indian/Pakistani restaurant, offers a welcome relief from tapas. It serves all the standard Indian dishes, including several vegetarian options, along with a daily €5 comboplate that's a great deal (just across from the La Línea TI on Plaza de la Constitución and Avenida del Ejército).

On Calle Real: This pedestrian street, several blocks north of the La Línea bus station, is lined with inexpensive cafeterias, restaurants, and tapas bars.

Gibraltar Connections

By Bus

The nearest bus station to Gibraltar is in La Línea de la Concepción in Spain, five minutes from the border (tel. 956-291-168 or 956-172-396). The nearest train station is at Algeciras, which is the region's main transportation hub.

From La Línea de la Concepción by Bus to: Algeciras (2/hour, less on weekends, 45 minutes), **Tarifa** (2/day direct, 1 hour; more possible with change in Algeciras, 1.5 hours), **Málaga** (5/day, 3 hours), **Ronda** (no direct bus, transfer in Algeciras; Algeciras to Ronda: 1/day, 2.75 hours), **Granada** (3/day, 6-7 hours, change in Algeciras), **Sevilla** (4/day, 4-4.5 hours), **Jerez** (1/day, 2.5 hours), **Córdoba** (1/day, 5.25 hours), **Madrid** (1/day, 8 hours).

By Plane

From Gibraltar, you can fly to various points in Britain: British Airways flies to London Heathrow (www.ba.com); easyJet connects to London Gatwick and Liverpool (www.easyjet.com); and Monarch Airlines goes to London Luton and Manchester (www.monarch.co.uk). The airport is easy to reach; after all, you can't enter town without crossing its runway, one way or another (airport code: GIB, www.gibraltarairport.gi).

COSTA DEL SOL

Tarifa

Mainland Europe's southernmost town is whitewashed and Arab-feeling, with a lovely beach, an old castle, restaurants swimming in fresh seafood, inexpensive places to sleep, enough windsurfers to sink a ship, and best of all, hassle-free boats to Morocco. Though Tarifa is pleasant, the main reason to come here is to use it as a springboard to Tangier, Morocco—a remarkable city worth ▲▲.

As I stood on Tarifa's town promenade under the castle, looking out at almost-touchable Morocco across the Strait of Gibraltar, my only regret was that I didn't have this book to steer me clear of gritty Algeciras on earlier trips. Tarifa, with 35-minute boat transfers to Tangier departing about every hour, is the best jumping-off point for a Moroccan side-trip, as its ferry route goes directly to Tangier's city-center Medina Port. (The other routes, from Algeciras or Gibraltar, take you to the Tangier MED Port, 25 miles east of Tangier city.)

Tarifa has no blockbuster sights (and can be quiet off-season), but it's a town where you just feel good to be on vacation. Don't expect a snazzy Riviera-style beach resort, à la Nerja. Tarifa is a functional, dreary-in-parts port city with an atmospheric old town and a long, broad stretch of relatively undeveloped but wildly popular sandy beach. The town is a hip and breezy mecca among windsurfers, drawn here by the strong winds created by the bottleneck at the Strait of Gibraltar. Tarifa is mobbed with young German and French adventure seekers in July and August. This crowd from all over Europe (and beyond) makes Tarifa one of Spain's trendiest-feeling towns. It has far more artsy boutique hotels than most Spanish towns its size, and its restaurant offerings are atypically eclectic for normally same-Jane Spain—you'll see vegetarian and organic, Italian and Indian, gourmet burgers and tea houses, and on each corner, it seems, there's a stylish bar-lounge with techno music, mood lighting, and youthful Europeans just hanging out.

COSTA DEL SOL

Orientation to Tarifa

The old town, surrounded by a wall, slopes gently up from the water's edge (and the port to Tangier). The modern section stretches farther inland from Tarifa's fortified gate.

Tourist Information

The TI is on Paseo de la Alameda (Mon-Fri 10:00-13:30 & 16:00-18:00, Sat-Sun 10:00-13:30; hours may be longer in summer and shorter on slow or bad-weather days, tel. 956-680-993, www .aytotarifa.com, turismo@aytotarifa.com).

Experiencia Tarifa: This organization, run by can-do Quino of the recommended Hostal Alborada, produces a good free magazine and town map featuring hotels, restaurants, and a wide array of activities (also online at www.experienciatarifa.com).

Arrival in Tarifa

By Bus: The bus station (actually a couple of portable buildings with an outdoor sitting area) is on Batalla del Salado, about a five-minute walk from the old town. (The TI also has bus schedules.) Buy tickets directly from the driver if the ticket booth is closed (Mon-Fri 7:30-12:30 & 14:15-18:00, Sat-Sun 14:00-20:00, hours vary slightly with the season, bus station tel. 956-684-038, Comes bus company tel. 956-291-168). To reach the old town, walk away from the wind turbines perched on the mountain ridge.

By Car: If you're staying in the center of town, follow signs for *Alameda* or *Puerto,* and continue along Avenida de Andalucía. Follow signs to make an obligatory loop to the port entrance, then swing right and park for free in the lot at the far end of Calle Alcalde Juan Núñez (on the harbor, at the base of the castle). During the busiest summer months (July-Aug), this parking lot can fill up, in which case you'll need to use a pay lot, such as the one to the east of the old-town wall (ask your hotelier for ideas). Or you can try finding street parking, which is most abundant in the new town just north of the old-town walls. Blue lines indicate paid parking, and yellow lines are no-parking areas.

Helpful Hints

Internet Access: Pandor@, in the heart of the old town, has 16 computers across from Café Central, near the church (€2.50/hour, generally daily in summer 10:00-23:00, in winter 10:00-14:30 & 17:00-19:00, tel. 956-680-816).

Laundry: Top Clean Tarifa will wash, dry, and fold your clothes. If you drop off your laundry early in the day, they can get it back to you on the same day (€13/load wash-and-dry, full service only, Mon-Fri 10:00-16:00, closed Sat-Sun, Avenida

Tarifa

ATLANTIC OCEAN

1. Hostal Alborada
2. Hotel La Mirada
3. La Sacristía
4. Casa Blan+co
5. Hotel Misiana
6. Dar Cilla Guesthouse & Apartments
7. La Casa Amarilla
8. Hostal La Calzada
9. Hostal Alameda
10. Hostal Africa
11. Pensión Correo
12. Hostal Villanueva
13. Restaurante Morilla
14. To El Puerto Restaurante
15. La Oca da Sergio
16. Ristorante La Trattoria
17. To Restaurante Souk & Surfing Sushi
18. Bar El Francés
19. Café Bar Los Melli & Bar El Pasillo
20. El Otro Melli
21. La Posada
22. Café Central & FIRMM
23. Casino Tarifeno
24. Mesón El Picoteo
25. Confitería La Tarifeña
26. Churrería La Palmera
27. Chilimoso Restaurante
28. Supermarket
29. Mercado (Farmers' Market)
30. Laundry
31. Internet Café
32. Girasol Adventure
33. Whale Watch Tarifa & Baelo Tour
34. FRS Ferry Office (2)
35. Tarifa Travel
36. Travelsur

COSTA DEL SOL

BEACH

TO BEACH

BULLRING

BERING

CASTILLEJOS

ALMADRABA

AVENIDA DE

AV. FUERZAS ARMADAS

PADRE FONT

HUERTA DEL REY

J.T. ARTIGAS

CRUZ ROJA

CALLE ALCALDE JUAN NÚÑEZ

DOUBLE ARCH

TO 14, BEACH FREE P & ISLA DE LAS PALOMAS

BOAT TO TANGIER (MOROCCO)

HARBOR

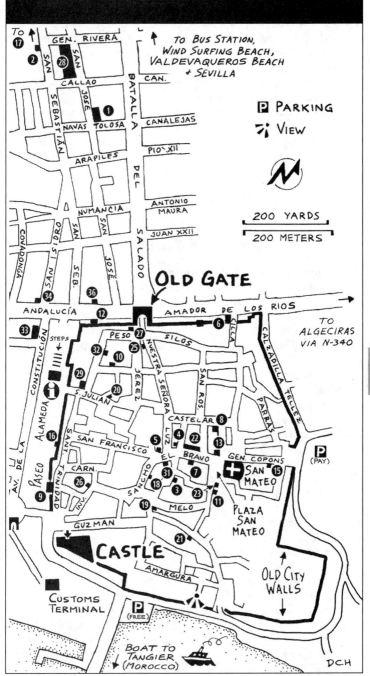

COSTA DEL SOL

de Andalucía 24, tel. 956-680-303).

Tickets and Tours to Morocco: Two ferry companies—FRS and InterShipping—make the crossing between Tarifa and Tangier. You can buy tickets for either boat at the port. FRS also has a couple of offices in town. If taking a tour to Tangier, you can book through a ferry company, your hotel, or one of several travel agencies in Tarifa.

Excursions: Girasol Adventure offers a variety of outdoor excursions, including mountain-bike rentals (€18/day with helmet), guided bike tours, hikes in the national park, rock-climbing classes, tennis lessons, and, when you're all done...a massage (€50/hour). The various activities generally last a half-day and cost around €25-35. Ask Sabine or Chris for details (Mon-Fri 10:00-14:00 & 18:30-20:30, Sat 11:00-14:00, closed Sun, Calle Colón 12, tel. 956-627-037, www.girasol-adventure.com).

Sights in Tarifa

Church of St. Matthew (Iglesia de San Mateo)

Tarifa's most important church, facing its main drag, is richly decorated for being in such a small town. Most nights, it seems life squirts from the church out the front door and into the fun-loving Calle Sancho IV El Bravo. Wander inside.

Cost and Hours: Free, daily 9:00-13:00 & 17:30-20:30; there may be English-language leaflets inside on the right.

Visiting the Church: Find the fragment of an **ancient tombstone**—a tiny square (eye-level, about the size of this book) in the wall just before the transept on the right side. Probably the most important historical item in town, this stone fragment proves there was a functioning church here during Visigothic times, before the Moorish conquest. The tombstone reads, in a kind of Latin Spanish (try reading it), "Flaviano lived as a Christian for 50 years, a little more or less. In death he received forgiveness as a servant of God on March 30, 674. May he rest in peace." If that gets you in the mood to light a candle, switch on an electric "candle" by dropping in a coin. (It works.) A bit closer to the main entrance, you'll see a sign offering you the chance to light a digital candle by sending a text message (for a pricey €1.50).

Step into the side chapel around the corner, in the right transept. The centerpiece of the **altar** is a boy Jesus. By Andalusian tradition, he used to be naked, but these days he's clothed with outfits that vary with the Church calendar. Underneath the dome, cherubs dance around on the pink-and-purple interior above an exquisite chandelier.

Head back out into the main nave, and face the high altar.

A statue of **St. James the Moor-Slayer** (missing his sword) is on the right wall of the main central altar. Since the days of the Reconquista, James has been Spain's patron saint.

The left side of the nave harbors several **statues**—showing typically over-the-top Baroque emotion—that are paraded through town during Holy Week. The **Captive Christ** (with hands bound) evokes a time when Christians were held captive by Moors. The door on the left side of the nave is the **"door of pardons."** For a long time Tarifa was a dangerous place—on the edge of the Reconquista. To encourage people to live here, the Church offered a second helping of forgiveness to anyone who lived in Tarifa for a year. One year and one day after moving to Tarifa, they would have the privilege of passing through this special "door of pardons," and a Mass of thanksgiving would be held in that person's honor.

Castle of Guzmán el Bueno
This castle, little more than a concrete hulk in a vacant lot, is interesting only for the harbor views from its ramparts (the

interior is undergoing a lengthy restoration and will most likely be closed for several years). It was named after a 13th-century Christian general who gained fame in a sad show of courage while fighting the Moors. Holding Guzmán's son hostage, the Moors demanded he surrender the castle or they'd kill the boy. Guzmán refused, even throwing his own knife down from the ramparts. It was used on his son's throat. Ultimately, the Moors withdrew to Africa, and Guzmán was a hero. *Bueno.*

Cost and Hours: €2; May-Sept Tue-Sat 11:00-14:00 & 18:00-20:00, Sun 11:00-14:00; Oct-April Tue-Sat 11:00-14:00 & 16:00-18:00, Sun 11:00-14:00; closed Mon year-round, last entry 30 minutes before closing.

Nearby: If you skip the castle, you'll get equally good views from the plaza just left of the town hall. Follow *ayto* signs to the ceramic frog fountain in front of the Casa Consistorial and continue left.

Bullfighting
Tarifa has a third-rate bullring where novices botch fights on occasional Saturdays through the summer. Professional bullfights take place during special events in August and September. The ring is a short walk from town. You'll see posters everywhere.

COSTA DEL SOL

▲Whale-Watching

Several companies in Tarifa offer daily whale- and dolphin-watching excursions. Over the past four decades, people in this area went from eating whales to protecting them and sharing them with 20,000 visitors a year. Talks are under way between Morocco and Spain to protect the Strait of Gibraltar by declaring it a national park.

For any of the tours, it's wise (but not always necessary) to reserve one to three days in advance. You'll get a multilingual tour and a two-hour boat trip. Sightings occur on nearly every trip: Dolphins and pilot whales frolic here any time of year (they like the food), sperm whales visit from March through July, and orcas pass through in July and August. In bad weather, trips may be canceled or boats may leave instead from Algeciras (in which case, drivers follow in a convoy, people without cars usually get rides from staff, and you'll stand a lesser chance of seeing whales).

The best company is the Swiss nonprofit **FIRMM** (Foundation for Information and Research on Marine Mammals), which gives a 30-minute educational talk before departure. To reserve, it's best to call ahead or stop by one of their two offices (€30/person, 1-5 trips/day April-Oct, sometimes also Nov, also offers intensive week-long courses that include boat trips, one office around the corner from Café Central—one door inland at Pedro Cortés 4, second office inside the ferry port, tel. 956-627-008, mobile 619-459-441, www.firmm.org, mail@firmm.org). If you don't see any whales or dolphins on your tour, you can join another trip for free.

Whale Watch Tarifa is another good option. In addition to a two-hour whale-watching trip (€30), they offer a three-hour orca trip in July and August (€45, Avenida de la Constitución 6, tel. 956-627-013, mobile 639-476-544, www.whalewatchtarifa.net, whalewatchtarifa@whalewatchtarifa.net, run by Lourdes).

Isla de las Palomas

Extending out between Tarifa's port and beaches, this island connected by a spit is the actual "southernmost point in mainland Europe." Walk along the causeway, with beaches stretching to your right and a bustling port to your left, to the tip, which was fortified in the 19th century to balance the military might of Britain's nearby Rock of Gibraltar. The actual tip, still owned by the Ministry of Defense, is closed to the public, but a sign at the gate still gives you that giddy "edge of the world" feeling.

▲▲Beach Scene

Tarifa's vast, sandy beach stretches west for about five miles. You can walk the beach from Tarifa, while those with a car can explore farther (following Cádiz Road). On windy summer days, the sea is littered with sprinting windsurfers, while kitesurfers flutter in the sky. Paddleboarding is also popular here. It's a fascinating scene: A long string of funky beach resorts is packed with vans and fun-mobiles from northern Europe under mountain ridges lined with modern energy-generating windmills. The various resorts each have a sandy access road, parking, a cabana-type hamlet with rental gear, beachwear shops, a bar, and a hip, healthy restaurant. I like

Valdevaqueros beach (five miles from Tarifa), with a wonderful thatched restaurant serving hearty salads, paella, and burgers. Camping Torre de la Peña also has some fun beach eateries.

In July and August, inexpensive buses do a circuit of nearby campgrounds, all on the waterfront (€2, departures about every 1-2 hours, confirm times with TI). Trying to get a parking spot in August can take the joy out of this experience.

Nightlife in Tarifa

You'll find plenty of enjoyable nightspots—the entire town seems designed to cater to a young, international crowd of windsurfers and other adventure travelers. Just stroll the streets of the old town and dip into whichever trendy lounge catches your eye. For something more sedate, the evening paseo fills the park-like boulevard called Paseo de la Alameda (just outside the old-town wall); the Almedina bar hosts flamenco shows every Thursday (at the south end of town, just below Plaza de Santa María); and the theater next to the TI sometimes has musical performances (ask at the TI or look for posters).

Sleeping in Tarifa

Room rates vary with the season. For many hotels, I've listed the three seasonal tiers (lowest prices—winter; medium prices—spring and fall; and highest prices—mid-June-Sept).

Outside the City Wall

These hotels are about five blocks from the old town, right off the main drag, Batalla del Salado, in the plain, modern part of town. While in a drab area, both are well-run oases that are close to the beach and the bus station, with free and easy street parking.

$$ Hostal Alborada is a squeaky-clean, family-run 37-room place with two attractive courtyards and modern conveniences.

Sleep Code

(€1 = about $1.30, country code: 34)

S = Single, **D** = Double/Twin, **T** = Triple, **Q** = Quad, **b** = bath-room, **s** = shower only. Unless otherwise noted, credit cards are accepted and English is spoken. Breakfast is not included (unless noted). Some hotels include the 10 percent IVA tax in the room price; others tack it onto your bill.

To help you easily sort through these listings, I've divided the accommodations into three categories, based on the price for a standard double room with bath during high season:

$$$ Higher Priced—Most rooms €100 or more.
$$ Moderately Priced—Most rooms between €50-100.
$ Lower Priced—Most rooms €50 or less.

Prices can change without notice; verify the hotel's cur-rent rates online or by email. For the best prices, always book direct.

Father Rafael—along with sons Quino (who speaks English and is generous with travel tips), Fali, and Carlos—are happy to help make your Morocco tour or ferry reservation, or arrange any other activities you're interested in. If they're not too busy, they'll even give you a free lift to the port (Sb-€40/60/65, Db-€50/70/90, Tb-€80/90/110, pay for first night when reserving, 10 percent discount when you book direct and show this book in 2014—not valid July-Sept, strict 15-day cancellation policy, basic breakfast-€2.50, larger breakfast with delicious tomato bread-€5, air-con, pay guest computer, free Wi-Fi, laundry-€14, Calle San José 40, tel. 956-681-140, www.hotelalborada.com, info @hotelalborada.com).

$$ Hotel La Mirada, which feels sleek and stark, has 25 mod and renovated rooms—most with sea views at no extra cost. While the place lacks personality, it's well-priced and comfortable (Sb-€45/55/60, Db-€65/75/90, breakfast-€5, elevator, free Wi-Fi, expansive sea views from large roof terrace with inviting lounge chairs, Calle San Sebastián 41, tel. 956-684-427, www.hotel-la mirada.com, reservas@hotel-lamirada.com, Antonio and Salvador).

Inside or next to the City Wall

The first three listings are funky, stylish boutique hotels in the heart of town—*muy* trendy and a bit full of themselves.

$$$ La Sacristía, formerly a Moorish stable, now houses travelers who want stylish surroundings. It offers 10 fine and uniquely decorated rooms, mingling eclectic elements of chic

COSTA DEL SOL

Spanish and Asian style. They offer spa treatments, custom tours of the area, and occasional special events—join the party since you won't sleep (Db-€117, superior Db-€137, extra bed-€35, can be cheaper off-season, includes breakfast, air-con, massage room, sauna, small roof terrace, very central at San Donato 8, tel. 956-681-759, www.lasacristia.net, tarifa@lasacristia.net, helpful Serafín and Sandra). They also rent 10 apartments at a separate location.

$$$ **Casa Blan+co,** where minimalist meets Moroccan, is the newest reasonably priced designer hotel on the block. Each of its seven rooms (with double beds only—no twins) is decorated (and priced) differently. The place is decked out with practical amenities (mini-fridge and stovetop) as well as romantic touches—loft beds, walk-in showers, and subtle lighting (high-season Db-€92-133, low-season Db-€52-69, small roof terrace, free Wi-Fi in lobby, off main square at Calle Nuestra Señora de la Luz 2, tel. 956-681-515, www.casablanco.es, info@casablanco.es).

$$$ **Hotel Misiana** has 15 comfortable, recently remodeled, spacious rooms above a bar-lounge. Their designer gave the place a mod pastel boutique-ish ambience. To avoid noise from the lounge below (open until 3:00 in the morning), request a room on a higher floor (Sb-€50/75/115, Db-€75/110/140, fancy top-floor Db suite-€200/230/300, low- and mid-season rates are €10-20 more on weekends, includes breakfast, double-paned windows, elevator, free Wi-Fi, 100 yards directly in front of the church at Calle Sancho IV El Bravo 16, tel. 956-627-083, www.misiana.com, info@misiana.com).

$$$ **Dar Cilla Guesthouse & Apartments** is an old Moroccan-style *dar* (or guest house), built into the town wall and remodeled into eight chic apartments surrounding a communal courtyard. Each apartment has a kitchen and is decorated in modern Moroccan style, with earth-tone walls, tile floors, and Moroccan rugs (Sb-€50/55/65, Db-€100/110/130, superior Db-€120/130/165, Qb-€190/210/240, extra person-€25, 2-night minimum, bigger rooms have air-con, free Wi-Fi, large roof terrace with beautiful view over the old town to the sea, just east of the old-town gate at Calle Cilla 7, tel. 653-467-025, www.darcilla .com, info@darcilla.com).

$$ **La Casa Amarilla** ("The Yellow House") offers 10 posh apartments with tiny kitchens, plus three smaller studios with modern decor (studio Db-€52/77/105, apartment Db-€70/100/120, reserve with credit card, free Wi-Fi, across street from Café Central, Calle Sancho IV El Bravo 9, tel. 956-681-993, www .lacasaamarilla.net, info@lacasaamarilla.net).

$$ **Hostal La Calzada** has eight airy, well-appointed rooms right in the lively old-town thick of things, though the management is rarely around (Db-€50-105, higher in Aug, extra

bed-€20, closed Dec-March, air-con, free Wi-Fi in lobby, 20 yards from church at Calle Justino Pertinez 7, tel. 956-681-492, www .hostallacalzada.com, info@hostallacalzada.com).

$$ Hostal Alameda, overlooking a square where the local children play, glistens with pristine marble floors and dark red decor. The main building has 11 bright rooms and the annex has 16 more-modern rooms; both face the same delightful square (Db-€60/70/90, extra bed-€25-35, air-con, free Wi-Fi, Paseo de la Alameda 4, tel. 956-681-181, www.hostalalameda.com, reservas @hostalalameda.com, Antonio).

$$ Hostal Africa, with 13 bright rooms and an inviting roof terrace, is buried on a very quiet street in the center of town. Its dreamy blue-and-white color scheme and stripped-down feel give it a Moorish ambience (S-€20/25/35, Sb-€25/35/50, D-€30/40/ 50, Db-€35/50/65, Tb-€50/75/100, laundry-€10, free Wi-Fi on terrace, storage for boards and bikes, Calle María Antonia Toledo 12, tel. 956-680-220, mobile 606-914-294, www. hostalafrica.com, hostal_africa@hotmail.com, Miguel and Eva keep the reception desk open only 9:00-24:00).

$$ Pensión Correo rents nine simple rooms (three sharing two bathrooms, one available with kitchen during high season) at a fair value. Room 8 has a private roof terrace, and rooms 6 and 7 have gorgeous views of the town (S-€20/30/50, D-€30/50/65, Db-€40/60/80, Tb-€50/75/90, Qb-€60/90/100, extra bed-€10, reservations more than 24 hours in advance require first night prepaid by credit card—refundable up to 3 days in advance, free Wi-Fi, roof terrace, Coronel Moscardo 8, tel. 956-680-206, www .pensioncorreo.com, welcome@pensioncorreo.com, Luca).

$ Hostal Villanueva offers 12 remodeled rooms at budget prices. It's simple, clean, and friendly. It lacks indoor public areas, but has an inviting terrace overlooking the old town on a busy street. Pepe (who speaks a smidgen of English) asks that you reconfirm your reservation by phone the day before you arrive (Sb-€25-30, Db-€35-55, free Wi-Fi, just west of the old-town gate at Avenida de Andalucía 11, access from outside the wall, tel. 956-684-149, hostalvillanueva@hotmail.com).

Eating in Tarifa

I've grouped my recommendations below into two categories: Sit down to a real restaurant meal, or enjoy a couple of the many characteristic tapas bars in the old town.

Restaurants

Seafood

Restaurante Morilla, facing the church, is on the town's prime piece of people-watching real estate. This is a real restaurant (€1.50 tapas sold only at the stand-up bar and sometimes at a few tables), with good indoor and outdoor seating. It serves tasty local-style fish, grilled or baked—your server will tell you about today's fish; it's sold by weight, so confirm the price carefully (€4-11 starters, €10-17 main dishes, daily 9:00-24:00, Calle Sancho IV El Bravo, tel. 956-681-757).

El Puerto, in a dreary and untouristy area between the port and the beach (near the causeway out to Isla de las Palomas), has a great reputation for its pricey but very fresh seafood. Locals swear that it's a notch or two above the seafood places in town (€8-14 starters, €10-22 seafood dishes and some meats, Thu-Mon 12:00-16:00 & 20:00-24:00, Tue-Wed 12:00-16:00 only, Avenida Fuerzas Armadas 13, tel. 956-681-914).

Italian

La Oca da Sergio, cozy and fun, is one of the numerous pizza-and-pasta joints supported by the large expat Italian community. Sergio prides himself on importing authentic Italian ingredients (€7-11 starters, €9-14 pastas, €7-10 pizzas, €14-16 meat and fish dishes, indoor and outdoor seating, daily 13:00-16:00 & 20:00-24:00 except closed Tue in winter; around the left side of the church and straight back, just before the Moorish-style old-folks' home at Calle General Copons 6; tel. 956-681-249, mobile 615-686-571).

Ristorante La Trattoria, on the Alameda, is another good Italian option, with cloth-napkin class, friendly staff, and ingredients from Italy. Sit inside, near the wood-fired oven, or out along the main strolling street (€7-18 starters and pastas, €6-15 pizzas, €14-25 meat dishes; daily 19:30-1:00 in the morning, July-Aug also Sat-Sun 13:00-16:00, closed Wed off-season; Paseo de la Alameda, tel. 956-682-225).

In the New Town

These two restaurants are in a residential area just above the beach, about a 15-minute walk (or easy car or taxi ride) from the old town. They're worth a detour for their great food, and for the chance to see an area away from the main tourist zone (though the sushi bar is on the beach and is no stranger to tourists). To get to either, begin by heading up Calle San Sebastián, which turns into Calle Pintor Pérez Villalta. When you see a big staircase immediately on your right, take it to reach Restaurante Souk, or turn left toward

COSTA DEL SOL

the beach to find Surfing Sushi in the large beige Surla building.

Restaurante Souk serves a tasty fusion of Moroccan, Indian, and Thai cuisine in a dark, exotic, romantic, purely Moroccan ambience. The ground floor (where you enter) is a bar and atmospheric tea house, while the dining room is downstairs (€6-10 starters, €12-16 main dishes; July-Sept daily 20:00-3:00 in the morning; Oct-June Wed-Mon 20:00-1:00, closed Tue; good wine list, Mar Tirreno 46, tel. 956-627-065, friendly Claudia).

Surfing Sushi, part of a cool surfer bar called Surla, serves up wonderfully executed sushi using only the freshest of ingredients. Situated just a few steps above the beachfront walkway, it's at the center of a sprawling zone of après-surf hangouts. They also offer delivery (€16-21 shareable sushi platters, daily 21:00-24:00 except closed Wed off-season, possible to order delivery sushi by phone at other times, Calle Pintor Pérez Villalta 1, tel. 956-685-175).

Tapas

Bar El Francés is a thriving hole-in-the-wall where "Frenchies" (as the bar's name implies) Marcial and Alexandra serve tasty little plates of tapas. From Café Central, follow the cars 100 yards to the first corner on the left to reach this simple, untouristy standing-and-stools-only eatery. This spot is popular for its fine *raciones* (€6-10) and tapas (€1.30-1.80)—especially oxtail *(rabo del toro),* fish in brandy sauce *(pescado in salsa al cognac),* pork with spice *(chicharrones),* and garlic-grilled tuna *(atún a la plancha).* The outdoor terrace with restaurant-type tables (no tapas served here) is an understandably popular spot to enjoy a casual meal. Show this book and Marcial will be happy to bring you a free glass of sherry (open daily long hours June-Aug; closed Wed-Thu March-May and Sept-Nov; closed Dec-Feb; Calle Sancho IV El Bravo 21A, mobile 685-867-005).

Café Bar Los Melli is a local favorite for feasts on rickety tables set on cobbles. This family-friendly place, run by Ramón and Juani, offers a good chorizo sandwich and *patatas bravas*—potatoes with a hot tomato sauce served on a wooden board (€5 half-*raciones*, €8 *raciones,* Thu-Tue 20:00-24:00, Sat-Sun also 13:00-16:00, closed Wed; from Bar El Francés, cross parking lot and take Calle del Legionario Ríos Moya up one block; mobile 605-866-444). **Bar El Pasillo,** next to Los Melli, also serves tapas (closed Mon-Tue). **El Otro Melli,** run by Ramón's brother José, is a few blocks away on Plaza de San Martín.

La Posada, a local-feeling place a block beyond the main tourist zone (and just up the street from Los Melli), takes pride in its fresh ingredients. There's a small dining room, a nondescript bar with a giant stone beer tap that's a replica of the city's first communal faucet, and tables out front near the real thing (€1.50 *montaditos,* €3 *tostadas,* €4-6 half-*raciones,* €7-11 *raciones;* July-Aug daily 13:00-16:30 & 20:00-24:00; Sept-June Wed-Mon 20:00-24:00, also open Sat-Sun 13:00-16:30, closed Tue; Calle Guzman el Bueno 3A, mobile 636-929-449).

Café Central is *the* happening place nearly any time of day—it's the perch for all the cool tourists. Less authentically Spanish than the others I've listed, it has a hip, international vibe. The bustling ambience and appealing setting in front of the church are better than the food (€1.30 tapas, €5 half-*raciones*), but they do have breakfast with eggs (€2-4), good €7 salads (study the menu), and impressively therapeutic healthy fruit drinks (daily 8:30-24:00, off Plaza San Mateo, near church, tel. 956-682-877).

Casino Tarifeno is just to the sea side of the church. It's an old-boys' social club "for members only," but it offers a musty Andalusian welcome to visiting tourists, including women. Wander through. There's a low-key bar with tapas, a TV room, a card room, and a lounge. There's no menu, but prices are standard. Just point and say the size you want: tapa (€1.20), *media-ración* (€4), or *ración* (€7). A far cry from some of the trendy options around town, this is a local institution (daily 12:00-24:00).

Mesón El Picoteo is a small, characteristic bar popular with locals and tourists alike for its good tapas and *montaditos*. Eat in the casual, woody interior or at one of the barrel tables out front (€1.30 tapas & *montaditos,* €3-7 half-*raciones,* €5-14 *raciones,* €7-15 meat and fish plates, long hours daily, a few blocks west of the old town on Calle Mariano Vinuesa, tel. 956-681-128).

Pastries, Beach Bars, and Picnics

Breakfast or Dessert: **Confitería La Tarifeña** serves super pastries and flan-like *tocino de cielo* (daily 9:00-21:00, at the top of Calle Nuestra Señora de la Luz, near the main old-town gate).

Churrería La Palmera serves breakfast before most hotels and cafés have even turned on the lights—early enough for you to get your coffee fix, and/or bulk up on *churros* and chocolate, before hopping the first ferry to Tangier (daily 6:00-13:00, Calle Sanchez IV El Bravo 34).

Chilimoso, literally a small hole in the old-town wall, serves fresh and healthy vegetarian options, homemade desserts, and a variety of teas. It's a rare find in meat-loving Spain. Eat at one of the few indoor tables, or get it to go and find a bench on the nearby Paseo de la Alameda (daily 12:30-15:30 & 19:30-23:00, just west of the old town gate on Calle del Peso).

Windsurfer Bars: If you have a car, head to the string of beaches. Many have bars and fun-loving thatched restaurants that keep the wet-suited gang fed and watered.

Picnics: Stop by the **mercado municipal** (farmers' market, Mon-Sat 8:00-14:00, closed Sun, in old town, inside gate nearest TI), any grocery, or the **superSol supermarket** (Mon-Sat 9:30-21:30, closed Sun, has simple cafeteria, near the hotels in the new town at Callao and San José).

Tarifa Connections

Tarifa
From Tarifa by Bus to: La Línea de la Concepción/Gibraltar (2/day direct, 1 hour, starting around 12:00; more possible with transfer in Algeciras, 1.5 hours), **Algeciras** (14/day, less on weekends, 45 minutes, Comes), **Jerez** (1/day, 2 hours, more frequent with transfer in Cádiz), **Sevilla** (4/day, 2.5-3.25 hours), and **Málaga** (2-3/day, 2.5-4 hours, Portillo). **Bus info:** Comes (tel. 956-291-168, www.tgcomes.es), Portillo (tel. 902-450-550, http://portillo.avanzabus.com).

Ferries from Tarifa to Tangier, Morocco: Two boat companies make the 35-minute journey to Tangier's city-center Medina Port about every hour.

Algeciras
Algeciras (ahl-*h*eh-THEE-rahs, with a guttural *h*) is only worth leaving. It's useful to the traveler mainly as a transportation hub, with trains and buses to destinations in southern and central Spain (it also has a ferry to Tangier, but it takes you to the Tangier MED port about 25 miles from Tangier city—going from Tarifa is much better). If you're headed for Gibraltar or Tarifa by public transport, you'll almost certainly change in Algeciras at some point.

Everything of interest is on Juan de la Cierva, which heads inland from the port. The **TI** is about a block in (Mon-Fri 9:00-20:00, Sat-Sun 9:30-15:00, tel. 956-784-131), followed by the side-by-side **train station** (opposite Hotel Octavio) and **bus station** three more blocks later.

Trains: If arriving at the train station, head out the front door: The bus station (called San Bernardo Estación de Autobuses) is ahead and on the right; the TI is another three blocks ahead (the road becomes Juan de la Cierva when the road jogs), also on the right; and the port is just beyond.

From Algeciras by Train to: Madrid (2/day, 5.5 hours, arrives at Atocha), **Ronda** (5-6/day, 1.5-2 hours), **Granada** (3/day, 4.25-5 hours), **Sevilla** (3/day, 5-6 hours, transfer at Antequera or Bobadilla, bus is better), **Córdoba** (2/day direct on Altaria, 3.25

hours; more with transfer in Antequera or Bobadilla, 5-5.5 hours), **Málaga** (3/day, 3.5 hours, transfer in Bobadilla; bus is faster). With the exception of the route to Madrid, these are particularly scenic trips; the best (though slow) is the mountainous journey to Málaga via Bobadilla.

Buses: Algeciras is served by three different bus companies (Comes, Portillo, and Linesur), all located in the same terminal (called San Bernardo Estación de Autobuses) next to Hotel Octavio and directly across from the train station. The companies generally serve different destinations, but there is some overlap. Compare schedules and rates to find the most convenient bus for you. By the ticket counter you'll find an easy red letter board that lists departures. Lockers are near the platforms—purchase a token at the machines (€3.20).

From Algeciras by Bus: Comes (tel. 956-291-168, www .tgcomes.es) runs buses to **La Línea/Gibraltar** (2/hour, less on weekends, 45 minutes), **Tarifa** (14/day, less on weekends, 45 minutes), **Ronda** (1/day, 2.75 hours), **Sevilla** (4/day, 3-4 hours), **Jerez** (2/day 2.5 hours), and **Madrid** (5/day, 8 hours).

Portillo (tel. 956-654-304, http://portillo.avanzabus.com) offers buses to **Málaga** (hourly, 2.25 hours *direcCo*, 3 hours *ruta*), **Málaga Airport** (2/day, 2 hours), and **Granada** (3/day *directo*, 4 hours; 1/day *ruta*, 5.5 hours).

Linesur (tel. 956-667-649, www.linesur.com) runs the most frequent direct buses to **Sevilla** (8/day, fewer on weekends, 2.5-3 hours) and **Jerez** (6/day, fewer on weekends, 1.5 hours).

Ferries from Algeciras to Tangier, Morocco: Although it's possible to sail from Algeciras to Tangier, the ferry takes you to the Tangier MED Port, which is 25 miles east of Tangier city and a hassle. You're better off taking a ferry from Tarifa: They sail direct to the port in Tangier. If you must sail from Algeciras, buy your ticket at the port (skip the divey-looking travel agencies littering the town). Official offices of the boat companies are inside the main port building, directly behind the helpful little English-speaking info kiosk (8-22 ferries/day, port open daily 6:45-21:45, tel. 956-585-463).

Route Tips for Drivers

Tarifa to Gibraltar (45 minutes): This short drive takes you past a silvery-white forest of windmills, from peaceful Tarifa past Algeciras to La Línea (the Spanish town bordering Gibraltar). Passing Algeciras, continue in the direction of Estepona. At San Roque, take the La Línea-Gibraltar exit.

Gibraltar to Nerja (130 miles): Barring traffic problems, the trip along the Costa del Sol is smooth and easy by car—much of it on a new highway. Just follow the coastal highway east. After Málaga, follow signs to *Almería* and *Motril*.

Nerja to Granada (80 miles, 1.5 hours, 100 views): Drive along the coast to Motril, catching N-323 north for about 40 miles to Granada. While scenic side-trips may beckon, don't arrive late in Granada without a confirmed hotel reservation.

COSTA DEL SOL

MOROCCO

MOROCCO

Al-Maghreb

A young country with an old history, Morocco is a photographer's delight and a budget traveler's dream. It's cheap, exotic, and easier and more appealing than ever. Along with a rich culture, Morocco offers plenty of contrast—from beach resorts to bustling desert markets, from jagged mountains to sleepy, mud-brick oasis towns. And there's been a distinct new energy since King Mohammed VI took the throne in 1999.

Morocco (*Marruecos* in Spanish; *Al-Maghreb* in Arabic) also provides a good dose of culture shock—both bad and good. It makes Spain seem meek and mild. You'll encounter oppressive friendliness, brutal heat, the Arabic language, the Islamic faith, ancient cities, and aggressive beggars.

While Morocco is clearly a place apart from Mediterranean Europe, it doesn't really seem like Africa either. It's a mix, reflecting its strategic position between the two continents. Situated on the Strait of Gibraltar, Morocco has been flooded by waves of invasions over the centuries. The Berbers, the native population, have had to contend with the Phoenicians, Carthaginians, Romans, Vandals, and more.

The Arabs brought Islam to Morocco in the seventh century A.D. and stuck around, battling the Berbers in various civil wars. A series of Berber and Arab dynasties rose and fell; the Berbers won out and still run the country today.

From the 15th century on, European countries carved up much of Africa. By the early 20th century, most of Morocco was under French control, and strategic Tangier was jointly ruled by multiple European powers. The country wasn't granted independence until 1956. In the late 1970s, Morocco itself became an invading country, grabbing Spain's Western Sahara territory and causing the relatively few inhabitants to clamor for independence. Western Sahara's claim

Islam 101

Islam has more than a billion adherents worldwide, and traveling in an Islamic country is an opportunity to better understand the religion. This admittedly basic and simplistic outline (written by a non-Muslim) is meant to help travelers from the Christian West understand a very rich but often misunderstood culture.

Muslims, like Christians and Jews, are monotheistic. They call God "Allah." The most important person in the Islamic faith is the prophet Muhammad, who lived in the sixth and seventh centuries A.D. The holy book of Islam is the Quran, believed by Muslims to be the word of Allah as revealed to Muhammad.

The "five pillars" of Islam are the core tenets of the faith. Followers of Islam should:

1. Say and believe, "There is only one God, and Muhammad is his prophet."

2. Pray five times a day, facing Mecca. Modern Muslims explain that it's important for this ritual to include washing, exercising, stretching, and thinking of God.

3. Give to the poor (one-fortieth of your wealth, if you are not in debt).

4. Fast during daylight hours through the month of Ramadan. Fasting is a great social equalizer and helps everyone to feel the hunger of the poor.

5. Make a pilgrimage to Mecca. Muslims who can afford it, and who are physically able, are required to travel to the sacred sites in Mecca and Medina at least once in their lifetimes.

Just as it helps to know about spires, feudalism, and the saints to comprehend European sightseeing, a few basics on Islam help make your sightseeing in Morocco more meaningful.

still has not been settled by the United Nations.

Unfortunately, most of the English-speaking Moroccans the typical tourist meets are hustlers. Many visitors develop some intestinal problems by the end of their visit. Most women are harassed on the streets by horny but generally harmless men. And in terms of efficiency, Morocco makes Spain look like Sweden.

When you cruise south across the Strait of Gibraltar, leave your busy itineraries and split-second timing behind. Morocco must be taken on its own terms. In Morocco things go smoothly

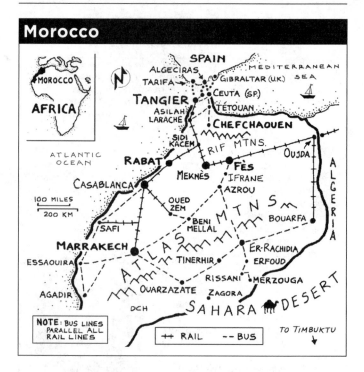

only *"Inshallah"*—if God so wills.

Politics and Safety: As throughout the Arab world, Morocco has had its share of political unrest in recent years. Widespread but mostly peaceful protests in 2011, influenced by the Arab Spring, called for greater democracy and economic reforms. A new constitution, adopted later that year, gave more power to the legislative branch and the prime minister—the ostensible head of government (although critics say King Mohammmed VI retained actual authority).

Morocco is also struggling to reconcile tensions between Islamist and secular factions within its government and in the region. Bombings attributed to Islamic fundamentalists killed 45 people in Casablanca in 2003 and 17 in Marrakech in 2011, and were met with widespread condemnation by the Moroccan people.

Americans pondering a visit may wonder how they'll be received in this Muslim nation. Al Jazeera blares from televisions in all the bars, but I've seen no angry graffiti or posters and felt no animosity toward American individuals there (even on my last visit, literally days after US forces killed Osama bin Laden). And it's culturally enriching for Westerners to experience Morocco—a Muslim monarchy with many women still in traditional dress and roles, succeeding on its own terms without embracing modern Western "norms."

If you're still concerned, check the state department's website for travel advisories: www.travel.state.gov.

Hustler Alert: Moroccans may be some of Africa's wealthiest people, but you are still incredibly rich to them.

This imbalance causes predictable problems. Wear your money belt. Assume con artists are more clever than you. Haggle when appropriate; prices skyrocket for tourists. You'll attract hustlers like flies at every famous tourist site or whenever you pull out your guidebook or a map. In the worst-case scenario, they'll lie to you, get you lost, blackmail you, and pester the heck out of you. Never leave your car or baggage where you can't get back to it without someone else's "help." Anything you buy in a guide's company gets him a 20 percent commission. Normally locals, shopkeepers, and police will come to your rescue if the hustlers' heat becomes unbearable. Consider hiring a guide, since it's helpful to have a translator, and once you're "taken," the rest seem to leave you alone.

Marijuana Alert: In Morocco, marijuana *(kif)* is as illegal as it is popular, a fact that many Westerners in local jails would love to remind you of. As a general rule, just walk right by those hand-carved pipes in the marketplace. Some dealers who sell it cheap make their profit after you get arrested. Cars and buses are stopped and checked by police routinely throughout Morocco—especially in the north and in the Chefchaouen region, which is Morocco's *kif* capital.

Health: Morocco is much more hazardous to your health than Spain. Eat in clean—not cheap—places. Peel fruit, eat only cooked vegetables, and drink reliably bottled water (Sidi Ali or Sidi Harazem). When you do get diarrhea—and you should plan on it—adjust your diet (small and bland meals, no milk or grease) or fast for a day, but make sure you replenish lost fluids. Relax: Most diarrhea is not serious, just an adjustment that will run its course.

Closed Days and Ramadan: Friday is the Muslim day of rest, when most of the country (except Tangier) closes down. During the major month-long religious holiday of Ramadan (June 28-July 27 in 2014), Muslims focus on prayer and reflection. Following Islamic doctrine, they refrain during daylight hours from eating, drinking (including water), smoking, and having sex. On the final day of Ramadan, Muslims celebrate *Eid* (an all-day feast and gift-giving party, similar to Christmas), and travelers may find some less-touristy stores and restaurants closed.

Money: Euros work here (as do dollars and pounds). If you're on a five-hour tour, bring along lots of €1 and €0.50 coins for tips, small purchases, and camel rides. But if you plan to do anything independently, change some money into Moroccan dirhams upon arrival (8 dh = about $1).

Information: Travel information, English or otherwise, is rare here. For an extended trip, bring guidebooks from home or Spain—Lonely Planet and Rough Guide both publish good ones. Buy the best map you can find locally—names are always changing, and if you need to ask someone, it's helpful to have towns, roads, and place names written in Arabic.

Language: With its unique history of having been controlled by so many different foreign and domestic rulers, Tangier is a babel of languages. Most locals speak Arabic first and French second (all Moroccans must learn it in schools); sensing that you're a foreigner, they'll most likely address you in French. Spanish ranks third, and English a distant fourth. The Arabic squiggle-script, its many difficult sounds, and the fact that French is Morocco's second language combine to make communication tricky for English-speaking travelers. A little French goes a long way, but learn a few words in Arabic. Have your first local friend help you with the pronunciation:

English	Arabic	Pronounced
Hello. ("Peace be with you")	Salaam alaikum.	sah-LAHM ah-LAY-koom
Hello. (response: "Peace also be with you")	Wa alaikum salaam.	wah ah-LAY-koom sah-LAHM
Please.	Min fadlik.	meen FAHD-leek
Thank you.	Shokran.	SHOH-kron (like "sugar on")
Excuse me.	Ismahli.	ees-SMAH-lee
Yes.	Yeh.	EE-yeh
No.	Lah.	lah
Give me five. (kids enjoy this...not above but straight ahead)	Ham sah.	hahm sah
OK.	Wah hah.	wah hah
Very good.	Miz yen biz ef.	meez EE-yehn beez ehf
Goodbye.	Maa salama.	mah sah-LEM-ah

MOROCCO

Moroccans are more touchy-feely than their Spanish neighbors. Expect lots of hugs if you make an effort to communicate. When greeting someone, a handshake is customary, followed by placing your right hand over your heart. Listen carefully and write new words phonetically. Bring an Arabic phrase book. It helps to know that *souk* means a particular market (such as for leather, yarn, or metalwork), while a *kasbah* is loosely defined as a fortress (or a town within old fortress walls). In markets, I sing, "la la la la la" to my opponents. *Lah shokran* means "No, thank you."

TANGIER

Tanja

Go to Africa. As you step off the boat, you realize that the crossing (less than an hour) has taken you further culturally than did the trip from the US to Spain. Morocco needs no museums; its sights are living in the streets. For decades, its once-grand coastal city of Tangier deserved its reputation as the "Tijuana of Africa." But that has changed. King Mohammad VI is enthusiastic about Tangier, and there's a fresh can-do spirit in the air. The town is as Moroccan as ever...yet more enjoyable and less stressful.

Morocco in a Day?

Though Morocco certainly deserves more than a day, many visitors touring Spain see it in a quick side-trip. And, though such a short sprint through Tangier is only a tease, it's far more interesting than another day in Spain. A day in Tangier gives you a good introduction to Morocco, a legitimate taste of North Africa, and a nonthreatening slice of Islam. All you need is a passport (no visa or shots required) and around €60 for a tour package or the round-trip ferry crossing.

Your big decisions: where to sail from; whether to go on your own or buy a ferry/guided tour day-trip package; and whether to make it a day trip or spend the night. Of these, the most important question is:

With a Tour or on My Own?: Because the ferry company expects you to do a lot of shopping (providing them with kickbacks), it's actually about the same cost to join a one-day tour as it is to buy a round-trip ferry ticket. Do you want the safety and comfort of having Morocco handed to you on a user-friendly platter? Or do you want the independence to see what you want to see, with a more authentic experience, fewer cultural clichés, and less forced shopping? There are pros and cons to each approach, depending on your travel style.

On a package tour, visitors are met by a guide, taken on a bus tour and a walk through the old-town market, offered a couple of crass Kodak moments with snake charmers and desert dancers, and given lunch with live music and belly-dancing. Then they visit a big shop and are hustled back down to their boat where—five hours after they landed—they return to the First World thankful they don't have diarrhea.

The alternative is to simply take the ferry on your own. Things are cheap and relatively safe. Since more than 90 percent of visitors choose the comfort of a tour, independent adventurers rarely see another tourist and avoid all the kitsch. You can catch a morning boat and spend the entire day, returning that evening; extend with an overnight in Tangier; or even head deeper into Morocco (if you do that, you'll need another guidebook).

My preferred approach is sort of a hybrid: Go to Morocco "on your own," but arrange in advance to meet up with a local guide to ease your culture shock and accompany you to your choice of sights (or you can book a tour with the ferry company and pay for the "VIP" option). While this costs a bit more than joining a package tour, ultimately the cost difference (roughly €10-20 more per person) is pretty negligible, considering the dramatically increased cultural intimacy. Doing it entirely on your own (no guide at all) can be a great adventure, but potentially more stressful.

Time Difference: Morocco is on Greenwich Mean Time (like Great Britain), so it's one hour behind Spain. It typically observes Daylight Saving Time, but its summer hours last about two months less than in Europe. Morocco "springs forward" in late April (about a month after Spain) and "falls back" in late September (about a month before Spain). Therefore, during the summer months, Morocco is either one hour (if they've changed) or two hours (if they haven't changed, or have already changed back) behind Spain. In general, ferry and other schedules use the local time (if your boat leaves Tangier "at 17:00," that means 5:00 p.m. Moroccan time—not Spanish time)...be sure to change your watch when you get off the boat.

Terminology: Note that the Spanish refer to Morocco as "Marruecos" (mar-WAY-kohs) and Tangier as "Tánger" (TAHN-hair, with a guttural h).

Going on Your Own, by Ferry from Tarifa

While the trip to Tangier can be made from various ports, only the ferry from Tarifa takes you to Tangier's city-center port, called the Tangier Medina Port (Spaniards call it the *Puerto Viejo*, "Old Port"). Boats from Algeciras or Gibraltar dock instead at the Tangier MED Port (Spaniards call it the *Puerto Nuevo*, "New Port"), about 25 miles east of the city center. (Note: Confusingly, because the city-center port is being remodeled, some Moroccans call it the "new port"—exactly the opposite of the Spaniards.) Tangier's city-center port has been closed to cargo shipping, and is in the midst of a massive renovation and beautification project, set to be completed in 2016, which will extend the pier to accommodate large cruise ships and create a marina for yachts.

I'll describe the trip assuming you're sailing from Tarifa to Tangier's city-center Medina Port—the most logical route for the typical traveler.

Ferry Crossing: Two ferry companies make the 35-minute crossing from Tarifa, Spain to Tangier, Morocco about every hour from 8:00 to 22:00: **FRS** (tel. 956-681-830, www.frs.es) and newcomer **InterShipping** (tel. 956-684-729, info.intershipping @gmail.com). FRS ferries depart Tarifa on odd hours (9:00, 11:00, and so on); InterShipping boats leave Tarifa on even hours (8:00, 10:00, and so on). Prices are roughly €33 one-way and €60 round-trip. Return boats from Tangier to Tarifa run from about 7:00 to 21:00.

Tickets are very easy to get: You can buy them at the port, through your hotel in Tarifa, or from a local travel agency. You can also get FRS tickets at either of their offices in Tarifa: One is just outside the old-town wall, at the corner of Avenida de Andalucía and Avenida de la Constitución (Mon-Fri 8:00-21:00, Sat 8:00-15:00, closed Sun, tel. 956-681-830, www.frs.es). The other location, with longer hours on weekends, is near the port on Calle Alcalde Juan Núñez 2 (daily 9:00-13:00 & 15:00-21:00). InterShipping has an office at the Tarifa's port, but none in town. You can almost always just buy a ticket and walk on, though in the busiest summer months (July-Aug), the popular 8:00 & 9:00 departures could be booked up with tours. Boats are most crowded in July, August, and during the month of Ramadan. A few crossings a year are canceled because of storms or wind, mostly in winter.

Procedure: The ferry from Tarifa is a fast Nordic hydrofoil that theoretically takes 35 minutes to cross. It often leaves late, but you'll still want to arrive early to give yourself time to clear customs (making the whole trip take closer to an hour). You'll go through Spanish customs at the port and Moroccan customs on the ferry. Whether taking a tour or traveling on your own, you

TANGIER

must get a stamp (available on board) from the Moroccan immigration officer. After you leave Spain, find the customs desk on the boat, line up early, and get your passport and entry paper—which they keep—stamped. If you're coming back the same day and know your return time, the immigration official may also give you an exit stamp (for your return from Morocco), which prevents delays at the port at departure time. The ferry is equipped with WCs, a shop, and

a snack bar. Tarifa's modern little terminal has a cafeteria and WCs.

Hiring a Guide: Even if you're visiting Morocco independently, I recommend hiring a local guide to show you around Tangier.

Tangier MED Port: Ferries from Algeciras and Gibraltar arrive at the Tangier MED Port, 25 miles from downtown. While this wastes time (it's about an hour each way from the boat to downtown Tangier), the connection is simple: A free shuttle bus picks up passengers at the Tangier MED Port terminal and brings them right to the entrance of the Tangier Medina Port, in the city center.

Returning to Tarifa: It's smart to return to the port about 30 minutes before your ferry departs. If you didn't get your passport's exit stamp on the way over, you must wait in line to get it stamped at the Tangier ferry terminal before you board the boat.

Taking a Package Tour

Taking a package tour is easier but less rewarding than doing it on your own or with a private local guide. A typical day-trip tour

includes a round-trip crossing and a guide who meets your big group at a prearranged point in Tangier, then hustles you through the hustlers and onto your tour bus. Several guides await the arrival of each ferry in Tangier and assemble their groups. (Tourists wear stickers identifying which tour they're with.) All offer essentially the same five-hour Tangier experience: a city bus tour, a drive through the ritzy palace neighborhood, a walk through the Medina (old town), and an overly thorough look at a sales-starved carpet shop (where prices include a 20 percent commission for your guide and tour company; some carpet shops are actually owned by the ferry company). Longer tours may include a trip to the desolate Atlantic Coast for some rugged African scenery, and the famous ride-a-camel stop (five-minute camel ride for a couple of euros). Any tour wraps up with lunch in a palatial Moroccan setting with live music (and non-Moroccan belly dancing), topped off by a final walk back to your boat through a gauntlet of desperate merchants.

Sound cheesy? It is. But no amount of packaging can gloss over this exotic and different culture. This kind of cultural voyeurism is almost embarrassing, but it's nonstop action.

The day trip is so tightly organized that tourists have hardly any time alone in Tangier. For many people, that's just fine. But frankly, seeing a line of day-trippers clutching their bags nervously like paranoid kangaroos reminded me of a self-imposed hostage crisis. It was pathetic.

You rarely need to book a tour more than a day in advance, even during peak season. Tours generally cost about €60 (about the same as a round-trip ferry ticket alone—they make their money off commissions if you shop, and get a group rate on the ferry tickets). Prices are roughly the same no matter where you buy. While some agencies run their own tours, others simply sell tickets on excursions operated by FRS. Ultimately, it's the luck of the draw as to which guide you're assigned. Don't worry about which tour company you select. (They're all equally bad.)

Tours leave Tarifa on a variable schedule: For example, one tour may depart at 9:00 and return at 15:00, the next could run 11:00-19:00 (offering a longer experience), and the next 13:00-19:00. If you're an independent type on a one-day tour, you could stay with your group until you return to the ferry dock, and then just slip back into town on your own, thinking, "Freedom!" You're welcome to use your return ferry ticket on any later boat. (Although FRS and InterShipping both have departures generally every other hour, tickets are *not* interchangeable between the two ferry companies).

You can pay extra for various add-ons. For an extra €15 per person beyond the cost of a standard tour, they will arrange a **"VIP tour"** for up to four people—you'll get a private guide and vehicle, plus lunch. This is actually quite economical, especially if you're traveling as a foursome and would prefer a more personalized experience.

If you want a longer visit, it's cheap to book a package through the ferry company that includes staying in a Tangier hotel for one night (only €30-35 more than the regular tour, €10 extra in peak season, includes guiding and 2 lunches and 1 dinner). If you stay overnight, the first day is the same as the one-day tour, but rather than catching the boat that afternoon, you take the same boat—on your own—24 hours later. There's also a two-day option that includes no guiding or meals (€25-30 more than regular tour, €12 extra in peak season).

Booking a Package Tour: If you're taking one of these tours, you may as well book direct with the **ferry company** (see contact information earlier, under "Ferry Crossing," or visit their offices at the port in Tarifa), or through your **hotel** (you'll pay the same, but the hotel gets a commission; if you know you want to visit Morocco with a tour, ask your hotel to book it when you reserve). There's not much reason to book with a **travel agency,** but offices all over southern Spain and in Tarifa sell ferry tickets and seats on tours. In Tarifa, Luís and Antonio at Baelo Tour offer Rick Steves readers a 10 percent discount (daily in summer 7:00-21:00, across from TI at Avenida de la Constitución 5, tel. 956-681-242); other Tarifa-based agencies are Tarifa Travel and Travelsur (both on Avenida de Andalucía, above the old-town walls).

Tangier

Artists, writers, and musicians have always loved Tangier. Delacroix and Matisse were drawn by its evocative light. The Beat generation, led by William S. Burroughs and Jack Kerouac, sought the city's multicultural, otherworldly feel. Paul Bowles found his sheltering sky here. From the 1920s through the 1950s, Tangier was an "international city," too strategic to give to any one nation, and jointly governed by as many as nine different powers, including France, Spain, Britain, Italy, Belgium, the Netherlands...and Morocco. The city was a tax-free zone (since there was no single authority to collect taxes), which created a booming free-for-all atmosphere, attracting playboy millionaires, bon vivants, globetrotting scoundrels, con artists, and expat romantics. Tangier enjoyed a cosmopolitan golden age that, in many ways, shaped the city visitors see today.

Tangier is always defying expectations. Ruled by Spain in the 19th century and France in the 20th, it's a rare place where signs are in three languages...and English doesn't make the cut. In this Muslim city, you'll find a synagogue, Catholic and Anglican churches, and the town's largest mosque in close proximity.

Because of its "international zone" status, Morocco's previous king effectively disowned the city, denying it national funds for improvements. Over time, neglected Tangier became the armpit of Morocco. But when the new king—Mohammed VI—was crowned in 1999, the first city he visited was Tangier. His vision has been to restore Tangier to its former glory.

While the city (with a population of 700,000 and growing quickly) has a long way to go, restorations are taking place on a grand scale: The beach has been painstakingly cleaned, pedestrian promenades are popping up, and gardens bloom with lush new greenery. A brand-new futuristic soccer stadium opened in 2011, and the city-center port is being converted into a huge, slick leisure-craft complex that will handle cruise megaships, yachts, and ferries from Tarifa.

I'm uplifted by the new Tangier—it's affluent and modern without having abandoned its roots and embraced Western values. Many visitors are impressed by the warmth of the Moroccan people. Notice how they touch their right hand to their heart after shaking hands or saying, "thank you"—a kind gesture meant to emphasize sincerity. (In Islam, the right hand is holy, while the left hand is evil. Moroccans who eat with their hands—as many civilized people do in this part of the world—always eat with their right hand; the left hand is for washing.)

A visit to Morocco—so close to Europe, yet embracing the Arabic language and script and Muslim faith—lets a Westerner marinated in anti-Muslim propaganda see what Islam aspires to be and can be...and realize it is not a threat.

Planning Your Time

If you're not on a package tour, pre-arrange for a guide to meet you at the ferry dock, hire a guide upon arrival, or head on your own to the big square called the Grand Socco to get oriented (you can walk or catch a Petit Taxi from the port to the Grand Socco). Get your bearings with my Grand Socco spin-tour, then delve into the old town (the lower Medina, with the Petit Socco, market, and American Legation Museum; and the upper Medina's Kasbah, with its museum and residential lanes). With more time, take a taxi to sightsee along the beach and then along Avenue Mohammed VI, through the urban new town, and back to the port. You'll rarely see other tourists outside the tour-group circuit.

After Dark: Nighttime is great in Tangier. If you're spending the night, don't relax in a fancy hotel restaurant. Get out and about in the old town after dark. It's an entirely different experience and a highlight of any visit. (But remember, this isn't night-owl Spain—things die down by around 22:00.)

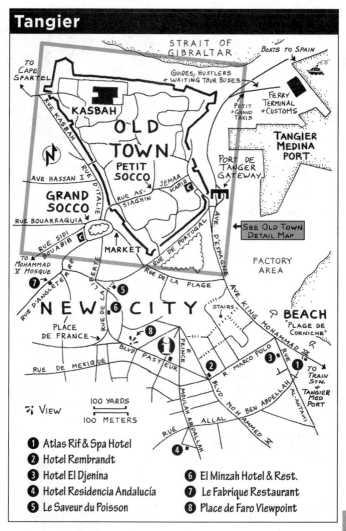

Tangier

STRAIT OF GIBRALTAR

BOATS TO SPAIN

TO CAPE SPARTEL

GUIDES, HUSTLERS & WAITING TOUR BUSES

FERRY TERMINAL & CUSTOMS

PETIT & GRAND TAXIS

KASBAH

OLD TOWN

PORT DE TANGER GATEWAY

TANGIER MEDINA PORT

RUE KASBAH

AVE HASSAN I

RUE D'ITALIE

PETIT SOCCO

JEMAA KABIR

RUE AS-SIAGHIN

GRAND SOCCO

RUE BOUARRAQUIA

RUE SIDI BOUABIB

MARKET

RUE DE PORTUGAL

AVE D'ESPAGNE

SEE OLD TOWN DETAIL MAP

FACTORY AREA

TO MOHAMMAD V MOSQUE

RUE DE LA PLAGE

7

5

RUE D'ANGLETERRE

RUE DE LIBERTE

RUE DE LA

N E W **6** **C I T Y**

STAIRS

AVE KING MOHAMMAD VI

BEACH

"PLAGE DE CORNICHE"

PLACE DE FRANCE

8

RUE DE MEXIQUE

BLVD PASTEUR

R. PRINCE

BLVD. MOH. BEN ABDELLAH

2 R. MARCO POLO **3**

1

RUE AL-ANTAKI

TO TRAIN STN. & TANGIER MED PORT

RUE MOULAY ABDALLAH

ALLAL

4

7 VIEW

100 YARDS
100 METERS

1 Atlas Rif & Spa Hotel
2 Hotel Rembrandt
3 Hotel El Djenina
4 Hotel Residencia Andalucía
5 Le Saveur du Poisson
6 El Minzah Hotel & Rest.
7 Le Fabrique Restaurant
8 Place de Faro Viewpoint

Orientation to Tangier

Like almost every city in Morocco, Tangier is split in two: old and new. From the ferry dock you'll see the old town (Medina)—encircled by its medieval wall—on your right, behind Hotel Continental. (The wall itself is being restored, with completion expected sometime in 2016.) The old town has the markets, the Kasbah (with its palace and the mosque of the Kasbah—marked by the higher of the two minarets you see), cheap hotels, characteristic guesthouses, homes both decrepit and recently renovated, and

2,000 wannabe guides. The twisty, hilly streets of the old town are caged within a wall accessible by keyhole gates. The larger minaret (on the left) belongs to the modern Mohammed V mosque—the biggest one in town.

The new town, with the TI and modern international-style hotels, sprawls past the industrial port zone to your left. The big square, Grand Socco, is the hinge between the old and new parts of town.

Note that while tourists (and this guidebook) refer to the twisty old town as "the Medina," locals consider both the old and new parts of the city center to be medinas.

Tangier is the fifth-largest city in Morocco, and many visitors assume they'll get lost here. While the city could use more street signs, it's laid out simply—although once you enter the mazelike Medina, all bets are off. Nothing listed under "Sights in Tangier" is more than a 20-minute walk from the port. Petit Taxis (described later, under "Getting Around Tangier") are a remarkably cheap godsend for the hot and tired tourist. Use them liberally.

Because so many different colonial powers have had a finger in this city, it goes by many names: In English, it's Tangier (or Tangiers); in French, Tanger (tahn-zhay); in Arabic, it's Tanja (TAHN-zhah); in Spanish, Tánger (TAHN-*h*air, with a guttural *h*); and so on. Unless you speak Arabic, French is the handiest second language, followed by Spanish and (finally) English.

Tourist Information

The TI, about a 15-minute gradual uphill walk from the Grand Socco, is not particularly helpful (English is in short supply, but a little French goes a long way). But at least you can pick up a free town brochure—in French only—with a town map (Mon-Fri 8:30-16:30, closed Sat-Sun, in new town at Boulevard Pasteur 29, tel. 0539-94-80-50). There's also a TI desk at the Tangier MED Port, and there may be one at the city-center Tangier Medina Port in the future.

The urban area around the Tangier TI has a few interesting features. The yellow building across the small street from the TI (toward the Grand Socco) is a synagogue. A block farther is the beautiful Place de Faro terrace, with its cannons and views back to Spain. (Nicknamed "Terrace of the Lazy Ones," this momentum-killing spot is usually lined with men relaxing and enjoying the views.) Beyond that, Rue de la Liberté leads directly into the Grand Socco square, the hub of old Tangier.

TANGIER

Arrival in Tangier

By Ferry

If you're taking a tour, just follow the leader. If you're on your own, you'll want to head for the Grand Socco to get oriented. You can

either take a taxi (cheap) or walk (about 10 gently uphill minutes through the colorful but confusing lanes of the Medina). Note that the entire port area is undergoing extensive reconstruction through 2016, so you may find some changes from the way things are described here.

A small blue **Petit Taxi** is your easiest way to get from the port into town (described later, under "Getting Around Tangier"); unfortunately, prices are not regulated from the port. An honest cabbie will charge you 20-30 dh (about $3) for a ride from the ferry into town; less scrupulous drivers will try to charge closer to 100 dh. Set your price before hopping in.

To **walk** into town, head out through the port entrance checkpoint (by the mosque) and bear left at the stubby wall, passing the big bus parking lot and the white Hotel Continental on your right-hand side. After a few minutes, at the end of the bus lot, look for a mosque's white minaret with green tile high on the hill, and head toward it by going up the street just beyond the long, high white wall (behind the buses). Go through the yellow gateway (Bab Dar Dbagh) marked *1921* and *1339*. Bear right/uphill at the T-intersection, then turn left/uphill on Rue de la Marine. You'll pass a school on the right, then the mosque with the green minaret on your left. Continue straight up to the café-lined Petit Socco square, then continue to the top of the street and turn left before the white gate to enter the Grand Socco. Leave mental breadcrumbs as you walk, so you can find your way back to your boat. If all else fails, head downhill.

By Plane

The Tangier Airport (Aeroport Ibn Battouta, airport code: TNG) is very new-feeling, slick, and well-organized, with ATMs, cafés, and other amenities. Iberia, Royal Air Maroc, easyJet, and Ryanair fly from here to Madrid (easyJet also has a route to Paris). Jet4you, another low-cost airline, is based in Casablanca, but offers flights from Tangier to Barcelona and Brussels (www.jet4you.com). To get into downtown Tangier, taxis should run you about 150 dh and take 30-45 minutes.

Getting Around Tangier

There are two types of taxis: Avoid the big, beige Mercedes "Grand Taxis," which are the most aggressive and don't use their meters (they're designed for longer trips outside of the city center, but have been known to take tourists for a ride in town...in more ways than one). Look instead for **Petit Taxis**—blue with a yellow stripe (they fit 2-3 people). These generally use their meters, are very cheap, and only circulate within the city. However, at the port, Petit Taxis are allowed to charge whatever you'll pay without using the meter, so it's essential to agree on a price up front.

Be aware that Tangier taxis sometimes "double up"—if you're headed somewhere, the driver may pick up someone else who's going in the same direction. However, in this case you don't get to split the fare—each of you pays full price (even though sometimes the other passenger's route takes you a bit out of your way).

Helpful Hints

Money: The exchange rate is 8 dh = about $1; 11 dh = about €1. While most businesses happily take euros or dollars, it's classier to use the local currency—and you'll save money. If you're on a tour, they'll rip you off anyway, so just stick with euros. If you're on your own, it's fun to get a pocket full of dirhams.

A few ATMs are around the Grand Socco (look for one just to the left of the archway entrance into the Medina); more are opposite the TI along Boulevard Pasteur. ATMs work as you expect them to. Banks and ATMs have uniform rates.

Exchange desks are quick, easy, and fair. (Just understand the buy-and-sell rates—they should be within 10 percent of one another with no other fee. If you change €50 into dirhams and immediately change the dirhams back, you should have about €45.) Look for the official *Bureaux de Change* offices, where you'll get better rates than at the banks. There are some on Boulevard Pasteur, and a handful between the Grand and Petit Soccos. The official change offices all offer the same rates, so there's no need to shop around.

Convert your dirhams back to euros before catching the ferry—it's cheap and easy to do here (change desks at the port keep long hours), but very difficult once you're back in Spain.

Phoning: To call Tangier from Spain, dial 00 (Europe's international access code), 212 (Morocco's country code), then the local number (dropping the initial zero). To dial Tangier from elsewhere in Morocco, dial the local number in full (keeping the initial zero).

Keeping Your Bearings: Tangier's maps and street signs are frustrating. I ask in French for the landmark: *Où est...?* ("Where is...?," pronounced oo ay, as in *"oo ay Medina?"* or *"oo ay Kasbah?"*). It can be fun to meet people this way. However, most people who offer to help you (especially those who approach you) are angling for a tip—young and old, locals see dollar signs when a traveler approaches. To avoid getting unwanted company, ask for directions only from people who can't leave what they're doing (such as the only clerk in a shop) or from women who aren't near men. There are fewer hustlers in the new (but less interesting) part of town. Be aware that most people don't know the names of the smaller streets (which don't usually have signs), and tend to navigate by landmarks. In case you get the wrong directions, ask three times and go with the consensus. If there's no consensus, it's time to hop into a Petit Taxi.

Mosques: Tangier's mosques (and virtually all of Morocco's) are closed to non-Muslim visitors.

Tours in Tangier

Local Guides

If you're on your own, you'll be to street guides what a horse's tail is to flies...all day long. Seriously—it can be exhausting to constantly deflect come-ons from anyone who sees you open a guidebook.

In order to have your own translator, and a shield from less scrupulous touts who hit up tourists constantly throughout the old town, I recommend hiring a guide. Stress your interest in the people and culture rather than shopping. Guides, hoping to get a huge commission from your purchases, can cleverly turn your Tangier day into the Moroccan equivalent of the Shopping Channel. Truth be told, some of these guides would work for free, considering all the money they make on commissions when you buy stuff.

I've worked with a variety of guides who speak great English, are easy to get along with, will meet you at the ferry dock, and charge fixed rates. They've promised me they won't make you do any more shopping than you want to—so be very clear about your interests. If one of these guides is busy (or takes a long time responding to your email), try the others. Any of these guides will

TANGIER

Women in Morocco

Most visitors to Tangier expect to see the women completely covered head-to-toe by their kaftan. In fact, only about one-quarter of Moroccan women still adhere strictly to this religious code. Some just cover their head (allowing their face to be seen), while others eliminate the head scarf altogether. Some women wear only Western-style cloth-ing. This change in dress visibly reflects deeper, more fundamen-tal shifts in Moroccan attitudes about women's rights.

Morocco happens to be one of the most progressive Muslim countries around. As in any border country, contact with other cultures fosters the growth of new ideas. Bombarded with Spanish television and visitors like you, change is inevitable. Another proponent of change is King Mohammed VI, who was only 35 years old when he rose to the throne in 1999. For the first time in the country's history, the king personally selected a female adviser to dem-onstrate his commitment to change. The king also married a commoner for...get this...*love*. And even more shocking, she's seen in public. (It's a first—locals don't even know what King Mohammed VI's mother looks like, as she is never in the public view.)

Recent times have brought even more sweeping trans-formations to Moroccan society. In order to raise literacy lev-els and understanding between the sexes, schools are now coed—something taken for granted in the West for decades. In 2004, the Mudawana, or judiciary family code, was shock-ingly overhauled, and Morocco became a trendsetter for women's equality in the Islamic world. The legal age for women to marry is now 18 (just like men) instead of 15. Other changes make it more difficult to have a second wife. Verbal divorce and abandonment are no longer legal—disgruntled husbands must now take their complaints to court. And for the first time, women can divorce their husbands. If children are involved, whoever takes care of the kids gets the house. Morocco took another step forward with its 2011 constitu-tional reforms, which now guarantee women "civic and social" equality.

make your Tangier experience more enjoyable for a negligible cost. They can also book your ferry tickets for the same cost as booking direct: They'll give you a reference number to give at the ticket office in Tarifa, then you'll pay them for the tickets when you meet in Tangier. While each has their own specific itineraries, the two basic options are more or less the same: a half-day walking tour around the Medina and Kasbah (generally 3-5 hours); or a full-day "grand tour" that includes the walk around town as well as a minibus ride to outlying viewpoints—the Caves of Hercules and Cape Spartel (7-8 hours, generally also includes lunch at your expense in a restaurant the guide suggests). Prices are fairly standard from guide to guide. If you're very pleased with your guide, he'll appreciate a tip.

Aziz Begdouri, who enjoys teaching about Moroccan society and culture, has been a big help to me with my guidebook-writing and TV production in Tangier (half-day walking tour-€15/person, groups limited to 4-5 people; 8-hour grand tour-€35/person; mobile 06-6163-9332, from Spain dial 00-212-6-6163-9332, aziztour@hotmail.com).

Salah Abdi grew up in the Medina and has devoted the past 30 years to showing tourists around his hometown. He is a delight, full of historical knowledge and American sports trivia, and his tours give you an intimate insider experience (half-day walking tour-€15/person, groups limited to 4-5 people; full-day grand tour-€35/person for up to 10 people; call to book at least a day in advance, mobile 06-4943-4911, from Spain dial 00-212-6-4943-4911).

Ahmed Taoumi, who has been guiding for more than 30 years, has a professorial style (half-day walking tour-€18/person, full-day grand tour with minibus-€35/person, also offers minibus side-trips to nearby destinations and discounted ferry tickets, mobile 06-6166-5429, from Spain dial 00-212-6-6166-5429, www.visitangier.com, taoumitour@hotmail.com).

If Aziz Begdouri, Salah, or Ahmed are busy, consider one of the following youthful go-getters who are a bit lighter on information, but enjoyable to spend time with and dedicated to making visitors comfortable: **Aziz ("Africa") Benami** (half-day walking tour-€15/person; full-day minibus and walking tour-€35/person, full-day tour including round-trip ferry to/from Tarifa-€79/person, lunch in traditional kasbah home-€15/person, mobile 06-6126-3335, from the US or Canada dial toll-free 1-888-745-7305, www.tangierprivateguide.com, info@tangierprivateguide.com) and **Abdellatif ("Latif") Chebaa** (half-day walking tour-€15/person, grand tour-€35/person, mobile 06-6107-2014, from Spain dial 00-212-6-6107-2014, visittangier@gmail.com).

Other Options: If you don't want to plan too far ahead,

and any guide will do, you can book a **"VIP tour"** through the ferry company in Tarifa for approximately the same prices listed above. I've also had good luck with the **private guides who meet the boat.** If you're a decent judge of character, try interviewing guides when you get off the ferry to find one you click with, then check for an official license and negotiate a good price. These hardworking, English-speaking guides offer their services for the day for €15.

Sights in Tangier

▲▲The Grand Socco

This big, bustling square is a transportation hub, market, popular meeting point, and the fulcrum between the new town and the old town (Medina). A few years ago, it was a pedestrian nightmare and a perpetual traffic jam. But now, like much of Tangier, it's on the rise. Many of the sights mentioned in this spin-tour are described in more detail later in this chapter.

○ **Self-Guided Spin Tour:** The Grand Socco is a good place to get oriented to the heart of Tangier. Stand on the square between the fountain and the mosque (the long building with arches and the tall tower). We'll do a slow clockwise spin.

Start by facing the **mosque**—newly remodeled with a long arcade of keyhole arches, and with a colorfully tiled minaret.

Morocco is a decidedly Muslim nation, though its take on Islam is progressive, likely owing to the country's crossroads history. For example, women are relatively free to dress as they like. Five times a day, you'll hear the call to prayer echo across the rooftops of Tangier, from minarets like this one. Unlike many Muslim countries, Morocco doesn't allow non-Muslims to enter its mosques (with the exception of its biggest and most famous one, in Casablanca). This custom may have originated decades ago, when occupying French foreign legion troops spent the night in a mosque, entertaining themselves with wine and women. Following this embarrassing desecration, it was the French government—not the Moroccans—who instituted the ban

Tangier's Old Town

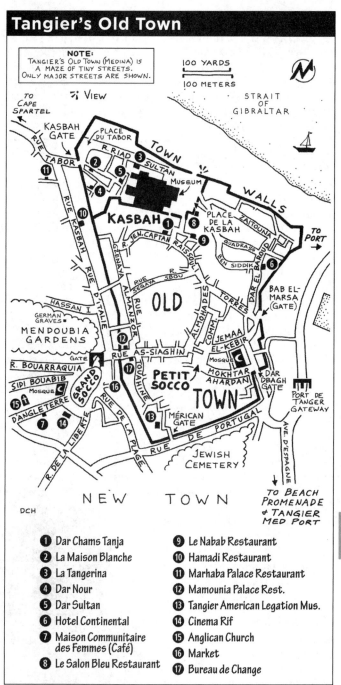

NOTE:
Tangier's Old Town (Medina) is a maze of tiny streets. Only major streets are shown.

100 YARDS
100 METERS

≈ VIEW

STRAIT OF GIBRALTAR

TO CAPE SPARTEL

KASBAH GATE

PLACE DU TABOR

R. RIAD

TOWN

SULTAN

Museum

WALLS

RUE TABOR

KASBAH

RUE KASBAH

RUE D'ITALIE

PLACE DE LA KASBAH

R. JEN. CAPTAN

RAISSOULI

PLACE ZAITOUNA

QUADRASS

BEN SIDDIK

DAR EL BAROUD

TO PORT

BAB EL-MARSA (GATE)

RUE SEGAYA

R. SBOU

RUE ALMANZOR

OLD

ALMOHADES

TORRES

COMM.

JEMAA EL-KEBIR

Mosque

HASSAN I

GERMAN GRAVES

MENDOUBIA GARDENS

Gate

R. BOUARRAQUIA

SIDI BOUABIB

Mosque

RUE AS-SIAGHIN

TOUAHINE

PETIT SOCCO

MOKHTAR AHARDANI

TOWN

DAR DBAGH GATE

PORT DE TANGER GATEWAY

GRAND SOCCO

RUE DE LA PLAGE

MÉRICAN GATE

RUE DE PORTUGAL

AVE. D'ESPAGNE

D'ANGLETERRE

R. DE LA LIBERTE

JEWISH CEMETERY

NEW TOWN

TO BEACH PROMENADE & TANGIER MED PORT

DCH

1 Dar Chams Tanja
2 La Maison Blanche
3 La Tangerina
4 Dar Nour
5 Dar Sultan
6 Hotel Continental
7 Maison Communitaire des Femmes (Café)
8 Le Salon Bleu Restaurant
9 Le Nabab Restaurant
10 Hamadi Restaurant
11 Marhaba Palace Restaurant
12 Mamounia Palace Rest.
13 Tangier American Legation Mus.
14 Cinema Rif
15 Anglican Church
16 Market
17 Bureau de Change

TANGIER

that persists today.

Locals say that in this very cosmopolitan city, anytime you see a mosque, you'll find a church nearby. Sure enough, peeking up behind the mosque, you can barely make out the white, crenellated top of the **Anglican Church**'s tower (or at least the English flag above it—a red cross on a white field). A fascinating architectural hybrid of Muslim and Christian architecture, this house of worship is well worth a visit.

Also behind the mosque, you can see parts of a sprawling **market.** (This features mostly modern goods; the far more colorful produce, meat, and fish market is across the square.) Those market stalls used to fill the square you're standing in; traditionally the Grand Socco was Tangier's hub for visiting merchants. The gates of town would be locked each evening, and vendors who did not arrive in time spent the night in this area. (Nearby were many caravanserai—old-fashioned inns.) But a few years ago, this square was dramatically renovated by the visionary king, Mohammed VI, and given a new name: "April 9th Square," commemorating the date in 1947 when an earlier king, Mohammed V, appealed to his French overlords to grant his country its independence. (France eventually complied, peacefully, in 1956.) In just the last few years, Mohammed VI tamed the traffic, added the fountain you're standing next to (there was never a fountain here before), and turned this into a delightfully people-friendly space.

Spin a few more degrees to the right, where you'll see the crenellated gateway marked *Tribunal de Commerce*—the entrance to the **Mendoubia Gardens,** a pleasant park with a gigantic tree and a quirky history that reflects the epic story of Tangier (particularly from the 1920s to the 1950s, when multiple foreign powers shared control of this city). At the top of the garden gateway, notice the Moroccan flag: a green five-pointed star on a red field. The five points of the star represent the five pillars of Islam; green is the color of peace, and red represents the struggles of hard-fought Moroccan history.

Spinning farther right, you'll see the **keyhole arch** marking the entrance to the Medina. (If you need cash, notice the exchange booths and ATM just to the left of this gateway.) To reach the heart of the Medina—the Petit Socco (the café-lined little brother of the square you're on now)— go through this arch and take the first right.

In front of the arch, you'll likely see **day laborers** looking for work. Each one stands next to a symbol of the kind of work he specializes in: a bucket of paintbrushes for a painter, a coil of wiring for an electrician, and a loop of hose for a plumber.

Speaking of people looking for work, how many locals have offered to show you around ("Hey! What you looking for? I help you!") since you've been standing here, holding this guidebook? Get used to it. While irritating, it's understandable. To these very poor people, you're impossibly rich—your pocket change is at least a good day's wage. If someone pesters you, you can simply ignore them, or say *"Lah shokran"* (No, thank you). But be warned: The moment you engage them, you've just prolonged the sales pitch.

Back to our spin-tour: To the right of the main arch, and just before the row of green rooftops, is the low-profile entrance to the **market** *(souk)*. A barrage on all the senses, this is a fascinating place to explore. The row of green rooftops leads toward Rue de la Plage, with more market action.

Continue spinning another quarter-turn to the tall, white building at the top of the square labeled **Cinema Rif.** This historic movie house still plays films (in Arabic and French). The street to the left of the cinema takes you to Rue de la Liberté, which eventually leads through the modern town to the TI (about a 15-minute walk). Just to the right of the cinema, notice the yellow terrace, which offers the best view over the Grand Socco (just go up the staircase). It's also part of a café, where you can order a Moroccan tea (green tea, fresh mint, and lots of sugar), enjoy the view over the square, and plot your next move.

Near the Grand Socco

These sights are near the Grand Socco, but still outside the Medina (old town).

▲Anglican Church

St. Andrew's Anglican Church, tucked behind a showpiece mosque, embodies Tangier's mingling of Muslim and Christian

tradition. The land on which the church sits was a gift from the sultan to the British community in 1881, during Queen Victoria's era. Shortly thereafter, this church was built. Although fully Christian, the church is designed in the style of a Muslim mosque. The Lord's Prayer rings the arch in Arabic, as verses of the Quran would in a mosque. Knock on the door—Ali or his son Yassin will greet you and give you a "thank you very much" tour. The garden surrounding the church is a tranquil, park-like cemetery.

Cost and Hours: A tip of about 20

TANGIER

dh is appreciated; daily 9:00-18:00 except closed during Sunday services.

Mendoubia Gardens
This pleasant park, accessed through the castle-like archway off of the Grand Socco, is a favorite place for locals to hang out, and also

has a surprising history. Walk through the gateway to see the trunk of a gigantic banyan tree, which, according to local legend, dates from the 12th century. Notice how the extra supportive roots have grown from the branches down to the ground. The large building to the left—today the business courthouse (*Tribunal de Commerce*)—was built to house the representative of the Moroccan king, back in the early 20th century when Tangier was ruled as a protectorate of various European powers and needed an ambassador of sorts to keep an eye out for Moroccan interests. The smaller house on the right (behind the giant tree) is currently the marriage courthouse (used exclusively for getting married or divorced), but it was once the headquarters of the German delegation in Tangier. France originally kept Germany out of the protectorate arrangement by giving them the Congo. But in 1941, when Germany was on the rise in Europe and allied with Spain's Franco, it joined the mix of ruling powers in Tangier. Although Germans were only here for a short time (until mid-1942), they have a small cemetery in what's now the big park in front of you. Go up the stairs and around the blocky Arabic monument. At the bases of the trees beyond it, you'll find headstones of German graves...an odd footnote in the very complex history of this intriguing city.

The Medina (Old Town)

Tangier's Medina is its convoluted old town—a twisty mess of narrow stepped lanes, dead-end alleys, and lots of local life spilling out into the streets. It's divided roughly into two parts: the lower Medina, with the Petit Socco, market, American Legation, and bustling street life; and, at the top, the more tranquil Kasbah.

The Lower Medina and Petit Socco

A maze of winding lanes and tiny alleys weave through the old-town market area. Write down the name of the gate you came in, so you can enjoy being lost—temporarily.

Petit Socco

This little square, also called Souk Dahel ("Inner Market"), is the center of the lower Medina. Lined with tea shops and cafés, it has a romantic quality that has long made it a people magnet. In the 1920s, it was the meeting point for Tangier's wealthy and influential elite; by the 1950s and '60s, it drew Jack Kerouac and his counterculture buddies. Nursing a coffee or a mint tea here, it's easy to pretend you're a Beat Generation rebel, dropping out from Western society and delving deeply into an exotic, faraway culture. More recently, filmmakers have been drawn here. Scenes from both *The Bourne Ultimatum* and *Inception* were filmed on the streets between the Grand and Petit Soccos.

The Petit Socco is ideal for some casual people-watching over a drink. You can go to one of the more traditional cafés, but **Café Central**—with the modern awning—is the most accessible, and therefore the most commercialized and touristy (7-12-dh coffee drinks, 20-45-dh meals, daily 6:00-24:00).

▲▲Market (Souk)

The Medina's market, just off the Grand Socco, is a highlight. Wander past piles of fruit, veggies, and olives, countless varieties of bread, and fresh goat cheese wrapped in palm leaves. Phew! You'll find everything but pork.

Entering the market through the door from the Grand Socco, turn right to find butchers, a cornucopia of produce (almost all of it from Morocco), more butchers, piles of olives, and yet more butchers. The chickens are plucked and hung to show they have been killed according to Islamic guidelines (halal): Animals are slaughtered with a sharp knife in the name of Allah, head to Mecca, and drained of their blood. The far aisle (parallel and to the left of where you're walking) has more innards and is a little harder to stomach.

You'll see women vendors—often wearing straw hats decorated with ribbons or colorful striped skirts—scattered around the market; these are Berbers, who ride donkeys to the city from the nearby Rif Mountains, mostly on Tuesdays and Thursdays. (Before taking photos of these women, or any people you see here, it's polite to ask permission.)

Eventually you'll emerge into the large white market of fish-sellers; with the day's catch from both the Mediterranean and the Atlantic, this is like a textbook of marine life. The door at the far end of the fish market pops you out on the Rue Salah El-dine

Bargaining Basics

No matter what kind of merchandise you buy in Tangier, the shopping is...Moroccan. Bargain hard! The first price you're offered is simply a starting point, and it's expected that you'll try to talk the price way down. Bargaining can become an enjoyable game if you follow a few basic rules:

Determine what the item is worth to you. Before you even ask a price, decide what the item's value is to you. Consider the hassles involved in packing it or shipping it home.

Determine the merchant's lowest price. Many merchants will settle for a nickel profit rather than lose the sale entirely. Work the cost down to rock bottom, and when it seems to have fallen to a record low, walk away. That last price the seller hollers out as you turn the corner is often the best price you'll get. If the price is right, go back and buy.

Look indifferent. As soon as the merchant perceives the "I gotta have that!" in you, you'll never get the best price.

Employ a third person. Use your friend who is worried about the ever-dwindling budget or who doesn't like the price or who is bored and wants to return to the hotel. This can help to bring the price down faster.

Show the merchant your money. Physically hold out your money and offer him "all you have" to pay for whatever you are bickering over. He'll be tempted to just grab your money and say, "Oh, OK."

If the price is too much, leave. Never worry about having taken too much of the merchant's time. They are experts at making the tourist feel guilty for not buying. It's all part of the game.

Al Ayoubi; a right turn takes you back to the Grand Socco, but a left turn leads to the (figurative and literal) low end of the market—a world of very rustic market stalls under a corrugated plastic roof. While just a block from the main market, this is a world apart, and not to everyone's taste. Here you'll find cheap produce, junk shops, electronics (such as recordable CDs and old remote controls), old ladies sorting bundles of herbs from crinkled plastic bags, and far less sanitary-looking butchers than the ones inside the main market hall (if that's possible). Peer down the alley filled with a twitching poultry market, which encourages vegetarianism. The upper part of the market (toward the Medina and Petit

Socco) has a few food stands, but more non-perishable items, such as clothing, cleaning supplies, toiletries, and prepared foods. Scattered around this part of the market are spice and herb stalls (usually marked *hérboriste*), offering a fragrant antidote to the meat stalls. In addition to cooking spices, these sell homegrown Berber cures for ailments. Pots hold a dark-green gelatinous goo—a kind of natural soap.

If you're looking for souvenirs, you won't have to find them... they'll find you, in the form of aggressive salesmen who approach you on the street and push their conga drums, T-shirts, and other trinkets in your face. Most of the market itself is more focused on locals, but the Medina streets just above the market are loaded with souvenir shops. Aside from the predictable trinkets, the big-ticket items here are tilework (such as vases) and carpets. You'll notice many shops have tiles and other, smaller souvenirs on the ground floor, and carpet salesrooms upstairs.

▲▲▲Exploring the Medina

Appealing as the market is, one of the most magical Tangier experiences is to simply lose yourself in the lanes of the Medina. A first-time visitor cannot stay oriented—so don't even try. I just wander, knowing that uphill will eventually get me to the Kasbah

and downhill will eventually lead me to the port. Expect to get a little lost... going around in circles is part of the fun. Pop in to see artisans working in their shops: mosaic tile-makers, thread spinners, tailors. While shops are on the ground level, the family usually lives upstairs. Doors indicate how many families live in the homes behind them: one row of decoration for one, another parallel row for two.

Many people can't afford private ovens, phones, or running water, so there are economical communal options: phone desks (called *tele-boutiques*), baths, and bakeries. If you smell the aroma of baking bread, look for a hole-in-the-wall bakery, where locals drop off their ready-to-cook dough (as well as meat, fish, or nuts to roast). You'll also stumble upon communal taps, with water provided by the government, where people come to wash. Cubby-hole rooms are filled with kids playing video games on old TVs—they can't afford their own at home, so they come here instead.

Go on a photo safari for ornate "keyhole" doors, many of which lead to neighborhood mosques (see photo next page). Green doors are the color of Islam and symbolize peace. The ring-shaped door knockers double as a place to hitch a donkey.

TANGIER

As you explore, notice that some parts of the Medina seem starkly different, with fancy wrought-iron balconies. This is the approximately 20 percent of the town that was built and controlled by Spaniards and Portuguese living here (with the rest being Arabic and Berber). The two populations were separated by a wall, the remains of which you can still trace running through the Medina. It may seem at first glance that these European zones are fancier and "nicer" compared to the poorer-seeming Arabic/Berber zones. But the Arabs and Berbers take more care with the inside of their homes—if you went behind these humble walls, you'd be surprised how pleasant the interiors are. While European cultures externalize resources, Arab and Berber cultures internalize them.

Tangier American Legation Museum

Located at the bottom end of the Medina (just above the port), this unexpected museum is worth a visit. Morocco was one of the

first countries to recognize the newly formed United States as an independent country (in 1777). The original building, given to the United States by the sultan of Morocco, became the fledgling government's first foreign acquisition.

Cost and Hours: Free entry but donations appreciated, Mon-Thu 10:00-13:00 & 15:00-17:00, Fri 10:00-12:00 & 15:00-17:00, during Ramadan holiday daily 10:00-15:00, closed Sat-Sun year-round, ring bell, Rue d'Amérique 8, tel. 0539-935-317, www.talimblog.org.

Visiting the Museum: This was the US embassy (or consulate) in Morocco from 1821 to 1961, and it's still American property—our only National Historic Landmark overseas. Today this nonprofit museum and research center, housed in a 19th-century mansion, is a strangely peaceful oasis within Tangier's intense old town. It offers a warm welcome and lots of interesting artifacts—all well-described in English. The ground floor is filled with an art gallery. In the stairwell, you'll see photos of kings with presidents, and a letter with the news of Lincoln's assassination. Upstairs are more paintings, as well as model soldiers playing out two battle scenes from Moroccan history. These belonged to American industrialist Malcolm Forbes, who had a home in Tangier (his son donated these dioramas to the museum). Rounding out the upper floor are more paintings, and wonderful old maps of Tangier and Morocco. A visit here is a fun reminder of how long the US and Morocco have had good relations.

• *When you've soaked in enough old-town atmosphere, make your way to the Kasbah (see map). Within the Medina, head uphill, or exit the Medina gate and go right on Rue Kasbah, which follows the old wall uphill to Bab Kasbah (a.k.a. Porte de la Kasbah), a gateway into the Kasbah.*

Kasbah

Loosely translated as "fortress," a *kasbah* is an enclosed, protected residential area near a castle that you'll find in hundreds of Moroccan towns. Originally this was a place where a king or other leader could protect his tribe. Tangier's Kasbah comprises the upper quarter of the old town. A residential area with twisty lanes and some nice guesthouses, this area is a bit more sedate and less claustrophobic than parts of the Medina near the market below.

▲Kasbah Museum

On Place de la Kasbah, you'll find the Dar el-Makhzen, a former sultan's palace that now houses a history museum with a few historical artifacts. While there's not a word of English, some of the exhibits are still easy to appreciate, and the building itself is beautiful.

Cost and Hours: 10 dh, Wed-Mon 9:00-16:00, closed for prayer Fri 11:30-13:30, closed all day Tue, tel. 0539-932-097.

Visiting the Museum: Most of the exhibits surround the central, open-air courtyard; rooms proceed roughly chronologically

as you move counterclockwise, from early hunters and farmers to prehistoric civilizations, Roman times, the region's conversion to Islam, and the influence of European powers. The two-story space at the far end of the courtyard focuses on a second-century mosaic floor depicting the journey of Venus. The big 12th-century wall-size map (in Arabic) shows the Moorish view of the world: with Africa on top (Spain is at the far right). Nearby is an explanation of terra-cotta production (a local industry), and upstairs is an exhibit on funerary rituals. Near the entrance, look for signs to *jardin* and climb the stairs to reach a chirpy (if slightly overgrown) garden courtyard. While the building features some striking tilework, you just can't shake the feeling that the best Moorish sights are back in Spain.

TANGIER

Place de la Kasbah

Because the Kasbah Museum (while modest) is the city's main museum, the square in front of the palace attracts more than

its share of tourists. That means it's also a vivid gauntlet of amusements waiting to ambush parading tour groups: snake charmers, squawky dance troupes, and colorful water vendors. These colorful Kodakmoment hustlers make their living off the many tour groups passing by daily. (As you're cajoled, remember that the daily minimum wage here for men as skilled as these beggars is $10. That's what the gardeners you'll pass in your walk earn each day. In other words, a €1 tip is an hour's wage for these people.) If you draft behind a tour group, you won't be the focus of the hustlers. But if you take a photo, you must pay.

Before descending out of the Kasbah, don't miss the ocean viewpoint—as you stand in the square and face the palace, look to the right to find the hole carved through the thick city wall (Bab Dhar, "Sea Gate"). This leads out to a large natural terrace with fine views over the port, the Mediterranean, and Spain.

The lower gate of the Kasbah (as you stand in Place de la Kasbah facing the palace, it's on your left) leads to a charming

little alcove, between the gates, where you can see a particularly fine tile fountain: The top part is carved cedarwood, below that is carved plaster, and the bottom half is hand-laid tiles. In this area, poke down the tiny lane to the left of the little shop—you'll find that it leads to a surprisingly large courtyard ringed by fine homes.

Matisse Route

The artist Matisse, who traveled to Tangier in 1912, was inspired by his wanderings through this area, picking up themes that show up in much of his art. The diamond-shaped stones embedded in the street (you'll see them on the narrow lane leading up along the left side of the palace) mark a "Matisse Route" through the Kasbah, from the lower gate to the upper; those familiar with his works will recognize several scenes along this stretch.

TANGIER

Tangier Beach

Lined with lots of fishy eateries and entertaining nightclubs, this fine, wide, white-sand crescent beach (Plage de Corniche)  stretches eastward from the port. The locals call it by the Spanish word *playa*. It's packed with locals doing what people around the world do at the beach—with a few variations. Traditionally-clad moms let their kids run wild. Along with lazy camels, you'll see people—young and old—covered in hot sand to combat rheumatism. Early, late, and off-season, the beach becomes a popular venue for soccer teams. The palm-lined pedestrian street along the waterfront was renamed for King Mohammed VI, in appreciation for recent restorations. While the beach is cleaner than it once was, it still has more than its share of litter—great for a stroll, but maybe not for sunbathing or swimming. If you have a beach break in mind, do it on Spain's Costa del Sol.

Just past the beach on the port side (between here and the Medina) is a zone of nondescript factories where local women sew clothing for big, mostly European, companies that pay about $8 a day. Each morning and evening rush hour, the street is filled with these women commuters...on foot.

Nightlife in Tangier

Most important: Be out in the **Medina** around 21:00. In the cool of the evening, the atmospheric squares and lanes become even more alluring. Then at about 22:00 things get dark, lonely, and foreboding.

El Minzah Hotel hosts traditional music most nights for those having dinner there (see "Eating in Tangier," later; 85 Rue de la Liberté, tel. 0539-935-885).

The **Cinema Rif,** the landmark theater at the top of the Grand Socco, shows movies in French—which the younger generation is required to learn—and Arabic. The cinema is worth popping into, if only to see the Art Deco interior. As movies cost only 20 dh, consider dropping by to see a bit of whatever's on...in Arabic (closed Mon, tel. 0539-934-683).

Sleeping in Tangier

I've recommended two vastly different types of accommodations in Tangier: cozy Moroccan-style (but mostly French-run) guesthouses in the maze of lanes of the Kasbah neighborhood, at

TANGIER

Sleep Code

(8 dh = about $1, country code: 212, area code: 539)
S = Single, **D** = Double/Twin, **T** = Triple, **Q** = Quad, **b** = bathroom, **s** = shower only. Unless otherwise noted, credit cards are accepted, English is spoken, and breakfast is included. Most hotels charge an extra tax of 15-25 dh per person per night (typically not included in the prices I've listed here).

To help you easily sort through these listings, I've divided the accommodations into three categories, based on the price for a standard double room with bath (during high season):

$$$ Higher Priced—Most rooms 1,000 dh or more.
$$ Moderately Priced—Most rooms between 500-1,000 dh.
$ Lower Priced—Most rooms 500 dh or less.

Prices can change without notice; verify the hotel's current rates online or by email. For the best prices, always book direct.

the top of the Medina (old town); and big, modern international-style hotels in the urban-feeling new town, a 10-to-20-minute walk from the central sights.

Remember, if you want to call Tangier from Europe, dial 00 (Europe's international access code), 212 (Morocco's country code), then the local number (dropping the initial zero). June through mid-September is high season, when rooms may be a bit more expensive and reservations are wise.

Guesthouses in the Kasbah

In Arabic, *dar* means "guesthouse." You'll find these in the Medina, or atmospheric old quarter. While the lower part of the Medina is dominated by market stalls and tourist traps—and can feel a bit seedy after dark—the upper part (called the Kasbah, for the castle that dominates this area) is more tranquil and feels very residential. All of my recommendations are buried in a labyrinth of lanes that can be very difficult to navigate; it's essential to ask for very clear directions when you reserve. If you're hiring a guide in Tangier, ask them to help you find your *dar*. (If you're on your own, you can try asking directions when you arrive—but many local residents take that as an invitation to tag along and hound you for tips.) All of these are in traditional old houses, with rooms surrounding a courtyard atrium, and all have rooftop terraces where you can relax and enjoy sweeping views over Tangier. Most include breakfast, unless noted; many also serve good, Moroccan dinners, which cost extra and should be arranged beforehand, typically that morning. Some also offer hammams (Turkish-style baths) with massages and spa treatments. Many lack stand-alone showers; instead, in Moroccan style, you'll find a handheld shower in a corner of the bathroom.

$$$ **Dar Chams Tanja,** just below the lower Kasbah gate, has seven elegant, new-feeling rooms with all the comforts surrounding a clean-white inner courtyard with lots of keyhole windows. While pricey, it's impeccably decorated, calm, and boasts incredible views from its rooftop terrace (five big Db-1,580 dh, two small Db-1,250 dh, sometimes discounts in slow times—check website, air-con, free Wi-Fi, hammam, massage service, Rue Jnan Kabtan 2, tel. 0539-332-323, www.darchamstanja.com, darchamstanja@gmail.com).

$$$ **Dar Sultan** rents six romantically decorated rooms on a pleasant street in the heart of the Kasbah (Db-1,210 dh, larger Db-1,224 dh, Db with terrace-1,446 dh, Jean Pierre promises a 10 percent discount if you book directly with the hotel and mention this book when you reserve, cash only, free Wi-Fi in lobby and cable Internet in rooms, Rue Touila 49, tel. 0539-336-061, www .darsultan.com, dar-sultan@menara.ma).

$$$ **La Maison Blanche** ("The White House"), run by tour guide Aziz Begdouri, has nine rooms in a traditional Moroccan house with modern amenities in the Kasbah (Sb-1,000 dh, Db-1,100 dh, all with bathtubs, air-con, free Wi-Fi, just inside the upper gate of the Kasbah at Rue Ahmed Ben Ajiba 2, tel. 0539-373-545, www.lamaisonblanchetanger.com, info @lamaisonblanchetanger.com).

$$ **La Tangerina,** run by Jürgen (who's German) and his Moroccan wife, Farida, has 10 comfortable rooms that look down into a shared atrium. At the top is a gorgeous rooftop seaview balcony (Db-600-935 dh in April and June-mid-Sept, otherwise Db-500-770; suite-1,520-1,650 dh in April and June-mid-Sept, otherwise 1,100-1,320 dh; prices depend on size, cash only, free Wi-Fi, wood-fired hammam, turn left as you enter the upper Kasbah gate and hug the town wall around to Riad Sultan 19, tel. 0539-947-731, www.latangerina.com, info@latangerina.com).

$$ **Dar Nour,** run with funky French style by Philippe, Jean-Olivier, and Catherine, has an "Escher-esque" floor plan that sprawls through five interconnected houses (it's "labyrinthine like the Medina," says Philippe). The 10 homey rooms feel very traditional, with lots of books and lounging areas spread throughout (Db-720 dh, junior suite Db-950 dh, suite Db-1,300 dh, cash only, free Wi-Fi in lobby, Rue Gourna 20, mobile 06-6211-2724, www.darnour.com, contactdarnour@yahoo.fr).

TANGIER

Modern Hotels in the Modern City

These hotels are centrally located, near the TI, and within walking distance of the Grand Socco, Medina, and market. The first two are three-star hotels and take credit cards; the others are cash-only.

$$$ Atlas Rif & Spa Hotel, recently restored to its 1970s glamour, is a worthy splurge. Offering 127 plush, modern rooms, sprawling public spaces, a garden, pool, and grand views, it feels like an oversized boutique hotel. Overlooking the harbor, the great Arabic lounge—named for Winston Churchill—compels you to relax (Sb-1,200 dh, Db-1,400 dh, 200 dh more July-Aug, 200 dh extra for sea view, see website for specials, breakfast-100 dh, air-con, elevator, free Wi-Fi in lobby, 3 restaurants, spa and sauna, Avenue Mohammed VI 152, tel. 0539-349-300, www.hotelsatlas .com, atlastanger@menara.ma).

$$ Hotel Rembrandt feels just like the 1940s, with a restaurant, a bar, and a swimming pool surrounded by a great grassy garden. Its 70 rooms are outdated and simple, but clean and comfortable, and some come with views (Sb-484-594 dh, Db-594-704 dh, higher prices are for sea view, 90-dh extra June-Aug, breakfast included, air-con, elevator, free Wi-Fi, a 5-minute walk above the beach in a busy urban zone at Boulevard Mohammed VI 1, tel. 0539-333-314, www.hotel-rembrandt.com, reservation@hotel -rembrandt.com).

$$ Hotel Continental—actually in the Medina (at the bottom of the old town, facing the port)—is the Humphrey Bogart option, a grand old place sprawling along the old town. It has lavish, atmospheric, and recently renovated public spaces, a chandeliered breakfast room, and 55 spacious bedrooms with rough hardwood floors and new bathrooms. Jimmy, who's always around and runs the shop adjacent to the lobby, says he offers everything but Viagra. When I said, "I'm from Seattle," he said, "206." Test him—he knows your area code (Sb-495 dh, Db-635 dh, Tb-765 dh, Qb-890 dh, about 100 dh more July-Sept, includes breakfast, free Wi-Fi, Dar Baroud 36, tel. 0539-931-024, www.continental -tanger.com, hcontinental@iam.net.ma). This hotel's terrace aches with nostalgia. Back during the city's glory days, a ferry connected Tangier and New York. American novelists would sit out on the terrace of Hotel Continental, never quite sure when their friends' boat would arrive from across the sea...

$ Hotel El Djenina is a local-style business-class hotel—extremely plain, reliable, safe, and well-located. Its 40 rooms are a block off the harbor, midway between the port and the TI. Request a room on the back side to escape the street noise (Sb-319-357 dh, Db-382-463 dh, higher prices are for mid-May-Sept, cash only, no breakfast, no air-con, elevator, free Wi-Fi, tel. 0539-942-244, Rue al-Antaki 8, eldjenina@menara.ma).

$ Hotel Residencia Andalucía is solid, clean, and minimal. It's buried in a totally non-touristy area in the new town, about a 20-minute walk from the Grand Socco. It has 19 rooms, a small reception, and a peaceful lobby (Sb-200-230 dh, Db-230-260 dh, higher prices are for mid-June–mid-Sept, cash only, Rue Omar Ben Abdelaziz 14, tel. 0539-941-334, Azdeen speaks a little English). Don't confuse it with the similarly named but very exclusive Hotel Andalucía Golf across town.

Eating in Tangier

Moroccan food is a joy to sample. First priority is a glass of the refreshing "Moroccan tea"—green tea that's boiled and steeped once, then combined with fresh mint leaves to boil and steep some more, before being loaded up with sugar. Tourist-oriented restaurants have a predictable menu. For starters, you'll find Moroccan vegetable soup *(harira)* or Moroccan salad (a combination of fresh and stewed vegetables). Main dishes include couscous (usually with chicken, potatoes, carrots, and other vegetables and spices); *tagine* (stewed meat served in a fancy dish with a cone-shaped top); and *briouates* (small savory pies). Everything comes with Morocco's distinctive round, flat bread. For dessert, it's pastries—typically, almond cookies.

I've mostly listed places in or near the Medina. (If you'd prefer the local equivalent of a yacht-club restaurant, survey the places along the beach.) Moroccan waiters expect about a 10 percent tip.

Le Saveur du Poisson is an excellent bet for the more adventurous, featuring one room cluttered with paintings adjoining a busy kitchen. There are no choices here. Just sit down and let owner Muhammad or his son, Hassan, take care of the rest. You get a rough hand-carved spoon and fork. Surrounded by lots of locals and unforgettable food, you'll be treated to a multicourse menu. Savor the delicious fish dishes—Tangier is one of the few spots in Morocco where seafood is a major part of the diet. The fruit punch—a mix of seasonal fruits brewed overnight in a vat—simmers in the back room. Ask for an explanation, or even a look. The desserts are full of nuts and honey. The big sink in the room is for locals who prefer to eat with their fingers (200-dh fixed-price meal, Sat-Thu 12:00-16:00 & 19:00-22:00, closed Fri and during Ramadan; walk down Rue de la Liberté roughly a block toward the Grand Socco from El Minzah Hotel, look for the stairs leading down to the market stalls and go down until you see fish on the grill; Escalier Waller 2, tel. 0539-336-326).

Maison Communitaire des Femmes, a community center for women, hides an inexpensive, hearty lunch spot that's open to

TANGIER

everyone. A tasty three-course lunch is only 60 dh. Profits support the work of the center (Mon-Sat 12:00-16:00, last order at 15:30, also open 8:00-11:00 & 15:30-18:00 for cakes and tea, closed Sun, pleasant terrace out back, near slipper market just outside Grand Socco, Place du 9 Avril, tel. 0539-947-065).

El Minzah Hotel offers a fancier yet still authentic experience. The atmosphere is classy but low-stress. It's where unadventurous tourists and local elites dine. Dress up and choose between two dining zones: The white-tablecloth continental (French) dining area, called El Erz, is stuffy (80-150-dh starters, 140-240-dh main dishes); while in the Moroccan lounge, El Korsan, you'll be serenaded by live traditional music (music nightly 20:00-23:30, belly-dance show at 20:30 and 22:30, no extra charge for music; 70-120-dh starters, 140-240-dh main dishes). There's also a cozy wine bar here—a rarity in a Muslim country (50-120-dh starters, 130-190-dh main dishes, decorated with photos of visiting celebrities). At lunch, light meals and salads are served poolside (all dining areas open daily 13:00-16:00 & 20:00-22:30, Rue de la Liberté 85, tel. 0539-333-444, www.leroyal.com/morocco).

Le Salon Bleu has decent Moroccan food and some of the most spectacular seating in town: perched on a whitewashed terrace overlooking the square in front of the Kasbah Museum, with 360-degree views over the rooftops. Hike up the very tight spiral staircase to the top level, with the best views and lounge-a-while sofa seating. French-run (by the owners of Dar Nour guesthouse), it offers a simple menu of Moroccan fare—the 80-dh appetizer plate is a good sampler for lunch or to share for an afternoon snack. While there is some indoor seating, I'd skip this place if the weather's not ideal for lingering on the terrace (30-40-dh starters, 80-120-dh main dishes, 90-dh fixed-price meals, daily 10:00-22:00, Place de la Kasbah, mobile 06-6211-2724). You'll see it from the square in front of the Kasbah; to reach it, go through the gate to the left (as you face it), then look right for the stairs up.

Le Fabrique has nothing to do with old Morocco. But if you want a break from couscous and keyhole arches, this industrial-mod brasserie with concrete floors and exposed brick has a menu of purely French classics—a good reminder that in the 20th century, Tangier was nearly as much a French city as a Moroccan one (50-140-dh starters, 120-250-dh main dishes; Tue-Sat 12:00-14:30 & 20:00-23:00, closed Sun-Mon, in winter open for dinner only; Rue d'Angleterre 7, tel. 0539-374-057). It's a steep 10-minute walk up from the Grand Socco: Head up Rue d'Angleterre (left of Cinema Rif) and hike up the hill until the road levels out—it's on your left.

Le Nabab is geared for tourists, but offers more style and less crass commercialism than the tourist traps listed below. Squirreled away in a mostly residential neighborhood just below the lower

Kasbah gate (near the top of the Medina), Le Nabab offers a menu of predictable Moroccan favorites in a sleek concrete-and-white-tablecloths dining room with a few echoes of traditional Moroccan decor (170-dh three-course meal is a good deal to sample several items, 40-55-dh starters, 110-130-dh main dishes, Mon-Sat 19:30-23:30, closed Sun; below the lower Kasbah gate—bear left down the stairs, then right, and look for signs; Rue Al Kadiria 4, mobile 06-6144-2220).

Tourist Traps

Tangier seems to specialize in very touristy Moroccan restaurants designed to feed and entertain dozens or even hundreds of tour-group members with overpriced and predictable menus of Moroccan classics, and often live music and belly-dancing. The only locals you'll see here are the waiters. For day-trippers who just want a safe, comfortable break in the heart of town, these restaurants' predictability and Moroccan clichés are just perfect. For other travelers, these places are tour-group hell and make you thankful to be free. Each local guide has their own favorite, but these are the best-known.

Hamadi is as luxurious a restaurant as a tourist can find in Morocco, with good food at reasonable prices (25-40-dh starters, 60-80-dh main dishes, long hours daily, Rue Kasbah 2, tel. 0539-934-514).

Marhaba Palace has the most impressive interior, with huge keyhole arches ringing a grand upstairs hall slathered in colorful tilework. It also has the highest prices—hardly a good value. It's near the upper gate to the Kasbah, so it's convenient for a meal just before heading downhill through town to the Medina and market (170-240-dh fixed-price meals, Mon-Sat 10:00-23:00, closed Sun, Rue Kasbah, tel. 0539-937-927).

Mamounia Palace, considered by most the bottom of the barrel, is right on the Petit Socco and more in the middle of the action. At least it has a Hollywood connection: The Moroccan teahouse scenes from the movie *Inception* were filmed on its upstairs balcony. A meal here will cost you about 100 dh for four courses (no à la carte, daily 11:00-22:00, tel. 0539-935-099).

Tangier Connections

In Tangier, all train traffic comes and goes from the suburban Gare Tanger Ville train station, one mile from the city center and a short Petit Taxi ride away (10-20 dh). If you're traveling inland, check the information booth at the entrance of the train station for schedules (www.oncf.ma).

From Tangier by Train to: Rabat (7/day, 3.5-4 hours),

Casablanca (station also called **Casa Voyageurs,** 7/day, 5 hours; a new train line will cut the trip to about 2 hours by 2014), **Marrakech** (7/day, 8.5-9 hours, transfer in Casablanca or Sidi Kacem; 1 direct overnight train, 10.5 hours), **Fès** (4/day, 4.5 hours).

Bus information is available at the sporadically functioning CMT bus company website (www.ctm.ma, tel. 0522-541-010).

From Tangier by Bus to: Ceuta and **Tétouan** (hourly, 1 hour).

From Fès to: Casablanca (10/day, 5.5 hours), **Marrakech** (4/day, 8 hours), **Rabat** (8/day, 3.5 hours), **Meknès** (10/day, 45 minutes), **Tangier** (6/day, 7 hours).

From Rabat to: Casablanca (2/hour, 45 minutes), **Fès** (5/day, 3 hours), **Tétouan** (5 buses/day, 4.5-6 hours, 4 trains/day, 6 hours).

From Casablanca to: Marrakech (9/day, 3.5 hours).

From Marrakech to: Meknès (2/day, 7 hours), **Ouarzazate** (6/day, 4 hours).

By Plane: Flights within Morocco are convenient and reasonable (about $110 one-way from Tangier to Casablanca).

Morocco Beyond Tangier

Morocco gets much better as you go deeper into the interior. The country is incredibly rich in cultural thrills, though you'll pay a price in hassles and headaches—it's a package deal. But if adventure is your business, Morocco is a great option. Moroccan trains are quite good. Second class is cheap and comfortable. Buses connect all smaller towns very well. By car, Morocco is easy. Invest in a good Morocco guide-book to make this trip. Here are a few tips and insights to get you started.

If you're relying on public transportation for your extended tour, sail to Tangier, blast your way through customs, ignore any hustler who tells you there's no way out until tomorrow, and hop in a Petit Taxi for the Tanger Ville train station one mile away. From there set your sights on Rabat, a dignified European-type town with fewer hustlers, and make it your get-acquainted stop in Morocco. Trains go farther south from Rabat.

If you're driving a car, crossing the border can be a bit unnerving, since you'll be forced to jump through several bureaucratic hoops. You'll go through customs at both borders, buy Moroccan insurance for your car (cheap and easy), and feel at the mercy of a bristly bunch of shady-looking people you'd rather not be at the mercy of. Don't pay anyone on the Spanish side. Consider tipping a guy on the Moroccan side if you feel he'll shepherd you through. Relax and let him grease those customs wheels. He's worth it. As soon as possible, hit the road and drive to Chefchaouen, the best first stop for those with their own wheels. Drive defensively and never rely on the oncoming driver's skill. Night driving is dangerous. Pay a guard to watch your car overnight.

Moroccan Towns

▲▲Chefchaouen
Just two hours by bus or car from Tétouan, this is the first pleasant town beyond the north coast. Monday and Thursday are colorful market days. Stay in the classy old Hotel Chaouen on Place el-Makhzen. The Hotel Parador (historic inn, but not the same as the Spanish government-run chain) faces the old town and offers good meals and a refuge from hustlers. Wander deep into the whitewashed old town from here.

▲▲Rabat
Morocco's capital and most European city, Rabat is the most comfortable and least stressful place to start your North African trip. You'll find a colorful market (in the old neighboring town of Salé), bits of Islamic architecture (Mausoleum of Mohammed V), the king's palace, mellow hustlers, and fine hotels.

▲▲▲Fès
More than just a funny hat that tipsy Shriners wear, Fès is Morocco's religious and artistic center, bustling with craftspeople, pilgrims, shoppers, and shops. Like most large Moroccan cities, it

has a distinct new town from the French colonial period, as well as an exotic (and stressful) old walled Arabic town (the Medina), where you'll find the market.

For 12 centuries, traders have gathered in Fès, founded on a river at the crossroads of two trade routes. Soon there was an irrigation system; a university; resident craftsmen from Spain; and a diverse population of Muslims, Christians, and Jews. When France claimed Morocco in 1912, they made their capital in Rabat, and Fès fizzled. But the Fès marketplace is still Morocco's best.

TANGIER

▲▲▲Marrakech
Morocco's gateway to the south, Marrakech is where the desert, mountain, and coastal regions merge. This market city is a constant

folk festival, bustling with Berber tribespeople and a colorful center. The new city has the train station, and the main boulevard (Mohammed V) is lined with banks, airline offices, a post office, a tourist office, and comfortable hotels. The old city features the maze-like market and the huge Djemaa el-Fna, a square seething with people—a 43-ring Moroccan circus.

▲▲▲Over the Atlas Mountains

Extend your Moroccan trip several days by heading south over the Atlas Mountains. Take a bus from Marrakech to Ouarzazate (short stop), and then to Tinerhir (great oasis town, comfy hotel, overnight stop). The next day, go to Er Rachidia and take the overnight bus to Fès.

By car, drive from Fès south, staying in the small mountain town of Ifrane, and then continue deep into the desert country past Er Rachidia, and on to Rissani (market days: Sun, Tue, and Thu). Explore nearby mud-brick towns still living in the Middle Ages. Hire a guide to drive you past where the road stops, and head cross-country to an oasis village (Merzouga), where you can climb a sand dune and watch the sun rise over the vastness of Africa. Only a sea of sand separates you from Timbuktu.

PRACTICALITIES

This section covers just the basics on traveling in Spain (for much more information, see *Rick Steves' Spain*). You can find free advice on specific topics at www.ricksteves.com/tips.

Money

Spain uses the euro currency: 1 euro (€) = about $1.30. To convert prices in euros to dollars, add about 30 percent: €20 = about $26, €50 = about $65. (Check www.oanda.com for the latest exchange rates.)

The standard way for travelers to get euros is to withdraw money from ATMs (which locals call a *cajero automático*) using a debit or credit card, ideally with a Visa or MasterCard logo. Before departing, call your bank or credit-card company: Confirm that your card will work overseas, ask about international transaction fees, and alert them that you'll be making withdrawals in Europe. Also ask for the PIN number for your credit card in case it'll help you use Europe's "chip-and-PIN" payment machines (see below); allow time for your bank to mail your PIN to you. To keep your valuables safe, wear a money belt.

Dealing with "Chip and PIN": Much of Europe—including Spain—is adopting a "chip-and-PIN" system for credit cards, and some merchants rely on it exclusively. European chip-and-PIN cards are embedded with an electronic chip, in addition to the magnetic stripe used on our American-style cards. This means that your credit (and debit) card might not work at payment machines, such as those at train and subway stations, toll roads, parking garages, luggage lockers, and self-serve gas pumps. Memorizing your credit card's PIN lets you use it at some chip-and-PIN machines—just enter your PIN when prompted. If a payment machine won't take your card, look for a machine that takes cash or see if there's a cashier nearby who can process your transaction. The easiest solution is to pay for your purchases with cash you've withdrawn from an ATM using your debit card (Europe's ATMs still accept magnetic-stripe cards).

Phoning

Smart travelers use the telephone to reserve or reconfirm rooms, reserve restaurants, get directions, research transportation connections, confirm tour times, phone home, and lots more.

To call Spain from the US or Canada: Dial 011-34 and then the nine-digit number. (The 011 is our international access code, and 34 is Spain's country code.)

To call Spain from a European country: Dial 00-34 followed by the nine-digit number. (The 00 is Europe's international access code.)

To call within Spain: Just dial the local nine-digit number.

To call from Spain to another country: Dial 00 followed by the country code (for example, 1 for the US or Canada), then the area code and number. If calling European countries whose phone numbers begin with 0, you'll usually have to omit that 0 when you dial.

Tips on Phoning: A mobile phone—whether an American one that works in Spain, or a European one you buy when you arrive—is handy, but can be pricey. If traveling with a smartphone, switch off data-roaming until you have free Wi-Fi. With Wi-Fi, you can use your smartphone to make free or inexpensive domestic and international calls by taking advantage of a calling app such as Skype or FaceTime.

To make cheap international calls from any phone (even your hotel-room phone), you can buy an international phone card in Spain (called a *tarjeta telefónica con código)*. These work with a scratch-to-reveal PIN code, allow you to call home to the US for pennies a minute, and also work for domestic calls.

Another option is buying an insertable phone card (*tarjeta telefónica*). These are usable only at pay phones, are reasonable for making calls within the country, and work for international calls as well (though not as cheaply as the international phone cards). Note that insertable phone cards—and most international phone cards—work only in the country where you buy them.

Calling from your hotel-room phone is usually expensive, unless you use an international phone card. For much more on phoning, see www.ricksteves.com/phoning.

Making Hotel Reservations

To ensure the best value, I recommend reserving rooms in advance, particularly during peak season. Email the hotelier with the fol-

From:	rick@ricksteves.com
Sent:	Today
To:	info@hotelcentral.com
Subject:	Reservation request for 19-22 July

Dear Hotel Central,

I would like to reserve a room for 2 people for 3 nights, arriving 19 July and departing 22 July. If possible, I would like a quiet room with a double bed and a bathroom inside the room.

Please let me know if you have a room available and the price.

Thank you!
Rick Steves

lowing key pieces of information: number and type of rooms; number of nights; date of arrival; date of departure; and any special requests. (For a sample form, see sidebar above.) Use the European style for writing dates: day/month/year. For example, for a two-night stay in July, you could request: "1 double room for 2 nights, arrive 16/07/15, depart 18/07/15." Hoteliers typically ask for your credit-card number as a deposit.

Given the economic downturn, hoteliers are often willing and eager to make a deal—try emailing several to ask their best price. In general, hotel prices can soften if you do any of the following: offer to pay cash, stay at least three nights, or mention this book. You can also try asking for a cheaper room or a discount, or offer to skip breakfast.

Eating

By our standards, Spaniards eat late, having lunch—their biggest meal of the day—around 13:00-16:00, and dinner starting about 21:00. At restaurants, you can dine with tourists at 20:00, or with Spaniards if you wait until later.

For a fun early dinner at a bar, build a light meal out of tapas—small appetizer-sized portions of seafood, salads, meat-filled pastries, deep-fried tasties, and so on. Many of these are displayed behind glass, and you can point to what you want. Tapas typically cost about €2 apiece, but can run up to €10 for seafood. While the smaller "tapa" size (which comes on a saucer-size plate) is handiest for maximum tasting opportunities, many bars sell only larger sizes: the *ración* (full portion, on a dinner plate) and *media-ración* (half-size portion). *Jamón* (hah-MOHN), an air-dried ham similar to prosciutto, is a Spanish staple. Other key terms include *bocadillo* (baguette sandwich), *frito* (fried), *a la plancha* (grilled), *queso* (cheese), *tortilla* (omelet), and *surtido* (assortment).

Many bars have three price tiers, which should be clearly

posted: It's cheapest to eat or drink while standing at the bar (*barra*), slightly more to sit at a table inside (*mesa* or *salón*), and most expensive to sit outside *(terraza)*. Wherever you are, be assertive or you'll never be served. *Por favor* (please) grabs the attention of the server or bartender. If you're having tapas, don't worry about paying as you go (the bartender keeps track). When you're ready to leave, ask for the bill: *"¿La cuenta?"* To tip for a few tapas, round up to the nearest euro; for a full meal, tip about 5 to 10 percent for good service.

Transportation

By Train and Bus: For train schedules, check www.renfe.com. Since trains can sell out, it's smart to buy your tickets a day in advance at a travel agency (easiest), at the train station (can be crowded; be sure you're in the right line), or online (at www.renfe.com; when asked for your Spanish national ID number, enter your passport number—but be aware that the website rejects nearly every attempt to use a US credit card; or from the US try www.raileurope.com). Futuristic, high-speed trains (such as AVE) can be priced differently according to their time of departure. To see if a railpass could save you money, check www.ricksteves.com/rail.

Buses pick up where the trains don't go, reaching even small villages. But because routes are operated by various competing companies, it can be tricky to pin down schedules (check with local bus stations, tourist info offices, or www.movelia.es).

By Plane: Consider covering long distances on a budget flight, which can be cheaper than a train or bus ride. For flights within Spain, check out www.vueling.com, www.iberia.com, or www.aireuropa.com; to other European cites, try www.easyjet.com and www.ryanair.com; and to compare several airlines, see www.skyscanner.com.

By Car: It's cheaper to arrange most car rentals from the US. For tips on your insurance options, see www.ricksteves.com/cdw, and for route planning, consult www.viamichelin.com. Bring your driver's license. You're also technically required to have an International Driving Permit—a translation of your driver's license (sold at your local AAA office for $15 plus the cost of two passport-type photos; see www.aaa.com).

Superhighways come with tolls (about $4/hour), but save lots of time. Local road etiquette is similar to that in the US. Ask your car-rental company about the rules of the road, or check the US State Department website (www.travel.state.gov, click on "International Travel," then specify your country of choice and click "Traffic Safety and Road Conditions").

A car is a worthless headache in cities—park it safely (get tips from your hotel). As break-ins are common, be sure all of your

PRACTICALITIES

valuables are out of sight and locked in the trunk, or even better, with you or in your hotel room.

Helpful Hints

Emergency Help: For **police** help, dial 091. To summon an **ambulance**, call 112. For passport problems, call the **US Embassy** (in Madrid, tel. 915-872-240, after-hours emergency tel. 915-872-200) or the **Canadian Embassy** (in Madrid, tel. 913-828-400). For other concerns, get advice from your hotel.

Theft or Loss: Spain has particularly hardworking pickpockets—wear a money belt. Assume beggars are pickpockets and any scuffle is simply a distraction by a team of thieves. If you stop for any commotion or show, put your hands in your pockets before someone else does.

To replace a passport, you'll need to go in person to an embassy (see above). Cancel and replace your credit and debit cards by calling these 24-hour US numbers collect: Visa—tel. 303/967-1096, MasterCard—tel. 636/722-7111, American Express—tel. 336/393-1111. File a police report either on the spot or within a day or two; you'll need it to submit an insurance claim for lost or stolen railpasses or travel gear, and it can help with replacing your passport or credit and debit cards. Precautionary measures can minimize the effects of loss—back up your digital photos and other files frequently. For more information, see www.ricksteves.com/help.

Time: Spain uses the 24-hour clock. It's the same through 12:00 noon, then keep going: 13:00, 14:00, and so on. Spain, like most of continental Europe, is six/nine hours ahead of the East/West Coasts of the US.

Siesta and Paseo: Many Spaniards (especially in rural areas) still follow the traditional siesta schedule: From around 13:00 to 16:00, many businesses close as people go home for a big lunch with their family. Then they head back to work (and shops re-open) from about 16:00 to 20:00. (Many bigger stores stay open all day long, especially in cities.) Then, after a late dinner, whole families pour out of their apartments to enjoy the cool of the evening, stroll through the streets, and greet their neighbors—a custom called the paseo. Tourists are welcome to join this people-parade.

Sights: Major attractions can be swamped with visitors; carefully read and follow this book's crowd-beating tips (visit at quieter times of day, or—where possible—reserve ahead). Opening and closing hours of sights can change unexpectedly; confirm the latest times on their websites or at the local tourist information office. At many churches, a modest dress code is encouraged and sometimes required (no bare shoulders or shorts).

Holidays and Festivals: Spain celebrates many holidays, which can close sights and attract crowds (book hotel rooms ahead). For more on holidays and festivals, check Spain's website: www.spain.info. For a simple list showing major—though not all—events, see www.ricksteves.com/festivals.

Numbers and Stumblers: What Americans call the second floor of a building is the first floor in Europe. Europeans write dates as day/month/year, so Christmas is 25/12/15. Commas are decimal points and vice versa—a dollar and a half is 1,50, and there are 5.280 feet in a mile. Spain uses the metric system: A kilogram is 2.2 pounds; a liter is about a quart; and a kilometer is six-tenths of a mile.

Resources from Rick Steves

This Snapshot guide is excerpted from my latest edition of *Rick Steves' Spain,* which is one of more than 30 titles in my series of guidebooks on European travel. I also produce a public television series, *Rick Steves' Europe,* and a public radio show, *Travel with Rick Steves.* My website, www.ricksteves.com, offers free travel information, a forum for travelers' comments, guidebook updates, my travel blog, an online travel store, and information on European railpasses and our tours of Europe. If you're bringing a mobile device on your trip, you can download free information from Rick Steves Audio Europe, featuring podcasts of my radio shows, free audio tours of major sights in Europe, and travel interviews about Spain (via www.ricksteves.com/audioeurope, iTunes, Google Play, or the Rick Steves Audio Europe free smartphone app). You can follow me on Facebook and Twitter.

Additional Resources

Tourist Information: www.spain.info
Passports and Red Tape: www.travel.state.gov
Travel Insurance Tips: www.ricksteves.com/insurance
Packing List: www.ricksteves.com/packlist
Cheap Flights: www.kayak.com
Airplane Carry-on Restrictions: www.tsa.gov/travelers
Updates for This Book: www.ricksteves.com/update

How Was Your Trip?

If you'd like to share your tips, concerns, and discoveries after using this book, please fill out the survey at www.ricksteves.com/feedback. Thanks in advance—it helps a lot.

Spanish Survival Phrases

Spanish has a guttural sound similar to the J in Baja California. In the phonetics, the symbol for this clearing-your-throat sound is the italicized *h*.

English	Spanish	Pronunciation
Good day.	*Buenos días.*	**bway**-nohs **dee**-ahs
Do you speak English?	*¿Habla Usted inglés?*	**ah**-blah oo-**stehd** een-**glays**
Yes. / No.	*Sí. / No.*	see / noh
I (don't) understand.	*(No) comprendo.*	(noh) kohm-**prehn**-doh
Please.	*Por favor.*	por fah-**bor**
Thank you.	*Gracias.*	**grah**-thee-ahs
I'm sorry.	*Lo siento.*	loh see-**ehn**-toh
Excuse me.	*Perdóneme.*	pehr-**doh**-nay-may
(No) problem.	*(No) problema.*	(noh) proh-**blay**-mah
Good.	*Bueno.*	**bway**-noh
Goodbye.	*Adiós.*	ah-dee-**ohs**
one / two	*uno / dos*	**oo**-noh / dohs
three / four	*tres / cuatro*	trays / **kwah**-troh
five / six	*cinco / seis*	**theen**-koh / says
seven / eight	*siete / ocho*	see-**eh**-tay / **oh**-choh
nine / ten	*nueve / diez*	**nway**-bay / dee-**ayth**
How much is it?	*¿Cuánto cuesta?*	**kwahn**-toh **kway**-stah
Write it?	*¿Me lo escribe?*	may loh ay-**skree**-bay
Is it free?	*¿Es gratis?*	ays **grah**-tees
Is it included?	*¿Está incluido?*	ay-**stah** een-kloo-**ee**-doh
Where can I buy / find...?	*¿Dónde puedo comprar / encontrar...?*	**dohn**-day **pway**-doh kohm-**prar** / ayn-kohn-**trar**
I'd like / We'd like...	*Quiero / Queremos...*	kee-**ehr**-oh / kehr-**ay**-mohs
...a room.	*...una habitación.*	**oo**-nah ah-bee-tah-thee-**ohn**
...a ticket to ___.	*...un billete para ___.*	oon bee-**yeh**-tay **pah**-rah ___
Is it possible?	*¿Es posible?*	ays poh-**see**-blay
Where is...?	*¿Dónde está...?*	**dohn**-day ay-**stah**
...the train station	*...la estación de trenes*	lah ay-stah-thee-**ohn** day **tray**-nays
...the bus station	*...la estación de autobuses*	lah ay-stah-thee-**ohn** day ow-toh-**boo**-says
...the tourist information office	*...la oficina de turismo*	lah oh-fee-**thee**-nah day too-**rees**-moh
Where are the toilets?	*¿Dónde están los servicios?*	**dohn**-day ay-**stahn** lohs sehr-**bee**-thee-ohs
men	*hombres, caballeros*	**ohm**-brays, kah-bah-**yay**-rohs
women	*mujeres, damas*	moo-**heh**-rays, **dah**-mahs
left / right	*izquierda / derecha*	eeth-kee-**ehr**-dah / day-**ray**-chah
straight	*derecho*	day-**ray**-choh
When do you open / close?	*¿A qué hora abren / cierran?*	ah kay **oh**-rah **ah**-brehn / thee-**ay**-rahn
At what time?	*¿A qué hora?*	ah kay **oh**-rah
Just a moment.	*Un momento.*	oon moh-**mehn**-toh
now / soon / later	*ahora / pronto / más tarde*	ah-**oh**-rah / **prohn**-toh / mahs **tar**-day
today / tomorrow	*hoy / mañana*	oy / mahn-**yah**-nah

In a Spanish Restaurant

English	Spanish	Pronunciation
I'd like / We'd like...	Quiero / Queremos...	kee-**ehr**-oh / kehr-**ay**-mohs
...to reserve...	...reservar...	ray-sehr-**bar**
...a table for one / two.	...una mesa para uno / dos.	**oo**-nah **may**-sah **pah**-rah **oo**-noh / dohs
Non-smoking.	No fumador.	noh foo-mah-**dohr**
Is this table free?	¿Está esta mesa libre?	ay-**stah** ay-stah **may**-sah **lee**-bray
The menu (in English), please.	La carta (en inglés), por favor.	lah **kar**-tah (ayn een-**glays**) por fah-**bor**
service (not) included	servicio (no) incluido	sehr-**bee**-thee-oh (noh) een-kloo-**ee**-doh
cover charge	precio de entrada	**pray**-thee-oh day ayn-**trah**-dah
to go	para llevar	**pah**-rah yay-**bar**
with / without	con / sin	kohn / seen
and / or	y / o	ee / oh
menu (of the day)	menú (del día)	may-**noo** (dayl **dee**-ah)
specialty of the house	especialidad de la casa	ay-spay-thee-ah-lee-**dahd** day lah **kah**-sah
tourist menu	menú turístico	meh-**noo** too-**ree**-stee-koh
combination plate	plato combinado	**plah**-toh kohm-bee-**nah**-doh
appetizers	tapas	**tah**-pahs
bread	pan	pahn
cheese	queso	**kay**-soh
sandwich	bocadillo	boh-kah-**dee**-yoh
soup	sopa	**soh**-pah
salad	ensalada	ayn-sah-**lah**-dah
meat	carne	**kar**-nay
poultry	aves	**ah**-bays
fish	pescado	pay-**skah**-doh
seafood	marisco	mah-**ree**-skoh
fruit	fruta	**froo**-tah
vegetables	verduras	behr-**doo**-rahs
dessert	postres	**poh**-strays
tap water	agua del grifo	**ah**-gwah dayl **gree**-foh
mineral water	agua mineral	**ah**-gwah mee-nay-**rahl**
milk	leche	**lay**-chay
(orange) juice	zumo (de naranja)	**thoo**-moh (day nah-**rahn**-hah)
coffee	café	kah-**feh**
tea	té	tay
wine	vino	**bee**-noh
red / white	tinto / blanco	**teen**-toh / **blahn**-koh
glass / bottle	vaso / botella	**bah**-soh / boh-**tay**-yah
beer	cerveza	thehr-**bay**-thah
Cheers!	¡Salud!	sah-**lood**
More. / Another.	Más. / Otro.	mahs / **oh**-troh
The same.	El mismo.	ehl **mees**-moh
The bill, please.	La cuenta, por favor.	lah **kwayn**-tah por fah-**bor**
tip	propina	proh-**pee**-nah
Delicious!	¡Delicioso!	day-lee-thee-**oh**-soh

For hundreds more pages of survival phrases for your trip to Spain, check out *Rick Steves' Spanish Phrase Book.*

INDEX

INDEX

INDEX

INDEX

INDEX

Rick Steves

www.ricksteves.com

Rick Steves guidebooks are published by Avalon Travel,
a member of the Perseus Books Group.

NOW AVAILABLE: eBOOKS, DVD & BLU-RAY

TRAVEL CULTURE

Europe 101
European Christmas
Postcards from Europe
Travel as a Political Act

eBOOKS

*Nearly all Rick Steves guides
are available as eBooks. Check
with your favorite bookseller.*

RICK STEVES' EUROPE DVDs

11 New Shows 2013–2014
Austria & the Alps
Eastern Europe
England & Wales
European Christmas
European Travel Skills & Specials
France
Germany, BeNeLux & More
Greece, Turkey & Portugal
Iran
Ireland & Scotland
Italy's Cities
Italy's Countryside
Scandinavia
Spain
Travel Extras

BLU-RAY

Celtic Charms
Eastern Europe Favorites
European Christmas
Italy Through the Back Door
Mediterranean Mosaic
Surprising Cities of Europe

PHRASE BOOKS & DICTIONARIES

French
French, Italian & German
German
Italian
Portuguese
Spanish

JOURNALS

Rick Steves' Pocket Travel Journal
Rick Steves' Travel Journal

PLANNING MAPS

Britain, Ireland & London
Europe
France & Paris
Germany, Austria & Switzerland
Ireland
Italy
Spain & Portugal

Rick Steves books and DVDs are available at bookstores
and through online booksellers.

Avalon Travel
a member of the Perseus Books Group
1700 Fourth Street
Berkeley, CA 94710

Text © 2013 by Rick Steves
Maps © 2013 Europe Through the Back Door. All rights reserved.
Portions of this book originally appeared in *Rick Steves' Spain 2014*.

Printed in Canada by Friesens.
First printing January 2014.

ISBN 978-1-61238-694-2

For the latest on Rick's lectures, guidebooks, tours, public radio show, and public television series, contact Europe Through the Back Door, Box 2009, Edmonds, WA 98020, 425/771-8303, fax 425/771-0833, www.ricksteves.com, rick@ricksteves.com.

Europe Through the Back Door

Managing Editor: Risa Laib
Editorial & Production Manager: Jennifer Madison Davis
Editors: Glenn Eriksen, Tom Griffin, Cameron Hewitt, Suzanne Kotz, Cathy Lu, John Pierce, Carrie Shepherd, Gretchen Strauch
Editorial Assistant: Jessica Shaw
Editorial Interns: Alex Jacobs, Zosha Millman
Researchers: Rich Earl, Suzanne Kotz, Robert Wright, Amanda Zurita
Maps & Graphics: David C. Hoerlein, Lauren Mills, Laura VanDeventer, Dawn Tessman Visser

Avalon Travel

Senior Editor and Series Manager: Madhu Prasher
Editor: Jamie Andrade
Associate Editor: Annette Kohl
Assistant Editor: Maggie Ryan
Copy Editor: Denise Silva
Proofreader: Kelly Lydick
Indexer: Stephen Callahan
Production & Typesetting: McGuire Barber Design
Cover Design: Kimberly Glyder Design
Maps & Graphics: Kat Bennett, Mike Morgenfeld

ABOUT THE AUTHOR

RICK STEVES

 Since 1973, Rick Steves has spent 100 days every year exploring Europe. Along with writing and researching a bestselling series of guidebooks, Rick produces a public television series *(Rick Steves' Europe)*, a public radio show *(Travel with Rick Steves)*, and an app and podcast *(Rick Steves Audio Europe)*; writes a nationally syndicated newspaper column; organizes guided tours that take over 10,000 travelers to Europe annually; and offers an information-packed website (www.ricksteves.com). With the help of his hardworking staff of 80 at Europe Through the Back Door—in Edmonds, Washington, just north of Seattle—Rick's mission is to make European travel fun, affordable, and culturally enlightening for Americans.

Connect with Rick:

f facebook.com/RickSteves   twitter: @RickSteves